Essays on the philosophy of music

This volume contains a selection of essays in translation by the German philosopher and man of letters Ernst Bloch (1885–1977), on the philosophy of music. For Bloch – often simply assimilated to the Marxist tradition, but whose thought shows a strongly individual and idealist cast – music was a primary focus of reflection. His musical knowledge and expertise were of a very high order and he was well acquainted with many of the leading composers and theorists of music of his time in Germany: even divorced from his philosophy his criticism remains of value and significance.

The first essay in this volume is drawn from Bloch's major early work *Geist der Utopie*, where it occupies a central place in the opening section. This substantial piece shows a spectacular synthesis of music history, music theory and philosophy: beginning with a historical account of the western musical tradition containing many original insights, it moves on to theoretical speculations which include a discussion of harmony and rhythm and culminates in a philosophical view that places music, as a human function and aspiration, at the heart of Bloch's general philosophy. Other essays in the volume include a discussion of the relation of music and mathematics, concluding with a contrast between the fugue and the sonata; a short history of attitudes to instruments and their significance, leading to a discussion of the human voice; and a novel and profound consideration of aspects of Wagner's dramatic and musical achievement – in many ways the focal point of Bloch's thought about music. The final piece is derived from *Das Prinzip Hoffnung*, and there Bloch traces music's emergence from a primordial longing – portrayed in the legend of Pan and Syrinx – and ends by characterising great music as embodying a supreme moral force, being charged with symbols of man's expectancy, or hope.

Throughout, whether discussing the complex and varied relations between text and music, or questions relating to the 'expressive' as opposed to the 'descriptive' functions of music, Bloch is intent on elucidating and placing musical experience.

David Drew's important introduction marks the centenary of Bloch's birth. It traces Bloch's career, discussing his very individual position in particular in post-war Germany, and concludes with an illuminating study of the crucial relationship between Bloch and his younger contemporary Theodor W. Adorno.

Contents

Translator's preface

Along with a dozen further pieces, the following essays were first assembled in German in an anthology titled *Zur Philosophie der Musik*. The opening essay constitutes a large extract from the revised version of Ernst Bloch's first book, *Geist der Utopie*. (As my Notes will indicate, in subsequent writings he sometimes quotes from the original, 1918, edition.) An Expressionist work in various respects, *Geist der Utopie* owes important stimuli to Georg Lukács – whose early Marxism included a mystical strain which found a ready response in Bloch. There was some talk between them of a joint book on aesthetics. Bloch, whose formal studies at university had embraced philosophy, music and physics, was to contribute a survey of music. In the event, such a survey occupies a central place in the first part of *Geist der Utopie*. Reconsidering this book when it entered his Complete Edition (as volume 3) in 1964, Bloch himself summed it up as a venture in 'revolutionary gnosis'. Its messianic reading of history, and its conception of music as potentially the prophetic art par excellence, are ultimately re-echoed by the final essay on music in the German and the present selection.

The final essay comes from *Das Prinzip Hoffnung*, originally titled 'Träume vom besseren Leben' (Dreams of the Better Life). Bloch wrote this in the United States, soon after he had emigrated there in 1938. Formally, stylistically, *Das Prinzip Hoffnung* yields nothing in brilliance to his earliest book. George Steiner, a critic rather better acquainted with world literature than Jean Paul's impecunious Wuz the Schoolmaster, assures us that there is no other work like it. 'There is', Steiner comments, 'no ready designation for its shape and tone, for its fantastic range and metaphoric logic.' Compared to Bloch's first book, *Das Prinzip Hoffnung* implies a delicate shift in focus: broadly speaking, from the religious self and its preoccupations to Man as a social being. In the interim, Bloch had equipped himself to demonstrate that – as one of his distinguished

vii

musician-admirers has put it – 'in a purely scientific sense hope resides in us' (Leonard Bernstein, *Findings*).

In contrast to the first and last essays, the other three in the present selection are inherently self-contained. The second and third essays appear in volume 9 of the Complete Edition (*Literarische Aufsätze*, 1965). The fourth appears within volume 10 (*Philosophische Aufsätze zur objektiven Phantasie*, 1969). Despite Bloch's emphasis on the role of individuality in musical creation, 'Paradoxes and the Pastorale in Wagner's Music' furnishes the only extended study in the German anthology of a single composer. Wagner's problematic genius was one with which Bloch repeatedly came to grips, as in *Geist der Utopie* and in his critique of cultural trends in the 1920s, *Erbschaft dieser Zeit*.

Two slips of Bloch's pen have been emended in the English texts. Beethoven's Seventh Symphony, as opposed to his Eighth, is evidently meant on p. 48; and the Nile music 'vor dem vierten Akt' of *Aïda* was Verdi's cue for Act 3 (p. 177). In the Notes at the end, some specific allusions and references are briefly elucidated. It was difficult to gauge the amount of material that the reader might welcome – I have simply tried to be helpful, without becoming tedious. As for the task of translation, there are well-known syntactical and psychological differences between German and English. When the original prose has the prevailing density of Ernst Bloch's, it makes the attempt to reconcile those differences all the more arduous. Since a good many passages defy 'naturalisation', my version will no doubt present a certain impoverishment. I can but hope that it still speaks effectively for its remarkable author, to the profit of anyone for whom ideas and music are vital, intimate concerns.

*   *   *

My thanks are due in the first instance to Robert Pascall, who selected most of the Essays for translation. He suggested many improvements to a draft of the English texts and was unfailingly generous in his encouragement. The project was patiently overseen by Jonathan Sinclair-Wilson in the philosophy division of the Cambridge University Press, and it found a musical copy editor in Penny Souster. She too made numerous valuable suggestions and continued to assist the book's progress after her appointment as music editor. Nicholas John, of English National Opera, helped to clarify a point in connection with *Tristan and Isolde*. Besides contributing the substantial Introduction, David Drew also provided a number of comments on the translation.

I would like, finally, to thank the library committee of the University of Nottingham for special facilities, and the arts division of Nottingham Central Library for procuring a copy of Bloch's *Geist der Utopie*.

P.R.P.

Introduction
From the other side: reflections on the Bloch centenary

By David Drew

Question: What is the basic idea in your philosophy?
Bloch: That I cannot see anything at very close quarters, anything that presents itself in front of my eyes. There has to be distance . . . Proverbs express
it very simply: 'The weaver knows not what he weaves'; 'At the foot of the
lighthouse there is no light'; 'The prophet is without honour in his own
country'.   1974[1]

To venture a guess at what will forever remain his secret, it is not entirely
improbable that, in pondering his road and its destination, Erasmus arrived
at conclusions which so filled him with fright that he preferred to lock them
away in his heart. He may (or he may not) have surmised that in the last
analysis he aimed at something beyond the pale of Christianity; that,
thought to the end, his true design was once for all to wreck the wall of fixed
causes with their dogmas and institutional arrangements for the sake of that
ultimate unity which the causes mean and thwart.
        Siegfried Kracauer, 'Erasmus', in *Ernst Bloch zu ehren*[2]

Marx and Nietzsche are the last German philosophers to have captured the popular imagination outside the German-speaking world.
If Nietzsche has lost – and lost perhaps to Freud – the dubious

---

[1] Bloch's oddly oblique answer to a question posed by a student journal of the day
   is not fully comprehensible without reference to his lifelong difficulties of seeing,
   and the blindness that finally overtook him.
[2] Siegfried Kracauer, 'Zwei Deutungen in zwei Sprachen', in *Ernst Bloch zu ehren*,
   ed. Siegfried Unseld (Frankfurt, 1965), p. 155. Known in the English-speaking
   world for his study of the German cinema, *From Caligari to Hitler*, and for his
   book on Offenbach, Kracauer (1889–1966) was one of the outstanding
   sociologists, essayists and editors in Weimar Germany. His difficult first meeting
   with Bloch in 1924 is recalled, in the light of their subsequent lifelong friendship,
   by Bloch in *Tagträume vom aufrechten Gang* (Frankfurt, 1977, ed. Arno
   Münster), pp. 47–8. Kracauer appends his Erasmus essay (in English) to his
   eightieth birthday tribute to Bloch (in German), claiming, with mock innocence,
   that he had not wished to arrive empty-handed and had therefore brought an
   essay written some years before. Be that as it may, its relevance to Bloch is so clear,
   so consistent, and so telling, that the essay can only be read as a second and crowning tribute in which every critical reservation honours its concealed subject.

honour of being in that sense a household name, that is no reflection on his real achievement, but only on the fact that it was in his name among others that hitherto unthinkable crimes were, within living memory, committed against the entire household of Western culture and humanity.

With the notable exception of Heidegger, almost every German philosopher worthy of the calling joined the great emigration from Hitler's Germany, whether literally or (like Jaspers until his removal), in spirit. For most, the traditional havens of Vienna and Prague, Basle and Paris, served their traditional purpose until, towards the end of the decade, circumstances called for a second and equally momentous emigration: westwards, to America.

That it was the America of Roosevelt's New Deal was generally influential. That it was also, for the Marxist left, expressly or tacitly the chosen alternative to Stalin's Russia, became crucial: a crossroads, and even for some a kind of personal cross. Of the leading German Marxist thinkers, only György Lukács[3] had (immediately) chosen Moscow; and there he was to remain until the end of the Second World War, true to the party he had joined in 1918 and apparently at one with the Stalinist consequences of the Leninism to which he had fully committed himself by the early 1920s. His friend and antagonist, exact contemporary and truest counterpart, was Ernst Bloch, who took the more familiar path through Paris and Prague, and in 1938 sailed for New York. Bloch's speech 'Zerstörte Sprache–Zerstörte Kultur'[4] – delivered to the Association of German

---

[3] György (or Georg) Lukács was born in Budapest in 1885 and died there in 1971. Though rightly claimed as a Hungarian, he is none the less a central figure in the intellectual history of the German-speaking world in the twentieth century. He completed his philosophical and sociological studies in Germany, and it was in Germany that his reputation was established before the First World War. His post-1918 commitment to Marxism and to revolutionary politics was signalled by the publication in Berlin in 1923 of a volume of recent essays collected under the title *Geschichte und Klassenbewusstsein*. For Bloch's review of that collection, see the Complete Edition (henceforth GA) 10, p. 620; for a curious epilogue to the long and complex Bloch–Lukács relationship, see the three-cornered discussion with the German philosopher Iring Fetscher in Rainer Traub and Harald Weiser, *Gespräche mit Ernst Bloch* (Frankfurt, 1975), p. 28. Leszek Kolakowski's study of Lukács in vol. 3 ('The Breakdown') of his *Main Currents of Marxism* (Oxford University Press, 1978) is critical, but strikingly sympathetic compared to his subsequent critique of Bloch in the same volume. Cf. Kolakowski's contribution – not listed in his bibliography – to *Georg Lukács. Festschrift zum 80. Geburtstag* (ed. Frank Benseler, Neuwied: Luchterhand, 1965). George Lichtheim's *Lukács* (London: Fontana/Collins, 1970) is an excellent short introduction.

[4] Ernst Bloch, *Vom Hasard zur Katastrophe* (Frankfurt, 1972), pp. 403–27.

Writers in New York in 1939, and published in Moscow that same year – ended with four English words: 'The Rights of Man'.

Unlike Adorno, Horkheimer, Marcuse, and their colleagues from the Hegelian-Marxist Frankfurt School, Bloch arrived in the United States without clear prospects of a post, and predictably failed to find one. After two years of hardship in New York and New Hampshire, he moved to Cambridge, Massachusetts, where he wrote most of his magnum opus, *Das Prinzip Hoffnung*. Apart from his address in 1939 to the Congress of American Writers, his appearances and his publications in the New World were confined to German exile circles.

In 1948, his sixty-fourth year, Bloch accepted the offer of a professorship of philosophy at the University of Leipzig, then in the Russian zone and recently re-constituted as the Karl-Marx University. The following summer he and his family arrived in what had already been established as the German Democratic Republic. In his inaugural address at the university[5] he spoke of the charts and the skills required in order to navigate 'the ocean . . . that lies before us' – an ocean of 'circumscribed possibilities'. Implicit in his 'principle, Hope' was the need to discriminate between short-term and long-term possibilities, and real rather than merely dogmatic limitations. For Bloch, in his public role as in his thinking, the problems of navigation were not simply a matter of enlightened confidence in the accuracy of existing charts – the 'Seekarte' of his inaugural speech – but also of constant deep-water soundings.

A collision between Bloch and the Ulbricht regime was nevertheless at some point inevitable. That should already have been clear from any but the most cursory or selective reading of his post-1918 work – including, in their proper context, his notorious apologia for Stalin's Moscow show trials.[6] The event that indirectly precipitated the collision occurred in February 1956, when Kruschev delivered to the Twentieth Congress of the Soviet Communist Party his com-

---

[5] Cited in Sylvia Markun, *Ernst Bloch* (Hamburg-Reinbek: Rowohlt, 1977), p. 82.
[6] 'Kritik einer Prozesskritik' (*Die neue Weltbühne*, Prague, 4 March 1937) 'Jubiläum der Renegaten' (ibid., 11 November 1937), and 'Bucharins Schlusswort' (ibid., 5 May 1938) are reprinted in Bloch, *Vom Hasard zur Katastrophe*; Oskar Negt's postface to the volume ('Ernst Bloch – der deutsche Philosoph der Oktoberrevolution') is primarily a defence of these articles in their historical context, and in relation to the much-criticised omissions and revisions in GA 11, to which *Vom Hasard zur Katastrophe* acts as an indispensable documentary appaendix.

prehensive indictment of Stalin's errors, crimes and general misrule – and above all, because it was intended to explain all, of the 'cult of personality'. Unwittingly Kruschev had dismantled part of the fortress upon which Russia's control of the Eastern bloc depended, and demolished ideological safeguards that have since proved irreplaceable.

Criticism of Bloch's 'revisionism' had been voiced in party journals, intermittently, since the start of the 1950s. Yet his seventieth birthday in 1955 – just six months before the epoch-making Congress – was marked by the kind of official celebrations that people's democracies reserve for the blameless great. Despite his age there was no talk of retirement, and seemingly no thought of it: the official as well as the real sense of the celebrations was that he was still at the height of his prodigious powers. So it was very much as a public figure that Bloch addressed a distinguished audience at the Humboldt University in East Berlin in November 1956, on the occasion of the 125th anniversary of the death of Hegel. In tones that would have rejoiced the heart of Brecht – who had died just three months before – he attacked party functionaries who sought to reduce the discussion of Marx and Hegel to the level of a 'hatter's competition', and who seemed to believe 'one could play the Ninth Symphony on a comb'.[7] The fervour with which Bloch now reiterated his attacks on rigid dogma and his pleas for a wise tolerance was unmistakably heightened by events in Hungary, where Russian troops were at that moment crushing the uprising in support of the anti-Stalinist government formed by Imre Nagy. Among the members of that government – all of whom were exiled to Rumania – was Lukács.

Lukács and his colleagues in the 'Petófi circle' had been the intellectual forerunners of the Hungarian uprising. Their connections with Wolfgang Harich, who together with Bloch had founded the highly respected journal *Die Deutsche Zeitschrift für Philosophie* (and who was also Bloch's editor in the state-controlled Aufbau Verlag), were well known in the GDR. Soon after Bloch had delivered his widely reported Hegel address and returned to Leipzig, Harich was arrested, together with other members of a 'revisionist circle' that included three ex-pupils of Bloch. The end-of-year issue of *Neues Deutschland* contained an article by Ulbricht criticising

---

[7] Cited in Markun, *Ernst Bloch*, pp. 93–4.

research and teaching at the Karl-Marx University in Leipzig, but not mentioning Bloch by name.

A month later, Ulbricht addressed the central committee of the SED on the subject of the Harich 'conspiracy', its connections with West German interests and the Petófi circle, and its open endorsement of the Yugoslavian 'experiment'. The awkward task of censuring Bloch himself was assigned to a second speaker, Kurt Hager. With a fine flourish of platitudes, Hager declared that as a teacher and thinker Bloch laid too much stress on the subjective, despised facts, ignored the disciplines of dialectical materialism, and concentrated on 'remote objectives rather than the current realities of the class struggle'. While granting that his philosophy 'obviously contains strongly humanistic and progressive tendencies' he concluded that 'it is basically a form of idealism, divorced from real life and the struggle of the working classes'.[8]

In due course Harich was sentenced to ten years' imprisonment for organising and leading a 'counter-revolutionary' group, and Bloch's three pupils received lesser sentences. The offices of *Die Deutsche Zeitschrift für Philosophie* were raided by the police, Bloch was removed from the editorial board, and a special issue containing Ulbricht's speech to the central committee was substituted for the issue planned by Harich and Bloch. At the central committee's bidding, Leipzig University held in April 1957 a two-day conference on Bloch's philosophy. Predictably its conclusions coincided with Kurt Hager's.

Compulsorily retired at the end of the 1955–6 year, Bloch was now isolated from student life, though by no means disgraced. He retained a second academic post, and in 1959 Aufbau published the first volume of *Das Prinzip Hoffnung*. By then he had already secured an alternative publishing outlet in the West, thanks to the links with the Suhrkamp Verlag in Frankfurt which Brecht had so wisely cultivated in earlier years. 1959 saw the publication by Suhrkamp of the first complete edition of *Das Prinzip Hoffnung*, and the first volume in what was to become a seventeen-part Complete Edition.

In 1960 Bloch was vociferously welcomed by large student audiences at the West German universities of Tübingen, Heidelberg, and Stuttgart. On his return to the Federal Republic for a summer

---

[8]   Ibid., p. 96.

holiday in 1961, he visited Bayreuth and became friends with Wieland Wagner. He and his wife were still there on 13 August, when Germany awoke to find that the Eastern sector of Berlin had been blocked off by a wall. Concluding that the risk of never recovering the manuscripts upon which the Complete Edition relied was less than the sum of the risks that returning to them would entail, Bloch and his wife resolved to stay in the West, where their son had already settled. With his appointment as Guest Professor in Philosophy at Tübingen later that year, he could at last resume the teaching responsibilities he had been deprived of in Leipzig five years before. In no respect did he modify his views to suit the new circumstances; nor did he avail himself of the tempting rewards and privileges which the West reserves for eminent fugitives from the East.

The special understanding Bloch established with the West German protest movement when it erupted in 1966 was manifestly related to the integrity of his bearing before and after 1961. Although most of the ideological fuel for the protest movement had come from the Frankfurt School – notably from Marcuse and Adorno – Bloch's unique experience and personal authority helped him exert a moderating influence that was specifically his own. The primitive Leninist position 'beyond' good and evil was one that Bloch refused to countenance, and although he was careful to cite the young Marx and even Lenin himself in support of his own moral and ethical scruples, the Judeo-Christian background was never disguised. A lifetime's preoccupation with the New Testament in particular had begun with the first (1918) edition of *Geist der Utopie* – for all its invocations of 'the profound designating power of heroic-mystical atheism'. It continued by way of the sixteenth-century revolutionary priest Thomas Münzer, was enhanced in the United States through friendship with the socialist theologian Paul Tillich (who had been Adorno's sponsor for a professorship at Frankfurt University in 1931), and culminated, exactly fifty years after the first publication of *Geist der Utopie*, in the passionately heretical *Atheismus im Christentum*, which belongs to the same year and the same climate as Bloch's friendly and much-publicised debate with Rudi Dutschke.

For many of Bloch's admirers and all his fiercest critics no heresy of his has been so shocking as his (subjective!) recognition of man's inherently religious nature. Whereas Lukács soon abandoned the metaphysics with which he set out in his pre-Marxist days, Bloch, whose friendship with him had been formed in those days and was to be commemorated in the dedication of his posthumous *Tendenz–Latenz–Utopie*, revised much but rejected nothing. Having finished the fifteenth volume of the Complete Edition in his ninetieth year and dedicated it to the memory of Rosa Luxemburg, he decreed that the sixteenth and last should be an un-retouched facsimile of the first (and later completely revised) edition of *Geist der Utopie*.

Theological initiatives were largely responsible for the short-lived discovery of Bloch in the USA in the late 1960s (as they were for his rather earlier and more durable recognition in France and South America). They were, however, questioned on strictly tactical grounds at the very start of the weightiest essay published in the USA in the aftermath of the events at Berkeley, Fredric Jameson's 'Ernst Bloch and the Future'.[9] Jameson begins by remarking that in his *Thomas Münzer* (1921) Bloch characterises the 'theologian of revolution' in a manner suggestive of his own aims, and that this is dangerous insofar as the idea of Marxism as a religion is 'one of the main arguments in the arsenal of anti-communism'. Bloch was by no means oblivious of that danger, and repeatedly sought to avert it. But within a year of Bloch's death the full force of Jameson's observation was demonstrated from an unexpected and influential quarter. The Polish philosopher Leszek Kolakowski had made his name as one of the young Warsaw revisionists in the early 1960s, and as such had been commended and approvingly quoted by Bloch. But the three-volume study of Marxism which Kolakowski published in England and America in 1978, after his emigration to the West, concludes with a volume entitled 'The Breakdown';[10] and it is in the chapter devoted to Bloch and the alleged irresponsibility of his quasi-religious utopianism that Kolakowski finally dismisses Marxism as a malignant will o' the wisp that has deluded mankind for generations.

Without visibly straining to be fair even in matters of detail, Kolakowski contrives to suggest that Bloch's philosophy is beneath

---

[9] Fredric Jameson, *Marxism and Form* (Princeton University Press, 1971), ch. 2, 'Ernst Bloch and the Future'; the phrase cited here is translated from the German version, 'Die Ontologie des Noch-Nicht-Seins' in Burghart Schmidt, *Materialien zu Ernst Blochs 'Prinzip Hoffnung'* (Frankfurt, 1978).

[10] Leszek Kolakowski, *Main Currents of Marxism*, vols. 1–3, tr. P.S. Falla (Oxford University Press, 1978). All references here are to the paperback edition of 1981, and to vol. 3, 'The Breakdown', ch. 12 of which is entitled 'Ernst Bloch: Marxism as a futuristic gnosis' (pp. 421–49). See Bloch, GA 11, pp. 472–3 for a telling passage from Kolakowski's *Der Mensch ohne Alternativen* (1964), in which his views are clearly at one with Bloch's.

serious consideration as such. Readers puzzled about why the author nevertheless lavishes some thirty pages on it will find the answer in the 'epilogue'; although Bloch is no longer mentioned by name, most of the ideological debris Kolakowski assembles as conclusive proof of Marxism's 'breakdown' derives from his demolition of Bloch, and the remainder is clearly related to it. By referring to chiliastic sects in this ostensibly impersonal context rather than in the Bloch chapter, where the reference properly belongs, Kolakowski effects a suitably dramatic transition from the evidence (which is abundant) of Marxism's false prophecies, to his crowning charge that Marxism panders to a 'psychological need for certainty' and that in this sense it 'performs the function of a religion, and its efficacy is of a religious character'.[11]

Dr Wayne Hudson, the author of the first and so far the only full length study of Bloch's philosophy in any language, avoids mentioning Kolakowski's critique until he has reached his own epilogue. 'Obviously' he writes,

Bloch is neither a philosopher nor a Marxist if he advances an intellectually irresponsible gnostic futurism, or a wholly out-of-date identity metaphysics. Indeed granted this interpretation, the problem is not to show that Bloch is not a Marxist, but to explain how he could ever have imagined that he was a Marxist at all.[12]

Since the latter 'problem' already answers itself in terms of its own premise it is no answer to Kolakowski but seems to be merely a baffle-screen for its equally questionable but strikingly resonant predecessor. To have shown that Bloch 'is not a Marxist' would no doubt have been child's play for Kolakowski, but would hardly have furthered his case that Bloch's philosophy is representative of the 'breakdown' of Marxism as a whole. In substance, though not of course in tendency, Kolakowski's objections to Bloch's outlook and methodology are intimately related to those that had been voiced in the GDR since the early 1950s. Bloch emerges as an incorrigible romantic.

Asked by a West German student journal in 1970 whether he was a Marxist, Bloch replied:

Properly speaking, a Marxist must also be a philosopher; and he who is a

---

[11] Ibid., p. 526.
[12] Wayne Hudson, *The Marxist Philosophy of Ernst Bloch* (London: Macmillan, 1982), p. 209.

philosopher must, in order to be one, be either a Marxist or, involuntarily, an ideologist of the ruling classes. If Marxism is not philosophy it is Vulgar Marxism, and will soon become counter-revolutionary. There is a fine phrase of Isaak Babel, the great Russian writer who was done to death by Stalin: Banality is counter-revolution. Marxism would become banal if it became schematic.[13]

To which the orthodox and the unbeliever alike would both perhaps reply that a philosophical Marxism, however admirable or deplorable its objectives, but especially if it develops an oracular tendency from its residue of idealism and mysticism, is so far removed from the *science* that Marx believed he had created as to be scarcely discussable in the same context.

Marx's famous and much misused quip that he was not a Marxist belongs within the field of Bloch's lifelong resistance to static concepts and closed systems. At an early stage he had steeped himself in the tradition of process philosophy, from its classical origins through Böhme and Leibnitz, through Schelling and Hegel, and finally to Bergson. Everything he subsequently acquired and developed from Marx was calculated to strengthen and define the processual in terms of tensions, tendencies, and latencies: above all, the 'tension of impeded precipitations' ('der Spannung des verhindert Fälligen') and the latency of 'not yet realised possibilities' ('noch nicht verwirklichte Möglichkeiten')[14] towards whose objective reality mankind's utopian dreams and experiments have everywhere and at all times called attention, whatever absurdities are immediately apparent in them, and however sure their ultimate failure. The itinerary, he insisted, is not decisive:

The main thing... is that the utopian conscience-and-knowledge grows wise from the damage it suffers from facts, yet does not grow to full wisdom. It is *rectified* by the mere power of that which, at any particular time, *is*, but is never *refuted* by it. On the contrary, it confronts and judges the existent if it is failing and failing inhumanly; indeed, first and foremost it provides the *standard* to measure such facticity precisely as departure from the right; and, above all, to measure it immanently: that is, by the ideas which have resounded and been inculcated from time immemorial before such a departure and which are still displayed and proposed in the face of it.[15]

[13] 'Ein falscher Sozialismus ist kein Sozialismus', in Rainer Traub and Harald Wieser (eds.), *Gespräche mit Ernst Bloch* (Frankfurt, 1975), p. 139.
[14] Ernst Bloch, *Das Prinzip Hoffnung*, GA 5, p. 727.
[15] Ernst Bloch, *Tübinger Einleitung in die Philosophie*, GA 13, pp. 96–7. John Cumming's translation of the section containing the paragraph cited here first appeared under the title 'The Meaning of Utopia' in *A Philosophy of the Future*

To be unmoved by such a passage, and to resist it, is in effect to resist all Bloch. But even those who feel compelled to do so on principle, or for some other reason, may yet recognise the injustice of the charge that facts for Bloch 'have no ontological meaning and may be ignored without hesitation'.[16] Nevertheless, Bloch's often-repeated contention that socialism has made 'too great a leap from Utopia to Science'[17] remains strikingly heretical in the context of his self-imposed isolation from an entire range of (economic) facts relevant to the theory and practice of Marxism, and hence to the discrimination of its functions, malfunctions, and alleged breakdown. In expressing his disquiet about the too-great leap. Bloch knowingly distanced himself from the mainstream of Marxist studies, but also from any fair-weather friends he might have found among those who were already proclaiming at the end of World War II that 'scientific' Marxism was dead, but not its 'moral radicalism . . . its feeling of social responsibility and its love for freedom'.[18]

The words are Karl Popper's in *The Open Society and its Enemies* – a key-work in post-war Hegel-and-Marx criticism and an evident precursor of Kolakowski. 'It is this moral radicalism of Marx', wrote Popper (in the era of Beveridge and Bevan) 'which explains his influence; and that is a hopeful fact in itself. This moral radicalism is still alive, and it is our task to keep it alive, to prevent it from going the way that his political radicalism will have to go.'[19] Between *The Open Society* and Bloch's so-called Open System, as between the 'might-have-been' evoked by Popper[20] in his assessment (via Marx's prophecies) of actual events from 1864 to 1930, and the 'not yet' evoked by Bloch in surveying the entire history of mankind up to and including the 1970s, there are some paradoxical affinities, and a chasm that can perhaps be bridged.

Kolakowski argues that because Bloch is aware that his notion of the Ultimum has no support from 'the existing rules of scientific thought' he instead 'invokes the aid of imagination, artistic inspi-

(New York, 1970) and is reprinted in Maynard Solomon (ed.), *Marxism and Art* (Brighton: The Harvester Press, 1979); an almost identical translation is given in Hudson, *Marxist Philosophy*, p. 53.

[16] Kolakowski, *Main Currents*, vol. 3, p. 433.
[17] E.g. Bloch, *Das Prinzip Hoffnung*, GA 5, p. 726.
[18] Karl Popper, *The Open Society and its Enemies*, vol. 2, *Hegel and Marx* (London: Routledge, 1945; fourth edition, 1962), p. 211.
[19] Ibid.   [20] Ibid., p. 198.

ration and enthusiasm'.[21] This, we are given to understand, would be a forgivable peccadillo if Bloch considered himself a poet. In that case, Kolakowski continues, the results of his 'anticipating fancy' could be shelved beside the frankly hallucinated poetry-philosophy of the 'surrealists' (meaning, presumably, Breton and his successors). Yet their philosophy, he concludes, is 'only' an offshoot of their art, whereas Bloch 'purports to be using the language of discursive philosophy, in which the ambiguity of basic concepts is suicidal'.

It is at this point that Dr Hudson's defence of Bloch wavers alarmingly. The problem as Hudson defines it is that Bloch's recursive modernism — a refunctioning procedure generally associated with the Frankfurt School — 'forces him to retreat into cypher talk at so many analytically crucial points that Open System runs the risk of being poetry philosophy, a theurgic aestheticist Weltanschauung: a system of faith in hope with splendid meta-mystical meditations, but little explanatory power'.[22]

Thrust into the dock where Freud (whom he revered) has repeatedly been arraigned for 'unscientific' procedures and where Marx has been condemned on every ground, Bloch can survive the denunciations more easily than the embarrassments of a defence that calls to the witness box friends and colleagues who will testify that he was a 'good' man, a brave, and indeed a noble, one. But suddenly there arrives in England — of all countries surely the least aware of Bloch's existence, let alone his greatness — an unexpected emissary who brings neither an ecumenical appeal for clemency nor even a pretext for one, but simply a collection of the essays he has translated from a volume published more than a decade ago — a volume whose significance had been quite overlooked in the English speaking world.

*   *   *

Perhaps as a present for Bloch's ninetieth birthday, certainly as a little gallery from which to observe from an unexpected angle the now-finished edifice of the Complete Edition, his wife Karola assembled, in 1974, an anthology of his musical writings, for publication in the Bibliotek Suhrkamp series under the title *Zur Philosophie der Musik*. The first half of the anthology is devoted to the complete

---

[21] Kolakowski, *Main Currents*, vol. 3, pp. 434–5.
[22] Hudson, *Marxist Philosophy*, pp. 151–2.

xxi

'Philosophy of Music' from the 1923 version of *Geist der Utopie*; the second half ends with a comparable excerpt from *Das Prinzip Hoffnung*; and between comes a sequence of articles and reviews from the inter-war period. The delight this 330-page volume must have given its now all-but-blind author was surely heightened by the companion volume his publishers, with extraordinary sensitivity, provided for it: a new edition of Busoni's *Entwurf einer neuen Ästhetik der Tonkunst*, incorporating Schoenberg's marginal notes transcribed from his own copy of the first edition. In his postscript, H. H. Stuckenschmidt described the *Entwurf* as 'a piece of the true Utopia'.

Busoni had published his *Entwurf* in Trieste in 1907, and dedicated it to 'Rilke, the musician in words'; Bloch had written *Geist der Utopie* in wartime Switzerland (where Busoni too sought refuge) between April 1915 and May 1917, and dedicated it to his first wife Else von Stritzky, a devout Christian who died in 1921 but remained a lasting influence on his work. One of the links between the *Entwurf* and *Geist der Utopie* is the notoriously 'unscientific' Schoenberg;[23] but it is also Schoenberg who helps account for the immense distance between these works – not so much the Schoenberg of the *Harmonielehre* (1911), which Bloch alludes to, as the Schoenberg who tried in vain to persuade Richard Dehmel in 1912 to collaborate with him on a mystico-revolutionary oratorio.

Geist der Utopie is one of the classics of German Expressionism. Just as its poetic leanings prefigure the poetry of Bloch's slightly younger contemporaries such as Rudolf Leonhardt and Johannes R. Becher, so do its tonal blends of revolutionary red and biblical blue produce heliotropic effects that seem to envisage the post-1918 paintings of Ludwig Meidner. Contemporary Anglo-American literature has nothing comparable; one has to go back through Shelley to Blake in the one direction, through Melville to the New England Transcendentalists in the other, to find distant equivalents.

In the music of Bloch's words there are certainly echoes from the Rilke Busoni admired. Far more important, however, is the place of

---

[23] The criticism of Schoenberg's achievement formulated by his young post-war admirers, notably Pierre Boulez and Karlheinz Stockhausen, is of a kind frequently encountered in Dr Hudson's exegesis, and summarised in his penultimate paragraph (p. 217), where Bloch is yet again reproached for neglecting to 'develop systematically' what is 'really new' in his work. Dr Hudson nevertheless feels that Bloch is now one of 'the bold men' from whom 'more careful thinkers' have much to learn.

honour *Geist der Utopie* reserves for music itself. In the 1918 edition, the seventy-odd pages preceding 'Philosophy of Music' end with an essay on 'The Comic Hero' – Don Quixote, briefly but illuminatingly compared with Don Juan. One of the main reasons for the essay's disappearance from the later edition seems to be structural: although the important Blochian motif of the idealistic day-dream makes its first appearance here, there is no natural progression from the Knight of the Sorrowful Countenance to that realm of heretical freedom which, in Bloch's world, is music's own, but which music has nevertheless had to reconquer again and again throughout history. (In that sense Mozart's Don would have served Bloch better; but his time is yet to come.) The removal of 'The Comic Hero' (whose laughter is 'the laughter of persecution') leaves the previous chapter's consideration of Van Gogh and his explosion of 'still' life into 'nameless mythology' and its references to Kokoschka and Marc, Kandinsky and Pechstein, even Picasso, to prepare for the modernist and revolutionary perspectives of 'Philosophy of Music'.

Not that wartime Switzerland can have afforded Bloch much opportunity of hearing the music of Kokoschka's and Kandinsky's peers. But he had already breathed the planetary air of Schoenberg's Second String Quartet, and known what it portended for music and the world. The word-play that enables him to conceive of a new age in which 'Hellhören' (second hearing, in a visionary sense) will replace the defunct art of 'Hellsehen' (second sight, or clairvoyance) reminds us that *Geist der Utopie* is almost exactly contemporary with Charles Ives's *Essays before a Sonata*, where the Hawthorne movement is described as music 'about something that never will happen, or something else that is not', and the oracular Beethoven is rediscovered through Emerson and Thoreau.[24] Early in 'Philosophy of Music' Bloch takes Nietzsche to task for seeing music solely as an art of socio-historical retrospection; near the end, he discovers in Jean-Paul a passage that corresponds precisely to his own view of music as the incarnation of the Utopian spirit. Why, asks Jean-Paul, does music's capacity to effect transitions more swiftly and potently than any other art 'make us forget a higher attribute of music, its

---

[24] Henry and Sidney Cowell, *Charles Ives and His Music* (New York: Oxford University Press, 1955), pp. 83–6; the 1969 edition of Ives's *Essays before a Sonata* (London: John Calder) includes later essays and documents that extend the Utopian perspectives into the field of populist politics – e.g. the 1938 letter to Roosevelt, and the proposals for 'A People's World Nation'.

power of nostalgia, not for an old country we have left behind but for a virgin one, not for a past but for a future?'

That quotation did not appear until the 1923 revision of *Geist der Utopie*. But the seeds from which were to grow the forest of *Das Prinzip Hoffnung* had already been planted and were sprouting in the 1918 version. At a point equidistant between the signpost 'Das Bachsche und das Beethovensche Kontrapunktieren' and an excursion to Kepler, Bloch returns by Shakespearean moonlight to Bayreuth, as if to the *locus delicti* of Romanticism. But the unhappy portents of his earlier visits are not fulfilled; for Wagner is now to be acknowledged as Beethoven's truest heir. Meanwhile, and still by moonlight, Bloch takes over from Wagner his own rightful portion of Schopenhauer's vision theory, and uses it to distinguish between the dream that 'sinks down' in contemplation of the daylight experience and the one that 'moves beyond' what has already existed into a 'not-yet-conscious-knowledge' – a knowledge which, by 1923, he can already describe as 'dawning'. By then, the dream that 'moves beyond' is clearly identified with that 'dream of a thing' which Marx apostrophised in one of Bloch's favourite passages, the letter to Ruge of September 1843.[25]

When all the philosophical sources of *Geist der Utopie* have been uncovered, when the contributions of Kant and Hegel have been measured against those of Nietzsche and Bergson, when Lukács has been credited with the traces of Dostoevsky and Kierkegaard, and Böhme detached from latter-day theosophists, when Dilthey and Simmel, the Kabbalah, the New Testament, and the Book of Revelations, have all been taken into account, a single absence and a single presence seem to dominate the Utopian whole. The absence, clearly located just beyond the line of vision, and announced by the trumpets and trombones of the final chapter-heading, is that of Marx; the presence is that of a philosopher without whom, as Bloch remarked many years later, there would have been neither Nietzsche nor Freud, nor, for that matter, Marcuse or Adorno – the one philosopher

---

[25] Karl Marx, ed. Siegfried Kröner, *Die Frühschriften* (Stuttgart: Alfred Kröner, 1978), p. 171. Alfred Ruge (1803–80) was a friend of Marx, Engels, and Heine, and the recipient of many important letters from Marx in the early 1840s. Bloch's references to the September letter are numerous: see for instance *Atheismus im Christentum*, GA 14, ch. 52, pp. 344–8; or the discussion 'Die neue Linke und die Tradition', in Ernst Bloch, ed. Hanna Gekle, *Abschied von der Utopie?* (Frankfurt, 1980), p. 277.

whose pessimism was so constructed that it could serve at all times as a crucible for the base and precious metals of Bloch's optimism: Schopenhauer.[26]

It was Schopenhauer who held that if it were possible to explain everything that music expresses, the result would be 'the true philosophy'. In effect, Bloch carries Schopenhauer's speculation to its extreme. For him, music at its best, and sometimes at its second best, *is* philosophy, requiring only the broadest of glosses and here and there an exemplary definition. Critics and commentators, including even the gifted Paul Bekker, who prattle about 'expressively pleading demi-semiquavers' and see in music a need or excuse for 'the play of supplementary imagery' are anathema to Bloch. And no wonder: for it is essential to his philosophical purpose that music is imageless and without narrative form; that it is wholly intelligible as formal process yet enigmatic as to its teleology; that it derives its energy from the anticipatory presence, from intimations of the 'not-yet'; and therefore (in a crucial phrase which appears only in the 1923 version but applies equally to the original) 'that music as an inwardly utopian art is completely beyond the scope of everything empirically verifiable'.

Or, as Charles Ives suggests in the Epilogue to his Essays, 'maybe music was not intended to satisfy the curious definiteness of man; maybe it is better to hope that music may always be a transcendental language in the most extravagant sense'. The Bloch of *Geist der Utopie* in general, and 'Philosophie der Musik' in particular, has long since abandoned the neo-Kantian pacts between philosophy and science. Like Lukács in *The Theory of the Novel* (1916) he is developing his own form of Diltheyan 'Geisteswissenschaft' and 'Geistesgeschichte', in which the play of intuition and mystical irrationalism is central.

Their effect is still felt when Bloch, greatly daring, enters the field of 'Musikwissenschaft'. His extensive debts to Riemann and his successors – notably Ernst Kurth and Hermann Abert – and again to such leading interpreters and practical musicians as Schweitzer and (with regard to Bruckner) August Halm,[27] are more amply repaid in

---

[26] The strength and durability of the inner bond between Bloch and Schopenhauer is attested by his lectures in Tübingen during the winter semester in 1964/5: see 'Recht und Unrecht des Pessimismus', in Bloch, ed. Gekle, *Abschied*, pp. 11–39.

[27] Unlike Riemann, Kurth, and Abert, August Halm (1869–1929) has been largely neglected in Anglo-American studies of the history and practice of musical analysis; for Bloch's debt to his work, see Tibor Kneif, 'Ernst Bloch und der

intuitive understanding and imaginative insights than in scholarly precision. Adorno's complaint[28] that Bloch is as impatient with musico-technical logic as with aesthetic discrimination cuts both ways and draws some blood, not all of it Bloch's. In 'Philosophy of Music' it is clear from the start that Bloch has no inhibitions with regard to academic proprieties in musicology, criticism, and appreciation. When in later years he was defending Wagner against 'impudent snobs', he remarked that they lacked, among other things, the ability to 'hear round corners'. That ability he himself possessed to a high degree – which is one reason why it is impossible to imagine him poring over scores to check his references. Yet the idea of furnishing 'Philosophy of Music' with pedantic footnotes – let alone 'correcting' the actual text – is plainly preposterous.

In that respect there is something to be learnt from the reception of *Geist der Utopie*. A lengthy review by Margaret Susman in the *Frankfurter Zeitung* of 12 January 1919[29] provoked a riposte from Paul Bekker (who was that paper's music critic, and can hardly have enjoyed Bloch's comments on his Beethoven book). Concentrating on Bloch's cavalier attitude to musical history, his shaky technical analysis, and his proneness to factual error, Bekker concluded that everything Bloch had tried and failed to realise in his 'Philosophy of Music' had been achieved by Spengler in the musical section of his precisely contemporary *Decline of the West*. As Bekker well knew, it was a highly provocative comparison, for Spengler's prestige and success owed much to the timeliness with which his impressively weighty work had provided the conservative-nationalist middle class with analgesics for the aches and pains of Germany's defeat.

Little knowing that Spengler was about to be arraigned by Alfred Einstein for musicological offences no less heinous than Bloch's, Margaret Susman returned to the fray, protesting, rightly, that Spengler's and Bloch's purposes were in no respect comparable, least of all with regard to the role their work allotted to music. She acknowledged Bekker's incontestable authority in musical matters, but questioned whether it entitled him to isolate the musical strata

musikalische Expressionismus', in Siegfried Unseld (ed.), *Ernst Bloch zu ehren* (Frankfurt, 1965), pp. 295–8; for Halm in general, see Regina Busch, 'August Halm und die Konzertform', in *Notizbuch* (Berlin, no. 5/6, pp. 107–52).

28 T. W. Adorno, 'Bloch's Spuren', in *Noten zur Literatur* II (Frankfurt, 1961), p. 140.
29 Susman's review, and her rejoinder to Bekker's riposte, are reprinted in the appendix to Unseld, *Ernst Bloch zu ehren*, pp. 383–93.

from a work of philosophy and then argue that their musicological shortcomings invalidated the whole structure.

If the function of music in Bloch's philosophy is that of parable and metaphor, detour and shortcut, the case against dissociating such excursions from their philosophical base is not inconsiderable. But the 1974 anthology was excused from answering it by the personal significance it manifestly had and by the historical one that the Busoni volume enhanced. Moreover it was on every side supported by the Complete Edition and its attendant commentaries.

The present anthology must, for the time being, stand alone. Its latticed structure should however offer many points of entry to whatsoever segments of the Complete Edition may be made available to English readers during the coming years. Like the 1974 anthology, it begins with the 'Philosophy of Music' from *Geist der Utopie*, and ends with a corresponding excerpt from *Das Prinzip Hoffnung*; between, there is a shorter selection from Bloch's inter-war writings on musical topics. The essays on *The Threepenny Opera*, on Stravinsky, and on Wagner which immediately and with challenging effect followed the 'Philosophy of Music' in the 1974 anthology have not been included, but on historical grounds certainly merit our consideration here.

All three essays reflect, from different angles, Bloch's friendship with the conductor Otto Klemperer.[30] Although their personal acquaintance did not begin until they were introduced to each other by Furtwängler in Berlin in the early twenties, Klemperer had read and been enthralled by the manuscript of *Geist der Utopie* as early as 1916 (thanks to his friend and Bloch's former teacher Georg Simmel). At that stage the manuscript probably still lacked its apostrophes to Marx. By 1924 and the first publication of the essay 'On the Mathematical and the Dialectical Character of Music', Bloch had evolved his idiosyncratic version of Marxism, and Klemperer was joyfully fulfilling the first of his major conducting engagements in the Soviet Union. The revolutionary production of *Fidelio* with which Klemperer opened 'his' Kroll Opera in September 1927 was influenced by his theatre-going in Moscow; and it was surely he who was responsible for commissioning from Bloch the introductory

---

[30] Klemperer's first reading of *Geist der Utopie* and his introduction to Bloch personally through Furtwängler, are described in Peter Heyworth, *Otto Klemperer: His Life and Times*, vol. 1, *1885–1933* (Cambridge University Press, 1983), p. 111–12.

essay in the programme-book. Later that season Bloch likewise introduced Klemperer's own production of *Don Giovanni*.[31]

At the Baden-Baden festival of German Chamber Music in May 1927 Klemperer (who was accompanied by his future Dramaturg at the Kroll, Hans Curjel) had been enraptured by Kurt Weill's *Mahagonny*, a Songspiel or scenic cantata to texts by Brecht. Bloch was not present at that occasion, but Weill attended the premiere of *Fidelio* together with his wife Lotte Lenya, and their friendship with Bloch was consolidated during the following year, after the epoch-making premiere of *The Threepenny Opera* at the Theater am Schiffbauerdamm, in August. October saw the Kroll premiere of Stravinsky's *The Soldier's Tale*, directed by Brecht's close friend Jacob Geis, designed by Piscator's discovery Traugott Müller, and conducted by Klemperer. Bloch's notes on *The Soldier's Tale* and *Oedipus Rex* (rescued from the previous season's Stravinsky programme) were the basis of his important later essay, 'Zeitecho Stravinskij'.[33]

Klemperer's admiration for *The Threepenny Opera* led to the commissioning of the suite, *Kleine Dreigroschenoper*, which he first conducted in January 1929 at one of the Kroll Opera concerts; Bloch's similar enchantment led to his marvellous essay on the 'Pirate-Jenny' Song, which he dedicated to Weill and Lenya and published in January 1929.[34] That same month, Klemperer conducted Jürgen Fehling's radically new production of *The Flying Dutchman*. No small element in the uproar created by that production in nationalist and proto-Nazi circles was Bloch's introductory and style-defining essay 'Rettung Wagners durch Karl May' (Rescue of Wagner through Karl May) (which was included in the 1974 anthology under the later title 'Rettung Wagners durch surrealistische Kolportage' (Rescue of Wagner through surrealistic Penny Dreadfuls)). Bayreuth, it seemed, was about to be stormed by Peachum and his beggars.

---

[31] Bloch's connections with the Kroll are documented in Hans Curjel, *Experiment Krolloper 1927–1931* (Munich: Prestel Verlag, 1975).

[32] The relationship between Bloch and Weill is discussed by the present writer in the closing section of his contribution to *The New Orpheus*, a symposium edited by Professor Kim Kowalke for the Yale University Press, due to be published in 1985.

[33] 'Zeitecho Stravinskij' was included in *Erbschaft dieser Zeit* and was reprinted in *Zur Philosophie der Musik*.

[34] Ernst Bloch, 'Lied der Seeräuberjenny in der "Dreigroschenoper"', in *Verfremdungen* 1 (Frankfurt, 1962).

From *The Threepenny Opera* to *The Flying Dutchman* would for most musical travellers of the day have been an inordinately long and dangerous journey; for Bloch it was surely no more demanding than the one that had taken him, on numberless youthful occasions, from his family home in the industrial port of Ludwigshafen to the old Palatinate capital of Mannheim on the opposite side of the Rhine.[35] The fairgrounds and circuses and amusement arcades of plebeian Ludwigshafen offered the young Bloch delights far removed from the patrician theatres and libraries of Schiller's Mannheim. In music as in the other arts his 'questionable' taste was a vital part of his own questioning of 'taste' and the hierarchies it stood for; but it was equally a part of his quest for the utopian spirit in whatever guise it might appear. There was no condescension about his tributes to those forms of popular art and *Kitsch* that reflected a universal truth. The chapter in *Das Prinzip Hoffnung* concerning fairs and circuses, fairytales and penny dreadfuls, is entitled 'Bessere Luftschlösser' ('better castles in the air').

Bloch's passion for aerial and low life excursions was one of his many bonds with Walter Benjamin, the outstanding critical mind among his younger German contemporaries and, like Klemperer, an early admirer of *Geist der Utopie*. It was surely thanks to Bloch and his essay on Offenbach's *Tales of Hoffmann* – written for the 1930 Kroll Opera production by Brecht's friend and colleague Ernst Legal – that Benjamin, whose genius was either unresponsive to music or else (in some sense that he never defined) intimidated by it, ventured his only essay on a musical subject – the Offenbach section of his great Karl Kraus study, first published in the programme book for the 1931 Kroll production of *La Périchole* in the Kraus version.

The closure of the Kroll at the end of the 1930–1 season was rightly seen to be representative of a reactionary trend evident at all levels of German culture and society. For Bloch and Benjamin, as for Brecht, there was no hope of reversing the trend unless Marxist theory was put into action, which meant collective and party action. The possible consequences of that for intellectuals who were unwilling or unready to repudiate their heritage of 'bourgeois' individualism and morality had already been examined in Brecht's first indisputable masterpiece for the theatre, *Die Massnahme* (The

---

[35] See Ernst Bloch, 'Ludwigshafen–Mannheim', in *Erbschaft dieser Zeit* (GA 4), pp. 208–11.

Measures Taken), a Lehrstück set to music by Hanns Eisler and first performed in Berlin in the autumn of 1930 under the baton of Karl Rankl (Klemperer's chorus-master at the Kroll). Functionally ambiguous as it is, *Die Massnahme* examines Leninist theory and practice in terms that cut straight across the two currents in Marxism characterised by Bloch as 'cold stream' and 'warm stream'. The fact that the 'measures taken' are in principle consistent with the new morality of revolution propounded by Lukács in the post-1918 era, has a direct and curious bearing on the debates with Lukács in which Bloch, Brecht, and Eisler were engaged during the 1930s. But *Die Massnahme* itself does not figure in Bloch's writings, and is not even mentioned in his 1938 essay on Brecht, 'Ein Leninist der Schaubühne', or its important predecessor 'Romane der Wunderlichkeit und montiertes Theater' which proceeds from Kafga through Proust and Joyce to the 'Leninist' Brecht.[36]

Die Massnahme happened to introduce (and today throws an inquisitorial light upon) an era in which most of the 'measures taken' were strictly reactionary. The closure of the Kroll was representative in that a plausible case could be made for it in terms understandable to all. Its effect on the flow of Bloch's musical writings was immediate: the only musical essay Bloch was to publish during the two years that remained to him in Germany dealt with an opera that Klemperer had taken a close personal interest in – Weill's *Die Bürgschaft*.[37]

Bloch's first major undertaking in exile was *Erbschaft dieser Zeit* (Heritage of this Time), a collection, or as he preferred to call it, a 'montage' of those essays and occasional pieces from the Weimar years that needed to be rearranged in the light of the catastrophe of 1933 and used as indications of the building materials required for the tasks of fortification and reconstruction. (In the original 1935 edition music was represented only by the essays on Stravinsky and on *The Threepenny Opera*, but the enlarged 1959 edition adds the inflammatory 'Rescue of Wagner through Karl May'). The book established the complex of watchtowers and dug-outs from which Bloch, Brecht, Benjamin, and a few others were to conduct their campaign against so-called Socialist Realism in the aftermath of the

---

[36] 'Romane der Wunderlichkeit und montiertes Theater', and 'Ein Leninist der Schaubühne', in *Erbschaft dieser Zeit* (GA 4), pp. 240–54.

[37] Bloch, 'Fragen in Weills Bürgschaft' in *Anbruch* (Vienna, 1932), vol. 14, pp. 207–9.

Comintern-backed 'International Writers' Conference for the Defence of Culture', held in Paris in June 1935.

As a result of one of the Congress's resolutions, Brecht, Lion Feuchtwanger, and Willi Bredel of the KPD were appointed editors of *Das Wort*, a new German language periodical to be published in Moscow. For various reasons, some of them purely practical, the editorial trio was unable to fulfil its proper functions, and by 1937 *Das Wort* was in effect directed by Lukács and his Moscow circle. In the September issue, Klaus Mann and Alfred Kurella led an attack on the 'heritage' of Expressionism with particular reference to the case of the poet Gottfried Benn, by far the most distinguished figure among the small group of erstwhile Expressionists who had attempted to come to terms with Nazism. Kurella, who in 1931 had published in Moscow an extensive critique of *Die Massnahme*, was one of Lukács's closest associates. He took as his starting point Lukács's own polemic against Expressionism, published three years before in another of Moscow's German language periodicals. The break with Bloch, and indirectly with Brecht and Benjamin, was now in the open.

Bloch was at this time working in Prague as a regular contributor to *Die neue Weltbühne*. His first published reaction to the debate was an article in the 4 November issue of *Die neue Weltbühne* entitled, simply, 'Der Expressionismus'. It made only passing reference to Lukács (and to Kurella under his pen-name Ziegler), but ended with a lengthy quotation from *Geist der Utopie*, every line of which Lukács himself must once have known almost by heart.

A month later Bloch continued the debate in partnership with the composer Hanns Eisler, whom he had first encountered in Berlin in 1930, but had lost touch with for the past four years. (Eisler spent the last three months of 1937 in Prague and then headed for New York, where Bloch was soon to join him.) The two imaginary dialogues they published in *Die neue Weltbühne* in December 1937 and January 1938 testified to their now consolidated friendship and to their sense of common cause against the Lukács circle.[38] The first, entitled 'Avantgarde and Popular Front' was between an Optimist and a Sceptic. The latter begins as a Lukácsian anti-modernist, but ends by agreeing with the Optimist that the anti-fascist masses and

---

[38] Ernst Bloch and Hanns Eisler, 'Avantgarde-Kunst und Volksfront' and 'Die Kunst zu erben', in *Vom Hasard zur Katastrophe*, pp. 325–35.

the 'new' (meaning politicised) avant-garde are interdependent and must proceed together. Though music was hardly touched upon in this part of the dialogue, Bloch had found a dramatic way of returning to the subject after more than five years' silence.

In the second dialogue, 'Die Kunst zu erben', the participants are the Art-lover (*Kunstfreund*) and the Art-producer (*künstlerischer Produzent*). Though it is still a joint work and not, as some commentators have assumed,[39] a quasi-naturalistic dialogue between Bloch as *Kunstfreund* and Eisler as *Produzent*, the points of view tend to be more characteristic of the individual participants than in the previous dialogue, and in some passages become wholly so. The direct leap from Offenbach to Wagner which the Art-lover accomplishes in order to affirm Wagner's status as the 'greatest musical phenomenon since Beethoven' was, for such a readership at such a time, a death-defying audacity, and quite unthinkable without the authority that Bloch alone could lend to it. Only a few sentences later Bloch does, in effect, take full responsibility for it by including the name of Eisler in a list – and most remarkable one – of key figures in modernism: Picasso, Stravinsky, Schoenberg, Eisler, Bartók, Dos Passos and Brecht (in that order).

The omission of some names unquestionably important to Bloch – notably Joyce's, since Mann's was scarcely admissible in this context – is less significant than the astonishing inclusion of both Stravinsky and Schoenberg. Stravinsky's barely concealed flirtations with fascism in the 1930s and Schoenberg's more forthright expressions of an old and true conservatism made their presence in the list highly provocative, and not least with regard to the Optimist's case for the natural alliance between modernism and progressive politics. Equally heretical, and equally typical of Bloch – but also of Klemperer – was the juxtaposition of Schoenberg and Stravinsky regardless of the fact that their work since the revolutionary years had divided the musical avant garde into two apparently irreconcilable camps. The possibility of a Hegelian construction on the antithetical basis of Schoenberg and Stravinsky, with Eisler and Bartók as the two halves of a proposed synthesis, is latent in the structure of the list, and seems consistent with the reference to the

---

[39] E.g. Albrecht Betz, *Hanns Eisler – Political Musician* (Cambridge University Press, 1982), p. 162.

'dialectically transitional' realities of the day which opens the final, and very Blochian, paragraph of the dialogue.

As outlines of a modernist and 'warm-stream' aesthetic in opposition to Lukác's neo-classicism, the Bloch–Eisler dialogues bridged the gap between Bloch's first and indirect response to the Kurella's attack and its famous successor, 'Discussionen über Expressionismus', which was published in *Das Wort* itself in June 1938.[40] By that time several distinguished figures (among them, Herwarth Walden and Bela Balász) had already published replies in *Das Wort*. But Bloch's essay dwarfed them all. Kurella was swiftly dispatched: noting the sinister congruence between his views on Expressionism and those promoted by the recent Nazi exhibitions of 'degenerate' art, Bloch turned to the much more formidable figure of Lukács, attacked his argument at its weakest points, and ended by condemning 'abstract methods of thought which seem to skim over recent decades of cultural history, ignoring everything which is not purely proletarian'.

Fittingly enough, the essay on Expressionism was Bloch's envoi to Europe. That same summer Bloch and his wife were reunited with the Eislers at the Connecticut home of a mutual friend, and there celebrated the first birthday of their son. The hard times that followed for Bloch as for so many of the emigrants were part of the background of *Das Prinzip Hoffnung*, but surely a lesser part than the times themselves. It is the date rather than the place or the immediate circumstances in which that great work was written that pertains to its historic character. At whatever stages in his American stay Bloch drafted the various parts of the main musical chapter (V in the present volume) their continuity with the 1918 'Philosophy of Music' is self-evident, not least in the 'Hollow Space' (*Der Hohlraum*, a concept first considered in the book's discourse on

---

[40] 'Diskussionen über Expressionismus' is in the second edition of *Erbschaft dieser Zeit* (GA 4); admirably translated by Rodney Livingstone under the title 'Discussing Expressionism', it opens the NLB anthology *Aesthetics and Politics* (London: Verso, 1977) where it is followed by Lukács's 'Realism in the Balance', a response both to Bloch and to the Bloch–Eisler 'Die Kunst zu erben'. Together with important essays and letters by Brecht, Benjamin, and Adorno, excellent introductory and linking presentations by the three editors, and a conclusion by Fredric Jameson, the anthology is an indispensable guide to the higher levels of the Expressionism debate and its aftermath. See also Erhard Bahr, *Ernst Bloch* (Berlin: Colloquium Verlag, 1979), pp. 43–50 and Markun, *Bloch*, pp. 49–52.

architecture) where the heroic Schoenberg of *Geist der Utopie* is at last reunited with his subsequent achievement.

On his return to Germany Bloch had little occasion or time to carry forward the musical aspects of his philosophy. The draft of *Das Prinzip Hoffnung* had been finished before he left Cambridge, and everything implicit in his dialogues with Eisler ten years before that related to musical politics in Ulbricht's Germany naturally devolved upon Eisler himself when he settled in Berlin in 1950. *Johann Faustus*, the libretto Eisler wrote in close discussion with Brecht in 1951 for an intended opera, was, among other things, a continuation of the dialogues with Bloch by other and very different means (including some derived from Bloch's 'own' Thomas Münzer). It was provocative in exactly the same sense, and sure enough its publication by Aufbau Verlag in 1952 made it a *cause célèbre*. Old enmities from the Expressionism debate were rekindled, party functionaries rallied once again behind the banner of Socialist Realism, and for two years Eisler was virtually persona non grata in the GDR. Nevertheless he returned in 1954 from his temporary refuge in Vienna to deliver at the East Berlin Academy of Arts a spirited defence of Schoenberg, whose very name was still anathema there. Within a year or so he was back in favour. But Brecht, who had decisively come to his defence, had only one more year to live; and Bloch, as we have seen, had little longer than that to wait before the arrest of Harich and his colleagues marked the beginning of his removal from official life in the GDR, and his stepwise migration to the West.

Exactly at this third cross-road of his life, and in the most highly charged atmosphere, Bloch encountered, and by sheer strength of character overcame the apprehensions of, a onetime friend and colleague from whom both he and Eisler had become estranged. With such unique precision did the meeting knit together the human and the philosophical threads in Bloch's life that it would merit some mention here, even if its complex background were not essential to an understanding of his importance for music today.

In 1958 Bloch attended the International Hegel Society's congress in Frankfurt. The principal speaker was Theodor W. Adorno, whom Bloch had probably not seen, and certainly not talked with, since they had parted company in the USA. Adorno had already arranged that he would not sit with Bloch at the opening banquet for prominent guests. When at last he took the platform to deliver his address,

Bloch seated himself discreetly at the back of the hall. During the subsequent discussion, however, he worked his way forward, to Adorno's evident consternation; and then, from an appropriate vantage point, he rose to his feet and delivered an impromptu speech of great brilliance, lasting some fifteen minutes. Of any quarrel with Adorno and his ideas not a word was said, though many had been expected. At the end of the session, Adorno nevertheless tried to make his getaway. But Bloch intercepted him, and with all the humour he alone could have mustered in such a situation, greeted him with the words 'Na, Teddy, wie geht's denn?'.[41]

Adorno had first met Bloch in Berlin in 1928.[42] Bloch, his senior by some eighteen years, was at that time lodging at the West End pied à terre of Walter Benjamin, a friend since their meeting in Switzerland in 1918, at the time of *Geist der Utopie*. Temperamentally and intellectually, Benjamin was the link between Bloch and Adorno, and although closer in age to Bloch – he was born in 1892, Adorno in 1903 – wholly accessible to the precocious Adorno, with whom he was to enjoy ten years of strenuous collaboration. Like Benjamin, though without the benefit of personal contact, Adorno had discovered Bloch through *Geist der Utopie*. Gripped by his first reading of it at the age of eighteen, he saw it as a magical and cryptic counterpart to Lukács's *Theory of the Novel*, and doubtless found in it further inducement for embarking on his studies in philosophy, music, sociology, and psychology at the Goethe University in Frankfurt.

After emerging from the University at the age of twenty-one with a degree in philosophy, Adorno studied composition with Alban Berg in Vienna. On his return to Frankfurt in 1926 he resumed his

---

[41] This account of the Bloch–Adorno meeting is entirely based on the more detailed one in Markun, *Bloch*, pp. 97–100. The author footnotes her quotation of Bloch's greeting in order to record that, whereas Bloch himself remembered saying 'Teddy', two eyewitnesses stated that he in fact said 'Wiesengrund'.

[42] See Gillian Rose, *The Melancholy Science – An Introduction to the Thought of Theodor W. Adorno* (London: Macmillan, 1978) and Martin Jay, *Adorno* (London: Fontana, 1984) for brief accounts of Adorno's career and invaluable consideration of his philosophical and sociological work. There is as yet no full-length biography in any language: Gerhard P. Knapp's brief monograph *Theodor W. Adorno* (Berlin, 1980: Colloquium Verlag) provides much biographical information that is not available elsewhere, but some important dates (for which no sources are given) differ significantly from those in Rose and Jay. The standard English-language work on the Frankfurt School in general is Martin Jay's *The Dialectical Imagination* (Boston: Little, Brown & Co., 1973).

philosophical studies, submitting as his inaugural dissertation for the University a development of neo-Kantian and Freudian ideas, but later withdrawing it on his teacher's advice, and starting a new dissertation on Kierkegaard, the father of Existentialism. During this first year in Frankfurt he established informal relations with Horkheimer's Institute of Social Research – where so much of his future lay – and continued his secondary career as a writer on music.

In the intellectual world of Weimar Germany, Frankfurt was Berlin's sister city; and by 1928 Adorno had already made Berlin his second home. Musically the presence of Schoenberg was a compelling, if also awe-inspiring attraction, balanced on the one hand by Adorno's friendships with several members of Schoenberg's masterclass at the Academy of Arts, and on the other by the tentative, inquisitive, and, for him, dangerous understanding he reached that same year with his slightly older contemporary Kurt Weill (whom Bloch had already met through Klemperer).[43] On the personal and intellectual levels, the decisive influences at this stage were, of course, Bloch's and Benjamin's. But that triangular relationship was soon modified by the intersecting influence of Brecht, and before long it was radically disturbed by the implications of *Die Massnahme*; for the interpretation of Marx that Adorno was now developing in conjunction with his Kierkegaard studies did not lead him as close to the KPD and the Soviet Union as Brecht, Benjamin, and Bloch allowed themselves to go.

Adorno's inaugural dissertation, 'Kierkegaard: Konstruktion des Aesthetischen', was sponsored by Paul Tillich and won him his professorship at Frankfurt in 1931. Although he was removed from his post soon after the Nazi seizure of power, he continued to publish articles and reviews – not all of them above reproach – in German periodicals. Towards the end of 1935 he decided to seek a temporary refuge abroad. Apart from some private visits to Germany, he spent most of the next two years as a research scholar at Merton College, Oxford, re-examining his first philosophical interest, the phenomenology of Husserl. Horkheimer had meanwhile moved his Institute to New York, but left outposts in London and in Paris, where Benjamin remained after Bloch's move to Prague.

By now thoroughly mistrustful of Benjamin's agreement with

---

[43] See the present author's essay in Kowalke, *The New Orpheus* for some discussion of Weill's pivotal role in the Bloch–Adorno relationship, 1928–32.

Brecht in political matters, Adorno nevertheless shared his reluctance to follow Horkheimer to the New World. That he did so at long last, in February 1938, was due to force majeure. Benjamin, finally disillusioned by the Hitler–Stalin pact, decided in 1940 to follow him, but had reached the Spanish port from which he was to sail for New York when a false report that he had been betrayed to the Gestapo caused him to take his own life. A sense of personal involvement in that tragedy undoubtedly contributed to Adorno's more than merely loyal advocacy of Benjamin's work in later years, and was also, perhaps, one of the factors behind his estrangement from Bloch.

In 1941 Adorno accompanied Horkheimer and his Institute to Los Angeles and there wrote the Schoenberg study whose manuscript he showed to Thomas Mann, with such momentous consequences for Mann's *Doctor Faustus*. Brecht was already in Santa Monica, and Eisler was to follow early in 1942 to work with Brecht on the Fritz Lang film *Hangmen Also Die*. Intermittently during the course of that year and the following one, Adorno and Eisler collaborated on the book *Composing for the Film*, commissioned by the Oxford University Press (which, thanks to Paul Tillich, was also interested in *Das Prinzip Hoffnung*). The book was finished in 1944 but not published until the autumn of 1947, by which time Adorno had arranged for his name to be removed from the title page. In accordance with the HUAC summonses issued the previous spring, Brecht and Eisler were at that very time testifying before the Parnell Thomas Committee in Washington.

In 1948 Adorno added to his still unpublished analysis of the dialectics of Schoenbergian 'progress' a complementary analysis of Stravinskian 'reaction'. A year later and shortly before his return to Germany with Horkheimer and his Institute, he combined the two essays, and prefaced them with a weighty introduction whose opening words characteristically, and with cogent symbolism, were taken from the then unknown and forgotten Benjamin. The result of this seven-year process was a book entitled, prophetically, *Philosophie der Neuen Musik*.[44] Its publication in Tübingen in 1949 profoundly influenced the development of New Music for the next two decades, and marked the beginning of Adorno's ascendancy in the musical and intellectual life of the Federal Republic.

---

[44] *Philosophie der neuen Musik* is volume 12 in Adorno's *Gesammelte Schriften* (Frankfurt, 1975).

The force of mind and personality that unites Adorno's critiques of Schoenberg and Stravinsky overrides the disparities of tone and method, but does not exclude an acute responsiveness to the climate of politically disengaged radical thought in the co-ordinated America of the 1940s, and therefore, by implication, to the related ideological conditions of Marshall Plan Europe. While the dialectical channels of his Stravinsky critique are plainly signposted according to his Hegelian system, the Marxist extensions that were fully operative ten years earlier are blocked off and overlaid by meticulously Freudian ones, constructed with a keen eye for every significant parallel. Thus the phenomenon of Stravinskian neo-classicism is no longer seen as reactionary in the political sense he and Bloch attributed to it in the 1930s, but as regressive in a strictly psychoanalytic sense which may or may not have political connotations.

It is not necessary to know the story of Adorno's relations with Bloch in the USA to be struck by the sheer opacity of the three-line footnote that refers, towards the end of *Philosophie der neuen Musik*, to 'Ernst Bloch's distinction between the dialectical and mathematical essence in music'.[45] Neither in 1949 nor when the book was reprinted six years later did Adorno trouble to inform his readers that he was referring to an essay Bloch had published in a long-forgotten journal in 1924, (pp. 183–94 in the present volume). Since there is no other reference to Bloch, this footnote might be dismissed as another of Adorno's displays of esoteric learning were it not for a previous denial of the very essence of *Geist der Utopie*, without overt reference to it or its author. 'The mere idea of humanity, or of a better world', writes Adorno (in 1948) apropos of *Fidelio*, 'no longer has any sway over mankind.'[46]

It was not from Schopenhauer, and still less from Spengler, that Adorno inherited the existential despairs of his post-war philosophy but from the Hegelian Kierkegaard. To compare his Schoenberg critique with René Leibowitz's *Schoenberg et son école* is to see why the actuality of Leibowitz in 1946 was about to be superseded by the prophetic Adorno of 1941. In dedicating the 'Prolégomènes' of his study to Simone de Beauvoir and Jean-Paul Sartre, Leibowitz had involuntarily drawn attention to the absence from his own admirably conscientious work of that foresight which ensured that

---

[45] Adorno, tr. Anne G. Mitchell and Wesley Blomster, *Philosophy of Modern Music* (London: Sheed & Ward, 1973), p. 198.
[46] Ibid., p. 19.

Adorno's relatively slender contribution would influence musical developments in the coming decades – while *Schoenberg et son école* was relegated to history. From Adorno's few words about Webern and the 'horror' that has 'cast its spell on the subject' an entire generation of composers was born; from the tremendous single-span paragraph on 'The Antimony of New Music', that same generation built pentagonal defences for the post-war avant garde, and wrested from Heads of State the funding for underground shelters in which the chosen few could preserve the spirit and machinery of progress from the twin catastrophes of commercialism and cultural reaction.

'You know that the subject of the "liquidation of art" ', wrote Adorno to Benjamin in 1936, 'has for many years underlain my aesthetic studies and that my emphatic espousal of the primacy of technology, especially in music, must be understood strictly in this sense.'[47] The Bloch who had declared eighteen years earlier that music is 'completely beyond the scope of everything empirically verifiable' understandably left to Adorno the task of evolving a rationale, a philosophy, and a sociology of music in the post-war, post-Schoenberg, world. Adorno's passionate concern with the problems of craftsmanship and the demands of 'material' was his legacy from the Schoenberg school and hence the Utopian vistas of New Music in its reconstructive phase.

But what then, and what next? 'The mere thought of hope is a transgression against it, an act of working against it': thus Adorno, in the tenth of the twelve 'Meditations on Metaphysics' which concludes one of his last major works, the *Negative Dialectics* of 1964.[48] He had headed the first Meditation with the words 'After Auschwitz', but in truth everything he wrote in the last twenty years of his life implies, or (frequently) insists upon, the transvaluation of values brought about by that particular paroxysm in the history of Western civilisation. Its implications for art and above all for music were never more clearly considered than in the posthumous *Aesthetic Theory* which Adorno intended, most fittingly, to dedicate to Samuel Beckett:

Art's Utopia, the counterfactual yet-to-come, is draped in black. It goes on being a recollection of the possible with a critical edge against the real; it is a kind of imaginary restitution of that catastrophe, which is world history;

---

[47] *Aesthetics and Politics*, p. 121.
[48] T.W. Adorno, tr. E.B. Ashton, *Negative Dialectics* (London: Routledge, 1973), p. 402.

it is freedom which did not come to pass under the spell of necessity and which may well not come to pass ever at all.[49]

Even in these inverted and retrograded forms, the themes are unmistakably Bloch's. They were indeed the basis of a wholly amicable discussion about 'contradictions in utopian longing' which Bloch and Adorno recorded for Südwestfunk in 1964.[50] Without deserting his own position, Adorno here accomplishes the considerable feat of suggesting complete accord with Bloch, above all in the key passage where he ventures to recall Bloch's 'conflicts' in Leipzig. Attributing to Ulbricht some 'philistine twaddle' to the effect that Bloch's Utopia is not at all realisable, he exclaims crossly that 'we do not *want* it to be at all realisable'. The 'we' is perfectly placed: it enables him to consolidate in a political sense his previous agreement with Bloch that modern medicine's vision of the 'abolition' of death is splendid as an incentive but repugnant as a realisable end. Pretending surprise at finding himself in 'the unexpected role of an advocate of the positive', Adorno remarks that the Utopian element missing from Eastern-bloc socialism has allowed it to become an instrument of oppression, and agrees with Bloch that the same element is missing in the West.

If Adorno's bearing in the radio discussion seems at times almost too friendly to be true, his finely measured tribute to Bloch on his eightieth birthday a year later is beyond suspicion.[51] Yet the truest, the most characteristic, and the most comprehensive of Adorno's tributes to Bloch was written in America, in 1947 – that is, at exactly the time when the two men, estranged for some years, were about to go in opposite directions. To suggest that it was an unconscious tribute is only to underline, in this most self-conscious of writers, its unfiltered authenticity.

The passage is the 'Finale' of *Minima Moralia*, at once the most personal and the most Benjaminian of Adorno's works. 'The only philosophy', it begins,

which can responsibly be practised in the face of despair is the attempt to contemplate all things as they would present themselves from the standpoint

[49] T.W. Adorno, tr. C. Lenhardt, *Aesthetic Theory* (London: Routledge, 1984), p. 196.

[50] Ernst Bloch, 'Etwas fehlt . . . Über die Widersprüche der utopischen Sehnsucht. Ein Gespräch mit Theodor W. Adorno', in Traub and Weiser, *Gespräche mit Ernst Bloch*, pp. 58–77.

[51] Adorno, 'Henkel, Krug und frühe Erfahrung', in *Ernst Bloch zu ehren*.

of redemption . . . Perspectives must be fashioned that displace and estrange the world, reveal it to be, with its rifts and crevices, as indigent and distorted as it will appear one day in the messianic light.[52]

So speaks the philosopher in whom, it is claimed, there was nothing of Benjamin's metaphysical leanings, let alone Bloch's. Adorno does not define the source or aim of the redemptive power, but maintains that this is of no account: for the sake of the possible, thought must comprehend even its own impossibility.

At the precise centre of the 'Finale' – fittingly enough, at the twelfth of its twenty-four lines in the English version – a single highly charged phrase marks the intersection between Bloch's orbit and Adorno's ecliptic: 'consummate negativity, once squarely faced, delineates the mirror-image of its opposite'. The consummate and unflinching negativity of Adorno's post-war philosophy, including his philosophy of New Music, delineates with the utmost clarity the mirror images of *Geist der Utopie* and *Das Prinzip Hoffnung*.

It has been suggested that Adorno's pessimism arises from his disappointed ambitions as a composer.[53] The theory does not bear examination. Aside from the not inconsiderable merits of his compositions, it is clear that Adorno never saw himself simply as a composer, but rather as an all-round musician – pianist and accompanist, critic and theorist. In this sense he had no cause for disappointment, and was never without the kind of admirers he merited. If his views on the 'difficulties'[54] of composition in the twentieth century, and especially in its second half, were a projection of his own difficulties, the same could surely be said of every contemporary composer who demands from himself, and from others, absolute probity of intent and execution at every structural and expressive level. It is only when Adorno confronts the specific question of what is and is not artistically justifiable in the aftermath of Auschwitz that the trajectory of his own composing career seems relevant. The silence which certain outstanding talents have from time to time or permanently imposed on themselves is that from which Adorno, in his *writings* about New

[52] T.W. Adorno, tr. E.F.N. Jephcott, *Minima Moralia – Reflections from Damaged Life* (London: Verso, 1974), p. 247.

[53] See Roberto Gerhard, 'Is New Music Growing Old?' (Ann Arbor, Michigan: School of Music Series, vol. 62, no. 18, 10 August 1960) for a rebuttal of Adorno that is altogether too urbane to touch on the delicate question of his compositions. In conversation (with the present author among others) Gerhard was less kind.

[54] E.g. T.W. Adorno, 'Schwierigkeiten – 1. beim Komponieren', in *Impromptus* (Frankfurt, 1968), pp. 93–112.

Music, was struggling to escape lest it might after all prove to be the last refuge of untarnished musical truth – the inaudible concord uniting Beckett and Barraqué, Cage and Boulez.

Premonitions of the end of Western bourgeois culture and recollections of all that Auschwitz portended for it are so deeply embedded in the texture of Adorno's thought that the 'finale problem' he acutely analyses in musical contexts becomes very much his own in philosophical and aesthetic ones. It is surely the humanist in him rather than the composer that so often recoils from closing his literary works on that pitchless extreme of discontent towards which his arguments constantly tended. Indeed, Adorno the composer could well have rejected as insufficiently integrated the Blochian motifs to which Adorno the philosopher resorts in order to sustain and give force to cadential structures that might otherwise dissolve into nothingness. The close of his *Versuch über Wagner* is particularly notable in that the tendency of the entire book has been directly opposed to the positive though by no means uncritical view of Wagner Bloch had been offering ever since *Geist der Utopie*. The antithesis is strengthened by Adorno's penultimate turn to Schoenberg and his Second String Quartet, which brings him to the selfsame threshold of New Music that Bloch had reached in *Geist der Utopie*, but allows him to draw from George's text conclusions that once again contradict Bloch's. Yet the fresh start announced in the Second Quartet inspires Adorno to modulate from his post-Nietzschean perception of Wagner's negative significance into the purely Blochian idealism of a final affirmation of music's 'age-old protest' and its 'promise of a life without fear'.[55]

Had this been the end of a chapter rather than of a book, Adorno might well have continued by remarking, as he did elsewhere, that art's promise of felicity is a 'promise that is constantly being broken'.[56] The disillusionment Adorno pursues and cherishes so ardently belongs within the dark circle at the foot of Bloch's lighthouse, and is as far removed from any modish cynicism as it is close to those apprehensions about which Kracauer – a lifelong friend of both men – speculated with such feeling. If at times Adorno reads like a repressed figment of Bloch's imagination it is because of an inseparable bond between them that became visible only in the years

[55] T.W. Adorno, tr. Rodney Livingstone, *In Search of Wagner* (London: Verso, 1981), p. 156.
[56] Adorno, *Aesthetic Theory*, p. 196.

1929–32, when Adorno's Marxian enlightenment was complemented by Bloch's discovery, through Adorno, of new musical significances.

It is of course in music that the strictly complementary nature of the two men is most apparent. Adorno's description of his own philosophy as 'atonal' was in no sense an affectation. It does however emphasise the fact, often overlooked, that he was fundamentally, in his innermost nature, a musician, in contrast to Bloch, who spoke of 'composing' *Geist der Utopie* but was from first to last a philosopher:[57] one for whom music was a system of geodesic lines traversing the many-contoured surface of his thought and pointing towards that transcendent future in which Adorno was to lose faith in the 1940s.

To read Adorno 'after Auschwitz' is to understand much about him; but to read him 'after Hiroshima' is to wonder why the musician who in 1936 affirmed his 'emphatic espousal of the primacy of technology' was so uncommunicative, a decade later, about an enormity equally symptomatic of our 'administered world' but much closer to the fissile core of Western musical experience – to the experience, that is, of present, past, and future time.[58] That failure is perhaps one of the reasons why in recent years the author of *Geist der*

---

[57] Music and physics were Bloch's secondary subjects at University. He was a competent pianist, and in his adolescence had thought of composition. Looking back on his musical beginnings in 1974, he remarked: 'I would probably have become a mediocre Kapellmeister but for . . . a certain talent for philosophy', see *Tagträume vom aufrechten Gang*, p. 31.

[58] Although one of Bloch's last public acts was to sign an appeal against the neutron bomb (Markun, *Bloch*, p. 121), the topic was no more prominent in his writings than in Adorno's. How far it is amenable to his 'Prinzip Hoffnung' is a question for a book, not a footnote; that the hard-headed technical, military, and political analysis it calls for can nevertheless be integrated with the moral and humanitarian considerations generally omitted from such analyses is illustrated by Farley Dyson's book-length essay which *The New Yorker* published in four parts (6, 13, 20, and 27 February 1984) under the suggestive title 'Weapons and Hope'. Dyson – a scientist, the son of an eminent musician, and politically a disciple of George Kennan – evolves a theory of disarmament based on the long-term goal of a (relatively) nuclear-free and peaceful world. Noting that it is purely utopian in present-day terms, but no more so than the abolition of slavery had once seemed to be, he examines with sympathy the idealistic proposals of today, analyses their weaknesses, and then, in the more or less harsh light of present realities, formulates the short-term aim which he sees as most likely to promote the interests of the long-term one. The principle is impeccably Blochian, the underlying spirit no less so.

Utopie and *Das Prinzip Hoffnung* has been discovered and wel-comed by European composers nurtured on Adorno.[59]
Wherever Adorno is known and understood, there can be no danger of Bloch's being misused as a rallying-point for further exped-itions by younger composers into those areas of Romanticism redis-covered by New Music in the years following Adorno's death. Bloch belonged to the last generation that experienced Romanticism as a contemporary, if decadent, phenomenon, and characteristically it was the Strauss of *Elektra* who inspired some of his last ruminations about music.[60] But to suggest on that account that his philosophy of music needs updating by Adorno's would misrepresent both systems, for their connectedness is not one of historical succession. Readers content to accept the present volume at face value, irrespective of its philosophical contexts and undeterred by its manifest lack of methodological (let alone Marxist) discipline, may find that the most persuasive arguments for proceeding from Bloch to Adorno are con-tained in the music of diverse composers who, since the death of Bloch, have proceeded in the opposite direction. Whether conscious or (more often) instinctive, their progress has clearly been animated by a sense of the far-reaching truth inherent in the reconciliation Bloch and Adorno themselves achieved on the human level – a sense, that is, of the bilateral and radial symmetries that makes each system

---

[59] An early, and possibly the first, article on Bloch by a leading member of the post-Adorno avant-garde is Dieter Schnebel's 'Forces de la musique nouvelle' in *Utopie – marxisme selon Ernst Bloch* (Paris: Payot, 1976), pp. 93–106. References to Bloch's writings now appear in contexts almost unthinkable ten years ago: see for example York Höller, 'Zur gegenwärtigen Situation der elektronischen Musik' (*Oesterreichische Musik-Zeitschrift* (Vienna), September 1984, vol. 9, pp. 452–8). This development clearly owes something to Schnebel. Theologically a follower of Karl Barth, and politically indebted to Bloch's version of Marx, Schnebel (b. 1930) is a priest and a teacher of religion as well as one of the leading figures in the German musical avant-garde. In 1965 he had written an essay which he dedicated to Bloch on the occasion of his eightieth birthday; 'Forces de la musique nouvelle' was its successor for the ninetieth anniversary. The original German version, entitled 'Gestoppte Gärung', is reprinted in *Dieter Schnebel* – no. 16 in the Musik-Konzepte series edited by Heinz Klaus Metzger and Rainer Riehn (Munich, 1981; Edition Text + Kritik, pp. 112–17). 'Gestoppte Gärung' is a brief survey of New Music in the 1970s, and has no direct connection with Bloch other than its dedi-cation. However, Schnebel ends his 'Festrede' in the same volume (pp. 82–6) by quoting from Bloch (whose name he here couples with that of Schweitzer); and in the same volume Norbert Nagler examines Bloch in the course of his essay 'Musik-philosoph der Freiheit' (see especially pp. 30–1).

[60] Bloch, 'Zur Musikphilosophie. Anagnorisis – Augenblicke des Weiterfindens in der Musik', in *Abschied von der Utopie*, pp. 185–93.

essential to the other. In, for instance, the recent opera[61] that ends where hope 'becomes a Death's head' yet 'begins again'; or in the Mass[62] whose panchromatic Sanctus represents for its composer a 'Utopia' that has to be obliterated by the forces blindly opposed to it at the start of the Agnus Dei in order that it may then be redefined as a remote possibility; or (perhaps most clearly because free of verbal interference) in the entire texture of a vast orchestral work appropriately entitled *Harmonika*,[63] the upwards spiral of Bloch's thought seems to link with the downwards spiral of Adorno's and re-form, once again, as a double helix around the axis of a still conceivable future.

London, 4 February 1985

BIBLIOGRAPHY

The Bloch Complete Edition (Gesamtausgabe, abbreviated to GA) is published by Suhrkamp Verlag in Frankfurt – the publishers of all books noted below and in the footnotes as originating in that city. GA comprises the following volumes:

1 *Spuren*
2 *Thomas Münzer als Theologe der Revolution*
3 *Geist der Utopie*
4 *Erbschaft dieser Zeit*
5 *Das Prinzip Hoffnung*
6 *Naturrecht und menschliche Würde*
7 *Das Materialismusproblem, seine Geschichte und Substanz*

---

[61] Alexander Goehr, *Behold the Sun*, the opera in three acts and ten scenes, text by John McGrath and the composer (London: Schott and Son, 1985; first performance, Duisburg, 19 April 1985). The opera concerns the Anabaptist Revolt in Münster in 1532–5, considered in the light of Norman Cohn's *The Pursuit of the Millennium*, with reference to Bloch's writings on the chiliastic sects.

[62] Wolfgang von Schweinitz, *Messe* for soloists, chorus, and orchestra (London: Boosey & Hawkes, 1984; first performance, Berlin, 1984). Schweinitz (b. 1953) studied with György Ligeti, and absorbed his version of Adorno's musical philosophy (see 'Points of View', *Tempo*, no. 132, March 1980, pp. 12–14).

[63] Helmut Lachenmann, *Harmonika* for solo tuba and orchestra (Breitkopf & Härtel, 1983; first performance, Saarbrücken, 1983). Lachenmann (b. 1935) studied with J. N. David and Luigi Nono, and is perhaps the outstanding figure in the second generation of the post-war European avant-garde. His article 'The Beautiful in Music Today' (*Tempo*, no. 135, December 1980, pp. 22–4) is a version of Adornoist aesthetics modified by Lukács and Christopher Caudwell; *Harmonika* is a landmark in his work, in that it reinstates 'traditional' vertical and horizontal controls but retains the highly individual character and radical function of his earlier work.

The challenge, even to readers fluent in German and trained in philosophy, is formidable. For the rest of us, no means of legitimate access to Bloch should be ignored so long as the dearth of translations continues. In the paperback 'edition suhrkamp' series nos 798 (*Gespräche mit Ernst Bloch* – see n. 3 above) and 920 (*Tagträume vom aufrechten Gang* – see n. 2 above) are helpful introductions: the earlier volume is a collection of press interviews and radio and TV discussions from the period 1964–75, when Bloch, in his eighties, was at the height of his influence in the Federal Republic; the later one (see n. 2 below) is a sequence of interviews given in France in the 1970s, half of which – deriving from a French television series made in 1974 but never transmitted – is loosely autobiographical, and a unique if erratic document. Both volumes have explanatory notes for the general reader (the *Gespräche* are furnished with a glossary of philosophical terms, which Bloch avoids in the French interviews). Also for the general reader, but more advanced than either of these volumes, are the 1965 Festschrift *Ernst Bloch zu ehren* (see n. 2) and the 1968 'edition suhrkamp' volume (no. 251), *Über Ernst Bloch*. Both contain essays of major importance. The only contribution to the *Festschrift* from England was by George Steiner (though his essay 'The Pythagorean Genre' is only tangentially related to Bloch). It was, however, in England that the first full-length monograph on Bloch was published: Wayne Hudson's *The Marxist Philosophy of Ernst Bloch* (see n. 12). As the first work of its kind on a subject at once dauntingly complex and deeply unfashionable, the book already commands respect by its very existence. If at times it betrays the author's uncertainties about his own position as well as about Bloch's, the control of a vast range of material is impressive, and the insights are many. No reader seriously interested in any aspect of Bloch should excuse himself from reading it – least of all on account of the pervasive technical jargon, unnecessarily dense though it sometimes is. Of the shorter studies in the English language, Fredric Jameson's (see n. 9) is essential reading; and Eric Hobsbawm's review of *Das Prinzip Hoffnung* in the *Times Literary Supplement* of 31 March 1961 was deservedly reprinted in his *Revolutionaries* (London: Weidenfeld and Nicholson, 1973). There is as yet no equivalent in English to either of the two brief monographs for the general reader published in Germany in the 1970s: Erhard Bahr's *Ernst Bloch* (see n. 40) and Sylvia Markun's *Ernst Bloch* (see n. 5). These are so different in tone and approach that the documentary–biographical methods they share do not result in any significant overlapping: the two books may with advantage be read in tandem.

For reasons not hard to find, the literature on Bloch and music is sparse, and in the English-speaking world non-existent. The title of Maynard Solomon's essay 'Marx and Bloch: Reflections on Utopia and Art' (in: *Telos*, St. Louis, no. 13, Fall 1972, pp. 68–85) carries resonances of his earlier *Telos* article (no. 9, Fall 1971) 'Beethoven, Sonata and Utopia' and is enough to attract the many admirers of his Beethoven biography (London and New York, 1977); but the essay itself is not specifically musical, and indeed its true function was revealed only when it was divided into two parts and included in Solomon's important anthology *Marxism and Art* (see n. 15).

In Germany, the first notable musicologist of the post-war generation to concern himself with Bloch was Carl Dahlhaus, whose article 'Der Ketzer. Marginalien zu den Schriften Ernst Blochs' appeared in the *Stuttgarter Zeitung* of 5 January 1963. Bloch's eightieth birthday was marked by Karl H. Wörner's 'Die Musik in der Philosophie Ernst Blochs' (*Schweizerische Musikzeitung*, no. 4, 1965) and the fifty-page essay 'Ernst Bloch und der musikalische Expressionismus' which Tibor Kneif contributed to the Suhrkamp Festschrift. In the two decades that have elapsed since the publication of Kneif's essay, nothing of remotely comparable stature has appeared. Hans Mayer's 'Musik als Luft von anderen Planeten', which Bloch's pupil Burghart Schmidt included in his massive documentary volume *Materialien zu Ernst Blochs Prinzip Hoffnung* (Frankfurt, 1978) fulfilled its original function as a *feuilleton* review of Bloch's *Zur Philosophie der Musik* in the context of the Busoni companion volume, but aspires no further than that. The chapter on

Bloch in Wolfgang Cramar's *Musik und Verstehen. Eine Studie zur Musikästhetik Theodor W. Adornos* (Mainz: Matthias Grünewald-Verlag, 1976) is of academic interest only: the book as a whole clearly owes its existence to a doctoral thesis, and its terms of reference are not such as to encourage any investigation into the finer points of the relationship between Bloch and Adorno.

I

The philosophy of music

DREAM

We hear only ourselves.

For we gradually become blind to the outside world.

Whatever we shape leads back around ourselves again. It is not so much exclusively self-oriented, not so much hazy, floating, warm, dark and incorporeal as the feeling always of being simply with ourselves, simply self-aware. It is material and it is experience with alien affiliations. But we walk in the forest and feel we are or might be what the forest is dreaming. We pass between the pillars of its treetrunks, small, spiritual and invisible to ourselves, as their sound, as that which could not become forest again or external appearance of day and visibility. We do not possess it, that which all this around us – moss, curious flowers, roots, trunks and streaks of light – is or signifies, because we are it itself and are standing too close to it, the spectral and still ineffable nature of consciousness or interiorisation. But the sound burns out of us, the *heard* note, not the sound itself or its forms. This, however, shows us our path without alien means, our historically inward path, as a fire in which not the vibrating air but we ourselves begin to quiver and to cast off our cloaks.

ON THE HISTORY OF MUSIC

How do we hear ourselves first and foremost?

As endless singing-to-oneself[1] and in the dance.

Both of these are anonymous. They do not live in themselves, and nobody has performed a personal shaping here. They possess, where one comes across them, the fascination of a primordial beginning. But first, other things had to be traversed, which ensured that the expression was fully and securely equipped.

1

Beginnings

These emerged only gradually. Very little is known of the earliest airs. Not even the songs of the ancient Greeks have survived in any greater number.

What remains today is for the most part barren and without charm. Nor can we form any particularly favourable impression of the sound of ancient Greek and early mediaeval bands. All players had to limit themselves to the one chant. The most that was allowed was to strike up the basic key-note and the interval of the fifth, the bagpipe's fifth, and then to sustain it. Church song too remained within the confines of monophony. Admittedly this was divided up at an early stage by means of the congregational responses. So it is possible that in its impressive psalmody, in the numerous articulations and jubilations of the Ambrosian and Gregorian psalter, in the decoration of its simple, delicate melodic line and in the truly basilica-like solidity of these chants, Church song may have meant more to the congregation than we who are outside of the religious ecstasy can now imagine.

For on the whole all this is dead wood. Much the same applies to the later, polyphonic music of the Middle Ages. It was the itinerant singers who began to invent afresh. They were untutored musicians, and this is reflected in the fact that they were the very first musicians to venture into polyphonic composition. Even during the ages of the strictest monophony, it was at least legitimate for the troubadour to strike an arpeggio. Moreover the harp, being unsuitable for free decoration as a distinctly audible figuration of the melody, led automatically to the blending of chords. So here there was not only freer movement and an expressive necessity. Independently and far more decisively than in the rational experiments made by the harmonists of the time, who excluded the troubadours from the academic school, musicians were clearly coming close to the major and minor tonalities and key-changes of the later period. But the benefits which this brought went begging or were rendered redundant by the later, related and altogether more magnificent masters of Italian cantilena. On the other hand, the contemporaneous experiments in polyphony (and they occurred only in European music) basically did not go beyond the mere theoretical spadework, outside the work's artistic conception, even in the music of the later Middle Ages. Certainly the learned monks discovered all kinds of things. With Hucbald, there is a first inkling of making notes sound together; with Guido d'Arezzo we have the beginnings of more precise notation, with Franco of Cologne, the mensural notation deriving from the custom of singing several notes in the upper part against one. Yet all this was nonetheless a pure academicism, whose intrinsic merits can no longer be properly assessed because we can no longer appreciate the technical difficulties of the period. And even in the theoretical context, the actual craftsmanship was far surpassed by the Flemish composers of the subsequent, already modern, epoch.

But even these composers present a barren prospect. Here the important Josquin comes to mind. Certainly he wrote some smaller pieces full of surprisingly intimate effects that depend entirely on the animation in the voice. But how dry the musical sustenance becomes wherever it is more ambitious! How dour the part-writing is; how unlyrical, expressionless and wanting in melody the artificial and highly respectable composing of Dufay or Ockeghem remains! The text exerts no influence, and the enormous cerebral labour remains fruitlessly locked in itself. It reminds one of the contortions of the 8: the winding figure that leads nowhere. Such work amounted to study scores of immense distinction which, when heard, may not have lacked a certain knotty strength, but which in essence only represented the technical preliminaries to a Baroque style that was to prove completely different. A jolt from below was needed to achieve simplicity, to guide composers back from the vain cerebration of these scores to the abodes of spiritual and textual necessity. Only by such means could the following statement by Luther be fulfilled in its wonderfully anti-formal sense: 'The other masters of song have to do as the notes want, but *Josquin* is master of the notes, and they have to do what he wants.'

The new influence came from the folk-song. If sung in three to six parts, it appeared in the form of a madrigal. Since this, too, remained light and mostly erotic in content, the primordially song-like aspect moved strongly into the lyrical upper voice. Soon afterwards the old modes became broken up chromatically. It was the Flemish composer Willaert who — under Italian influence, significantly — first wrote chromatically and within the new division of the major chord and minor chord. Willaert replaced the previous subtle, variously interwoven texture with the clear, simultaneously sounding chord. Thus he discovered what the Venetians called the *aurum potabile*, i.e. the new possibilities of a harmonic music, in the middle of the purely

3

contrapuntal era. Only a short time after, Hassler introduced the new harmonic sound to Germany in order to infuse the polyphonic treatment of the Protestant chorale with its splendour. Here melody surfaced once and for all. That is to say, the *cantus firmus* which previously lay in the tenor, and hence in a middle voice, was placed in the upper voice so as to subordinate the remaining parts – which now became filler-parts – more and more decisively to the upper part as bearer of the lyrical main melody. Initially this occurred in the most practical manner. The accompanying parts progressed with the upper part as evenly as possible in a simultaneous harmony, rather than each voice, *ex cantus firmi una voce plures faciens*, going its own way by means of imitation, inversion, cancrizans or the other rules of canon and counterpoint. And now, from *Orlando di Lasso* onwards, complete freedom was achieved. Orlando is master of the drinking-song no less than the sobriety of his deeply moving penitential psalms. Everything has become ripe for expression on the grandest scale. The house of tonality has been built, and the actual truly 'musical' breadth, laws of perspective, transcendence of the sound-world, foreshadowed. The individual styles, melodic in the case of the Italians, contrapuntal in the case of the Flemish composers, coalesced to provide the desired medium for an expression attained only with passion and deliberate subjectivity. All severity, one-sidedness and stark alternatives were now a thing of the past. The battle between *trouver*, discovery, and *construer*, contrivance, had been spent and was to remain so for a long time to come. In the person of Orlando, this battle was resolved so fully and decisively that henceforth all the parts sang, and the troubadours and the 'academics' were at one. This enabled both the first, the melodic element (still stemming largely from the scale and not from the chords, and therefore in search less of harmony than of the manifold orderings of counterpointing) and the second element, counterpoint itself – that old art of rational combination, formerly so unconcerned with the beauty of its melismatic and thematic material – to experience their complete union in the joy of music-making. If, however, Orlando was temperamentally akin to Rembrandt, *Palestrina* was temperamentally akin to Raphael. With Palestrina the notes become more tranquil and are organised with a most splendid propensity for a more chordal concurrence and repose. Consider the way in which he groups the few human voices (sometimes, in the Roman chorales, leading back to the most intense harmonic simplicity; and sometimes, as his *Stabat Mater* and, even more, the celebrated *Missa Papae Marcelli* demonstrate, leading into the spatial strength of note-progressions, progressions supplying their own homophonic colouring). For this is already extraordinarily harmonic, not in the dramatic sense but in the sense of what is still conceived of as rhythmlessly seraphic (a carpet for Bruckner and late-period Wagner). Hence only chordal hearing, i.e. a unifying that is vertical below and horizontal only above, where the overall impression of the melodic element occurs, can be reckoned an adequate means of grasping these works. As music's first geniuses, Orlando di Lasso and Palestrina discredited the academic school's construction as an end in itself. The melodic expression, the melody, was elevated to sole content of contrapuntal writing. This writing tended mainly towards the passionate and linear in Orlando's case, the pious and chordal in the case of Palestrina.

The method

Hence from this point onwards one can no longer be limited. For everything pertaining to technique now takes second place. The note is fixed, the seat is established. What is to follow cannot be accomplished by technical mastery. One can be a diligent musician and still fail to produce anything vital, because a mere craftsman will be baffled by precisely that which makes technique worthwhile in the first place.

The technical succession

There is also something else that forces us into vitality. It is quite clear that even with regard to the more significant artists, nothing detracts from them more than to introduce them into, or assign them to, some line of technical development – the history of mere formulae with an intermediary, supporting, technical function. How tedious E.T.A. Hoffmann's *Undine* has become for anyone who is unfamiliar with this approach, and perhaps even more so for one who *is* familiar with it, now that Weber has made a far better job of the whole thing in his *Freischütz*! It makes no difference how much he learnt from the earlier work instrumentally. But how unpleasant, even in Weber, the once so novel harmonisations can sound, particularly in his *Euryanthe*! For on hearing these, we cannot suppress the nagging, absurd idea that Weber was plagiarising *Lohengrin*. Once something has been discovered, it will have forfeited all its interest for later ages. There will be no chance of our imaginatively re-experiencing the original interest at the problematic or newly created stage, if that problem was no more than a technical one. The true uniqueness of the great composers, therefore, is not determined by the history of musical techniques. Otherwise it would be the forerunners who would comprise that prime quality, which they do not possess within them but for which they tirelessly prepare the way in respect of formal structures. The more great masters owe to the rules that have preceded them, the more accurate it is to say that they are novel *not* in technique but in their supremely personal use of it. Do we need to stress that Mozart is unthinkable without the Mannheim composers and the *opera buffa*? Is it the set of rules, rather than what he did with them, that accounts for Gluck's superiority to the old Florentine and old French opera? Must we still go out of our way to add how much Bach himself adhered to what was old? How clearly he departed from the Neapolitan school's increasingly mild type of harmony simply in order to assimilate the old Flemish and Italian composers, rather than Scarlatti? In the course of this, incidentally, a certain *bel canto* was always preserved; and, formally, dances and chansons play a major role. And with regard to the other question, that of counterpoint: where Bach harks back to the past in a way almost comparable to Brahms, he surpasses the contrapuntal learning of the old masters simply in the way he uses it and not somehow in terms of technique. An even stranger case is that of Beethoven, whose new manner was not new at all in technique. For many influences contributed to the sonata. While Haydn may have first created this poly-thematic structure in practice, it is extremely revealing that this objectively tranquil master is the one who lives on as father to the revolution, and that he had a far greater liking for technical experiments than Beethoven had. In contrast, Beethoven himself, who was Haydn's pupil, encountered nothing technical whatever that his specific musical style required him to revolutionise.

Thus here we have nothing to classify or to construct in any kind of 'progressive' way. Great musical personalities are incomparable and are truly born to something better than the shackles of technique. We have only to recall, for instance, Hanslick's malicious prattle about Gluck, against whom he played off Mozart; or about Mozart, against whom he played off Rossini; or about Rossini, against whom he played off Meyerbeer. Then we realise how this exclusively technical pitting of one composer against another lends itself to vileness and the shallowest lack of respect. Especially when, as in this case, the critic suddenly applies the brake at the most resolutely modern point in the music, abandons his precept of day-to-day progress and resorts to history as a stick with which to beat the composer in his own vileness – in which alone our critic remains consistent. If two characters never sing at the same time in *Rhinegold*, this is for reasons exclusive to the work. And, in its essential character, *Tristan* no more harks back to early Florentine monody than *Don Giovanni*, conversely, is a standard music-drama. The other critics, in Hanslick's place, were not much better. The more wretched Wagnerians liked to classify all the old masters of the opera recitative and aria merely as more or less untalented precursors of a Wagnerian style that professedly renders even – or especially – Beethoven's Ninth Symphony redundant. And our repugnance to this attitude shows that a historical classification in terms of craftsmanship, of technique, falls down in the face of all the essential works in the history of music. Indeed it illustrates more graphically the incomparable nature of the individual vitality communicating itself than would be possible without attempting a purely technical-formal 'theory of progress in the craft'.

The sociological context

In music, it is rather a matter of building for any truly great master a personal dwelling, in which he can live for himself as a specific 'condition' beyond the compass of his talents. Herein he is free, housing solely his spiritual self. Needless to say this is quite different from the fashion for establishing a relationship to the contemporary context. After the failure of the technical approach, there is no hope of making some headway by forming links with something similar from the past or by means of other comparative tools. Only the minor and lesser masters have certain colleagues among painters or poets who share their lives and express the same thing in a different way. Nicola Piccini may be Rococo-like, but it would be shallow to claim that Gluck goes with the Louis Seize style, or Mozart with the Austrian Rococo, or Beethoven with the Empire style, or Wagner – well now, to whom or to what might Wagner correspond without reservation? Nietzsche half sensed this at least when he wrote: 'Music is of all plants the last to appear. Indeed, once in a while music peals forth into an amazed and modern world like the speech of a vanished ֩ epoch and comes too late. It was not until the art of the Flemish composers that the soul of mediaeval Christianity found its full resonance; not until Handel that music resounded with the best in the soul of Luther and his fellow-spirits, the great Judaeo-heroic streak which created the whole Reformation movement. Only with Mozart was the age of Louis Quatorze and the art of Racine and Claude Lorrain repaid in gold of the realm; not until Beethoven and Rossini was there a musical finale to the eighteenth century, the century of enthusiasm, of shattered ideals and fleeting happiness.' Certainly external circumstances may have encouraged this profound lack of historical simultaneity. Bach, to be sure, is still understandable 'sociologically', to a minimal degree, from Germany's 'relative backwardness' compared to Western Europe in general. German book-bindings preserved their mediaeval, folio-like appearance amid the elegant formats of the Renaissance and indeed the Rococo age. In the same way polyphony, organic articulation, the superseded line-drawing were retained for a long time in Germany and went by the light of late-Gothic piety amid all the triumphing of the concertante, homophonically individual, emancipated single part. However, all this 'explaining' from external factors is itself external in the last analysis. It does not help us to grasp the phenomenon of Bach as a whole, his profound historical isolation and sociologically inexplicable plane of existence. And even Nietzsche, while grasping music's lack of historical simultaneity, makes it seem all too much of a mere revenant. He relates music itself in too historical a way to past events instead of illuminating it from the perspective of the future, as a spirit *of utopian rank* which, accordingly, is simply constructing a dwelling of its own amid history and sociology, constructing the framework of its own discoveries and inward planes of existence, though with countless elective affinities and free assimilations. It is quite a strange fact, and an anomaly in world-history, that the ancient Greeks and the people of the Middle Ages remained almost silent musically, that Bach should suddenly appear in the age of Watteau, or of Tiepolo, as the heir to a past stretching back seven centuries, a sombre, prolific, perplexing, often Gothic master; and that the very young art of music – a permanent syncope even in modern history – quite patently follows a different rhythm to that of the morphologically, sociologically given cultural frame appropriate to it. Beethoven evolves solely from within himself. Mahler, to all outward appearances, to some extent created his Eighth Symphony in advance for another society. Similarly, Wagner dreams up Eva and the populace on the Festival meadow, a personally chosen, utopian Bayreuth appointed as inspirational by the artist himself, far removed from all contemporary sociology, its contents and form-will. If, then, a composer could feel so independent of the will of his age (and it is a magnificent, mysterious thing that the two greatest composers of the nineteenth century were both revolutionaries), it is surely not the essential part of music – that which goes beyond Mendelssohn, Schumann and mere ceremony – which can be classified in terms of economics and sociology. Thus to wish to make absolute an economic or other standardising study would be a mistake, salutary though it is in all areas other than music. One man's meat is another's poison; it can even be the same force that makes everything flourish in economic and public life but causes one disaster after another in the pure life of artistic creation. One may think otherwise and wish to confine the most diverse activities to the same socio-historical trotting pace, with a view to harnessing twenty horse-power and perversely combining the non-simultaneous, indeed qualitatively incomparable, under the same reins of the epoch. But this outlook will necessarily become all the more shallow and godforsaken the more energetically things begin to move, and the more startling the way such movements seem to explain one another – movements which have fitted so homogeneously into the genetically polyhistorical, the world-historical or even morphologically synoptic concept. Thus we affirm that neither individual, negative, i.e. non-necessary – and, in substance, causally impotent – conditional interconnections of an economic kind nor the inter-human relation, which has public life as the only objectivity and its perennial 'sociology of ---' as a distinct internal limit of competence, can somehow so present the historical divisions and sociologies of music as to make a statement derived from the actual development and facts of this art, regarded as a sphere of its own. To draw inferences largely in social terms or even thereby to encompass the matter completely is only possible in certain instances. The inter-humanly, i.e. socially, engaged mode of study needs to coincide with its object – public morality as an active inter-human relation, or economics, the law and the State as a form of the inter-human relation. Where this is not so, where it is impossible to conclude with the State and to put the other values – art, religion, science and philosophy as the supreme products of public life – into one class, the basic aim of the study has a different, wider-ranging structure. It exists only, as it were, in the sight of an *a priori* beholder, hence claiming for its major representatives, subject-matter and works *a solitary, historically eccentric* typicising according to *a priori* practical and factual problems. It is true that the individual act of genius is not entirely undeducible. But this is different from the outlook of a human group unified over a length of time, where – as occasionally occurred in ancient Greece and in the Middle Ages – the will of the age and the will of genius coincide as though by secret arrangement. Here, great individuals are suddenly involved in a strange rising and falling of the same line; from above them, they hear promptings which their 'I' obeys, and supra-individual tidings which determine the shaping of their work; and the unique determination of genius turns into a symbol for a supra-historical canonic diapason. Here, therefore, a series of relations is disclosed which is truly part of the 'philosophy of history', far removed from any economically sociological pragmatism or morphological synopticism. The great individuals become categories, and the whole sequence of geniuses, especially those of music, starts to cross over to a categorical system concerned with the awareness of ourselves, with God's awareness of Himself.

The explosive youth of music

In music, however, we have, with impunity, been growing ever younger. And it is not skill and maturity but academicism that has disappeared in the process. So from this point of view, too, the customary glorification of the past in all musical matters is sure to be confounded. Admittedly even the most novel types of picture tend to be judged more indulgently than the most modern styles in musical composition at any given time. But people soon get over their shock. Those who wanted in all seriousness to line their ears with sheet-iron on first hearing *Figaro* soon became used to it; and once people had got out of their rut and had discovered and grasped the new structural rules, the dispute over the principles of the beautiful and the melodious was quickly settled. Techniques progressed, small forms disintegrated, form with a deeper expressive basis flourished. Expression was soaring, so markedly that the decline and subsequent powerful upsurge of talented painters in the nineteenth century has no musical parallel whatever. How little mere age signifies in music will be sufficiently evident from two examples. When a young man is supposed to discover the magic that will dissuade him from suicide and restore all his lost vitality, Balzac legitimately uses as the setting for this miraculous shagreen an entire antique shop filled with all the successive fashions, inventions, furniture, designs and relics of the past.[2] When, on the other hand, three libertines have joined forces with a desperate crowd of vagabonds in order to violate nuns and to go in for iconoclasm, and St Cecilia appears in person to rescue her convent,[3] it seems rather pointless of Kleist – musically amateurish, in fact – to have her performing, as he very explicitly states, an ancient Italian mass. A contemporaneous piece by Palestrina would have served her better (and indeed, if we ignore the anachronism, a movement from a Bruckner symphony more magically still). The essential point is this: that one has to depart from all the visual art produced in Balzac's time, or at least race frantically through it, if it is to serve as a significant background to events, whereas the contemporaneous, musical, world of sound can be closely associated with any conceivable exploit or miracle. This is because music is permeated – not only in the self-evident technical skill, but also in the strength of the personal expression – by a single stream of equal-ranking figures. This stream remains unaffected by any rise and fall. It rendered Bach and, in a quite different, more surprising way, Wagner anachronistic, and it made possible in any contemporary music the same high degree of imagination, otherwise traceable only in the past.

But does this new improvement to the note proceed aimlessly? Is not the thriving state of sound, a sound increasingly disporting itself, perhaps an expression of the fact that we have lost the upper ribbon which attaches itself to the objective realm but whose fluttering and dipping ends can still be seen for a while within the subjective? And the more visible these are, and the nearer they come to the ground, the closer the proximity of downfall, animation and end? Above all, does the whole puzzling fact that music has grown increasingly younger, freer and wider in scope, also contain a guarantee of its inexhaustibility and immunity from the *Zeitgeist*? Many factors apparently combine to answer this last question in the affirmative, but only at the price of numerous reservations. And these, while in no way vindicating conventional praise for the past in musical matters, do render problematic the pure youthfulness of music, which is empty

11

and system-free. We have already said that the creator's talent always partakes of the technical assiduity that is self-evident here. In fact it can even be claimed that the power of melodic invention and the love of individual detail in chamber-music part-writing have increased since Beethoven. Nonetheless, all this constantly depends on just one person's eyes, eyes without an image. There is neither a School nor the firm intellectual beauty of a musical style – the only possible style for us – and music is unwilling to make the start. We find only artists and not an art; but the individual artists do not automatically have the right to categorise themselves. Or, if they do, then only in the sense that the great individuals of the past who now stand as categories have formed a categorical framework which conveys to the younger men, disregarding their more magnificent youth, the checks and balances of a sphere which provides the youthful, future-oriented, subjective condition with a substantial foundation. Because they go deeper, musical structures do not possess youthfulness simply as an attribute. Rather, they grow younger precisely by virtue of the fact that they are growing older and rest upon themselves, thus attaining the new-and-old of the secret behind this repose. Hence they are not senselessly participating either as artists or as works of art in the empty, formal, onward march of time. Instead, the new gains roundedness so as to discover its measure and discipline; it becomes something commanding respect, and ultimately a homecoming. And in the end it is exactly what is most reckless and painful, most 'breakaway' and paradoxical that is closest to what is old, most primevally basic, simplest, given, longed for in a previous world, lost in the adult one. In its unpredictability and in the effect this has, the working loose of the inessential and the increasing subjectifying, the validation of quest and adventure, of the spirit of the modern age with itself, to itself which are almost always vital to musical history obey an expressionistic idea. This is directed at what is essential, and it causes invention [*trouver*] to triumph over contrivance [*construer*] time after time. So it is only the undying, unyielding youth, the ceaselessly regenerating youth in a genius who brings maturity with him, but always the very *maturity* which substantiates the 'youthfulness' in the first place. Vagrant dissonances, the intensification of the climaxes and even our so anarchic-seeming atonal music actually form only the lower contrary motion of an upper expressionism which asserts itself therein, and of an intuitive vision of its Gothic exuberance that was scarcely attained in the initial stages. Yet this is all as it is simply by dint of its direction, its remembrancing [*Eingedenken*], its secret *system* of emerging, increasingly emerging youthfulness that is revolutionary out of ultimate orthodoxy. If, therefore, the modern note is in itself the better one, it is certainly not so because of its young looks or its surprisingness, attractive only to those who crave change. It is better because the times – the developing modern times, the time of Advent understood as a symbol – need and love the musician.

The problem of a philosophy of musical history

For this reason the agents of sound, to prevent any dissipation, must always be held together. This act of combining, while handled progressively on the principles of drawing and aiming, is comprehended not only in terms of time but also, and even more so, in terms of space. It is so handled that the individual points which it touches as form acquire an absolute fixity of being. So here it is a matter of comprehending particular subjective states of genius which become canonical for anybody with the gifts of a Mozart, a Bach or a Beethoven. But for this purpose, everything that is merely historically conjoined must be thoroughly separated in favour of a new complete overview. That which is given, apparently with such great differentiation, has grown comprehensive enough to place Mozart prior to Bach, or to prepare from the Mozartian, Bachian, Wagnerian forms a sequence of musical composition and its objects which cannot be transferred to history. It must be postulated again every time, just as the great masters have freely juggled with the differing forms of the song, the fugue or the sonata, as required by the 'spirit' of the pertinent passage. Purely from the temporal standpoint, and hence going by the view which says that each composer destroys his predecessor, the differences are, of course, quite enormous. Nowhere is the change so forcible, and above all the space of time in which this change occurs so markedly rapid and brief, as in music; and in no other art is the road so hopelessly – or, if we prefer, so hopefully – straightforward. Everywhere else there are models, scattered over a broad area, which cover related things, unique encompassings of the absolute and the receptive. The Grecian column but also the Gothic column, the Homeric epic but also the Old Testament are such basic forms, just as Platonic philosophy but also Kantian philosophy are.

13

That is to say, in these fields it suffices to have been the first to make a significant contribution, thereby providing an indestructible model which is at least exhaustive as a carpet: a certain encircling or a certain encompassing, detailing of the possible contents. But only recently, despite the individually effective directional norms already presented by Mozart, Beethoven and indeed Bach, has the new completeness of the better overview been accomplished in music as well. Now as before, a master can feel like a wheel rolling of its own volition, but the senseless turbulence within the progressive criterion has vanished. From vanity and from the most anarchic possible rivalry with what has gone before, there is emerging an edifice and a place in the edifice, so that every idea can find its specific location in the historically given form-complex: a place which is by no means necessarily settled by the position of its actual historical occurrence and very probably calls for further improvement to its content, a stronger imaginative power and a further, utopian dimension. Only recently, since Brahms and to a far greater degree since Bruckner, does the ultimate start appear to have been made. Restless modernism, together with the sheer ceaselessness of its straight line, appears to want to go over to the parabola made up of significant figures, to the *open system* and the occupied or (if the genius has the freshness of a metaphysical irruption) projected areas in this periodic system of musical forms, or rather, signet-categories [*Siegelkategorien*].

There is a clear intention here, and this creates divisions; in addition it creates a pure order. For what takes shape here, I shall introduce Lukács's concept of the *Teppich* or 'carpet' as the pure form which is corrective in nature and his concept of reality as the fulfilled, impinging, constitutive form. Thus, complemented half by a process of explication, half by remembrance, according to the direction of the energy applied, we can distinguish between three schemas. The *first* is endless singing-to-oneself, the dance and finally chamber music, that music which is descended from higher things and for the most part become unauthentically 'carpet-like'. The *second* takes a longer run: it is the uniform song [*geschlossenes Lied*], Mozart or the *Spieloper*, moving in a narrow secular ambit, the oratorio, Bach or the Passions, moving in a narrow sacred ambit, and at the summit the fugue. Now the fugue, to be sure, is already changing into dramatic form [*Ereignisform*] in respect of its unending melody, but it is decisively separated from that form through its

14

purely architectonic, undramatic counterpoint. This, then, is always the abode of the forms of uniform or at least uninterruptedly flourishing, monothematic melody. Our *second* schema has not descended from above into the object-less realm but has its object in a region of the self which is to some extent lighter, more easily attainable, more low-lying. Only, however, so that compared to any more powerful movement, and hence the corresponding dramatic form, it looks like a prelude, like a 'carpet' that is certainly authentic, like pure form and like a constraint [*Korrektiv*] which, with its beautiful and stationary unity – i.e. animated purely lyrically and otherwise simply fitted together, is now meant to throw light upon the *third* schema, upon *dramatic form*, the turmoil of the weighty, more chaotic, dynamically symbolic symphony. The *third* is the open-ended song, the *Handlungsoper*, Wagner or transcendent opera, the great choral work and Beethoven-Bruckner or the symphony as the broken-loose dramatic forms, great in the secular if not yet the sacred domain. Altogether dramatically animated, altogether transcendentally objective, such forms assimilate all that is artificially and genuinely 'carpet-like' and fulfil it in being drawn to the tempo, the rumbling and flashing, in the upper regions of the self. Here an analogy with the triple, syllogistic construction of form in the other arts suggests itself. There are the still-life, the portrait and the large landscape; the linear ornament, plastic art and the multi-dimensional ornament of eidetic figural composition and architecture; the short story, lyric poetry and, beyond it, great epic and dramatic poetry. Indeed, we might wish to take the syllogism of sheer composition even farther. For there is also that strange sequence of religious forms we find in the emotional craving for miracles, in Protestantism and the established, mediated faith of the Church. All these abstract beginnings, individual centres and concrete fulfilments of abstractness are obedient to a rhythm similar to that of musical forms and obey a related syllogism: from contentedly elegant play, as the stage of personal inclination, to full, inwardly changing individuality as the stage of warmth and the soul, and up to the adamantine brilliance of the system as the stage of might and depth and spirit. What occurs more centrally still – thereby exploding, to be sure, the merely formal play of the dialectical arrangement – is a relation which we can only suggest at this point. And by that, we mean the relation of the Grecian Mozart, the Gothic Bach, the Baroque Beethoven and Wagner and the seraphic, unknown musician to the

15

corresponding indicators in a philosophy of the history of inwardness set up in the world.

Fulness and its schema

I

How, then, did we hear ourselves first and foremost?

As endless singing-to-oneself and in the dance.

Both of these, we stated, are still anonymous. They do not live in
themselves, and nobody has performed a personal shaping here.
They possess, when one comes across them, the fascination of a
primordial beginning. But first other things had to be traversed
which consciously extracted this primordial style of music from its
purely immediate disposition – and indeed ensured that the
expression was fully and securely equipped. Then, certainly, we can
again encounter the cry and the dance, when an artist is musing upon
them.

They are arrears or hopes, call them what you will. Here we can
let them rest, together with chamber music, which can be partly a
very hackneyed exercise and partly a most fruitful contrapuntal
subtlety and rescue of the sonata from its all-too-careless, all-too-
precipitate plunging in. It also remains to be perceived later what
significance endless singing-to-oneself and then, above all, the dance
attain in Bach and Wagner.

II

The song

In the song, however, everything is still proceeding quite calmly.

Soon, singing became delicately rounded off. This sounds genuine
in the open air, but with Silcher it becomes spurious. It is the stillborn
art of the spurious folk-song or popular song [*Bürgerlied*]. Music
that was sung departed at an early stage from the cry, the dance and
magic airs. At any rate the Minnesingers seem to have taken their
invention from a very subdued source. The surprising thing is that
even such late artists as Schumann, Schubert in his earlier works,
indeed even Brahms, have had a significant influence in this field.
Through them, the uniform song has been pinned down as a pliant,

homophonically melodious form with the simplest of tempi. They run riot, these songs, but they are buoyant, always end in subjective impressions; they are German and yet, paradoxically, uniform in a finite, civilised, if not strophically melodic, way. It may be that the quiet Biedermeier pleasure in singing, soon to become so corrupt and so much at the mercy of *Liedertafel* societies, contributed a great deal to this bourgeois victory in the middle of an age which had totally different goals in view – not in Zelter's case, admittedly, but certainly in that of Schubert. The aria is a straightforward matter, as is Italian cantilena: easily learnt, cosily self-contained, truly folk-like and still entirely attuned to the lute. It thrives in opera, thrives on the fact that every display-piece has a beginning and an end. Thus from Pergolesi to Offenbach it has its finished, 'carpet-like' form, one that is equally easy from the singer's angle and from the angle of opera.

On Mozart

Mozart is the principal figure in this scintillating line.

He is capable of singing in a light and enchanting way, in uniform song. Within it he has the ability to speak of himself, and of us as far as we are attainable therein, quite uniquely. Calm descends in a different way with Mozart: the night is revealed and gracious figures draw us into their ranks. But then again, it is not yet that night in which a transformation takes place, in which the light is put out and the mountain fairy appears, and across all the walls there steals a shimmer of light, like a rosy dawn not long before sunrise. Rather, the candles are still burning and everything is still illumined by them, their light being more kindly and radiant than that of the daylight, occasionally skirting Rococo-like the world beyond, but otherwise iridescent, lit only from outside. These gaily coloured musical shapes show an extremely buoyant, aerial movement. But there is nothing frenzied and nothing explosive, not even in the more agitated *Figaro* ensembles. Above all there is no action other than that intended and presented solely in the recitative, passing into song and through it and back into it once more. In this way a scene quickly filters into an aria as the concentrated registering, the concentrated emotion of a situation, as the duration of the expression of a feeling, without the ulterior motive of collectively storming away from the specific physical self and its moderate bounds. Whether delicate or sorrowful or merry, this last music of nobility is calm and plastic. Charmingly coming and going, neatly answering, weaving its neat pattern of replies, the melody does not even desire to make any distinction between Don Giovanni's merry banquet and his mystical downfall, with regard to its constant unity and plasticity of line and form. Almost everything about this temperately nurtured action and concentrated aria couched in gentle melancholy remains silvery, porcelain-like; even the excited, liberated, jangling march is disguised in chinoiserie. And just as the recitative is self-confined in a fairly 'carpet-like' way, so the portrayal of the inner life, of its actions as depicted solely in the recitative, and of the outpourings of its lyrically exhausted fulness does not go so deeply into the more turbulent, more real self, the dramatically erupting or mystically recognised self, that Mozart's operas could leave the ambit of the puppet-play, the *Spieloper*, fairy-tale opera, or, in the supreme event, the 'carpet' for the musical drama of clemency. Certainly there are some unforgettable passages. Take the dialogue with the Priest and the suddenly irrupting gravity of the priestly melody in A minor, or the fugal writing and the way in which the stony *cantus firmus* of the Two Men in Armour in front of the temple rises erect above it like a solemn seal of baptism. These two powerful sound-structures from the *Magic Flute* offer a second view, tearing apart the 'carpet' like some immense, staring, gorgonian vision, mindful of itself beyond all the playful, sportive and superficially paradisical elements of pure form elsewhere. But even this constitutes childhood and basically unverified dreaming. It is adolescent music immediately behind which the settling down of the adult state is at hand, and which this 'carpet-like' immanent art did not make decisively real in other passages or compel to be serious.

Hence Mozart remains the principal figure in the music of the South, which almost constantly admits of reshaping into visual qualities and plastic delight. For even where there was greater movement, he did not want the melodic line to be interrupted or to recede into the distance. We come to understand, even in the broad and atmospheric Mozartian *sonata*, how quickly the soul summarises itself here. There are melodic rewards to be found in these structures and often – as in the peerless *Magic Flute* overture or the finale to the 'Jupiter' symphony – the rewards of chamber music; but rarely, if ever, symphonic rewards. These works are perfectly charming in their invention, often with an amazingly large span of the most noble intervals, and so fertile and rich in all their detail that Schubert is the only other composer to approach this richness of melody. But nothing has happened by the time the theme reappears, no energy is charged and discharged; snowbound passes, the mist and the forest are lacking, there is no going astray and no warm light in the distance. The music is an amiable exercise and passes by like a string of pearls. The counter-subject generates neither light nor heat, nor that music of emotional entanglements at which, after all, composers normally excelled in the *opera buffa*. So much is quiescent in the small, non-interacting, successive moods of the small secular self and the simple dynamisms of its body-soul, short both in time and in space. Hence, without being hypocritical and with affection for the 'carpet', it is necessary to state that here the development is unwilling and unable to contain any tension and deliberately to aim for the great line that would be sure to proceed from the expansive, necessarily expansive, blaze of the contrasts in its themes. With Mozart, the whole design shows an arithmetical streak that fundamentally contradicts the more agitated symphony of Beethoven as a deliberate formation fitting together visibly and organically. Just this prompted Wagner's accurate observation that Mozart combined the most graceful sensitivity with a surprising gift for arithmetic, which is what produces the characteristic value of this enchanting, but not devastating, musical Hellenism. On the secular level, it has a refining influence, but on the sacred level it is almost unquestioning.

The Passions

Admittedly, there was no immediate wish to be agitated beyond this extent.

Yearning, in the case of *Bach*, was not a spreading fire but a depth of soul remaining within itself.

Hence it was not desirable for it to appear agitated and open straightaway. With Bach too, the narration is largely in unchanging recitative. Only when the voice becomes choked, as it were, and tears hinder its intimate account of the sacred events, are the more excited sounds of *lyrical* heart-searching released. But without leaving their known, equally settled location or even – as was the custom with Keiser and the contemporaneous Hamburg school – straying into the operatic realm, these lyrical structures are constantly under the sway of the chorale. In the *chorale* the agitated element returns to a uniform, lyrical, hence undramatic, context, though already its ultimate purpose is to bridge the way to this as being supra-dramatic as well. For when Jesus says: 'I say unto you that one of you shall betray me', and the disciples, excited and confused, cry in a most violent allegro: 'Lord, is it I?' and then, after a wondrous pause, the congregation sings the chorale 'It is I, I should atone', this moment in the St Matthew Passion reverberates with the most intense feeling. Kierkegaard himself could not have found a more powerful sermon for this sense of being addressed *ad hominem*, for Christian action and the subjectifying of Christianity. In this way, then, the chorale's lyrical disposition overrides both the purely private lyricism of the characters in the story and the external drama – which we shall discuss in a moment – of the actual choruses. For the chorale, like some of the contemplative arias, is essentially the form of expression proper to a higher or theocratic community which dwells beyond events, so to speak. In the overriding 'carpet' of its no longer private (or, as indeed, is inherently impossible) agitated, progressive or dramatic lyricism, a lyricism truly supra-dramatic and *ontological*, it corresponds to that highest stage-level which the mediaeval mystery plays erected for their Heaven, above the levels of Earth and Hell. A totally different picture, to be sure, is presented by the actual *choruses*. Here Bach, like the powerful, epical, Handel, writes counterpoint that is no longer in the homophonic shape of the old Protestant chorale but savage, jagged and divided in rhythm. There is at least action here, and we certainly receive the impression of a passionate agitation. This applies to the 'Crucify!', the rabidly uttered demand for Barabbas and the furious chorus of 'Lightning and thunder have vanished on clouds' as well as all the choruses of the Jews and earthly community in which the crowd is making demands or accusations, so as to intervene in the action in a completely different way from the recitativo narration and, indeed, to engender a more passionate action than the Biblical action itself. At the same time, however, the word is thereby abandoned, just as much as the calm, closed type of form in the narrower sense is finally shattered. Now, the human voice can only be employed in the chorus as a musical instrument, just as the more fully developed vocal music was spontaneously bent on transmitting its agitation to the richer and at the same time more stable colours of orchestral instruments – bent, indeed, on dissolving among these, or at least on figuring simply as the uppermost and most expressive part of the orchestra. So when Bach transferred the old vocalism to the organ and orchestra, there was an obvious sequel. It was that the 'voices', which had already lost all their specifically lyrical quality in the complex use of the chorus, were really subjected to the rhythm of a new style resulting from their union and contrapuntal development. And as a melodic, or rather, melismatic device placed in more difficult circumstances, this was bound to weaken considerably the undisturbed, uniform solo line of the melody, which had previously been merely accompanied, though with a certain amount of filigree. The consequence of this disruption of uniform melody was, in the case of Bach's music, the fugue. And soon after Bach, it produced the great surprise: the sonata leading to Beethoven.

Bach, his form and his object

The *Lied* or song therefore becomes extensive, unending, but internally unending, as it were, in the fugue.

Here everything is to be played absolutely lyrically and is distinctly filigrane. But are we therefore to regard Bach purely in diatonic terms and be wary of the mixing of sound in general? For superficial, pedantic minds, of course, this is the easiest approach. Hence there is no smart assistant choirmaster who never saw himself in the role of a Bach trumpet and never tried to turn these inscrutably lofty works into downright parochial ones. But it has rightly been said that the harpsichord's pinched, short-lived tone did not fulfil a single one of Bach's requirements. By the same token, it is by no means entirely true that for Bach it was only the organ, the organ of voices, the orchestral organ, which always represented the corresponding sound-image. And there can be no shadow of doubt that it is only our pianofortes, the incomparable Steinway pianos produced for the modern Bach, clear, booming and silver-edged, that have taught us how to play the master afresh, how to view the many decorations but also the seemingly unswerving part-writing. They have taught us the heights, the rich effects to be attained by the well-tempered clavier: effects that are lyrical, i.e. not simply harmonic, but not alien to harmony either. Bach embraced both endless singing and the ancient, rhythmically much-divided dance; at this point the earliest 'carpet' starts to give ground. But the fundamental thing for the master of the new inward burgeoning is the thematic seed of this singing state of dividedness. He cherishes his theme, in which he as no other composer compressed what was to come, tension and the

21

sharpest outline of tension. He goes on lovingly considering the theme from all angles and prospects until it blossoms forth and until, in the great modulations of the fugue, it has become an unlocked shrine, an internally unending melody ('internally' meaning within the context of the theme), a melismatic universe in respect of the developed individuality of his theme. For precisely this reason, Bach's layout is not purely diatonic, however clear its filigrane nature. Obviously the harmonic element in itself becomes irrelevant with Bach insofar as it is manifested in a fortuitous, pleasantly meaningful simultaneity of the parts. But it is surely not irrelevant to the extent that the pertinent motions and their framework, which is to say the counterpoint, are now also the paramount factor and, as such, emphasised. To the extent that it represents a complete horizontal transparence, it is certainly the essence of Bach more than it is of Beethoven and Wagner. And yet, even in Bach, there is in the layout an active desire. There is the pervasive flow of a succession of themes rich in associations, a twofold thematicism already inherently rich in tension which finds itself far less strongly dependent on the constant polyphony's non-decisive part-writing than on the transitional, turning and corner points, but above all the rhythmically stressed anchor-points in the harmony. And as we can see, this is not straightforwardly homophonic but a different, deliberately chosen harmony, one that underlines, that emphasises by virtue of its mass. The one reflects upon the other, even though Bach remains the master of the single voice, multiplying the old homophony by two or by five, the intrinsic master in the spinning out of lines and in this procedure's seemingly unlyrical, supra-lyrical domain. The blending, harmonic-rhythmic element still has an influence: it prevents a revelling in the mechanics and the formal aspect of counterpoint even where Bach's wide gaps between parts play an important role in preventing a vertical blending, i.e. the being and changing of whole columns of notes or hosts of chords, no matter whether rhythmically diminished or caught up by and released from the dominant. But it is only the song, the theme, that seeks to become extensive and unending within the fugue melody which is, as it were, internally unending. It is by virtue of this above all that the element of diatonic counterpoint is reduced to a mere means, to something reflexive, permitted only because the lyrically flourishing melismata acquire a sharper profile from the juxtaposition. For it is in the contrapuntal or, rather, dialinear system of balances that they can best represent their protected, unbroken simultaneity, that *lyricism* of theirs which no longer has any individual relevance but simply means soul, developed soul. And that lyricism, in spite of all the dramatic community choruses, is the core of Bach's Church music. Where this balance is self-supporting, it is easy to recognise, within the framework of Bachian counterpoint, the hidden, connected, multi-layered lyricism of the Passions, built into the niches of three-dimensional counterpointing. It is akin to the uneven surface of the bas-relief, where we can feel the presence of air, the arrangement of figures in the landscape and, in fact, the whole actual landscape that is set in the rise and fall of the uneven background.

As follows from this, even a fugue played with vitality and melismatically is a 'carpet' or a constraint. It can be described as the carpet *in front of* all the confusion of the excited, chaotic, melodically disrupted symphony. Hence it forms the carpet of fulfilment, a fulfilment under constraint that is just as valid as the *Spieloper* and the chorales of the theocratic community. At this juncture, however – to avoid missing anything out and thus going against our principle – it seems appropriate to pause in order to stress two prototypical features of Bach: one is the *intrinsic* soul (but with the difference that now, in the keyboard, organ and orchestral works, both the shape and the limit of the lyricism are made clearer by the recourse to a basically architectonically contrapuntal mountain-range than they are in the Passions). And *hence* the *scope* of this lyrical factor. *Hence* the mixing and the balancing of the lyrical and shaped element in a basically *architectonic*, Gothically architectonic, harmony and counterpoint which represents the special house of this lyricism, or what we might call its spatially constitutive system. Accordingly, then, we may very well speak of an impinging relationship within this area. Even so, the uniform lyricism in which, ultimately, the whole of Bach's harmony, Bach's symphony, is based or incorporated clearly restricts this area's constitutive object to the more readily perfectible 'carpet' or constraint of something more difficult, more real and more absolute.

In Mozart it is the secular self, and in Bach the sacred self, which becomes the object. Mozart turns feelings into animated sound, with lightness, freedom, élan, elasticity and brilliance. Bach shows the self and its stock of emotions in a more measured way, grave, imposing, taut, with solid rhythms and a depth which lacks Mozartian brilliance. Hence Mozart presents the – always small – secular,

Luciferan self, and Bach the – again always small – sacred Christian self, the self of goodwill or the released Adam attainable through the more subjective, Protestant outlook which comes closer to it; and consequently not yet the self glimpsed in the Convocation, the Glory or the released Lucifer, which is hidden behind a quite different dynamic. It is the inwardly illumined receptacle of the Christian desire for action, in the sense that Bach's music expresses the struggle to save one's soul. It marks the stage of charity and hope behind which – parallel to Bach, but inaccessible to him – rise the three upper quick-nesses [*Lebendigkeiten*], the stages of Faith, Illumination and the Apocalypse. And these are found within a religious phenomenology which is not more sublime, but both more difficult and more definitive.

III

Finally, however, for what purpose do we hear ourselves? Well, soon we come to feel freer. For the note wants to press on to actions as well.

Looser in disposition, it accumulates tension and energy. The tendency of the third schema arises, that of venturing all the way out. The early cloister is opened, and the chaotic world, the external dream before the genuine cloister shines in.

Carmen

So we now move more easily in that direction. This is not to say that the individual songs roam far afield with no dividing-lines, no boundaries. If we take *Carmen*, for instance, each wild and exotic song is still uniform in its construction. But it is characteristic of these songs that they are not simply strung together but, without being actually broken up, are at least open and readily mobile. For they can follow the course of the action with lightning speed, instead of decorating it lyrically and holding it up. In this way, the note goes out into the wide world to make room not only for the playful enthusiast but also for the impetuous man of action who loses and preserves his identity in quick feats of daring, although he does not yet actually 'find' himself. Here we need only recall the typical change in the expression of the *Carmen* motif which is wrought by the changing tempo. The way in which Escamillo and Don José sing to each other before and after the duel also offers, in the ardently changing sequence, a good example of animated unified ideas. All the same, it is because of the simple melodies that this sequence can be limited to round, smoothly rounded, forms.

Open-ended song and *Fidelio*

The open-ended song [*offenes Lied*], of course, is a different matter. It was started above all by Schubert in his final years. Nothing is traditional, tied to the strophe any more. The accompanimental parts are so very free, flexible and prepared for any illustrative underlining. The vocal line expressively matches the meaning, and the way the song flows to its climax becomes the essential style of the whole. That holds true for Hugo Wolf; less so for Strauss, who grows shallow, Biedermeier-like and trivial whenever he wants to move us with tender notes. But he does become the greater of the two when it is a matter of writing austerely, of setting fervent, serious, high-soaring texts by Klopstock and such poets. The open-ended song also saves the day where action is evoked. This was especially the case after it started to grow more and more richly filigrane, full of scrupulous filling-out. The note was too colourless in recitative and too long-winded in the lyrical sphere. Now sonorous exclamations come with it and convert the song into a shorter melodic *fait accompli* which is sufficiently varied to be even capable of reproducing the sensations and outbursts of active characters, the whole charging of the atmosphere with haste, destiny, decision. Hence whenever the character becomes involved in the action, and the latter, in turn, more seriously involved with the character, it is necessary to break the lyrical matrix more decisively and leave it open. This is true of Weber. It is even more true of the extremely important Marschner of *Hans Heiling*, with its splendid aria-writing and unique melodrama. And above all it applies to Beethoven's *Fidelio* and the mystery of its melody. Gradually, of course, this practice has become so widespread and the means of dressing out trivia and offering a melismatically improvised surrogate for melodically uniform ideas so often that we no longer have any *Spieloper* at all. Instead, everything is drawn into an area which ought to be reserved for only the most violent passion and action. For only then is such agitation legitimate; it would still be 'opera of action' in the formal sense, but capable of bringing things right to the boil, and clearly distinguished from the *Carmen* type through its symphonic character. Even the *Flying Dutchman*, *Tannhäuser*, *Lohengrin* and above all the *Mastersingers*, which moreover preserves a perfect operatic structure, are operas of action with dramatic action as the basic aim, as are large chunks of the *Ring*. But just as everything lyrical in Beethoven's music becomes pregnant, so to speak, with an endless, erupting agitation, so *Fidelio*, as the *a priori* model of the symphonically dramatic genre, contains not a single song that remains sheltered within the four walls of melody, however animated. And this applies even more to the fury of Beethoven's ensemble scenes. The extravagantly treated note, the surging sound and the constant admixture composed of tension, chaos and destiny overflow into a style of music which is largely non-melodic, which is melismatic in terms of recitative, thematic in terms of motifs and develops purely symphonically as a whole. This kind of music – in automatic mockery of any prepared text – not only follows the action but itself engenders action, action as yet undefined and anonymous. The opera composer has then to endow this with practical meaning in theatrical terms, and with a textual 'rationale'.

Missa solemnis

All this is intensified in Beethoven's use of the choir. To sing in communion was what people needed in earlier times, the need to make mutual confession. These were solitary voices calling in the dark, responding to one another and thus attaining to harmony in the deeper sense of the word. To be sure, we have seen that now the human voice can only be used instrumentally in the choir. But we have also established that even so, it preserves its integrity as the supreme, most powerfully expressive part of the orchestra. The word, hitherto so important, loses ground in the process. It becomes a network and canvas into which notes are stitched and which, as these interweave, can no longer be indicated or reproduced at all. Certainly the four or at the most eight parts prevent too great a mobility; but they are human voices which are not only capable – especially since Beethoven – of working out any heightening of tension with the most tremendous seriousness. Especially when what matters is weight, calm, the spiritual and mysterious – by which we mean the climaxes and end-product of dramatically conceived symphonic writing, they are also in a position to propagate the full supradramatic, mysterious aura of the calling, if not the divine audience, of a worshipping community. Now, the old religious community has burst apart, and we can no longer enjoy or even create a choir, the work of this community, as a religious force: we can only have it as a longed-for strength and unity. There is now a different gathering together, a different seeking and finding on the part of the souls firmly united in this gathering. There is a different longing for organisation and above all for the coherence of something global which will bring men together and will, in the choir, endow them with a thousand voices in order to seek for the one God, to proclaim their vigil to the heights, to invoke salvation with a thousandfold, now musically transcendent, cry. The choir is a means to this end, offering itself for this purpose, stormily and cathedral-like, with the ascending line of new faith that runs, in increasingly passionate versions of Baroque, from Bach's B minor Mass to the 'Pater omnipotens' of the *Missa solemnis* and finally to the sacred music of Bruckner, particularly his F minor Mass. It leads to an ever firmer awareness – which we must pursue just as strongly on the philosophical plane – that the community has less to praise the Holy Spirit than to bear witness to it.

The birth of the sonata

Many other things bringing fresh life had become apparent. The animation engendered by the rise of opera now yielded its own special product, the sonata. We know how decisively the style of composition changed shortly after Bach. Indeed, Bach himself looked like a strange, sylvan giant among the masters of the *style galant*. For a long time the solo voice of the violin and of song participating individually in the concert had already been raised, lightly and vigorously. No longer a servant to polyphony, this voice roamed at will, farther and farther from the hierarchic structure of the mediaeval *a cappella* style. J. S. Bach's son Carl Philipp Emanuel had already helped to establish the new style, the explosion of homophonic individuality; and *Haydn* succeeded and surpassed him in sonata writing, just as he was typically preceded in Scarlatti's tripartite opera overtures. Here the song coursed freely in a texture which had become completely fluid, and its line dominated the whole sonata. The other parts were there to surround the melody on every side, submerging and ostensibly dissolving it, only to revert with a still greater alacrity to their subordinate, merely ornamental, developmental status. Hence parts were exclusively developed no longer. Instead, Haydn used inner parts and especially instrumental groups that enabled him to achieve what orchestral effects and harmonic colouring he pleased. Thus even in its external aspect, the theme became less important; it no longer sought to engender the development. On the contrary, it wanted the development to impart to it ever greater vitality and brilliance, the result being a lighter fabric woven with an impetuosity quite impossible in the fugue. It has rightly been said that while one bad bar will ruin the fugue, a single good bar will redeem the sonata. Be this as it may, there was no going back once the free entry of the part had been finally achieved. It was just not feasible, having paid the price for accomplishing so much, to turn back or even simply to turn over the new pages – which, sad to say, grew very 'poetical' in the end – in order to recover, bar for bar, the deliberately, unimaginatively solid writing of the fugue. Even if one did not care for the new tactic of taking the listener by surprise, it was absolutely established that, with the existence of the *Eroica*, one's marching orders had been received; and that the veritable spirit of the times, and of time, had issued them. The more attentive listener, incidentally, may not be hard put to surrender himself for the whole duration of a sonata by Beethoven as completely as he would to a Bach fugue, though in a different way. The Beethovenian sonata, after all, is as full of demagogic devices as it is of promises, of genuine climaxes and far-reaching feelings of tension based on the dominant. What we find so startling about it – the lightning changes in dynamics, the miracle of the horns, comparable to an organ pedal in the rich, satisfying, resonant way they fill out the sound, and then bitter cold . . . a changing of the guard, we imagine, and tales of the night . . . belief . . . the star . . . and now here it comes, the phantom or ghost, with all the resources of the percussion, trombones, organ and, sustaining an extreme fortissimo, the full orchestra – all this adds up to a new way of life for instrumental and dynamic expression. And this caused the new design to be created – harmonically-dramatically created – in terms of colour and luminosity, so to speak, thus introducing a rushing wind, a Venetian glow into the character of thematic change, initially so slender and meagre. Haydn, to be sure, only used the exhilarating colour-sequence to the extent that the music no longer simply sang and a conflict raged in the upper melody, whose line was often punctuated by melismata from below. To this extent there was also a second melody, a contrast and the incentive for development and alliance contained in that contrast. This does not seem to add up to much, especially as Haydn did not actually invent the duothematic form. Even in Bach, we already clearly discern the prototype of sonata form in the principle of contrast expressed through a second theme, especially in the introductions to his partitas. But what occurred in a single, rounded section in Bach's music was persistently maintained by Haydn, whose composing made it the basis for a veritable polythematic philosophy. And this directly preordained the hazardous world of the freer, dramatically symphonic style of the absolute sonata, the Beethovenian sonata.

Brahms and chamber music

Those composers who liked to murmur and were at the same time easily understood became false in this world. The demure song-writers also put in a fresh appearance here, became 'symphonic' and smoothed the ripples that had been started. Only one stood out from the others and sought the very trail that Beethoven had blazed: Schubert, who, at the end of his life, loathed the homophonic songs of his past, and died almost the moment he grasped his real talent, a talent both for revelling in long drawn-out passages and for construction that sets him on a par with Bruckner. As 'symphonists', the remainder seem very different from one another. There was poor Mendelssohn, always blithe and polished; Schumann, that unfortunate symphonist *manqué*; Chopin, the keyboard star of the *ancien régime*; and the virile, incomparably more magnificent Brahms, a giant by contrast. They did all share, however, a deplorable streak of decorum and moderation. Occasionally, Chopin avoided this, as in his extremely interesting chromaticism (showing affinities with Wagner); but it is evident elsewhere, in the empty contrast of drawing-room brilliance and a noble, but largely insignificant, fioritura art. This was a streak which caused Brahms, the passionate, deep and sombre Brahms, to be mistaken time and again for the spokesman and leader of a prim, middling, German bourgeoisie. Hence the 'correct' musicians, people whom the academies continued to produce until recently, an unworthy if not wholly undeserved band of pernicious, mediocre talents following in Brahms's footsteps. At that time, music was in serious danger of degenerating from a matter of universal scope into the academic concern of the German middle-class parlour, of well-bred people with all their inhibitions and barren sentimentality. But it is highly regrettable that Brahms, of all musicians, withdrew so cosily into an avoidance of all brilliance. He does have colour: his orchestral sound has been compared, not unfavourably, to the North German heathland, which appears from a distance like a broad, monotonous expanse, but whose greyness, as we enter, suddenly dissolves into a myriad little blooms and specks of colour. Brahms did not of course go in for painting or writing 'mood-music'. Instead he achieved his wish to compress the melismatic content and derive pleasure from organic construction, using the more deliberate old polyphonic devices and aiming at an organically plastic articulation, rendered more difficult by a dense criss-crossing of the diatonic lines. What is not feasible, however, is to stretch the layout so high-mindedly and to revel in plasticity when being well-constructed is secondary to being rhythmically and emotionally well-arranged. Hence nothing could be more spurious or a worse sequel to Beethoven than to do as the Brahmsian conservatories tended to do. That is, to reduce the master – the universal spirit of music who wrecked keyboards, swept in like a hurricane and turned even the strongest orchestra to jelly in the face of his music's *a priori* exorbitancy – to the level of well-bred piano and chamber music.

That is why we have already described the latter in all seriousness as 'carpet-like'. It tells us what a composer can do or has learnt, and the few parts say it all. Much of it, we should add, may be on shaky ground and searching for bridges to the domain of the real. It is possible for there to be a specific four-, five- or six-part movement which requires no further parts and which claims for itself the autonomy it denies to other structures that are plainly slipping into the symphonic realm, such as the octet. But none of this means anything by itself and in itself until the neatness and transparency are employed in the larger context. No discerning listener will be able or willing to grant to the string quartet a soul of its own when all it expresses, however lucidly, is its ostentatious formal beauty. Where this is not the case, as in Beethoven's last quartets, it is a small matter to position the light not at the front, but from behind, as the interior, rearward expansion of the structure of a great musical composition demands. A stained-glass window must not be illuminated from the front and by day, or naturally it will never stand comparison with the genuinely plastic arts. No, Beethoven here inserts the magical stained-glass (to borrow

Wagner's excellent metaphor) in the silence of night, between the world of phenomena and the most intimate, hermetically radiant world of the essence of all things. The hermetic portrait thereby acquires animation for the first time. It now testifies to a world which is not accessible to regimented form, only to inspirited, vitally evolving form, and thus to the organically eidetic transparence of music. Everywhere else, however, musicians were only taking a cold, pedantic pleasure in the interweaving of themes and in deciding how they should enter, meet and greet one another, how they were to be weakened or intensified, proceed with one another and unite as though – and not even 'as though' – they were real people meeting and thus instigating fateful dramatic events. Such are the pleasures and self-justifications of the connoisseur, a person who has pursued snobbish or pedantic middle-of-the-road policies only too often. If these pleasures are legitimate at all, then only inasmuch as chamber music completely withdraws to the realm of pure form, the preserve of accuracy and melismatic beauty of the individual: that inventive, blossoming solo playing of every instrument which nurtured the individual detail to be found, after Beethoven, in Bruckner's truly symphonic writing, which ventures out into the active, 'effective', real domain. To this extent, then, the quartet style is, now that the case has been fully investigated, a 'carpet' and constraint. Not with regard to the poorer examples, which are simply behindhand, but all the more in the case of the better, contrapuntally newly blossomed chamber works. For in these, nearly all the transparence may be regained for the purpose of imparting their *sophrosyne*, their prudence, to the more democratic and also more transcendent structure of the symphony.

Beethoven, his form, his object and the spirit of the sonata

Now, though, everything false and stifling melts away. The leadenness disperses, and the distortions vanish, and Beethoven is the sequel until an end beyond our divining. 'How elated we feel at the thought of you, infinite one!'[4] Certainly we sense that something even more splendid will appear, but that is a desire and not something achieved; and so our soul bubbles up to the stars in the initial rough, tempestuous, eloquent sea of this music. Beethoven is Lucifer's benign offspring, the daemon that leads to the ultimate things.

Thus for the first time, we may now breathe freely. Singing which takes on a rounded form, to be sure, is almost wholly over, and this also applies to its thematically abbreviated form, at least in large-scale movements. The only exception is variation form, still flourishing with its melodic diversions. Needless to say, the long drawn-out Adagio still exists, although it no longer implies suffering or calm and is growing rhetorically sentimental. The variation process is, as Paul Bekker neatly defined it, the fraying out or unfolding without inner conflict – hence the largely passive extension – of a theme still presented as song and melody, and displayed as a series of feelings. To this we can add the rondo, likewise still nearly always melodic, but different in that the basic principle is to present several ideas. It is so worked that here the loose string of variations, while avoiding the stricter form of the sonata, builds up to an almost rhapsodic variety of moods which are, to some extent, the intermediate stages between feeling and thematic ideas. Thus rondo form represents a mixture of lyrical variation and dramatic sonata elements. The association becomes more animated and at the same time stricter in the scherzo: the most idiosyncratic Beethovenian form inasmuch as it assimilates the old minuet with a show of enigmatic delight, compounded of laughter and mockery, in its wild and furious or ironically buoyant dance rhythms. But now we come to the essence, the great and consuming sonata movements themselves. Passion, pain, cheerfulness and liberation are and always will be the components of the sonata, as the authentic and encompassing Beethovenian form. The headings Allegro, Adagio, Scherzo and Finale generally correspond to these, although on occasion, to be sure, there is a marked change in meaning. The first movement itself is frequently anything but an allegro, while the last occasionally incorporates rondo and even variation form. Normally the latter is diametrically opposed to strict, antithetical development. But when located in the final movement, it nonetheless constitutes the most significant part of the sonata besides the opening movement, precisely because it expands at will, loosely, more freely.

Perhaps, at this point, we should also mention the Beethovenian piano concerto as a specific form as well. To some extent it reflects the customary pattern of the gloomier labyrinths contrasted with light, liberated play on the plateau. For, with Mozart, the keyboard part was still integrated in the concerto: it may strike up the theme, but otherwise it only plays below the orchestra. With Beethoven, on the other hand, there is no motif that is not taken up again by the piano and no passage that is not finally obliged to leave the orchestra in order to attain its full splendour in the piano, the instrument raising it to fresh heights and to its crowning glory. Beethoven's other piano writing, above all in the later sonatas, is less unequivocal. If we were persuaded to orchestrate individual sonatas, and especially the 'Hammerklavier', the result would be a symphony. The two forms are closely related; in both the sonata and the symphony we find the same organically articulated events which led Beethoven's contemporaries to believe that here was an opera in disguise. In fact the dramatic principle behind his symphonic construction is undeniable. All this wholly action-oriented, supra-thematic bustle leads, of course, to the dramatically increasing puzzle of what it is that ushers one into the depth of the whole when it is not the singing theme. For the moment that Beethoven realised his talent as a leader and commander with the power to overwhelm, this thematicism yielded to a seething ferment, the exhortatory urge and the propensity to dramatic form. Thus the theme itself in Beethoven's music is far from leading a separate life of its own. There is the greatest difference in these symphonic works between the impetuosity of the individual movements and the powerful steadfastness of the whole. Hence it is not feasible, either, to attribute all their success to the much-praised incisiveness of Beethoven's themes. For these are often based simply on the rudimentary facts of triad, dominant and tonic, as August Halm has demonstrated in the image-filled D minor Sonata, where the upper line consists of a turn, the allegro theme of a scale and the largo theme of a chord. That the themes are delineated so sharply is due primarily to *rhythm*, which makes them precisely identifiable in the first place, and then, after the development's lengthy digressions, to the instantaneousness, the sudden reappearance of the old keynote and character, which provide cohesion. Here a fog is cast over the blaze. There are shafts of darkness, and we traverse the development as though traversing a mine, from which we emerge towards the glimmering first theme, which looks at first like a distant arc-lamp and suddenly expands into the full daylight of the open air, the longingly sought-after tonic of this first theme, which is profitably regained only now, after its eclipse. But all this has its seeds in something other than the theme. It derives from something slighter or greater, from the ebb and flow of excitement, from the vacillating and wavering, ceasing, dying, doubting, resurging and all the new dynamic expressive devices of a wildly changing, unreservedly committed emotion singing out and venturing forth, its changes of lighting and the worldly spectacle of its development. In other words, it derives from *harmonic-rhythmic* thinking. This means the correctly chosen, well-prepared, correctly timed chord, the comprehended power of the cadence, the instantaneity of the regained tonic and the *organisation* of its entry which, being a question of strength, is likewise a question of rhythm. It means the abstract tension of the two themes, as the two different witnesses to a dynamic state, the two contrasted principles. Thus both the development's buried treasure and the massiveness of the climaxes in Beethoven are produced by a new *succession* rich in correlatives: such a horizontalism is no longer *linear* but made up of *complexes* realised through remembrance and vertically built in their detail. They are, in conclusion, the product of a specially devised, *dramatically form-modelling counterpoint*, the like of which had never been seen before.

In this way we see right into the animated and self-generating interior breaking out in the secular realm. The self packs its bags, the heroic man is urging with all the strength of his synthetically extended character. His very voice becomes a series of calls for help, calls of rebellion out into the middle of a night in which the drowning soul finds scarcely any illumination. Indeed, all stellar and angelic spaces, however broad, have gradually sunk into oblivion. But now, loudly and without inhibition, the cry of the Beethovenian subject is raised. This is satisfied by nothing in the life of appearances, surpasses the highest reach of any worldly embrace and, like the genius of music itself, is neither prefigured nor received anywhere in the world. It ranges over the whole gamut of passion and imagining, yet in the end is always driven back upon itself, upon the longing for its brother and its visionary Father. Here we find a passion for quitting the purely inner life, the hermetic calm of inwardness. And this passion transforms the self into a truly cosmic structure so high and so deep that sun, moon and stars could rise and set within it without colliding and there is space to encompass the whole of humanity. Although something even more splendid may yet arrive, these are the waves of the outer mystical sea that surge as high as the stars; this is the great Roman Empire constructed from inwardness, with its discovery of the happening, the existence of magic and the philosophy of history – a realm which engendered Wagner and Bruckner and where alone the prophet of music may one day appear. Let us put it another way. Beethoven may be essentially only an outline, still wanting in fulness. And one has only to hear the perpetually amazing Paris version of the *Tannhäuser* overture – and perceive the glowing mists of the subterranean realm and finally, counter to this and above it, rising from the gigantic columns of the Pilgrims' Chorus, the victorious temple of the Church – to be lured into believing that, basically, Beethoven was only an expiring Moses, laying plans for the appropriation; that here with Wagner, the Promised Land is beckoning from afar: the lyrical melisma in the nonetheless dramatic counterpoint. Yet all this can be seen at a glance, whereas Beethoven cannot. He is as superior to Wagner as Kant is to Hegel, and as the restless *a priori* in man is to any kind of prematurely fulfilled objectivism. For only with Beethoven does the self advance into the discovery of that certain ground which perhaps extends as far as the ultimate deity. And the symphony of Beethoven, the wrestling, the turmoil of elemental feelings experienced in it and through it, the *makanthropos*[5] and his eloquent sea, this sea contained in a single distracted figure, this erupted, external dream of essential humanness casts upon a reluctant Heaven the most powerful beam of heroic-mystical atheism, transitory and born of despair. Here the 'we' and the generality finally coincide in the spirit of music. It presents a cluster of faces of the kind portrayed in carvings of the *majestas Christi*; that truly symphonically expanded space where the 'we' apprehends itself, where the universal ground shared in the spirit of brotherliness resounds, and where the 'it' of this musical happening becomes definable as the individual *multiversum*. Now all this is manifested in Beethoven – that supreme chosen vessel of the dynamic, Luciferan spirit – entirely at one remove still, as a sheerly tensed, heroic, synthetic, Luciferan, sacred vision and not within confirmed Christian ontology. But Bach had spoken from the viewpoint of the lyrically attained self of hoping, though in an intricate and consummate fashion, and as a permanent constraint for everything transcending dramatic form. Beethoven in contrast stirs up the rubble and the magic of the end quite differently. He does so with a violence which can indeed enter upon the three higher stages, Faith, Illumination and the Apocalypse, as the stages of the complete self. Here, and in just this way, it is no longer the first Jesus and not yet the second Jesus that is Beethoven's guardian spirit and object. The role is filled by Lucifer: the fighter in the front rank, the *seed* of the Paraclete, the active substance of humanity itself.

Strauss, Mahler, Bruckner

All music-making still feels weak when confronted by this. It certainly dreams of, broods over, speaking differently.

Perhaps not so certainly in the case of those who are alive now – Pfitzner, a subtle, gaily coloured flower, or Reger, a vapid, perilous talent and a falsehood into the bargain. Raw as he is, Reger never knows whether he is supposed to write waltzes or passacaglias; whether his mission is to set the 'Island of the Dead' or the Hundredth Psalm. Music and speech do not present themselves thus if one sits at their source in the morning. How empty it all is, even if Reger – the most un-Bachian figure imaginable – professes to be a believer, because a natural borrower and composer of variations follows this course as a matter of formal necessity. He is nothing, commanding only a superior sleight-of-hand. The annoying thing is that he is not only nothing, but a source of constant fruitless irritation.

Different feelings altogether are aroused in us by *Mahler*, that vehement, severe, Judaic man. At the time of writing, our hearing is still not good enough to sympathise with this great figure and to understand him. Basically, he is still regarded as just an important conductor. Many a wretched journalist has the temerity to ask quite unblushingly if Mahler ever had a vocation to compose, as though talking about the first tentative efforts of a harmony student. Almost none of the symphonic works is being performed at the moment. And when they are, the result is often an embarrassed silence, or else that infinitely base prattle about Mahler's Jewishness or pseudo-Titanism with which frivolous consumers of music come to terms with the purity of a serious artist, whose nature is of course foreign to them. Certainly he is not effortless; nor do we claim that the contrivedly simple-minded and folksily German, sentimental lumber of many Mahler songs, particularly those from *Des Knaben Wunderhorn*, is gratifying or easy to bear. But that is another question, a minor one which is totally irrelevant to the remaining Mahler and the overwhelming majority of Mahler's works. We are now thinking of the *Kindertotenlieder*, the last canto of the *Song of the Earth*, the Second, Third, Seventh Symphonies and the supremely earnest introduction to the closing section of Goethe's *Faust* in the Eighth: unforgettable music for anyone whom it has transported to the lofty and terraced mountain landscape of the anchorites. However often the axle of the cart – the natural talent – may buckle under this enormous load, nobody has previously been borne closer to Heaven with the force of a most soulful, effervescent and visionary music than has this yearning, holy, hymnic man. Deep inside, one's heart is pierced at the 'Ewig, ewig', when faced by the primal light. For this artist entered his empty, insipid, sceptical age like a messenger from afar, sublime in his outlook, unprecedented in the strength and masculine ardour of his pathos, and truly on the verge of bestowing music's ultimate secret upon the quick and the dead.

Where Mahler and Richard Strauss are concerned, it is as though a blood transfusion has taken place. Mahler is Germanic, or at any rate wants to be thoroughly recognised as a German master, though with no success, for his music bespeaks veritable Jewishness, Jewish woe and Jewish fervour; and *Strauss* has to stomach being compared to Meyerbeer. It is very difficult fully to come to terms with Strauss. He is banal and presents the picture of an industrious man who can enjoy life and take it as it comes. But to compensate for and notwithstanding this, Strauss is good company to the highest degree. Even when he is merely crafty and composes fashionable successes, even amid the most frightful kitsch, he is eminently upper-class with his free and easy, sovereign, worldly manners, from which all trace of the old German petty bourgeoisie has disappeared. He is, furthermore, without principles and takes his material wherever he finds it. Now and again, though, he does find something good, relying upon his effortless, harmless and basically wholly naive pleasure in musicmaking. Strauss can hit upon a new, supple singing line one day, curves with the richest intervals the next; now a new method of interspersing little motivic fragments like metal dust (where Liszt's example saves him from Debussy's mere boneless sound-vibrato), now the force and brilliance of a thematic incisiveness, of a gale raging round the thematic blocks and a rhythmic élan that are without parallel even in his mentor, Liszt. However vulgar, frenzied and ear-tickling, however lascivious, fulsome and eudaimonic his orchestral pyrotechnics may be, Strauss thereby achieves an expressive flexibility which undoubtedly represents an artistic plus, compared to the chronic, perpetual solemnity and the Pilotian[6] grandeur of the frowning Wagner school. For the most part, of course, Strauss only takes us by surprise because basically he is not developing but marking time in constantly different ways. There is no core to him that could bear fruit less arbitrarily than from the 'Ständchen' up as far as

Elektra and then, to meet the new plutocracy's demands for uniform melody, down again to the *Rosenkavalier*, so as finally to seek refuge, it seems, in a very euphonious, very erotic fairy-tale mysticism. Strauss triumphs predominantly only with bravado and sensuality, the legacies of an early, colourful cabaret style of rustic sturdiness which he turned to account after his own fashion, with extraordinary intelligence. Hence everything sounds quite excellent, and there is often a marvellous exultation in this music. The bravado mounts to a contrasting joviality, the sensuality at any rate to a certain specious mysticism, inferior and eudaimonic though this is. Eulenspiegel's foolery, the extinguishing of the light in the Sendlingergasse, the piping of the dances in *Zarathustra*, the reeling Narraboth's seduction, the way that Don Juan's hubris cuts through any theme of lingering, the ineffably lovely ascent of the Transfiguration from Death through a threefold suspension to the bliss of its tonic, the lighting up of the silver rose, the pitting of Orestes's sombre chords against all the previous disturbance in the women's voices, the way the recognition scene in *Elektra* arises from the motif of the messenger of death, the god's descending upon Ariadne – all these, certainly, are skilfully executed, executed with surpassing skill even. And it takes an exceptionally vigorous, resourceful artist's mind to make such radiant use of its talent. All the same, the resources used here are basically only muscular talents. A soul is lacking, however lyrical-erotic the prevalent mood throughout, for the pitiful, Mendelssohnian, Jokanaan motif already reveals the religious shallowness and lack of substance. In its deepest passages, Strauss' music wears at best the melancholy expression of a brilliant hollowness. It has enough animation to convey conflict and the most excitable of objects, but it is not animated with the gravity that could also produce real breadth and events spanning several movements. None of this ventures forth, in spite of the powerful, exultant gesture, but remains a chromatic shadow tracing all the details of the 'programme' including the undramatic details – which, indeed, it traces the most vividly. There are hedonistic reasons behind Strauss' fondness for the soft, flowery, atmospheric Viennese libretto. Where dramatic writing is called for, his scented candles consume any genuine reality in their fragrance and in the merely reflexive imagining of trivial characteristics. Thus what makes a constant impression, as a working principle, and moreover constitutes the life-blood of Strauss' system and method, is this music's extraordinarily descriptive power. It encourages the pictorial expression of even the smallest and certainly the most trifling, least musical details, but occasionally the semblance of something more profound as well. In addition, with an energy that blends all the details together again, this power gives rise to the marvel of a purely lyrical, undramatic symphonic writing that is lyrically descriptive in a 'pagan' way. Hence it is no accident that Strauss should favour the single-movement, Berlioz-Lisztian form, whereas not only Schumann and Brahms but also, and more important, Schubert, Mahler and Bruckner, the true heirs to the spirit of Beethoven, preserved the symphony with several move-ments, the form which has dramatic breadth, the Beethovenian prototype. So it may now seem that much has come from Strauss which appeared different on a first reading, stronger and less arti-ficial. And this is not the result of a reassessment but simply by dint of the fluid, volatile, period-bound, reflexive content. We recall Georg Simmel, all of whose work likewise illustrates only the chromatic, highly-strung, purely susceptible border-states of living; and Rodin or Bergson are the inspired 'reagents' of this condition. So it is feasible to assign to Strauss, along with these other two heralds of a mutable age without a hub, the place occupied by the three refuted wayward philosophers at St Thomas's feet in the fresco of the Spanish church in Florence. On the other hand it is possible to revere Bruckner, who dedicated his Ninth Symphony 'to the dear Lord', at least as the precursor of a St Thomas.

With *Bruckner* singing finally returned to the world, with a clear conscience to boot. He learnt a thing or two from Wagner, but the over-heated character, the 'blood-drenched' score, has now dis-appeared. We perceive active sprightliness and an internally chang-ing radiance of a spiritual kind, of spiritual realities, a vibrant calm, although Bruckner extracts even more from the 'cosmic' than from the 'intelligible' realm.

Yet he is as solicitous as he is versatile and deep. What we love about him are his warmth, good cheer and all the pleasure in travel for its own sake, which had been lost.

External, merely nervous excitement disappears in the process. But we have had our fill of over-excited musical execution, of bluff-ing and of misconceived Faustian behaviour, which only seeks to make the extravagant gesture absolute because it is the most readily imitable external aspect of talent. It is possible, too, for one's paragraphs to become too short or too empty – did not Wagner himself commend the adagio as a specifically Germanic tempo? Further-more, Bruckner requires no sacrifice of genuine temperament or indeed of genuine, substantial and objective intensification. Quite the contrary: this is rooted very strongly in his devout upward striving and also, as we can all hear, in his orchestral language's glowing splendour, which is that of the Austrian Baroque.

Here we have a composer who works carefully and neatly, who pays attention to good part-writing. *Thereby one of the first types, the chamber-music 'carpet', is regained.* Bruckner's achievement was, in short, to reintroduce a melismatic, chamber-music culti-vation of the parts and thereby to disinfect the symphonic organism. That is to say, he rid it of all extrinsic fever-heat mounting only in accordance with the will and not in accordance with the work. Here, as Karl Grunsky rightly stresses, every intensification of the sound is the appropriate expression of tensions which are strictly prepared and sustained musically, not only in a largely rhythmic form, as in Beethoven, but in a worked-out form which has been fully thought through in respect of modulation and counterpoint. For this very reason, to be sure, all kinds of malicious charges have been levelled against Bruckner: ponderous and incongruous diction, longueurs, and then again fits and starts, at least in the outer movements. Where this is not simply due to defective hearing (it was, of course, easier for Brahms to be coherent, as it was for the Lisztian school, where the emotional or straightforwardly descriptive force of the 'programme' often replaces any more strictly musical development), this reproach may be easily limited to the problem, and also the problematic aspect, of the Brucknerian finale, apart from a few slight sins of omission, or ellipses.

The finale, to be sure, is frequently woven together in a curiously broad and formless, sketchy fashion. But by its very nature the end is a very difficult chapter, even for Beethoven. A first movement's ideas are absolutely disciplined and successively presented according to precise rules. But the symphony's conclusion is the old merry last dance, the traditional form of abandon, far looser in structure, intent on leaps and flights, with contrasts jostling pell-mell and extravagant caprices in the development, which only the need for a supremely brilliant, or devastating, triumph of the main theme will restore to order. This was so with Beethoven; and it is more so with Bruckner, who leaves the finale unbridled and like a synthesis achieved only in the horizontal dimension. For this finale is mostly so worked that, by slackening its hold, it returns the listener noisily and formlessly to the everyday world. Although he may now reapproach the gateway, the climaxing has itself deferred to the world outside, which alone ultimately concludes the concert. Here the close, while outwardly linked to the end of the adagio, confirms only the scherzo, which represents the restoration of balance and the most worldly part of the symphony. Because the victory comes at the end, even the finale of Beethoven's C minor Symphony gives the impression that the intervening storms, the sweets, indeed the victory itself enjoyed to the full with such insatiable appetite, are not to be taken as altogether real. At any rate, the music indicates the end all too plainly and of its own accord diverts from itself simply by insisting on that point. In one respect, however, Bruckner goes farther than even Beethoven and the classical conclusion. With Bruckner the finale is not intended to disperse the audience. Rather, it is developed in such a way as to transport us to music's own sphere, to be an entrance into the most spatial and objective part of music. Presented with images that he will recollect, the listener is released from the pressure of the temporal world in a contemplative review of the passions, territories and the established primary colour of the whole performance, in the expectation of visionary prospects and with the consciousness of standing at the birthplace of that which is lyrically essential in the symphony. Certainly, having subsided so heavily into the epic domain, it is no longer dramatic. But it is probably right that the dramatic element should be engendered only in the first movement and that the last movement, the finale, should introduce no fresh eruptions – for which, after all, there had been time and exposition enough – but should postulate a different heightening, a new adagio (which even in its lyrical form is, as we know, the most difficult music to write). So the finale supplies sacred, Brucknerian epic qualities in the most relaxed and eucharistic conclusion.

Here the obstacle, even with Bruckner, remains the more profound problem – one which cannot be overcome at the present level of musical creativity – of the musical finale as a *happy ending*. Climax and resolution are necessary, but very often this results in the exaltation having the appearance of being simply a neat arrangement. This applies to Beethoven and of course to Bruckner as well: an approach to Heaven which is made according to formal rules, not actively verified. Certainly the rejoicing stems from Beethoven's ultimate experience. It is no mere appendix to the heightening of tension, no conventionally registered climax. But it does not stem from the music-making itself in an inexorable way. Thus in purely musical terms, the appended rejoicing cannot signify anything at all – yet if we are not satisfied with the idioms, we must ask ourselves: how could it be otherwise? Through darkness to light! or Beethoven would not be that man who . . . well, who endured long periods of gloom and unheroic depression. Not unless one belongs to those blithe Hegelian rationalists for whom things must always turn out well in the end and suffering represents only a stimulus, a gloriously exciting ritual of prolonged travel. And then nothing could matter less than this rejoicing in purely musical terms, either. For it is only present in a biographical sense and does not achieve any conviction from the actual musico-metaphysical angle by being well placed formally and coming at the end with the impact of the tonic. Joy is always a paradox in everything great; musically speaking, it is not actually produced by the development, the heightening of the dominant, i.e. induced in a deeper sense, induced as a necessity. Rather there must be an individual voice, a 'productive' development, a music of yearning, calling, believing, a birth of faith out of music, coming from the quietest, innermost, farthest depths of the musician's soul. This could finally strike up the *Sed signifer sanctus Michael* – à goal which even the greatest composers up to now have only rarely managed to achieve, and then mainly in such a way that the productive vision was more wont to occur in the adagio than in the finale with its fancifully epic structure. For the latter is too far removed from the burning spiritual core, the pure auto-vision focused on a single point, and from genuinely lyrical ontologism.

Recently Bruckner has found in August Halm a devoted interpreter of his talent and situation. Halm has shown that Bruckner provides what Beethoven failed to provide, since with Beethoven song was lost in the grand design, in the energy-laden motif and in the power to control large masses. Bruckner's achievement in this respect renders superfluous the impure goad of poetic stimuli. Rather, it is this master's feat to have separated for good the benefit of the Wagnerian style, 'eloquent' music, from the penalties of the programme or the music-drama and to have thus internalised it – significantly, this also applies to the completely different music of Brahms – as form and substance combined, indeed as the route to other waters than those of poetry. So Bruckner, the heir to Schubert and purifier of Wagner, is equally related to Bach and Beethoven. These, in turn, he relates to each other, because the well-developed individuality of the detail and of the Bachian theme is now most lovingly preserved in the form of Beethovenian strategy and social organisation.

On Wagner

Yet this all first blossomed through one person. Nobody has started off on a worse footing than Wagner. He was uncertain and lacking in taste, and something of this was to remain with him. But nonetheless: what preceded him has been very largely recovered through him. He stirs up and beats together so much of what was previously shaped that it takes on a present reality through which it finds its starting-point.

Forerunners

Not long before, the uniform song was still the widespread and dominant form. But at this point singing-to-oneself regained its status. Wagner brought a completely new kind of melody or, to put it more aptly, a new path into woodland and long-neglected mountain territory. Until he arrived, the only melody still known was the simple, homophonically written song-tune with its modest beat. The lesser Italian vocal pieces or, better still, since we are at present discussing the Germanic tradition, Mendelssohn's *Songs without Words* and Meyerbeer's arias make perfectly clear the poverty of this style, which maintains a homophonic accompaniment underneath and whose stable, weakly syncopated rhythm suppresses almost any polyphony unified in a different way. This applies even to Mozart, the greatest master in fundamentally homophonic lyricism, although in his case it was necessary to the gentle seriousness of the lyrical *Spieloper*. Only in one case, Schubert's, does the situation appear different. Here it has seemingly grown possible for the old uniform song melody to survive in symphonic writing as well. But on closer examination we will observe – as also occasionally, by the way, in Schumann's more accomplished songs, such as the remarkable 'Zwielicht' – a dualism in Schubert, who lived at the time of the worst song-fanaticism. It is a far cry from 'Wohin?' to 'Der Erlkönig' or 'Die Nonne', just as it is from those Schubertian melodies that depend only on one voice to the different, no less prolific and long-drawn melodies of the instrumental works. For all these no longer have anything to do with all too weakly disposed, sentimentally melodious homophony. Schubert conceived them in an eminently melismatic, polyphonic style, even though – like Weber in spite of the powerful ghost-scenes or like even the exuberant Berlioz and the early Wagner himself – he lacks energy and conflict in his counter-melodies and a penetrating *melos* that would cut through the regular divisions of the beat. Soon afterwards, something new and strange arrived, which was only unexpected in terms of the wretched state of music-making at that time: speech-song and unending melody.

False polemics

This melody, it is true, was no longer so easy to retain in the mind. One could not hum to it, nor was it inherently transportable at all. To be sure, the bourgeois music-lover of the time was accustomed to enjoying as 'melody' in its own right the stuff of contemporaneous homophonic song-making, which could be readily and thoroughly trivialised. Only this accounts for the crass misunderstanding of the relationship to Bach already established by the Rome Narrative in the middle of *Tannhäuser*, which Wagner still made so insufferably homophonic. Just think of all the objections raised and all the vile charges that people dug up! And today we have again reached the point where the idlest gossips are appointing themselves moral-aesthetic judges of a matter in which even Beethoven would not have passed censure without some humility. Think of all the objectors. First there were those petty-minded, unseeing scoundrels who experience only their own vileness in anything significant they find. Then came the lovers of the Florentine landscape and of everything consciously favouring the garden, as opposed to the Gothic forest. They railed against the continual modulating, against Wagner's uninventiveness and weak design, against melody always expended in interrupted cadences, extreme susceptibility without punctuation and the tediously dry psalmodising into which, allegedly, the singers were forced over a shapeless, fluctuating, at best realistically pic-torial, orchestra. Truly, if we ever heard anything that was simple and old, and that conserved and added to our native tradition, it is this downfall of uniform and birth of unending melody. And it is not as though these are merely superficial links, for in what respect could they have been broken beforehand? Was it, perhaps because of an 'inability' to manufacture old operatic set pieces, these that fell apart? Wagner, we may be sure, did not break these up just with a view to reassembling them in an endless chain, jumbling them in a coldly calculating way and anxiously avoiding any half and full closes. What or where is the evidence for a mere conglomerate of the kind which may still be perhaps true for Weber? For these 'preludes' which are so close to Bach contain no single note which could escape from the permanent tension based on the dominant, or would even want to. This represents the new melismatic-polyphonic form – so much so that after the arrival of Weber, the appearance of the Beethovenian symphony and the assimilation of Bachian polyphony, it would have taken Wagner an act of violence to withstand this intrinsic line of development. Certainly all this is, as we have said, no longer so easy to retain in one's mind. Nor does it bring many rewards to the upper voice, especially with regard to recitative which is simply narrative. Moreover, it is only at the end that the form of the delayed resolution, in its literal sense, becomes recognisable as a shape, a visible entity and 'form' with all the virtues of its huge phrases, its sparing use of the cadence and a tension based on the dominant for an entire Act which, it seems, coheres only poetically. But this in itself does not entitle us to mention in the same breath the broad and legitimate movement of unending melody and the totally different – and, to be sure, technically dubious – fusion of the *Gesamtkunstwerk*, or to reject the first along with the second. The superseding of the small forms of the old operatic design by means of a new large form of totally different dimensions is one thing. Quite obviously, it is not the same as the juxtaposition of partly related elements so that each one denies the structure and roundedness of the others and thus, in the exchange of musical and poetic components, engenders this hybrid structure of the *Gesamtkunstwerk*, which only Wagner's genius could turn into a vital, though theoretically irregular, category. From the technical standpoint, of course, Wagner needed both constituent parts. He needed the open pattern of speech-song and arioso recitative and also the huge, problematic support of the *Gesamtkunstwerk* as his defence against all roundedness and graphicness. Such boundless totality was his means of achieving that music of destiny which was intended to match it.

Speech-song, syncopated rhythm
and chordal polyphony

Singing now becomes just one voice amongst many. This singing can be flexible, brief and merely narrative. Song can also flourish in arioso, with breadth and all the emotional unburdening that one could desire: elevated, sonorous and with its fair share of pathos. Granted, Wagner's melodic through-composing is often ponderous and tiring; there is a lack of give-and-take, and sometimes one misses the old separation of batter and filling, speech and song. Nonetheless, all the voices are resonant now, and song is submerged as often as it pleases, being amply overrun by the other voices if they have more to give, in their mutual play and interweaving. Hence we may state that with Wagner the human voice, which formerly conveyed everything but has now ceded to the orchestra its whole development towards vocal polyphony, renounces the meagre role of influencing the course of events purely melodically. Now that it is completely free and unhampered, it reverts to *singing-to-oneself*, to its starting-point and original roving, psalmodising, condition.

What followed was lightened by dance and syncopation. Beethoven basically discovered it, and Wagner developed it so fully that we can experience all its varieties in his music, as in the almost continually syncopated *Tristan*. It means a dragging or urging forwards, a retarding or anticipating of the melodic impulse; or, as Grunsky first accurately defined the syncope in answer to Hugo Riemann, a new way of emphasising and freshly accentuating metrically unstressed passages, a new element to the beat, a bracing and matching of the stressed against the unstressed and vice versa. By means of the friction arising through the presence of different time-divisions, it thus becomes possible to execute several rhythms simultaneously, even if these can only be sensed in the jolt at the end of the beat. By this means, but not of course through this alone, the beat is frequently subdivided. Indeed it is a useful exaggeration to say that one beat now turns into a myriad, and with unstable, strongly syncopated, poly-rhythms there is now room for any kind of polyphony. Once again, each of the many, simultaneously sounding parts has something to play, has its solo to play. Melisma is tied to harmony, harmony to rhythm and the latter to the totality of the new periodic structure of the syncope, no longer heard in a vacuum, unblended, extra-

46

harmonically, but purely harmonically and in terms, moreover, of music-drama.

By all this we no longer mean a gentle floating. It is more likely that the old peasant dance preserved a more powerful movement. Even today we find with all savage tribes an interchanging, mysterious whirling, and there is perhaps no significant difference between this and the dancing of dervishes or David's dance in front of the Ark. This rotating is not only physically intoxicating as representations of hunting, desire and convulsive movements of various kinds, but is moreover of an altogether stellar character. The dancing dervishes are secretly participating in the dance of the houris, indeed of the angels, in a round-dance and spinning around their own axis until spasms, swooning and sidereal ecstasy set in. For the houris are regarded as the spirits of the stars that control destinies. By thrusting himself into this imitative rotating, the dervish seeks to conform to the constellations, to absorb and to draw down upon himself the efflux of the *primus agens* around which the constellations revolve and whose eternal splendour is most directly beheld by the stars. Thus the dancing dervish would, as ibn Tofail has explained, undertake the various types of rotating movement as a duty. Even Dionysius the Areopagite praised the rotating motion of the soul as its withdrawal into itself, no longer in order to copy the circle of the starry spirits in the revolution of the heavenly spheres, to be sure, but rather – with the beginning of the divorce from all Dionysian or Mithraic ecstasy – in order for the soul to withdraw in a cyclical motion into its *own* ground's beauty and goodness. So in the end, any outward convulsion was rejected as pagan by the early Christian communities. That is to say, the singing which accompanied the dancing survived as a religious stimulant; but just as the lascivious sound of musical instruments was abhorrent, so too did the vigorously and variously divided measures of the ancient dance seem at odds with the still waters of the Christian temperament. This gave rise to the time-change of the chorale, which was merely suggested harmonically – anti-pagan in its total lack of tension, unless we already claim to find a tension in the calmest of motions towards the tonic. It is also probable, although we can hardly say for sure now, that the conception of the stressed note before a rest as a rhythmically articulating fermata in the chorale is not an ancient one. This picture did not change until the appearance of the Italian and French masters of the *style galant*. They however did not, in their desire for livelier movement, hark back to the old peasant dances. Instead there is a parallel with the stiffness of recent times, when the only dance was the waltz. The *galant* composers adopted (it was, to be sure, a graceful generation, and as the gigue proves, the leap from the village fair to the ball did not necessarily mean the loss of all the more artful measures) a certain delicate, elastic and yet most exquisitely restrained motion in even time which both maintained the energetic progress of the music and forestalled the further consequence, the polyphonic promiscuity of the syncope. Even earlier, admittedly, the introduction of proportional notation had opened the way to a more divided beat. But all this was a vast stride into the realm of the impracticable, the musically and artistically irrelevant, the study score and mere theory. Hence things could only change when Bach, first and foremost, also assimilated the ancient folk-dance. This, after all, goes far back in time, has faithfully preserved many primitive features and, as all Hungarian gipsy music still confirms, is not all that far removed from polyphonic music's more diversified rhythm. Bach, then, used rhythm in a manner – here let us just recall the aria 'Erbarme dich mein' from the St Matthew Passion or the numerous 'reworkings' of French dance forms in the partitas – which sounds like the primitive rhythmicality of clashing stones and drumming in pagan ritual, though now recreated, of course, involuntarily and unconsciously. But it is just this use of rhythm which also revived that strange, unbidden act of self-intoxication which is not only spiritual. We know how accurately Wagner explained Beethoven through the dance, through the act of grasping, breathing, the motion of the pulse. Not that this prevented Wagner, illogically, from ultimately deriving the dance form from the tonal connection, because he went only by its social, tritely eurhythmic occurrence. It is quite remarkable that Wagner, having coined his famous description of Beethoven's Seventh Symphony as the apotheosis of the dance, still denies Beethoven's art the power to exceed certain limits of musical expression, and does so precisely because of this debt it owes to the dance. Certainly dance-rhythm, insofar as Wagner defined it for himself solely as an aural ballet, a kaleidoscope for the ear, pitched the passionate and tragic tendency so deep in this form that the question of a reason, an empirical causal connection totally foreign to the tonal events, becomes inevitable. So Wagner was never inclined to set any particularly great store by the rhythmic element. Despite his own indefatigable posing of rhythmic problems, along with his avowed love of the sonorous gesture and all theatrical symbolism – all he saw in rhythm was a point of contact, a *tertium comparationis* with the visual plastic world whereby, like light on a physical body, music would only be apprehensible in the lower sense of an empirical reality. What matters here, however, is just one crucial point. In spite of all these anti-social, indeed anti-worldly, reservations, Wagner could still be termed a musician invoking and reviving the Dionysian revels, as long as the latter only appear in a wholly idealised form as dramatic action and are accordingly capable of being related to music's passionate, tragic and transcendent propensities. Thus *the singing-to-oneself, assimilation of the dance and chamber-music subtlety* that found its orchestra in Wagner-Bruckner also meant *a regaining of the whole original, still anonymous, genuine 'carpet', that of the whole repository of the primitive and right.* But, precisely because the syncopation is supported by the assimilated dance, this fiery rhythm not only underlies Wagnerian polyphony like a carpet with a technically and objectively non-obligatory corrective value. It is also accompanied, in practice, by the paganism embodied in it from ancient times. One purpose of this was to communicate its Dionysian character; another was to dictate to music all manner of delirious self-destruction, tyranny of the lower body and physiologically earthbound, indeed starbound, Dionysian-Mithraic, astral, transcendents.

The *third* and most important factor leading to the colourful, polyphonic and also dramatic fabric of unending melody is harmony. In song every note is already animated and active. That is to say, in homophonic writing the note is actively oriented towards a chord. Throughout, the tonal progression derives from a feeling for the dominant and cadence, by which it is led and melodically drawn. Hence for as long as people have sung, even without any knowledge of harmony, the driving and hidden cause was always the scale, then the intervallic relations within it, and so finally harmony. 'The startling effects which many credit to the natural genius of the composer are often achieved with the greatest ease by the use and resolution of the diminished seventh chords.' Those are Beethoven's own words.[7] And as we shall show in due course, they undoubtedly serve, when allied to a harmony with a different type of rhythm, to throw light on many passages in his work, for example the entire first movement of his last sonata. At any rate all the notes are actively moving, all going somewhere, leading or being led; the third strives upwards, the seventh downwards, until the key asserts its will and the concluding consonance appears. But even the latter is not actually there: where consonance first sounds, without harmonic preparation, it is the most nondescript sound imaginable. When it truly 'appears' at last, even after the tremors of the most grandiose general pause, it is still possible – as Bruckner has demonstrated with the utmost splendour, especially in the first movement of his Seventh Symphony – for there to be such enormous tensions, such immense climaxes upon the dominant and its repercussions before the consonance, that Halm can rightly say that no consonance occurs. It exists only as a hypothesis, and the history of music is the history of dissonance. Where else, therefore, could a cause, a necessity or a guiding rule for the outcome be located but in the chord and the harmony? Bach was a great composer, and the fugue is an unforgettable reminder of him. But basically his continuing influence for both Beethoven and Wagner derives from his richly filigrane harmony. Despite the astonishing neglect of his works, he was bound to regain attention, an attention commensurate with the abandonment of homophonic melody and return to polyphonic activity, which became strict again, needing all voices in order to achieve polyphonic chordal vitality. Certainly the masters of homophonic melody are far removed from the earlier period's part-writing, which had an extraordinary wealth of gradations. But we have only to look at individual structures in Haydn (who can often become mysteriously serious and profound), such as the chorus depicting the downfall of the spirits of Hell, or the overture to the *Creation*, to perceive a harmonic style which is so surprisingly daring, so thoroughly romantic, and at the same time so consistently derivative of Bach's harmonic 'coincidences', that one tends to regard all subsequent music, all classical-romantic chromaticism and polyphony, as the mobile and now engrossing workings of a spring that was wound up in Bach less demonstratively. One thing is certain. In the Haydn-Beethoven sonata there was, after an initial homophonic loss, once more a developing tendency towards richer and richer solo playing, individually inward-looking music-making and linear melisma of a chamber-music type. Also, Bachian counterpoint – that is, counterpoint treated harmonically-rhythmically, with the target of the chord – clearly has repercussions in Wagnerian polyphony, a polyphony of a higher order which is now contrapuntal not in an architectonic but in a dramatic sense. It is not just that the fresh orchestral colour provides

50

contrast and nuance and, even sensuously speaking, its own counterpoint again. With Wagner, the development takes pride of place. And in its restless harmony – which is above all fleetingly constructed and never as the aim of a fixed motif or theme, as in Beethoven – it attains to a form of mounting dramatic polyphony assimilating Bach's latent verticalism, i.e., oriented towards the chord rather than away from it. Hence chordal vitality is not a product but a *prius*, and by no means just of a theoretical kind. Set against the harmonic approach, counterpoint – at any rate when devoted to the gathering and composing of the *fugue* – is a method of a secondary order surpassed by the *harmonic* and *symphonic* methods. For in the divided layering of its melodies, it has to take into account *pari passu* the chordal 'results', dissonances, along with what is stressed and compressed in chordal-rhythmic terms. So it may only be a different way of expressing the same thing whether we consider the structure of a Wagnerian work from the viewpoint of harmonic economy – which, to be sure, would sorely need a rhythmic theory to complement it – or seek to outline the still unwritten structural theory of Wagner's style from the angle of a new counterpoint. This means counterpoint developed not so much through juxtaposing and superimposing but rather in a *succession*, counterpoint which has shed all that is merely 'incidentally' harmonic in the fugue and has acquired the additional advantage of harmonic tensions, rhythmic contrasts, thematic developments – in short, all the relations of the 'symphonic' complex. Hence it is primarily Bach the richly filigrane, polyphonic, vertical harmonist who first flourishes again in Beethoven and who culminates in Wagner, for the time being at least. Ultimately, though, the *linear* working still has a far stronger influence through the *chamber-music 'carpet'*, and the *ontological* realm still makes a far more vivid impact in Wagner through the Palestrinian, seraphic *chordal, 'carpet'* than through the carpet of the Bachian fugue, of lyrically contrapuntal *equilibrium or repose*. This, of course, is the carpet and constraint, the ultimate musically possible and expressible assimilation, to be regained only at the still invisible end of music. There is a double singing and storming, that which occurs within the scale and that which occurs within the chords, i.e. that of the linear Bach and that of the overlapping, vertical Bach, introduced into the symphony's range of contrasts. And Wagner, however vehement or ceremonious in his mastery of the scale, primarily assisted open-work chordal vitality to achieve supremacy over linear counterpoint. He did so inasmuch as it is the former which most intensifies, fuses and safeguards the mutual glow of the melismata. At the same time this chordal vitality causes *the new harmonic counterpoint's richly connected succession* to be articulated in the most fruitful way.

So the sonata's storming has also re-acquired a gravity and a fulness of fragrance. Thus the three ways, the cry or regained carpet of singing-to-oneself, the syncope or regained carpet of the primitive dance, dramatically applied harmony or the regained carpets of chamber-music subtlety and seraphic chordal effulgence, have been ultimately secured in dramatic-symphonic practice. It is surprising to what extent the symphonic impulse tends first to destroy the lyrical element and then to present it in a dynamic fresh outpouring and intricacy; how much it was the delight in melisma which led to music that was truly active, to the veritable animating and humanising of its mechanics. It was only Wagner's aversion to writing a single note which could not have symbolised a Bachian lyricism right within his dramatic, meta-dramatic sonata form that initiated, as Nietzsche says, the opening up of the unknown area of music not only with ethos but also with transcendental pathos, and thus with mystical gain.

The transcendent opera and its object

The fulfilment of Mozart, however, was yet to come.

He too, the delicate instigator of tender motions, has now become fully effervescent. We are not referring to *The Flying Dutchman*, *Tannhäuser* or *Lohengrin*, nor to the marvellous structure of *The Mastersingers*, which, in spite of some transitional features, all represent operas of action on the lines of Beethoven's *Fidelio*. Still less do we mean the *Ring* cycle, which falls foul of the pagan dance and thus frequently strays into vacuity and into the despondently brutish. But on the other hand we may regard *Tristan and Parsifal in particular as dividend-paying fulfilments of the Mozartian fairy-tale opera*, as enhancing that delicate instigator of tender motions who did not need mankind to challenge fate in order to achieve the great secular self and its conversion in the act of redemption. In redemption, however, mankind steps forward from fate again so that in the area of music which constitutes homeland and myth, the meta-dramatic lyrisma of redemption may appear the actual object of transcendent opera. And this begins in *Tristan*.

Now we make inroads into ourselves, as gentle as they are profound. Other people are agitated and constantly leading outwards.
Tristan and Isolde have escaped the daily hubbub, and they do not
act. This is our own deep-seated dreaming, occurring where words
and steps no longer hurry. It is we who share in the journey, taking
on a chromatic opacity, moving in a state of yearning and flounder-
ing towards the dream that takes shape in the advancing Night.

This can already be seen in the way that the Prelude removes us
from time. For it spins only the one a-historical, abstract Yearning
motif, completely without reference, freely hovering, but ready to
descend and take bodily form. Its region grows bright, but everything
directly behind remains distant and calm. Only the first Act is energetic, leading the two characters away from Day. Here the action is
still shrill and mocking, all too deliberate, and the death-potion leads
to the wrong gateway. But neither Isolde nor even Tristan would
require this potion in order to find one another. They only go
through the motions of passing one another by, outwardly, in the
uncertain shimmer of the Day which still hides what has already
appeared from this couple, these Night-seers. Isolde believes that she
feels hate, when only betrayed love is raising its head. Tristan is so
stiff, so excessively concerned with decorum, so peculiarly weak and
also awkward and contorted, that the potion only gives to the couple
what they long possessed, what amounts to fate and now also
penetrates time to become destiny, conveyed through a symbolised
leap. Here there is not only another twist to the story as in the *Ring*,
where Hagen seasons the corresponding drink for Siegfried so that
something distant should not escape him: a distant thing which is
part of the plot, which can be repeated and which is a reawakened
memory only because Siegfried, in the plot, knows the place where
the wood-bird, Brünnhilde's rock and the magic fire are located.
What happens with or behind the Irish potion is never action. The
potion is not even a key or a catalyst or that accident which is really
no accident and which tragic necessity uses as the accomplice of fate,
but only — supposing that even this uncharted land can be a homeland — a glimpse within time, a temporal distillation, of what is going
on for ever, in the supra-temporal, mythical world of love. Here two
people are striding into the Night; they are passing from one world
into the other; and, as we can perceive towards the end of the first Act
and throughout the last two Acts, this is all that happens, and all we
hear is the music of this striding and final disappearing. Wagner

wanted us to recognise this when he called *Tristan* a pure 'action' [*Handlung*]; it is an ineffable movement, an enormous adagio scarcely touched by any opposing outside element that Tristan and Isolde could consciously register as a conflict, a catastrophe at all. This is what the word 'action' means on the title-page, not that it is one, but only that it is distinct from the authentically dramatic agitation and significance, the daylight destinies of the antithetical, symphonic movement or even music-drama.

Only the final scenes are agitated, reaching an outwardly visible conclusion. This may be necessary in terms of stagecraft, but along with Pfitzner we cannot help thinking that it means the intrusion of Day once more, precisely where we have developed the most sensitive reaction to the latter. After what has been stated, moreover, it will be clear that repetition does not now have that effect of which it is normally assured in the symphony. One has the sense of an incipient sinking at this point, of leaving the pure spiritual path which cannot brook any recurrence. All this sounded much lovelier in the great closing duet of Act 2 than in the orchestral writing at the close of Act 3, which *cannot* have experienced anything en route, inasmuch as any actual progress was lacking, and which is therefore unable to figure as the regained present, the reprise and conclusion of a symphonic development. And it must be said in general, with all due respect for its merits, that the orchestral piece 'Isolde's Liebestod' which Wagner inserted in such a very deliberate and finale-like, as it were transportable, manner begins to descend into something intolerably weak and a-mystically sweet. As in the case of the resolved triads, the massive and interminable solemnity at the close of *Parsifal*, it risks a fall from its immense heights that will be all the more abrupt, the greater the discrepancy arising between a good theatrical ending and the quite different finality of a birth of redemption from the spirit of music. There was so little more said, and the Love-night engulfed us with such world-redeeming profundity in Act 2 that we no longer want to see the actual dying on stage, presented there in the form of corpses, a ring of attendants and an emotional benediction; the appropriate, though less representable, sight would be the lovers' meeting in the universal Night. When Siegfried dies and the vassals carry his body slowly away over the rocks, funeral music plays for as long as the cortège is visible. But mists soon climb up from the Rhine to conceal the stage. Then we hear the singular, exuberant rejoicing of an intermezzo which has not the least thing in common with a traditional 'consolation' or other music of mourning. Only when the mists disperse again, and the scene reverts to those of us who remain behind, to our world, does the funeral music also return, more terrible and heavy than before, just as the lower, visible world around Siegfried's body replaces the unrepresentable paradox, which can only be preserved in music. True, the mists only appear so that the Act is not interrupted by a scene-change. But precisely by screening our eyes, but not our ears and hearts, from the rejoicing, Wagner evinces a restraint which, better than at the end of *Tristan*, matches his own demand for a weakening of the visual faculty as the music intensifies.

Yet in *Tristan* too the note has already become distant and 'Night-seeing'. Melot, Brangäne, Kurwenal and even Marke sing in a different way, though (and this is significant) not all the time. Brangäne remains foolish and trivial, with no inkling of what is happening; Melot, her counterpart, becomes the short-sighted judge and betrayer; and only the two benign characters, Kurwenal and Marke, show some discretion, grown humble in the face of the totally impenetrable, Kurwenal without even asking questions or permitting the inquisitive shepherd's question in the face of the mysterious ground of unfathomable depth which turns Tristan into a transgressor and which, even in the Yearning motif, is expressed so inadequately. The utterances of the Day characters, those generally stupid awake and adult people, sound perceptibly different from the utterances of the Night-dedicated couple. Less so at the beginning when we can still hear, couched in jagged or inflexible rhythms, Isolde's shame and Tristan's honour. But what an immense difference there is in Act 2! The anchor is raised, the wheel left to the tide's mercy, sails and mast to the winds', while world, power, fame, glory, honour, chivalry, friendship, all quotidian goods are vanished like an insubstantial dream. All is ready for the voyage to the most mysterious of lands, and the garish Day motif which the nefarious Melot first sings – it is related harmonically to the 'Who dares to deride me?' of the beginning – and which opens the second Act, cuts perceptibly with its abrupt interval and its thrashing, dour and also pronouncedly plastic rhythm into the slow movement, the largely chordal, rhythmically hesitant adagio of Night. Indeed, with the latter itself, we have the undeniable feeling that there would not even be music of this extremely quiet type if Isolde and Tristan could die, if yearning did not still bind them to this world in that other one.

That is why in his first draft Wagner wanted the roaming Parsifal, another and profounder seeker of Grace, to reach the death-bed of the mortally wounded Tristan. The light was not yet out, and it was not yet night in the house, or else one would hear nothing further; but there remains the impulse, the amorous desire, the eternally self-regenerating Will – if no longer the will for earthly reproduction, the procreative will, the convulsive mother who does not want to die as would be necessary if the sacred child is to live. And the shepherd's old and earnest air is heard: to yearn, to yearn in the act of dying, not to die for yearning – for Isolde, still living in the Day, for Tristan, who could not meet Isolde in the realm which fills him with holy fear because Night tosses him back to Day. Again we perceive that most intimate, but still somehow exoteric, music which dwells at this ultimate frontier. This, to be sure, would not be inevitable, for the note has no limits. It is quite peculiar that Tristan and Isolde can escape from us at all, that even in sound, which equips them so thoroughly, they no longer have anything to say to us. For never was music so eminently suited to conveying Night in its entirety, as a condition and concept which permeates the whole work and constitutes Tristan's authentic language. But it does seem to be only twilight, though a remote twilight, and not Night to which the music of *Tristan*, still earthly and linked to action, relates. However much we occasionally seem to perceive a glimmering of the delirium's end – soundless dreams of motley shades, a spiritual life, the Liebestod, the dimension of Love, the *passio*, steeped in miracles, the lyrically ever-enduring, meta-dramatic glory – all this nonetheless withdraws again in its insufficiency to the broad and indistinct perspective of the universal, of love in general and similar formless centres. Certainly the self was never more thoroughly shattered and more firmly transferred to the Other. 'You stepped forth from my dream, I stepped forth from yours': in order thus to achieve in the other, after changing places and with the other's image in each one's heart, the lyricism of feelings of strangeness, the self-awareness alive in the other. But the 'and', the one reality connecting the love of Tristan and Isolde, cannot at the same time distance them; it causes the two souls to intermingle, renders their faces and figures ultimately unrecognisable. In accordance with the Indo-Schopenhauerian theory of the musical object, it thus expels from the subjects all selfness, all that is Luciferan, only for this to be replaced – 'in the world-breath's drifting universe, drowning, sinking, unconscious' – by an expansion of the brahmin's pagan, subject-alien and Asiatic universality. That is why even Wagner's visionary sound of Night is at an ultimate loss. Admittedly *Tristan*, and *Parsifal* too, give us the full lyrical splendour, the full, supra-dramatic incandescence of the lyrical self. Consequently they provide an objective, ontological fulfilment of the Mozartian fairy-tale opera and indeed even of Bach's Passions with their Adamite-Christian lyricism. But however thoroughly the quieter, more deeply Christian splendour of the adagio already overlies this, the fact remains that what is behind the yearning process – repose, out-and-out soul, the Bachian fugue as *musica sacra*, the metaphysical adagio, music as 'space', the music of the Paracletian self, architectonic counterpoint of the highest order – all this remains unachieved because of the profoundly un-Christian mysticism of the universal and general in Wagner.

Anyone who has truly crossed the frontier will never return unscathed. He will be repelled, as though there was blood in his shoes, or else, depending on the personality, he will be a visionary. Tristan too has forgotten everything and become a complete stranger, within the five hundred thousand years he spent looking into the Night. 'Which king?' he asks Kurwenal, who has to point across to Marke, as though there had ever been another king for Tristan. 'Am I in Cornwall?' he finally asks, no longer recognising Kareol, his ancestral castle. And then again: 'O King, I cannot tell you this; these answers you can never learn'. Indeed when Tristan suddenly wakes up, staring aghast at Melot and the courtiers who are rushing in, and seems slowly to comprehend Marke's words, his own immeasurable disgrace and deadly sin, he is still refusing to register anything other than a feeling of sympathy and mounting sorrow for Marke. To Tristan, the illusion in which the others are living has become just as puzzling as his Night is to them. They are daylight phantoms, waking dreams, deceptive, disorderly and completely pointless in their sharp banality. Here there no longer burns a light that can provide a release, with breadth and chromatically mythological history. The first man to enter into the realm of the invisible and genuine saw nothing, the second went mad, and [the first-century] Rabbi Akiba met only himself. Nor does the night that Tristan was in precede another morning in the world we know.

But there is also another hero and his retinue. There is also another sun, not opposed to Night but behind it. Full of a different yearning, the four main characters in *Parsifal* are on their way there.

Kundry still survives in fairy-tales as the cunningly kind-hearted ogre's wife or as the devil's grandmother. Even today the tale of 'The Magic Table' preserves the whole myth of the grail with its thieving landlord, the magic cudgel or sacred spear, Bricklebrit the ass or the grail of the moon and the magic table, the authentic, supreme sun-grail itself. We also know that Klingsor and Amfortas were originally a single character, viz. the demon of the clouds that conceals the light. Rather less easy to unravel are the origins of Parsifal, a hero who is at first fruitful and then completely abstinent. At an early point he already takes the place of Thor, the god of thunder who on the gods' behalf has repeatedly to remove the solar cauldron from the clutches of Hymir the giant, who lives in the oriental world of primitive waters. So in Indian and mediaeval legends – which, as Schröder first neatly pointed out, all derive from these primeval astral motifs – Parsifal too is basically the cauldron-stealing, grail-seeking, sun-conquering hero, the master of rain and above all of the magic of light. The only Christian feature to have been added is the complete purity of heart, the innocence. Otherwise the original astral myth still shines through to the extent that Parsifal either has first to look for the spear or else promptly slays the giant of the clouds with the spear as the instrument of thunder in order to obtain the lunar dew, the draught of *soma* or nectar, but above all the pitcher of light, the ambrosia. And that is nothing less than the grail with the solar food, later the vessel in which Joseph of Arimathea collected the solar blood, the blood of the Saviour. Wagner strengthened and deepened the whole story, adding the theme of consecration through love. We have Kundry, sinful, confused, leading two lives, divided through a death-like sleep between good and evil, the womb of sensuality and endless birth, eternally mocking, eternally without faith, but also the meekest of servants, a healer and a seeker of herbs. Klingsor: the thief, magician of a bogus daylight; Amfortas: the defeated man, afflicted by the boundless craving of his heart, an inconceivably heightened Tristan desirous of death, a thief in his way, but filled with a holy desire for the promised redeemer, the Orphic reviver of the sacrosanct. Finally, there is Parsifal: poor, inexperienced, the pure fool, the fool with a knowledge acquired through sympathy, a universal clairvoyant whose eyes are opened by immense suffering, who conquers the dragon, that symbol of woman and rebirth, and who, another and higher Siegfried, now understands not so much the language of birds as that which has no language, the anxious waiting of Creation for the revelation of the children of God. In him, what is chaste and pure has become absolute. Parsifal, then, is no longer the exuberantly overflowing youth of astral myth who divides clouds and brings a purely natural fertility. On the contrary, he transforms the magic garden into a desert, and the fallow land in the region of the grail is blessed with a sun altogether different from the daytime sun and an altogether profounder dawn than that of a merely natural, earthly summer. But all the same, one is going towards the sun once more, and the secret footpath upon which it rediscovers the mountains where it rises is plainly there. Where the Love-night failed, the holy night has succeeded: succeeded, that is, in attaining at its fountain-head the beautiful Meadow, the enigmatic light of Good Friday morn. Day is losing its outward brightness. 'As the sun departs in gladness from the empty show of day', wrote Wagner's friend in the third of the Wesendonck Lieder with its curious dialectic, whereby it can constitute a night-mysticism and yet also rescue the daytime constellation. Similarly, the music of *Parsifal* reaches a point where it is not pure action and thus dramatically tracing the paths of error and suffering. It becomes quiet and endeavours to confer on the heavenly glow of the morn its immutable, meta-dramatic, ontological interpretation. On the last noon, at the obsequies, during the growing twilight down below and the increasing illumination from on high, with the pious, enigmatic blasphemy of 'redemption for the Redeemer' – here at any rate, this ontological *Parsifal* music seeks only to introduce us on that most inward of days to the word 'soul', which is no longer of this world but still hardly of the next, still hardly impervious to the age-old resplendence of the old thrones and dominions and powers. This light, again surpassing all resounding words or harking only to that single word 'soul', is one which shatters bolts; and nothing can approach it more nearly than music's new self-perceiving and remembrancing. Hebbel divined it in his memorable lines about the deaf man and the dumb man, to whom God has confided a word –

> . . . a word he cannot fathom,
> One man only can he tell it,
> A man he has not met.
>
> Then will the dumb man speak,
> The deaf one will perceive the word,
> He will at once decipher

Its sombre, godly letters.
'Ere morn they will depart.

You people, pray in earnest
For these two men to meet.
For if they should, this pair of
Lonely wanderers, why then
All things will reach their goal.[8]

For the time being, of course, to give even the remotest glimmer of this daylight may be even less successful than the music of Night. Although the note in *Parsifal* does absolutely point upwards, and thus does not draw the universal down into a broad mysticism of oceanic depth as much as in *Tristan*, it was still unable to become a vision of the sun. Its music was even less capable of 'eloquence' or of providing clear points of contact with the higher world that were not only suitably evocative and formally mythical but also substantial and inherently mythical. And the music's inability in this respect, the fact that it does not make an expressive statement but at best only a disclosure and that the metaphysical adagio is still a mere, vaguely ceremonial musical *sphere* without any categories, demonstrates afresh – within this mounting polemic which is based on admiration, on an absolute yardstick – how far away Wagner's music still is from achieving an ultimate, sacred status. It falls short of the fulfilment of music as an annunciation, as an explanation starting beyond all words of our secret nature – which the music of Wagner is the first since that of Beethoven to have delved into so deeply.

By the same token, there is ultimately no disguising the fact that Wagner's oeuvre has also impinged on areas which cannot be so musically desirable. A ring with a curse on it spells ruin equally for all who possess it. Likewise, Wagner's all too enthusiastic re-adoption of the ancient pagan-ritualistic action – instead of the pure consummation of Mozart's 'fairy-tale' music and the Christian music of Bach – left the rest of him, especially the Wagner of the *Nibelung trilogy*, hopelessly at the mercy of the dream of sheer natural will as the musical object.

For no character in this cycle behaves as he would like to behave and might indeed do so *qua* human being. Is this boastful character really a hero, and is that one a god? Neither of them is what he so volubly professes to be. Siegfried experiences suffering and follows his trivial impulses with emotion and comical horn-calls. From the start, theatrical considerations prevent Wotan with his eye-patch from being a god, and this tedious figure has nothing superhuman or mysterious about him. Mystery is restricted to the Norns and Erda, and it is not displayed with any conviction. The musical note, as we said, now lapses almost entirely into vacuity and into the despondently brutish. This work contains no insight that could help us to escape personal limitations other than by revealing a world of cardboard, greasepaint and grotesque heroic poses. Sentient and active human beings too often become painted marionettes for the acting out of the rapacious, dishonourable, self-alien, superficially general and abstract features of this delirium. It is all performed with an ebullient, clamorous presentation, with lifeless speech-song, endless, emotionally tedious and superfluous conversation, with embarrassing overtones of Wilhelm Jordan and Felix Dahn[9] and a lyricism which, in spite of many splendid and inspired details that one would only too gladly see elsewhere, cannot obliterate the tortured aspects of this saga, the fact that Wagner laid it aside for a long period before resuming it, or its artificial, academic-seeming and mechanically integrated character. Certainly the note in itself is incomparably purer here than in the subsequent new idiom compounded of notes and words, words that thrust themselves forward only too self-righteously and yet are never comprehensible in performance. With Wagner, the sonority not only inspires the invention of many details, indeed entire figures – consider Loge, who only comes to life with the flickering flames, or the Oblivion motif that uncannily drags us down with it, or the sombre grandeur and solitude, the veritable music of finality and death in Brünnhilde's closing song. The master also discovers in his orchestra – which extends right through the world of consciousness and also right underneath it – basic means of movement and motivation, i.e. leitmotifs in more than one sense, which the rational libretto cannot include. Thus often there is certainly a clairvoyant anticipation at work here, an activity which is very capable of illuminating the impersonal and indescribable twilight of the active powers of the will in the mighty lower and upper expansion of consciousness, in the multi-layered structure of melismatic polyphony, given that in their concatenations, the promptings of the will can hardly ever fall into the more complete consciousness of the upper voice, and thus into the express motivating of people. But all this does not remove mere impulsiveness. Wherever there is a convenient place for this peculiarly subjective lyricism of the animal, the sound reverts to its semi-military tam-tam beat or else to its broad espressivo, which is universal on a common and inferior level. As we see, for all its extensive raging, this sonority engenders only passion and no genuine action, far less destiny that is personally compelling, metaphysically significant. It is by accident that this and that happen to Brünnhilde and Siegfried. Their destiny is sad but not inevitable or tragic, and the gods that perpetrate it are called gods without their being such. It was rightly observed that Wagner's heroic women in love never become mothers with the sole exception of Sieglinde, and even the latter only in order for the ardent splendour of love to recur without further refinement in Brünnhilde and Siegfried. So too – in spite of all the breadth of the work, despite the encounters between men and gods, despite the extreme flexibility of it all, the imaginative animation of Nature, the hugeness of the fates, eschatologisms of the background, the *ragnarok* – the whole thing lacks any vision, any extension forwards and upwards, any genuine action of a dramatic or indeed meta-dramatic kind. It is totally and utterly sub-human, and it can only use its magical mandrakes to produce a futile, purely physical narcotic, instead of redemption. In lieu of the much swollen human heart, the finally explained, musically explained baroque quality persisting in men, we have underground trapdoors, generalities, acts of treachery and Nature myths. The Nibelung cycle lacks truth and remains 'art' in the pejorative sense, finding no place in the philosophy of history and in metaphysics. Decadent barbarians and decadent gods are the *dramatis personae*, not the yearning for Siegfried, the Germanic messiah, not the distant, ultimate God of the Apocalypse and the apocalyptic 'drama of clemency' invoked by ontological music.

Wagner, then, has now given up all conscious willing without achieving another willing that would break fresh ground. There is a roaring, a flashing, the fog is eloquent and yet not eloquent, for everything is blurred, and the pre-arranged word interrupts. But it *can* be achieved, that other type of willing, if first the fist is clenched that will open the inner door, if not break it down. Beethoven pursued this course, with virile, courageous, morally objective energy, and this alone can render things mystical, legitimately mystical, again. Wagner too sought to achieve this effulgence, but he did not allow his torrid sound to have a complete say so that it might find its innately spiritual language; instead he countered the opacity in the most specious way through the rationality of the word. Even in terms of poetry, the result was no effulgence of the word. The sound-haze simply became even more oppressively thick, and, in accordance with the perpetually billowing, uncompleted sound, the remedy of the Gluckian and classicistic elucidation that Wagner superficially, sentimentally, adopted ran solely to the expression of 'a confused idea' of unsuitable fervour. Here Wagner was not prepared to wait for his *most original discovery*, the *Tonwort* or 'eloquent music', to arrive of its own accord. But it is precisely the inspired composer who must, in a completely detached way, be ultimately capable of remaining absolute and of seeing whither his art, only partly known so far and only to be explored through persistence, is leading him, into what immeasurably inner areas of his world radical expression is taking him. And he must not be influenced by the poetic element, which, even in the transcendent opera, can rather be only a variable and which in the end loses any correlation when confronted with the different, supra-rational correlation of music. Otherwise everything will be dragged down to such depths that we no longer come into consideration at all and it is only the unconscious, pathological will that rules. The pent-up sound takes its revenge by holding back, by becoming hypertrophied in its primitive Maenadic, chthonian, sub-daylight state instead of supra-daylight, remembrancing warmth. Given that the prematurely interrupting poetry is stored up here, it thus shifts the dramatic characters back into a region where they can only be blossoms on a tree, the tree of the soul, and indeed no more than bobbing ships which passively share in the grief, the struggle, the love and yearning for redemption of their sub-human sea and only experience the universal wave of the Schopenhauerian Will washing over them at every critical moment, instead of a mutual encounter and their own profound destiny. Certainly the individual souls will offer some resistance – not, however, that of the individuation principle but rather the useful check that is necessary to any stage representation, even an undramatic one. This is not the new solitary self which can only talk of its own concerns and must leave it to the others whether to go along with this. Nor is it the self of the folk-song or *Minnesang*, which speaks of the lover or the greybeard as a collective type. Indeed, individual souls can no longer even be regarded as mere arenas for the battles waged between the forces of sensuality and reason, forces that are abstract but that nonetheless still lead back to human beings. Instead the lower chinks are opened, the lower level replaces the higher, the sea comes into the heaven's inheritance. The self pitches back – even, at times, in the *Master-*

singers – in such a feverish, delirious and glowworm-like state, in midsummer night, midsummer day and unconsciousness, in such waves, clouds of vapour and base slumbers that it no longer speaks out of itself and certainly not out of the Beethoven-Comtean *grand être* as the socially mystical entity of mankind. It now speaks out of the ancient Nature-god's belly, though quite without the latter's sidereal clarity and ancient, pliant mathematics. Hence a passive submission replaces the sturdy commitment, the rigour, severity, consciousness of sin and the strictly individual postulates of the Christian faith. Pagan is the word for everything that Wagner's Nibelung music, this music peculiarly riddled with smut, gold and narcotics, provided in terms of its breadth, bogus ecstasy and impersonal glory in the service of its Nature principle, which was disturbed by Christianity but not shattered by it. That this should have occurred and that the demonstration of the object of transcendent opera, when measured by its most dangerous and least successful type, should proceed so abruptly into the feverishly inessential and most profoundly undramatic is therefore by no means due, as is repeatedly evident, only to Dionysian dance rhythms directed towards the false object. Ultimately it is also due to the spreading over the music of a layer of pre-arranged poetry, inasmuch as this sought to suppress the powers of the note. It forced music – now deposed, but unassailable in the genius of Wagner – to spread in the sole remaining unconscious realm with such total, innate absoluteness that it would lose its sight and the not yet conscious, supra-conscious element, the heroic-mystical phantom of man and the genuine unendingness of the inwardly real and ontological. To be sure, there are demands which cannot be met from a historical standpoint, the standpoint of the higher world-clock. But to some extent Wagner robbed himself of his finest hour, which was a great and hallowed one and in which the enormous impulses of his sacred *Tristan* and *Parsifal* dramas became efficacious. What he failed to achieve are those fulfilments we are still awaiting of Bachian ontological lyricism and the fugue, of the Bachian melismatic-contrapuntal equilibrium, the aim of purification, of the pure and simple present, the undefiled rose of the Virgin, the unriven heart of the Son, the conquering of any drive towards space and the homecoming of a weary, anonymous Kaspar Hauser to the throne-room of his heavenly splendour. Certainly we can say that Wagner turned aside from the self's Luciferan orientation, which had been innate to music since Beethoven. But the course of Wagner's note, the born illuminator of the soul's higher realms, reverted on the basis of the arrantly false Indo-Schopenhauerian definition of music into the meretricious and the mysterious, pathologically poisoned; whereas, given the complete freedom and consistency of objective music, the incipient speaking in many tongues and hence the Luciferan-Paracletian willing of the man-linked spirit of music itself could have proclaimed the true mystery, the mystery of the intelligible realm. Yet by the same token, these realms would not have been heralded as *realms of the note* at all without Wagner's precedent. *Tristan* is their beginning, the celesta in *Parsifal* their presentation.

This is the end of a long train of events. It produced things of immeasurable splendour; yet the bitter feeling which nagged Mozart, Schubert and Beethoven before they died – namely, that it seemed as though they had yet to begin, as though they had not yet written a note of music – remains conceptually valid, but with the difference that the bitterness is turning into rejoicing and hope. The note is not yet 'eloquent'; it is emphatic enough, but nobody can fully understand it, for it is a fervent stammering like that of a child. And by making suppositions, prescriptions of its own or simply by obtruding, 'poetry' interferes with both the note and itself, its own, similarly subordinate, indeed vanquished, power, at any rate in the music-drama. Nothing is finished apart from the 'carpets', those boundary markers and constraints for the future, and then, minus the Bachian fugue, their filling-in and fulfilment in an increasingly concrete roundedness. The symphony that Wagner raised to the peak of expressive exactitude still awaits the object which it itself engendered in absolute music, namely Bachian music that has reached its goal, the music of space, of a melismatic-contrapuntal equilibrium transcending all chordal-polyphonic drama, the music of the fully Christianised soul and its true basic sound-figure. There is much to be hoped for, and a grand situation is developing. The time is imminent when the overflowing inner life, the breakthrough and the divining of a most immediate, ultimate latency, can no longer express itself other than in the musical, ethical and metaphysical domain. When that time comes, it will no longer be necessary to content oneself with the Areopagite's precept – that the divine darkness is the inaccessible light in which God dwells – as the supreme formulation of all the associative and transcendental factors in art.

ON THE THEORY OF MUSIC

All we hear is ourselves.

Admittedly, this sound has always been quite faint. Many would find hearing easier if they knew how to talk about it. This is connected with the extremely uncertain and derivative character of human feelings. For it is in men's nature only to be comfortable on the basis of communication. They must have means of accounting for their feelings, because this calls for a far slighter participation, a far slighter personal commitment, and also because one can obtain an exchange, a substitute or abstract surrogate for the understanding one lacks. If this were not so, then listening to music would also be less distracted and nervous. The question of why precisely the latecomers to a concert are remarkably apt to attract everyone's attention would neither arise nor, indeed, have to receive an answer so embarrassing for the listeners concerned. Above all it would be hard to see why, given every human being's natural inclinations to music, we so rarely find an avowed love of this art among the intellectual high-fliers in particular. The average citizen lives with music because he likes to be sociable and he reads the concert notices. On the other hand, painting with its abstruse concepts seems quite remote to him, an area in which one is liable to make involuntary blunders. There were, however, periods when the same was true of the intelligentsia in respect of painting, until Winckelmann and, more recently, Riegl finally broke the deplorable spell of personal passiveness and weakness of judgement through circuitous logical means. The ability to hear, on the contrary, is still quite weak. For in the musical world, unfortunately, there are no old Winckelmanns, and the new one goes by the name of Leopold Schmidt. For all his versatility, one August Halm does not make a summer.[10] Paul Bekker is a shrewd man, but he very often lets us forget it, and his yarn-spinning book on Beethoven does not always do him credit. Grunsky and also Friedrich von Hausegger can be recommended, while Richard Wagner's piece on Beethoven – a piece by a writer far removed from these others – is of exceptional importance. But it is to Riemann that one will turn for detailed instruction in all theory, although Moritz Hauptmann's profound writings are even more thorough in this respect. Busoni in particular has recently aired the subject of opera again, and Pfitzner has also provided critical stimuli. August Halm himself, to whom we owe much and who displays great learning and acumen, is questionable in that he evaluates all music all too often from the purely technical angle, criticises it too pedantically and analyses it too persistently simply in terms of well-chosen themes and their dynamic movement. His tone with regard to Beethoven also leaves something to be desired. To be sure, this led to such significant and necessary achievements as Halm's critical analysis of the first movement of Beethoven's D minor Sonata. But he neither knows nor acknowledges that naive, expressive music-making which does not lend itself to form-critiques, reflects a human being and not a technical category, and may sound different from a psycho-dramatic exposition *à la* Bekker. Even the eternal life becomes merely a world of stricter and higher laws in Halm's over-exaggerated form-concept of music in general, which does not gain in clarity or depth through an appended mythologising on the lines of Carl Spitteler. Nonetheless, it is greatly to be hoped that men of intellect, too, will more readily permit themselves to be encouraged in the enjoyment of music, once their susceptible minds have been provided with firm concepts for their objective further guidance.

Practice and Composition

Inflexion

We must bring ourselves to the process.

Then we will grasp at once what is being called to us. The glance and particularly the inflexion are quite clear and direct in themselves. We feel that this is what we are; this concerns us, we too would call out or behave in this way. Our own throat, gently innervated in sympathy, permits us to see and understand from within, as it were, what is being directed at us, what is speaking here.

In addition we know of no better way to express ourselves than through inflexion. The latter runs deep, and where a glance would coarsen the expression and make one flinch, where silence says more than speech, it is song which amplifies even the slightest and most elusive motion. It separates the inflexion, as the most fleeting and yet strongest potential means of being intuitive, from the human being, as it were, and collects it in a continuous, condensed structure. Here, therefore, so much depends on the note we have struck. What it contains of the actual person singing, and thus what quality the singer or player 'puts into' the note, is more important than what his song contains purely in terms of note-values. For the latter in itself effects only a quite general mood which is largely subject to the practitioner's discretion.

Attack

All too little would become clear without the attack. It is still crucial to see the person who is making the musical utterance or attack.

This is why the same thing may be sung in such very different ways. We know how often a song has changed owners without the conscious registering, on any listener's part, of the frequently colossal nature of this change. Otherwise how could the most diverse stanzas be set to the same melody? True, composers now attempt to avoid this, but even Schubert's 'Lindenbaum' has this drawback, which does not necessarily distort the meaning. Besides, who would now want to limit himself to formal analysis after learning that one and the same melody was initially the basis of the folk-song 'Mein Gemüt ist mir verwirrt, das macht ein Jungfrau zart' (My heart is all confused, a tender maiden charms me), later attached itself to the text 'Herzlich tut mich verlangen nach einem sel'gen End' (My heart is desirous of a blessed end) and, finally, still survives in the chorale 'O Haupt voll Blut und Wunden' (O sacred head sore wounded)? The same B flat–F sharp–G which stands for 'yearning' in Susanna's closing aria in *Figaro* accompanies, without any kind of rhythmic modification, the splendour of midsummer's day and consequently a completely jubilant state of fulfilment in Pogner's discourse, without the one being preferable to the other in respect of the intended content. Admittedly, it may be objected that the two uses do not occur in the same composer. It may also be objected that Mozart, in accordance with his partly Italianate character, did not present a perfect model of consistent organisation. But Bach, on the other hand, is a thoroughly German composer and shaped the richest, most potently expressive melodies to boot. Yet now we find in Bach, and thus precisely in a unified oeuvre, that the same song which illustrates hypocrisy in Cantata No. 179 is used as a plea for mercy in the Kyrie of the Mass in G. And the aria expressing carnal desire and its rebuttal ('I will not hear you, nor will I know of you, infamous craving, I know you not') in *Hercules at the Crossroads*, a *dramma per musica*, is transferred to a cradle-song for Mary in the *Christmas Oratorio*. Here the spurning of temptation, just pitched a third lower and accompanied by woodwinds and organ along with the strings of the operatic version, but in no respect changed, turns into the most eager counsel ('Make ready, O Zion, now gently prepare to take to your bosom the most lovely, the dearest'). When sung in a different way, however, it contains a noticeably different meaning which follows the 'sense'. And just as the word 'pray' need not remind us of prey or prairies or praise, or the word 'altar' of alteration, as they do in the empty shock of a pun, so we do not need to become aware of the melodic identity behind this change of meaning, even where the relevant passages are heard in fairly quick succession. It matters relatively little that if it is good, as nearly always with Wagner, declaimed song will form a certain natural, always identical analogue to the speech intervals, the sense-intervals; or that individual melismatic turns of phrase in absolute music – especially descending motifs or sighing or yearning with a suspension – will possess certain universally occurring, substantially identical meanings.

So all along we gather only from ourselves and not from the note-progression what the latter signifies. Until it is performed, sound remains blind. Granted, speech-song faithfully mirrors the living sound of the spoken word. But it is, after all, only intelligible by reference to the sub-text, and even the most accomplished recitative could not indicate of its own accord the prevailing climate in the higher textual regions at any given time. The position is similar, indeed far more unfavourable for the language of melismatic movement in absolute and accompanying music. The note climbs and subsides again, in short phrases, a seemingly clear and yet similarly ambiguous case. In one instance it can signify real resignation, as in the beautiful figure accompanying Hans Sach's words 'Schön Dank, mein Jung' after the *Wahnmonolog*. But it can also mean that the line is building up energy and that, having reached the summit, it turns and pours this energy out in excess, as in the jubilant melody to the words 'Und die belohnende Lust' in Strauss' setting of Schiller's *Hymnus*. The only objective difference is a certain, intrinsically indeterminate breadth of the intervallic compass within which take-off and meteoric return take place. One can, of course, retort that the two connected examples we have given are not very incisive melodically; but in cases where they are, the player of vitality, the inner clavichord becomes far more important still. The player's own stirrings of sorrow or joy will often even run counter to, and be out of proportion to, the written notes. A falling line frequently has no bearing at all on the mood, as in the Adagio of Beethoven's Fifth Piano Concerto, where the music descends through two and a half octaves twice in succession and instils in us just poise and security in aiming at and hitting a target, rather than the melancholy which the notes delineate. Often too, as in the 'huldreichster Tag' motif from the *Mastersingers* which descends, with a little twist in the middle, exactly the length of the triadic articulation of an octave, the expression is diametrically opposed to the falling motion. If, in the overture to this opera, the rising march theme of the horns encroaches upon the falling 'huldreichster Tag' theme of rejoicing in the violins, it is truly not this contrary motion in the orchestra which decides the musical outcome. Granted, where further critical interpretations are concerned, it is possible that some of them support musical practice, support it in a conventional way. Sometimes they simply leave the music to its own devices. Then the low notes are always sombre, ponderous, weighty, bulky, the high notes always bright, airy, light, also supra-terrestrial, angelic, sidereal; and apart from this, dynamically faint music will be inherently bodiless, shadowy, spectral, while dynamically strong music will be inherently powerful, gigantic, enormous; in addition there are the varyingly agitated, flowing, storming, jagged, iron rhythms. Sometimes interpretation is more thorough and imaginatively bestows on the sequence of notes a certain evolutionary history in an upward direction, with a 'moral' emphasis. According to this, a descending motion into the bass represents cessation and an incipient fading away, whereas – as Köstlin earnestly followed up in Vischer's *Aesthetics* – the rising motion, envisaged as actually engendering music, illustrates its vital, creative element, the extracting of sound from intrinsically silent matter.[11] But the same applies to this naturalism as applies to speech-song: that there would be no such association without prior human practice, and that not even the most analogous form-quality could indicate by itself what spirits are ever lurking in the upper regions of its logic.

So here again it is solely the attack, the delivery, which enables one to be a speaker winning all ears.[12] Sound wants to turn towards the human being. With all music it is important to heed the *expression* which is only added to the written notes through the act of singing them, through a violin section's bowing, a pianist's attack, but above all through that creative practice without which neither dynamics nor rhythm could be tackled in the way the composer intended. This attack is summed up in conducting, inasmuch as primarily, the latter comprises fascinating sonorities, volume, intensification, pacing and counterpoint (which offers graphic shapes or colours suggestive of moods) as the individual elements of the will communicated. Conducting, however, involves something further. We refer to the rediscovery of the creator's original vision, which only exists in the 'work' as a rough indication, as a mere code for its realisation. The essence of a born conductor – in contrast to the pedant who plays what is written in a lifeless, tradition-bound but actually disrespectful way, and also, of course, the egocentric charlatan who debases another man's work by using it as an aphrodisiac to counter his own sterility – is to remain open to suggestion until the music suddenly plays of its own accord. A miraculous transformation, a sovereign and blessed inner feeling of the passage of genius will have occurred, and the ambience, the work's atmosphere, the practice and soul of the work flares up and combines in a Beethovenian blaze. Then one will have reached the mysterious point where the lifeless components of the melisma and also of harmony and counterpoint rejoin in the pristine vision. Here it is Bach or Beethoven – not, therefore, some bogus classified specimen, but the pertinent composers themselves as essential symbols and objects – that will immediately become intelligible. So in the end, we evidently depend even more strongly than before on the performer's inflexion, his manner of speech and musical gesture. This alone is capable of reinforcing the weak affective, or otherwise significant, explicitness of fully formed elements or analogously demonstrable typifications. Nowhere does it appear so imperative to demand personal participation and, furthermore, a good interpreter. For not only can he make or mar everything: his receptively spontaneous intermediation also underlines and opens up the special experiential character of music, the merely approximate, conceptually shifting and permanently processual nature of the musical object.

For what happens in the note is still empty and uncertain. It is also hard to associate music with feelings that are already precise. From the slurring together of its vibrations, we cannot always make out whether a melody can unequivocally express anger, yearning or love *at all*, i.e. whether it is these specific emotional contents of ours, previously experienced, at which the music is aiming, and in which it could easily be bettered by a statue. Something other than the sound is responsible when horns sound like huntsmen, trumpets like kings, and indeed even when certain rhythms – now light and brisk, now slow and heavy – introduce humour or majesty or similar categories with external associations and occupying regions inferior to music. On the one hand music is not a thing apart; it is, as it were, too promiscuous for that – viewed from the angle of poetry, which is reflexive and in relation to which music has no ambition not to be promiscuous. On the other hand, music is not a merely generalised thing either, since it is in turn too strong for that, too unabstract, too gripping, too fraught ontologically. Something surges, 'from airy tones wells up a mystery',[13] here all the demands are initially only approximate. And this is because in music, which everyone understands without knowing what it signifies, no palpably clear life of its own has yet stirred. It lacks any means of furnishing very precisely defined categories in place of the dramatic necessity we are about to discuss and hence in place of the mere *outline* of symphonic drama and rising spheres of the self. A piece of music, when viewed from the technical angle, will be perfectly in order and tell us nothing, like an algebraic equation; but when viewed from the poetic angle, it says everything and decides nothing – a peculiar dichotomy in which, seething as the content is, any centre and any reconciliation accessible to the understanding are still lacking. Here it is pointless to confine ourselves to the technical element, which will remain a lifeless stereotype unless it is interpreted through its creator. It is also pointless to confine ourselves to the poetic aspect so as to force the 'infinitely hazy character of music', as Wagner put it, into categories which are not proper to it. The only remedy is to listen well and to wait expectantly for whatever may yet take shape in music – this pealing of bells from a wholly invisible tower – in terms of eloquence and of supreme explicitness both supra-formal and supra-programmatic. Beethoven already presents a fist, and his art is not lacking in the plainest moral will, which is to say the moral will *sui generis*, appertaining to music. But the future is still open, and it will, with a *non-liquet* matching the incompleteness of the available material, oppose that fundamentally false Schopenhauerian definition of music as 'Will altogether' which fits Wagner now and then, but which essentially perpetuates the temporary state of uncertainty.

The creative musical setting

Only sound that originates in ourselves, therefore, can bring us nearer to an answer.

In the first place, the functional note renders every happening sharper, more penetrating, more sensuous.

For as hearers we can keep closely in touch, as it were. The ear is slightly more firmly embedded in the skin than the eye is.

Not that the note condescends, but it fits in so well that it enables us to perceive something as a reality. Hence there is a good reason why we jib at viewing a silent film. For the latter extracts only the optical impression of black-and-white, and since this is presented just as it is, the elimination of the ear gives rise to the disagreeable impression of an eclipse, a life that is silent and sensually diminished. But the ear now assumes a peculiar function: it serves to represent all the other senses, it contrasts the sound of rustling, friction between objects, people's speech with our other impressions in a vital fashion. And so the sound-accompaniment to a film, however vague or exact it may be, is felt to provide, in its own way, nothing short of a complement to the picture. Equally it can be maintained that the sounding frieze through which the opera illustrates the stage libretto does not by its very nature lead away from the latter. It renders it vivid, impressive, striking. And it does so all the more grippingly the farther the music moves out into the broad area of action, of dramatic agitation and indeed of the normally recondite and the supersensual.

In the second place, however, the functional note realises things in palpably different ways according to whether it is leading into the realm of the merely striking or into that of the truly significant.

Hence everything must begin in the appropriate way underneath and achieve a greater density. Singing, or the note, must render real by being differentiated, not only through contrast but by introducing a more ardent human being, by the act of utterance.

In effect the note must be able to husband itself and must be held back, with a minimum of passion, in every passage where only straightforward, though animated, life is speaking. To demonstrate to excess is to prove nothing. It was precisely the advantage – one easily obtained, to be sure – of the 'numbers' opera that it had recitativo accompaniments to the action and introduced the aria, in which music is sovereign, only where the action became denser, more 'real', where events contracted and it was hence imperative for the characters to sing. Through-composed opera, on the other hand, lays stress on everything. The result is not only that much which relates to the plot will remain unintelligible, but also that the music will very often forego the most sparkling and finest effects of a sudden heterogeneity, a distinct multi-layering of the real. It is only so as not to lose this that Wagner and the through-composed opera seek indefatigably to rise and fall and work up to ever-new climaxes, thereby inserting differences of level into the landscape of the through-composed style, which in itself is a uniformly mountainous one. But this often renders an opera insufferably over-excited and pathos-filled where there is no call for it at all in terms of the words, the urge of reality. How a differentiated and yet flowing build-up might still in fact occur is shown, for instance, by Verdi's *Otello*. From the peace, depth, maturity, fulness of the recitative (often on one note for a whole phrase) and then the song, the lyrical dialogue, the wildest of outbursts, the sound of mounting catastrophe, the chords marking the end of the hero's career, we can surely perceive in this unique work of genius an operatic union of the graduated with the through-composed dramatic style. Thus all that is again needed at the end of the symphony's evolution, paradoxically enough, is what the Mannheim school, when it started around 1750, achieved in terms of darkening, brightening, 'soft-pedalling', diminuendo, crescendo, and consequently the creation of orchestral contrast. This is because the accompanying polyphony has gradually become monotonous. From pure over-intensification, it has finally turned into a new ground-bass that lacks all economy of musical realisation.

Only at the very top of the texture, even when the highest register is used sparingly, does the energy reinforcing the practical application seem to abate. And this takes place where the tone produces a floridness, blurs the intensity and gives to any transports of emotion a comfortably real garb, which in this case means a musical turning inside-out. This may have either a good or a bad result. If the trumpeting does no more than simply evoke a mood, if the hero, as Schlegel says, goes to his death on a trill and if – as Schiller says reproachfully of the semi-melodramatic conclusion to *Egmont* – 'we are transferred from a most true and moving situation to an operatic world in order to witness a dream', then the effect will have been realised in a poor and superficial manner. But we will react differently to those passages where the composer is speaking of a reality in the better sense, where we forget about the primadonna and the basely melting sweetness of the *Heldentenor* and where, for instance, Wagner's music delineates things 'lyrically' once more and comes close in its adagio to the Mozartian fairy-tale opera, that first carpet of the ontological. This, however, in no way signifies the extinction of music's power to reinforce, intensify and render actual, its vast method of realisation with the aim of a sounding silence, the realising of depth. On the contrary, its object has just shifted deeper. It is now the quieter, deeper core, some final decisive peripeteia and fate-rationale which comes under the spotlight of musical 'reality' – under the spotlight of an unchanging characteristic intensification which presents, renders mythical, the significant instead of the striking. That is to say, this reveals precisely the other, deeper layer of reality and stages the utopian reality of transcendent opera instead of the verismo reality of the *Spieloper*, adventure opera, opera of intrigue: phantoms and masquerades, the distorting mirror for comic opera and the magic looking-glass for the serious opera. We mean the music that has to resound as soon as the supersensual enters the scene, in order for the impossible nature of the music to combine with the impossible, visionary, nature of the action and thus for both, as Busoni's good theory of opera puts it, to become possible. In this way, then, the 'aria' of the 'numbers' opera and moreover of Bachian concentration, of supra-dramatic 'lyricism', also returns with inexorably greater weight and on a very high level of reality, with an *a priori* claim. This accords with the penultimate nature of all agitation, the absolute hierarchic plus and *telos*-content of the act of interposing, intervening, of faltering, mystical, self-bewilderment [*Selbstbetroffenheit*]. Whenever the solidity and transparence of the simple word-structure disappear, whenever the beam of a musically penetrative awakening, realisation, accentuating, generates *suo modo* the magic atmosphere of untragic drama, there also comes into being that mythical musical area of ultimate reality which transcendent opera shares with the drama of clemency. Such an area, as being the myth of love or sanctity, exhausts the spiritual ontologies beyond any possible world-destiny, any continuing epic of the world.

In the third place, music that is personally innervated will impose a subtle necessity with regard to the action; the dramatic note goes on 'composing' and even involves *a dramatic outline of its own making*.

Granted, more than once it has been hotly contested that the note goes this far. Thus Pfitzner separates the elaboration of melodic detail from the complete, substance-giving line of a poetic kind.

His argument undoubtedly possesses its charms. If I want to give the gist of a musical work, I will whistle the first theme. But if, on the other hand, I am to give the gist of a literary work, I will never quote the first sentence but will describe the basic features of the plot or the overall plan. A composer who said that he was planning a sonata or symphony for which he did not yet have a single theme would seem just as foolish to us as an author who wrote down some lines or sentences and said that they would go into a drama, but that he did not know yet what would happen in it: a drama, therefore, whose great overriding idea had not yet come to him. Thus the individual detail is reckoned to be the musician's real concern. And this finely conceived detail, the small, tangible entity, the inspiration that is already fully fledged at birth without being in need of a subsequent symphonic unravelling, indeed without ever changing in effect through a change of context is, according to Pfitzner, the true yardstick in music. Conversely, he argues, the poet's true concern is the all-pervading, omnipresent element – the first thing to aim at, the great intangible entity or inspired poetic idea which, instead of being 'composed', is gradually precipitated or 'condensed' in a downward direction, yet whose only value is as a binding intuition of the whole that *substantiates* the detail. So if we are to unite these two utterly different working methods, it can only be done to advantage when the elementary principle exclusive to the particular art-form is emphasised and then balanced with its complement. Hence there is a bad kind of music-making which aims at becoming broadly descriptive or even conceptual, and there is a bad libretto which has either put too much stress on detail or has, as a mere peg for duets, arias and ensembles, neglected the basic essentials of the action. Therefore music's genuine mission, according to Pfitzner, is to be accidental. It must renounce the autonomous creation of forms, the skilfully distributed putty of symphonic working, which abolished the former separation of the inspired idea from conventional tutti phrases in favour of a uniformity of the whole that is an indistinguishable amalgam of inspiration and reflection. Not without reason, Pfitzner states, has the history of musical forms had a chronic difficulty in accommodating the material of musical inspiration. Poetry's mission, on the other hand, is to be substantial. It must renounce sensuous detail, i.e. it must make way for music. From that realm of logical forms and complexes which is only accessible to itself, it must furnish music – in an action as terse as possible and often condensed to symbols – with both the basis for the mood and also the dramatic foundation, necessity and fate-concept. That is why Pfitzner likes his own music and Schumann's and plays him off against Liszt; and why, to his mind, *Der Freischütz*, above all the Wolf's Glen music, is the prime example of perfect opera. The basic question of opera composition is solved, and with a conception which is both poetically and musically elementary, i.e. specifically musico-dramatic, Pfitzner thinks we can avoid the dangerous confusion latent in a music-making that seeks to engender drama.

Much of this argument is as accurate as it is sharp-witted. But it is remarkable how sharp-witted a false notion can often be. For if what Pfitzner says were true, then it would be precisely the minor and lesser composers who have worked with the surest instinct, the best inspiration. Certainly there exists an empty, calculated way of working and a fraudulence which adopts a Beethovenian manner when all is hollowness and the thematic fabric is not even reflexive but has become what the tutti phrases were, namely stereotyped. There are equally telling objections to the Beethovenian aria itself: that it is lacking in sonority, lacking in song, becomes all too meagre in the individual parts and, for all its verve, often fails to counterpoint organically. Likewise Pfitzner is correct in noting some lifeless passages in Wagner where the recitative has nothing to say because even the text lacks verve and where the leitmotif is inserted in the music not for the purely symphonic reasons of a reprise but only conceptually, as a kind of pedagogic compass-bearing. But should we wish to see in this a confirmation of the dangers besetting the borderline between music and drama, we can learn something from the fact that this 'debt of the sonata to the ideal of music' has not been repaid by Schumann or Pfitzner or any other homespun composer whose music, however highly deserving of respect and well acquainted with inspiration, nonetheless converts the brief moments of the inspired idea into the inspired idea of the brief moment *pro domo*; only Bruckner and Wagner have repaid the debt. There is no question of somehow skipping Beethoven. Besides, it is in Beethoven that we find inspired ideas that are supremely productive of movement, and indeed developments of them whose dialectical drama, starting from the tension of these thematic 'inspirations', itself belongs purely to this music's dramatic dimension. For it is a music which needs symphonic room, and breadth, in order to be as it is, and which time – which carries it forward and is included in it – assists to a productive overall vision of at least the individual movement, if not the whole symphony. And even the composer of *Der Freischütz* and the Wolf's Glen music (extolled by Pfitzner as especially individual and decidedly melodic), even Weber feels so little inclined to conform to Pfitzner's theory that he comments in an aphorism, like a truly symphonic thinker: 'When one reads a poem, everything hurries past our soul more quickly; a few words suffice to change and determine the passions; the composer cannot switch like that, his language needs longer accents, and the transition from one feeling to another places a number of obstacles in his way.' Equally it can be stated that even if a repugnance to large-scale forms is deemed to be particularly musical, symphonic spinning-out has still shattered more forms than musical addings which are inspirations of the moment. And lastly, it must be argued against Pfitzner's nominalism that the sonata and the corresponding birth of Wagnerian drama from the spirit of the symphony present not just a shell, not one of the extra, engrossing, chronic difficulties of accommodating the material of musical inspiration. What they present is the wholly legitimate body of a special *melos* and its similarly productive, inspirational, drama-dictating counterpoint.

Hence, to do justice to the power of music with regard to dramatic action: here the note actually *draws*, broadening in flight, whereas the word is just used. We have only to observe how a good song comes about to see how little it is a matter of simply bringing the detail to life. Thus with Pfitzner himself, with Hugo Wolf, Bach and Wagner, the note is only outwardly fitted to the word in each case, far from appearing atomistically, so to speak. Here there is an absolute concentration on the essentials; to such a degree that, as Rudolf Louis rightly observes, with Hugo Wolf the whole piece is largely evolved in a thoroughly musical spinning-out. It relates not so much to the textual detail and the corresponding mood as to a basic mood found at the start of the text or in the course of it, which is now translated into music and displayed as the accompanying polyphony of this basic overall mood. This is, to be sure, a delimitation, but precisely one which shuts out the detail. Instead, it constitutes a clear reference to the whole into which, conversely, the poetry of the song or the opera has now to insert its detail. Here, after all, there does not always need to be such a stylistic difference as exists in Pfitzner's *Palestrina* – between the lyrical visions of the first Act and the merely cantankerous counterpoint of the Council scene in Act 2; there is feeling, but beyond it there is also a mysticism of *travel* and of *time*. Although, therefore, one must not overestimate a symphonic accompaniment's power to determine the action from the angle of content, we now certainly do find from *Fidelio* onwards a purely musical necessity. And by means of melismatic-symphonic agitation, this not only follows the action, but itself generates action, action still vague and anonymous, the air, the tempo, the mood, the soil, the level, the sombre, quivering, supra-conscious, magical, mythical background to the action. Into this action must now be admitted, with the details left optional but bound together as a whole, the practical stage application and textual 'rationale' which copies it only, as it were, in the lower domain. It goes without saying that a concise, synoptical, often symbolically illustrative story will be more suitable than a finished drama created independently of the music. Schiller's *Kabale und Liebe*, therefore, will result in a more questionable libretto than a Strauss-Hofmannsthal collaboration or the dramas that Wagner designed to be wholly subservient to music, because music-drama's own richness and also, in principle, its more mysterious depth will not bear any drama already finished, finished in purely poetic terms.

In the fourth place, the whole of the action that can be spoken is latently overtaken in this way by the sounds originating in us, by the subjective streak in the note.

The poor word is in itself already easily disturbed. It is superfluous and cuts a ridiculous figure by comparison with the note it seeks to clarify, and whose mood it seeks to breathe, wherever it appears.

Furthermore it is not without reason that when sung, nearly everything ends too high-lying and that in opera, even the poorest boatman has a golden oar to row with. Nobody can understand all the business about the poisoned ring and Emma's ghost, but Weber's music almost makes a meaningful poetic work out of *Euryanthe*. Indeed elsewhere the illusion is so extensive that in the *Magic Flute* Pamina seems like Dante's Beatrice and all the cheap production tricks look like occult visions. This is because Mozart's music lends depth to the mere theatricality and external oppositions, and returns to that theosophical material which had only survived in a confused form and was largely gibberish in the actual text by Schikaneder. It is also not without reason that we can be startled by a mere students' drinking-song, which is what the opening chorus of the *Tales of Hoffmann* with its truly infernal pulsing and pounding apparently represents, just as relations are never 'right' or easy between music and text in this unique masterpiece. Or again, the same thing is evident when first a journeyman and then the apprentices break off in the middle of their dance and announce the Mastersingers in a harmonically splendid series of fourths, as though Wagner were dealing not with staid dignitaries but with the entry of heavenly hosts. The voice in every great song, every profound setting of words, is like the voice of that ghostly traveller from Hoffmann's *Kreisleriana* who tells of many distant, unknown countries and people and unusual destinies on his far wanderings, and whose speech finally 'died away into a wondrous sounding in which he intelligibly uttered unknown, extremely mysterious things without recourse to words'. The one settled factor in all this is that the note overtakes the word and thus cannot comply with the constantly visible element of the text in accordance with the whole, the established level in the last place, because this whole lies beyond the whole of the literary composition. For that reason, to be sure, one is also unable to say that any literary work, if measured against the ultimate whole, may be placed within the area of dramatic music with its vague postulates other than in a more or less arbitrary and approximate way. It may imitate music's secret, immoderate power of action by ways broadly connected to it, but with its demystifying, 'more logical' resources it cannot readily prove itself up to the mark that music requires. Even when the fourths sound less special, and even where there is a loftier basis to the spectacle than with the mere entry of the Mastersingers, the transcendent drama that is present will always be poorer in mysteries than the music that is preparing its destinies, its myth. This alone is the *true* dividing-line between the symphonic and the dramatic relation.

Consequently there can be no point, even in a hermeneutic respect, in the impulse to translate this recondite content back into everyday language. It is principally in doing this that people say the silliest things about the personification of sound. These, as even Bekker, the biographer of Beethoven, needed telling, are reminiscent of the most awful commentaries on 'the picture of the month' from the period of the *Gartenlaube*.[14] Here we find twaddle in full spate about expressively pleading demisemiquavers, the brightly smiling trill of the violin, the thrice-heard unison G sharp after the scherzo in the C sharp minor Quartet which is said to ask, as it were: what am I doing in this world? This is the province of the smug philistine who, with his explanatory chatter, thinks that he has not only said something but has also settled the matter for good by describing the Symphony in A major as, to quote the enchanting words of a musical handbook, 'the Song of Songs of Dionysian heroism'. Devices by which a piano teacher tries to improve his pupils' lame imaginations have been elevated by Bekker to the exegetical science of musical poetics: and Beethoven is then supposed to have written it. More than that, it is supposed to be Beethoven made plain, rendered clear to the imagination, the most repugnant stuff with a neat little word for every bar, compared to which the most banal newspaper serial seems like the *Aeneid*. There are various ways of putting it: if Beethoven's other biographer, Adolf Bernhard Marx, interprets the course of the musical events in the *Eroica* as an imaginary battle – the first movement showing the battle itself, the funeral march portraying the crossing of the battlefield at dusk, the scherzo constituting camp-site music full of mirth and song, and the last movement a swift and happy return for peace celebrations and the pleasures of the home – then all well and good, because the actual music has nothing at all to do with this. By shutting out from the depths of its being this play of supplementary imagery based on popular conceptions, it neither denies nor confirms its putative accuracy. It is irrelevant whether this or that composer himself believed he was necessarily depicting a cheerful peasant. It is not even of much use to investigate how far Beethoven personally, when receiving his inspiration or when savouring the finished product, seems to have supported this lame fantasising. Certainly in later years he would complain that the earlier period was 'more poetical' than the present one: 'everyone sensed at the time that the two sonatas, opus 14, portrayed a dialogue between two people because it is, as it were, obvious'. We also know how strongly impelled Beethoven was to give the earlier works poetic headings, in connection with his lament for the dwindling imagination of music-lovers. The motto . . . *non licet bovi* applies equally to Jove as personified by Wagner, a composer who doted on poetry, and who often produced the most questionable of interpretations. Thus, in his view, the Andante of Mozart's G minor Symphony closes by finally acknowledging the bliss of a death through love. The unexpected sweetness of the finale to the *Eroica* now 'symbolises' the perfecting of the hero in love, while in the Prelude to *Lohengrin* an angelic host is heard descending with the Grail – all interpolations of a most random, arbitrary kind, which Wagner's own genius refutes. If, therefore, even Beethoven claimed that his *Namensfeier* overture was not a composition but a poem, this confusion of genres is connected in the first place with the urge towards the 'intellectual' sphere, a sphere that was closer to science (the same thing led Goethe to value the writing of poetry less highly than achievements in the theory of colours). Secondly, we may be sure that by the 'poetic', Beethoven only meant that free indulgence in moods and enthusiasms which we understand by poetry in contrast to prose, the prose of philistine, dreamless, unsymbolic life. Be that as it may, Beethoven is not a poet but both less and more than a poet. As for the programme symphony that apparently succeeded his music, with its additional ideas of bleating sheep, a stifling sickroom, ticking clocks, rushing waterfalls, the coolness of the forest and other narrowly conceived photography with humdrum captions, this programmatic type of poetry reveals itself to be a mere bridge to the inner, imageless pathos, the intrinsic wordlessness of music. So, without belonging to those who wish to confine themselves to form and who regard their derivatively heard or created form-residua as 'absolute' music, keeping guard *à la* Hanslick and Herbart[15] against the 'indirect' tradition, one must protest most firmly against essays of the programme-music type. They put a false complexion on matters because they put forward a kind of interpolation which is accidental, territorially inferior to music, as a legitimate way of speaking about music or as its translation into adequate categories, whereas this art will never be any more familiar than is a strange land.

But even the well-chosen word, the word that has poetic value, will necessarily fall short of the note. Hence it matters little in the final analysis if Wagner should now give the impression that even historically speaking, one must in turn proceed from the note to the word and not vice versa. Above all in the *Ring of the Nibelung* and on principle, in theory altogether, he will not allow the note to finish speaking. Instead of trusting in the as yet unsuspectedly 'eloquent', expressive future of music, he resorts to the crutches of the text in the most unconditional way. Just as instrumental music originated in the chorus, so it must seek at all costs, according to Wagner, to dissolve in turn into the drama, as though absolute instrumental music were a reprobate that, out of the dialectical difference of merely metallic sound, was now calling again for the return and synthesis of the word, for the sublimation of its mere logograph in the 'chorus' that had returned in a dramatic form. And yet Wagner himself, while finding it so wonderful that the composer should appear upon the ruins of the art of opera-writing as the authentic, real poet, repudiates his own theory. For he says that with regard to Beethoven's and Shakespeare's treatment of *Coriolanus* in music and drama respectively, Shakespeare only seems like a Beethoven continuing to dream in a waking state, with this glowing and unbearably rich life above him as an indication of the musical vision. But apart from that, Wagner is also labouring under a historical error when he overlooks the fact that the earliest operas took shape during the orchestra's one great efflorescence. And what was later discharged from the chorus and developed further in the separate instrumental form is not a historical centre whose beginnings in the chorus were bound to return dialectically as an ending in the drama. Instead, without detriment to the Florentine and all later opera, without detriment even to the music-drama and in spite of the brilliant cultivation of the instrumental forces serving it, the chorus has remained absolutely the uppermost and most powerfully expressive part of the orchestra, abandoning more and more the 'logic' of words, programme music and drama, and forming the mightiest climax of the pure symphony that has flourished along with the chorus. Thus it is and always will be the fate of even the well-chosen word, even a word of the greatest poetic value and completely involved musically, to end up as the note's poor relation. 'O namen-namenlose Freude', sing Leonore and Florestan; even at its simplest and most rudimentary stages, music quietly overpowers poetry and turns it into a reflection of itself. Even the simplest or most abused note is incapable of mere textual illustration. The dark primordial sound of music dissolves every word, even every drama within itself, and the deepest transformations, a multitude of mysterious shapes concealing future revelations, are crowding past us in the singing flames of great music. Hence there is no *great* music at all which, *ultimately*, might still have room for a creation of a different type, a drama of the spoken word, or whose prerequisites do not exceed the limits of even the most masterly and polished poetry. Similarly, the visionary hearing for which we hope, the successor to defunct clairvoyance, must formally and objectively be distinguished no less clearly from what is merely poetically mythical than the Apostles' gift of tongues differed from the simple literary and Julian wish to believe in belief. Granted, Nietzsche asks if we can conceive of a person who could register the third Act of *Tristan* purely symphonically, unaided by any word or image, without expiring at that echoing sound of countless cries of pleasure and pain. Why shouldn't one? we may ask in reply; music is not there to protect us from the mystical or to be protected from it. The projected image of Apollo which *The Birth of Tragedy* would have rising above the Dionysian ocean remains for Nietzsche, as for Wagner, an admitted delusion, a noble deception in face and form and *universalibus post rem* instead of *ante rem*, behind which the primal reality of Dionysus and, if one looks more deeply, of Christ immediately bangs shut. Hence the logical purpose of this Nietzschean *quid pro quo* is totally incomprehensible. Music has sovereign power and intends to become absolute, and fundamentally there is no other music than music which is absolute and therein eloquent *per se*, lending itself only to purely speculative interpretation. In the long run, what is designed and fully thought out in a truly symphonic fashion does not know any intermediate areas of its worlds where the gods of poetry, akin to the real gods in Epicurus, might lead their hermeneutically superfluous existence.

Interpretation, or On the relation between absolute and speculative music

Now of course the aforegoing statements do not mean that any discussion of the musical note is necessarily doomed to failure. A good listener is rare, certainly. And here we must stress another point before we go into the details of the tonal, harmonic, rhythmic and contrapuntal nexus. Everything is always based upon one pair of eyes only. It will never be possible directly with these resources, and without instituting a new self, to infer or to unlock that which is accessible to the receptive person and which alone animates the artist: soul, expression and content.

The 'what' of expression in general

Just what do I seek when I hear something? I am seeking, when I listen, to grow richer and greater in content. But I shall receive nothing if I join in by merely sitting back and relaxing. I shall only receive it by fetching it myself, going further, in terms of content, beyond passive enjoyment. The artist himself will not touch us, will say nothing, if the means are all that interest him in the course of the work.

For even in the medium of art, one can be a prophet and preacher. More important than the fact that the bystanders hear singing when a man cries out in the fiery belly of the Pharsalian bull, and far more important that the mechanism through which his cries are transformed into song, communicated to us, are the cries themselves, their undeflected genuineness and depth. So it is not feasible in the long run to look to the formal product alone for the shaping conviction. That would be to brand as dilettantish anything which does not press outwards and does not feel satisfied in the technical sphere to such a degree that the vision experiences its growth to full stature, and the confirmation of its genuineness, only in this outward manifestation of the work. Nothing could be falser, more accidental and more limited in terms of art-history; it is equally removed from anything that needs to express itself, from the great artist as much as the child who paints and the peasant who carves. Granted, in Lukács's *Soul and Form* we find a full statement of this more and more purely formal-objectivistic view, with a neo-classical emphasis. But there it derives from a method which, although it adheres to works and forms, does not ultimately signify these but, through their prompting and thus ironically, indirectly, essayistically, has as its object the most recondite, most intimately achieved profundity. In particular cases, no doubt, this procedure can have extraordinarily fruitful results. As a whole, however, as a systematic method, as a divination of the works' native territory based on a thorough analysis of form, it still gives too much weight to the insignificant. It cannot avoid arbitrariness in establishing the internal limits of cryptographic form-relation, and it perpetuates the laboured, unauthentic, Flaubertian element in the modern, merely stylistic and alienated compulsion to create. The 'what' of artistic creation is amply defined, rather, by how the artist is and not by virtue of how he does it, quite apart from the fact that a sober, purely technical working definition is incapable of doing justice to the needfulness, the exuberance of the artistic will and its object. Amusing, ugly, lovely, meaningful – all these reflect the limited sensitivity and emotional utterances of a shallow audience. Green and red, movement and repose, contrapposto, false relations and the Neapolitan sixth – these are similarly broken-winded phrases, formulae which do of course apply and are necessary for communication, for the pedagogic *horos* of the incomplete work of art; trees which indicate the forest but do not constitute the forest. At best, they are auxiliary concepts matching the spirit of the forest, the substance of the work, a substance that, *qua* content, is already eminently artistic. Nor must we think it possible to give individual modes of representation a self-significant background by serving them up in historical terms, by regarding the forms of the novel, dialogue or other outlets for talent as fixed upon a revolving firmament of intellectuality within the philosophy of history, one that permits a fluctuation of the possible forms of expression; and hence by reinterpreting the history of artistic 'whos' and the 'whats' therein as a history of mediaeval-realistic 'hows'. Here we are dealing not with colour, stone or language as the materials, which already seem aberrant enough. It is a question of the actual forming process, the concerns of precision, those questions of the will to influence and to communicate which, for an artist, can come even before the question of the *content* which is our one consideration. But an artist does not always need to concentrate on the work in itself so hard that his experiences have to enter into an inseparable alliance with the technical forms of the specific genre, just in order to achieve the pre-established harmony between vision, form and the concrete materiality which is first acquired therein.

Those people who listen will have found another way home. Precisely from this point onwards, the artistic drive may again resemble a visionary gift transposed to another context. Certainly that which is not expressed does not survive, but it is the will, the content, that governs the means. And it appears that these days we no longer need to stand aloof from what is said [*das Gesagte*] in such a strict, genre-conscious way in order to perceive it as a finished statement [*Ausgesagtes*]. In terms of the self and the 'we', therefore, it has again become possible for the modern artist – and without our being befogged by the rainbows and processions of clouds that are now only too close – to present us with a work of art, the essence of the work of art, without the hindrance of a distancing form-concept. Thus the uncouth will often become strangely profound. No decent author, says Jean Paul, is seen in a vest; what we take for a vest is a vestment. The means themselves are the leaven, emerging simply as some act of realisation which is left to the artist's discretion, and this forming process has not the slightest influence in respect of the content. Elpore sets out with the intention of remaining Elpore and of

86

being fully recognised as such, even if she steps too close to the dreaming Epimetheus.[16] There gradually shines forth what is inherently significant to us, the other self and the other object which determines the artist and art's proper sphere; and not a form that gathers, say, what is transcendent into artistic immanence. If the essential will increases, to be sure, the formal perfection of its objects will also be increased: euphonious sound summons up many images and they are true ones. But here it is the envisioned *essence* which is constructing its physical shape. If the latter, the form of the realisation, the work's external reality, seems denaturalised or highly abstract, this is a later impression and moreover, chiefly abstract only in relation to the natural occurrence of the object represented. For in itself the modern, expressionistic formation of the essence is just as 'naturalistic' and purely descriptive, if not so perfectly descriptive of things astrally perfect, as are the tombstones bearing the name of Horus, the relief of Bel Merodach or the winged bulls of Assyria and the prophet Ezekiel. Here there is a fresh directness and absoluteness at work which has formal architectonics arising seemingly independently – neat execution, a Flaubertian concern with smoothness – as the object's lower determinant, certainly, and as the foreground *prius* in the envisioned object. But it is not now the case that the work is as long as the expressive statement, as in style-oriented ages, or that the perfectly descriptive formal symbol smothers the imperfectly expressive-descriptive signet-symbol [*Siegelzeichen*]. On the contrary, wherever we find great, personally expressive work, it is the will – the subject and its content – which alone can be ultimately discerned from the means, the formulae, which lack value and background; it is the authentic element in the abstractness, beyond means and also beyond any anchorage and any object in the formal, lower sense; it is the intimating personal signet or even the incipiently matching secret of the 'we', the *ideogram*. In one way only can form be discussed in an objective sense. This is where the formal, constructional, objectifying element is not a medium but itself an objective component, as is especially the case with stage effects, with rhythm and especially with the different types of counterpoint that determine the shaping subjects as categories of their innate being, as indeed with all artistic problems of time and of place involving remembrance. Here the shaping subject has truly entered into a 'form' as its deeper aggregate condition, a 'form' accordingly representing the lower, quasi-epistemological, metaphysically skeletonic part of the object arrangement itself. *But this, of course, is still separated from the authentic life, content and depth of the aesthetic substance by a leap to self and truth, to personal energy and expression, to the ideogram of revealed inwardness, of the figure of life and figure of humanity.* Now it is precisely the unusual strength of our period that we can apparently grip the reins more loosely or rather, more unconsciously, and still travel to the right destination. Artists are showing an astonishing barbarity in that the purely picturesque, say, is able, if it becomes an inner necessity, to leave things out as it pleases or to become of a purely musical character and to show other such signs of 'decadence', which are monstrous from a scientifically precise standpoint. When plaster casts and precious ornaments of the inessential first appeared, it used to be similarly said, as a reproach, that some ancient building or other was not particularly 'pure in style'. Here one is pursuing that bold but not at all *Sturm und Drang* aim (there is far too much affliction in it for that, far too little joy in the sheer excess of energy, far too severe a responsibility towards the object), that extremely direct aim which precisely the very greatest stylists alone have hitherto accomplished, rueful and clairvoyant, in the works of their old age: that of being subjective, supra-formal, descriptive of the essence. The 'work', too, will give this impression. For the eyes have become strong, there is no longer a need for the 'salutary' toning-down and elaborate detour which diminishes the supra-liminal charms of transcendence and distributes them over a large area so that they cannot suddenly assault us, or whatever phrase one uses in order to turn productive weakness into an Olympian pedagogy, in accordance with the classicistic idolatry of form. In other words, there appears a new, more direct, archetypal stress on the fact of having something to say which will scarcely flinch at the charge of dilettantism. Indeed the dilettantish, that which is dilettantish *a priori* and purely 'aesthetic in content', will attain a metaphysical level – provided only that the real incompetence of individual paltriness and negative expression is kept at bay. At this level we have: the dismissal of all passive enjoyment; the advantage of the work's expressive statement of the self; a moral nominalism opposed to any indirectness with autonomous power; a descriptive 'naturalism' or, to put it more neatly, an expressionistic realism of the 'subject'; and finally the strength of the message [*Ansage*] or how it was and how it might have been, ought to be, the majesty of the perception, the specific perception of an 'aesthetic' reality and of the utopianly possible ideas that its sphere commands.

That is why, from this point onwards, art can again resemble a visionary gift transposed to another context. How far removed all art was in its first heyday from the intention of demonstrating and of having a beautiful effect! It was forbidden to approach the masks out of season, and indeed there were statues of gods which could only be venerated at all in a completely darkened area, the fulfilment of a world different from that visible to our eyes. Like the whole of music, the primitive, and also Gothic, artistic volition has not the least thing in common with the volition of art conceived as an intended effect, as a small, insubstantial stylistic segment of a world without disappointments. In respect of this art and of all great art, we are never dealing with the objective or even normative form-problems of aesthetic 'pleasure'. This is the least important thing on earth, because the very concept of *aisthesis* does not signify a strongly emotional sensitivity [*Empfindung*] but exactly the same thing as perception [*Wahrnehmung*], phenomenology, adequate fulfilment. What we are dealing with, time and again, is the content-'what' of man writ large and of pure ground that has been kept open, yet has retained its mystery.

The last, to be sure, is no longer given to people listening today as readily as in the blessed times of the gods' proximity. But at any rate their artists are again aiming the arrows, the now slow-moving arrows of expression, in an esoteric direction. And just as the sacred can drop no lower than to the artistic plane, so conversely the chromatically darkened visionary feeling of expressionistic art with the utopian orientation of its content, its object, can be venerated as the nearest place to the house of a parousia or Second Coming. To conclude, it is only that the artist, even one who intends to be a preacher, to be perceptive and substantial in the most volcanic artistic manner, is always confined to the realm of appearances. The isolated, aesthetic effigies amount to stirring, but primarily only coruscating paintings on glass which give a hint, a broad indication, of human beings, but also dismiss them again. Hence the criterion of purely *aesthetic* illumination, viewed in respect of its ultimate categories, is as follows. *How might things be consummated without their ceasing apocalyptically?* How might each thing and each person be driven to its or his highest limit, towards the leap of faith, be portrayed, which is to say mirrored, even if expressionistically reduced and direct, and yet – most importantly of all – be completely illuminated, so long as the higher inward light is still hidden? So long as the leap implicit in its projection of the heart of Jesus into things and men and the world – a projection which effects a totally different change – is still awaited? Where this ultimate aesthetic striving does not end up weakened and hence a barrier, a delusion, paganly immanent, the great work of art becomes a reflected splendour, a star of anticipation and a song of consolation on the homeward journey through darkness. Yet it remains no more than remoteness, semblance, reflected splendour, avowed contradiction of all perfection on Earth. It is incapable of rendering man, in need himself, at home in the glory so desperately anticipated. Earlier, when we were still close to the mystery, that is to say before our eyes had clouded over, and before we had our modern styles and stylisations, the descriptive artist's view encompassed winged bulls, upper column placings, the secret of the transept, fairy-tales, the epopee's transcendent connections, divine life itself as it was displayed to the world in splendour. The self-same thing – *lighting itself up in a different, gloomier, hazier, more twilit and warmer fashion, behind defunct logic and theology, as an incipient mystery of 'we' and primal ground* – might now form the Dostoievskian and Strindbergian sphere of a pure spiritual reality, a purely moral 'transcendence' of the encounters, convexities and vistas of a humanness transcending society. This life too, this sermon, comes to us in colour, in the coloured reflection.[17] But if we glance into the hidden sun itself, this is no longer art, on the verge of fulfilment while effected nonetheless within the world, but the statement 'it is I', an inner God-seeking devoid of images, and at bottom of works, where the objective element occurs as an auxiliary construct so rarely that only the rebirth, the fitting out of the heart may still be there as the work. This would then constitute – behind all art – a morality and metaphysic of inwardness and its world. It would be a new, medium-less standing-by-itself-in-existence of subjectivity and its non-world, clearly separating the immanence of the artistic object from the transcendence of the direct or religious object we have proposed.

The philosophical theory of music

Nonetheless even the aforesaid does not mean that all discussion of music is, when it delves deeper, necessarily doomed to failure. There is no danger of losing one's footing: a good listener has his appointed, still artistic, place. It is just a matter of finding a vantage-point from which to view those utopian lands of meaning which are located in the windows of the work, so to speak. Of course it may still be asked whether we regard such an extension, even though carried out purely predicatively, as necessary in the first place. For in purely aesthetic terms the arch of a great work is totally continuous or rather, as a closer study will establish beyond doubt, it possesses an aesthetically adequate key-stone in its own artistic world of form, signet-world [*Siegelwelt*] even, without allowing a transcending interpretative structure to be more than inherent within it. But here we are on the one hand, and there stands the work on the other. However much we have been temporarily in thrall to it, we can easily move away from the work again so as to become free for new contexts situated below or above it. Hence it must be legitimate for a mentality which will not yet be appeased on any account, and to which the mechanical apparatus in any sphere is something squalid, to regard even musical structures as mere stations on a journey and to go on pursuing them as mere *vestigia anabaseos* until they, too, appear within the dance of the constellations of the history of philosophy, indeed the dance of the whole universal process.

It is not difficult to advance into this other form of hearing. Admittedly, all that is initially given from outside, besides desire, is a presentiment. Even this largely works only hedonistically, passively, in repose and thus seems still totally lost in a void. It already has the depth, but at this level, as the *first* simple revelling in sound, it is not yet usable; it is false, incidental, arbitrary. For only what is formally finished is manifest – which, after all that has been said, is certainly not to ask for the shutters to be kept closed so that all we can do is make a critical note of the small and limited gleam in the chink. The full daylight which is active behind the shutters also contains 'form'; it possesses form at least as a lower object-determinant, and the latter subsequently gives rise afresh to the concepts of individual composers, of composers as concepts. Here the creator and his 'what' are active as relevant form, not arbitrarily or just the way things turn out; on the contrary, it always turns out to be in a historio-periodic system of musical 'I'-objects and spheres. Here sound operates above all as a *means* of expressing oneself, as a means that has to be broken but that is a buoyant conveyance nonetheless. Here harmony operates as a *formula*; and entering fully into what is personally meaningful, the specific rhythmicising, their elegant, polyphonic, dramatic counterpoint, operates as a *work-form*, as a *species*, as the *signet-character* of great composers. Rhythm and the three existing kinds of counterpoint are already lower object-determinants in themselves. So they determine that historio-periodic system of ascending musical 'I'-objects and spheres which has been evidenced in the great composers so far. But these forms are, of course, only *lower* object-determinants, and the musical object that has really to be brought out is not decided. The most intricate web does not in itself compose, nor indeed is it meant to, and dramatic-symphonic movement posits only an area of very general readiness into which the poetically executed music-drama can now be fitted 'at one's discretion'. And by the same token, there yawns between the most transcendable species and the ultimate signet-character of great composers or indeed the ultimate object, the ideogram of utopian music in general, an empty, damaging hiatus which renders the transition more difficult. Even in rhythm and counterpoint illumined theoretically and set in relation philosophically, it is not possible to come directly to the kind of presentiment accessible to the weeping, shaken, most profoundly torn-apart, praying, listener. In other words, without this special learning-from-oneself, feeling-oneself-expressed, human outstripping of theory which can only be discussed at the end of these investigations as the interpolating of a fresh subject (though one most closely related to the composer) and of this subject's visionary speech, which in terms of the philosophy of history is metaphysical – without this, all transcending relations of the species to the apeiron, the ground of matter, will remain stationary. Thus with the presentiment, a stage which *no longer belongs to the history of music*, the note itself reappears as the solely intended, explosive aha!-experience of the parting of the mist; the note which is heard and used and apprehended, heard in a visionary way, sung by human beings and conveying human beings. It no longer appears as a means, and certainly not as an astral shrine, but rather as the supreme aura of receptivity, the ultimate material of the soul, the core, the latency, the symbol of the self upon which music is borne; as the *highest phenomenal aspect* of musical expression and the musical ideogram, of the musical spirit-realm. So whereas poetry short-circuited music, it can genuinely extend interpretation, it can trace lines on the archetypal map in a way that is recollective and far from any mere commentary. Admittedly 'our very deeds, and not our sufferings only, restrict the progress of our lives'.[18] But there is also another human streak playing a part, a conception of the artistic character which is more encouraging, the 'ultimate' artist as a metaphysician of art, that is, as an ultimate custodian of the artistic object, as creator of the *Gesamtkunstwerk* of a *substantial* kind, in the homogeneous medium of the speculative conception. Consequently there is an intrinsically creative aesthetic which not only comments but is spontaneous, speculative. It is only in the latter's interpretation that truly 'absolute' music is established, that the envisioned, utopian castle of music reveals itself.

Means, formulae, forms and phenomenal aspect of the transcending theory of music

The note as means

Thus nothing in this realm can sound by itself.

It is only within us that it can flower and awaken. The note is intensified by us, qualitatively coloured and dispersed immediately by us. It is only we who exalt it – more than that, who stabilise it and allow it to be animated with our life. True, it is no accident that precisely this delicate, transparent body is chosen. Certainly intoxication lies not in the wine but in the soul; nonetheless, there is palpably at work in the natural note a preternatural buoyancy and eloquence which renders it pre-eminently suitable as the material of music. But, of course, where the interval of the fifth is concerned, all is fine, because it is selected, because it prompts further, non-natural relations, and only in breach of these direct propensities is man capable of singing.

The theory of harmony as formula

It is thus a question of feeling extensively.

Anyone who simply hears music, and one can be very moved in doing so, will not even notice how the notes are compounded, and it is not very important to know this. With the artist what flourishes, except on special occasions, is the knack. But it is more than a mere knack, and much that looks unconscious actually derives from an extremely cold-blooded calculating process working with well-tried devices. That is why there is also wont to be such a strong emphasis on this and why composers are traditionally divided into pupils and teachers, with all the critical assurance to which a language of formulae and technical knowledge entitles them. For this reason, then, we cannot speak theoretically without heeding the special theoretical science developed by composers themselves. Could it not now be hoped that a mind in which technical knowledge came into contact with logical knowledge would, on the purely factual level, by drawing on both areas, be bound to discover something extraordinary? There is in fact a certain inevitable raising of the eyebrows, if not a kind of hope thinking ahead on straightforward lines, in philosophical circles (perhaps it still stems from the old reliance on mathematical ingenuity), as soon as one is confronted with concepts like the third or Neapolitan sixth or false relation and indeed the whole shape of the theory of harmony, which in itself seems so intellectually abstract. And like the young Wagner, not only the title-character in Grillparzer's story *The Poor Musician* but also Hoffmann's Kapellmeister Kreisler have moments when they are seized with horror by music's numerical relationships in themselves, to say nothing of the mystically intensified rules of counterpoint, a Sanskrit of Nature. And yet when Kreisler, that Kreisler who is always delving into the infinite, confronts the full, resounding reality of music transferred from the border region of form to the real centre, the scaffolding will have long since collapsed, and he is again at one with the deeply moved layman. The *reality* of modulation is the actual miraculous element which dwells in the interior spirit. In the same way we have a large number of excellent books on theory, and if, in the ensuing exposition, we refer especially to Schönberg's for a practical answer to the question, this is not – much as it suits us – because the book was written by a creative composer who only strove for a system of representation and not a system of Nature. It is for the deeper reason that here, significantly, precisely the most successful methodical musical mind takes care that form does not override its object as a purpose in itself.

Anyone with the requisite ability may compose as he pleases. Here, everything comes down strongly in favour of the composer who writes out of inner necessity. For this composer, however, if he knows what he is doing on the technical level and what he can achieve on a personal level, there is no longer anything that is ugly, forbidden or dissonant at all. He may compose according to a free, fluctuating schedule, indeed he may write any harmony, even if it does not appear obtainable by harmonic processes at all and can be explained by the part-writing alone. It is thus not linguistically permissible to talk of notes that are alien to harmony. Any consonance is possible and may therefore be postulated for the harmony purely *qua* consonance.

Nowhere does a *key* exist independently, any more than a dissonance does. It is seemingly impossible to imagine a score without it, quite apart from the fact that the entire effect of the dominant has been shaped and comprehended only on a basis of preserved tonality. Nonetheless Schönberg, in the last movement of his F sharp minor Quartet, for example, did not provide a key-signature although the movement belongs principally to the realm of F sharp major, even if its most expressive structures, the chromatic fourth-chords, have been detached from any key, from all *tonality*. The note from which everything proceeds is at liberty to hover in the air. As Schönberg says, instead of closing the piece on the same note there is also the possibility of making the relationship more noticeable on one occasion and more blurred on the next. What this engenders is a kind of unending harmony which no longer needs to communicate the country of origin and destination every time, and which has even less need to shrink from journeys of discovery in the broad spaces of the tonal vacuum. Moreover, it has long been the case that it is not the cadences which govern the harmonic developments of a piece. For that reason it is also unnecessary to set up other keys to assist the fluctuating tonality, and thus to elevate to a system such new, subordinate and, now and then, surprisingly handy means as the exotic whole-tone scale. There is nothing to which the chromatic note-row would not stretch just provided that we stop approving of all possible deviations from the old scale while still upholding the dictum of the dominion of tonality. If the latter is our aim, then we must leave out all the leading notes which cannot be tied. Above all we must observe certain proportions in the modulations, as the classical composers did. But we cannot behave as though we had a free hand and exploit all the possibilities of this freedom if we are not prepared to take upon ourselves its genuine risks and responsibilities. Schönberg expressed it quite neatly by saying that it seems nothing short of a disturbing asymmetry if the relation to a key-note is still intended to be maintained after exploiting the harmonic possibilities of the augmented triad and particularly of vagrant chords not just sporadically but continuously, under the pressure of a permanent expressive dictate beneath which, basically, there could still lie the axiom of tonality. The song closes, then, with something new, unending or unfulfilled. It travels without arriving, the sense being in the path it takes, and the previous centre of the key-note, the stationary part, the sustained pedal-point or even just the need for one, heard in imagination and only realised again in the reprise, disappears in fluctuating or suspended tonality. Instead there are many groups of tonics. Indeed, each chord can achieve harmonic definition through its own tonic; there are intermittent tonic relations or simply changing centres. And the collective impression which permits the conclusion of a work, leading it inexorably back from a position of ideal infinitude to real finiteness, does not need to be a harmonically given ending, even if neither animated nor artistically contrived form hitherto allowed the work's internal limit, the actual shape of its form, to be dictated other than spontaneously, on the basis of its own predilection, growth and *a priori*. Hence the limiting factor here must be taken from something other than the tonic of the whole. There can be no doubt that this something can never be a premature breaking-off, since it is not working its way towards a finally attainable goal. It will, on the contrary, achieve its zenith and possible full stop in the strongest, most genuine expression of an inner violence, boundlessness, infinitude, and hence in a tonic which can be discussed in harmonic terms no longer but rather is explicable in terms of rhythm. As a rule with Schönberg, the harmonic element, where things could depend on a deeper substantiation, nearly always turns into the contrapuntal. Something which may arise almost spontaneously, chordally unsought, although constantly distributed as such within the parts, cannot be justified or substantiated in harmonic terms. If, for example, we set two parts in the C major scale in contrary motion over a stationary c–e–g harmony, this will engender an abundance of the most splendid and interesting dissonances. Yet the sudden and fantastic chordal wealth would have no other source than the simplest contrapuntal exercise. In counterpoint itself, however, anything can be placed against anything else. For that reason – while still presupposing a contrapuntal diligence from the purely technical angle, of course – it can further be properly decided only from the whole man, the ethic of the artist, whether a passage difficult to grasp in harmonic-contrapuntal terms contained a 'mistake' or whether the treatment is unprofitably laboured or if, on the other hand, we have to accept an unknown rule, i.e. a unique likeness of the pertinent inner animation, fulness and sound-density which is only necessary to the one particular example, and which in itself is empty and untransferable. Thus it would be no less of a mistake to seek in the contrapuntal field, in the travelling of the counterpoint, an especially cogent reason for harmony's empty wealth of combinations, its theoretically endless chordal permutations.

This is the happiest verification of our emphasis, once and for all, on the inner necessity that will shatter not only dissonance and tonality but also every *autonomous* harmonic *expressive relation*. Naturally the simpler the mood of a song, the more clearly one can indicate its vein of sorrow or happiness. It is always clear with Zelter, but anything but clear when Schubert sets his bitter 'Heidenröslein' in the major. For what feelings are these which can be immediately characterised as delight by the brighter major key and as its absence by the darker minor? As Schubert himself asks, is there such a thing as 'happy' music? And what a tremendous superficiality there is in this black-and-white treatment of pain and joy and of that profounder feeling which is neither the one nor the other but simply what Shakespeare so ambiguously praises in music as 'moody food of us that trade in love'. The simple-minded duality of minor and major which is registered emotionally as softness or brilliance and based in the blending of the partials to a lesser or greater extent, based also, perhaps, in the characteristic downward evolution of the minor triad, as the drop from an upper key-note to the depths – this division according to mood has already lost its significance in numerous works. Probably nobody would ever infer sorrow and joy from the minor and the major if the onomatopoetic names were not derived from the round or angular shape of their usual symbols (the German b and h) as the *B-molle* and *B-durum* of mediaeval notation. Thus Bach is very often totally indifferent to the mood which the keys are assumed to express. Indeed occasionally he even uses the minor for firmness and the major, especially where the third predominates, for mildness and melancholy. Moreover, just as the ancient Church modes have dissolved, so the minor and major scales left over from them will also dissolve one day, perhaps in the new leading-note affinity of the chromatic scale. Already the augmented triad which appears in the minor in the triad on the third degree of the scale cannot be retained as a minor chord simply from considerations of mood. Not only can we continue with it in the minor or major as we

97

choose; like Schönberg's 'vagrant' chords, i.e. chords alien to key, roaming on the frontiers of key, it has a by no means unequivocal association with any characteristic mood embodied in either the minor or the major. True, in Hugo Wolf and also Puccini, the augmented triad is used as a brooding chord. But Wagner's totally contrasting use of it, in his Sleep motif and then in a resolved form in the cry of the Valkyries or chordally in the *Nothung* motif, makes us prick up our ears. To precisely this important chord which is so very typical of richly expressive modern harmony, it will be seen, there attaches an extensive arbitrariness of character and a certain hermaphroditism tending to either the minor or major. Hence when a chord sounds very expressive, Schönberg is also perfectly correct in wishing to locate the cause of this expression in nothing other than the novelty of it. The brilliant and harsh diminished seventh was once new; it gave an impression of novelty and so could represent anything – pain, anger, excitement and all violent emotion – in the music of the classical masters. Now that the radicalism has worn off, it has sunk irretrievably into mere 'light music' as a sentimental expression of sentimental ideas. Consequently a new sound is only penned when a composer's concern is to express something new and remarkable that moves him. This can be a new chord, but even Schönberg believes that an unusual chord is only placed in an exposed spot in order for it to do its utmost, to state what is new, namely a new person, in a new way, and thus in order for the new consonance to assist a new emotional world to achieve symbolic expression. What is new in the effect, the mental associations of a chord, can only be grasped by saying that it is unusual. Already for that reason, or rather only for that reason, it becomes capable of expressing even the most agitated and powerful of feelings. It is no more possible to comprehend it otherwise than it is conceivable to deduce in some essentially ulterior, constitutive, sense the element of necessity in the choice, the formal-causal associations, i.e. the harmonic expressive relation of such a chord, outside of this sheer symbolic practicality it has. Thus what else could it be, this strange identity of the inner and tonal instinct, this coincidence of expressive truth and constructional truth, this 'natural' physical system of chords tempered or permitted by psychology, but the unerring continuation of 'tonal', i.e. manlent instinct, the man-lent vitality of notes, in a harmonic *logic of expression* which cannot be demarcated any farther by conventional means?

Certainly one's choice in the matter is influenced by the discipline and order of traditional procedures. But after that, the sole remaining rule-maker – both in the composing context and in that of the theory of the object – will be the expressive dictates of the person of genius, his vigour, flowering and truthfulness. Then any harmonic system will ultimately become unimportant. What at first seemed to amount to nothing but prohibitions and laws will become simply a barrier for the untalented composer and an education for the talented one. The latter must tell himself soon enough how far he may go and what is to be the nature of that subjectively irrational element which may override rules and, ultimately, the bar-line, dissonance, harmony and tonality as well. The fact that a person amounts to something, that he truly needs this or that particular form, that this or that unmistakable original colour and personal aura surround him, that he is due to appear in the philosophy of history as the person he is: these are basically the only reasons we can give for distinguishing Kaulbach from Michelangelo or Bungert from Wagner, for separating the copy from the original at all.[19] We can ignore the petty distinctions drawn by a mere rule-book of a conciliatory, demagogic type, which actually make it impossible to discredit Kaulbach with such concepts as 'decorative pose' or 'historical scene-painting' without seeming to strike at Michelangelo and to condemn him as well. The mere formula which fits best in each instance does not necessarily carry much personal significance. Certainly it is no supra-personal symbol, and even if it were, this would apply solely within the limited context of an epoch. It would not mean that what was hitherto most apt to the expression and thus traditionally historical could, irrespective of its expressive-symbolical connection and necessity at the time in question, cross the bridge to theory, into a harmonious object-relation set apart from the imperative of choice.

Relations of rhythm as form

The musical beat, otherwise, does not seem to be wholly divorced from the reflecting process [*Abspiegeln*].

It is not only that we find our way about it by virtue of breathing. At best, this inwardly empty quality might apply to the allaying, expelling, elevated atmospheric function of a line of poetry. But there is palpably a deeper life operating in musical time. Not only does it elapse in a different way from the outer time in which it occurs; it also has the immediate effect of going, gaining, acting out events.

Thus in a particular part of a bar, a sharply struck timpani blow, say, is due to occur. If it fails to do so or occurs elsewhere it can destroy the whole complexion of the piece. Here a miss is as good as a mile: one can slow down the simplest popular song to a hymn and conversely, merely by speeding up the tempo, one can turn Wagner's Pilgrims' Chorus into an unspeakably banal waltz, indeed even evoke memories of an old student drinking-song. Or we can attempt to ignore what it says in the score and to put, say, the twenty-first bar of Beethoven's D minor Sonata at the beginning, thus erasing the 'now' and 'at last!' in this bar, the whole admirably planned triumph of the D minor tonic achieved at this juncture. Then it will be manifest, if not all the colours disperse, how with Beethoven in particular nearly everything depends on tense expectation, on something that happens at just the right time.

Of course this power can confuse more often than it enlightens, with its ability to make our pulses throb audibly. From this viewpoint one understands Wagner's hatred of rhythm, which does also relate to other things besides the simple time-beating of the Italians. Accordingly we as the mere spectators are proffered, as it were, the hand to reconcile us with the dream. Through his dividing and phrasing, through the rhythmic arrangement of his notes, the musician comes into contact with the plastic visual world. The bar-lines in fact cut into the mere brightening, darkening and shifting, the magical flux of the tonal patterns, the process being similar to that whereby the movement of visible bodies intelligibly communicates itself to our perception. Thus the outward gesture which has established itself in the dance through expressively changing, orderly movement seems to mean the same to music as physical bodies, for their part, mean to light, which would not shine if it were not broken by these. For music could not be apprehended without rhythm, without the coincidence of plasticity with harmony. Hence, according to Wagner, it is the most external aspect of the note which is now turned towards the world and calls for the well-furnished spectacle of opera as a logical extension of this external side. The internal aspect, on the other hand, makes its impact as the direct dream-image of the essence in repose, liberated from the manifestation and the relations of its rhythmicality. This would mean, therefore, that the temporal element can have the pedagogic function of an individual scenic clarification. But just as the *Ring* cycle leads us into the realm of the gross, broadly spread, inferior and visible, whereas Palestrina and the chorale style indicate a change of beat through scarcely more than a slight change in the harmony's primary colour, so truly ontological music as a whole would be obliged to banish rhythm, just as the early Christians did. With this we cannot fully agree, very pertinent through these objections seem to some empty formal accomplishment, to some examples of a certain virtuosity – not only rhythmic, to be sure – in quartets, and to some confusion and intermixing of Dionysian dance rhythms in Wagner's own music. Moreover we no longer need to curse periodicity at all costs, if we are consecrating it. It is not just that Beethoven and the syncope have arrived already, and precisely the music of *Tristan*, that surging and utterly elusive sound, is extremely well formed in its periods and rhythmically sophisticated. No, philosophically we are also moving towards a practical approach where time signifies something other than absolute worldliness [*Diesseitigkeit*], than this world's passage and an action which is merely penultimate, as dramatic as ever. This is simply because the essence roaming with us and through us is no longer 'in repose' and immutability is no longer the only theological posture. In this way, the soul's deeper self-reckoning can take place in a new thronging, an intuitive rubato versed more and more deeply in Beethoven and Wagner, a mysteriously agitated and syncopated adagio as organically abstract rhythm, without any betrayal of graphicness or even pagan biology. Already there are instances where – as in the jerky motion peculiar to the Priest's adagio in the *Magic Flute*, to the awakening of Tristan, to Parsifal's homecoming and the mystical hour of noon, but above all to the entire prelude to the second part of Mahler's Eighth Symphony – some correspondence or other seems to set in with the occult tempo, the strangely punctuated rhythms of occult striding or climbing. There, we usually also hear the second music, that other type of sounding, the secret respiration, secret atmosphere of music, spontaneously vibrant and full of the beyond like the air in Tintoretto's *Last Supper*. Not only here, however, but also where the whole course of a piece is concerned – in its deep-seated, as yet scarcely discovered *rhythmic tonic-relation altogether*: here the time-shaping, above all, becomes substantial. It constitutes not a formula but a form, no crutch on a naturalistic base or mere, trivial outward beauty either, but pointers to a spiritual action which essentially takes place inwardly, in the area of the musical object itself.

In Beethoven's music in particular, the rhythmic tonic takes precedence over all harmony. It assumes the latter's office and, as the explosion of tonality advances, becomes increasingly destined for victory. For how else could Beethoven be understood, without this music within the music? He drives restlessly on, lets go in order to build up energy in the meantime, compresses his material quietly and imperceptibly so as to set it alight later all the more fearsomely. He leads it, pulls it awry, sends hither and thither, treating his small melodic structures like lifeless creatures, and he sees, does this tremendous strategist of time, masses of music before him and under him from which he selects those that best suit his purposes. Whole groups of notes follow one another like a single lean, economical, stretching family line. But now, at the crucial moment, with a single bar of genius more than richly endowed with rhythmic-dominant power, comes the flash of prodigality, and the enormous masses discharge their load. By doing this, by composing not themes but a whole movement, a whole sonata, Beethoven makes the changing states of our energy a contributory factor. He chases time into hitherto passive counterpoint and produces, by means of this dramatic form, the likeness of a history where not only does the sequence of our innermost ages recur; the existence of time, previously so wraith-like, also spontaneously raises its head. If the temporal still intermittently occurs in the novel, enjoying great importance but becoming visible only through the hero, through his age, his disillusioning, maturing or whatever, the sonata compresses time like a special material and lets us actually hear this mysterious facet of the work. It glows and stamps within; there is an anonymous calling out, waiting, knocking, entering, arriving, hesitating and effusive meeting such as normally only takes place on the stage of the very tersest drama. But first and foremost the arrival is the prime secret of Beethovenian music, and this is essentially a rhythmic secret. The light and heavy rhythmic divisions, the groups, half-subjects and periods of the phrasing are now autonomous flowing substance. Each thing in the Beethovenian sonata derives its time, its verifiable inevitability according to its position in the moment, its gravity and dignity, its genesis and appearance, from the metaphysical schedule. And this time's apparently subjective schema is not just straightforward coherence or the mere cunning management of formulae but – since all effect originally has metaphysical ground behind it – additionally a signet-like simile, an extremely objective rhythm and the most inward, most real, effective schema of our Luciferan nature. Here we have flame and the most secret time-signals. The first movement presses dramatically into the beyond. The second reposes within its own self, in the lyrical fulness of its immediate understanding. And the third movement, particularly the coda, opens the inner door, the march as hidden chorale, and offers its late, sombre, ecstatic confession – a very last syllogism of the discovery of the soul.

So in point of fact, the musical beat is naturally full of objective-metapsychical reflections and relations.

We do the roaming, it is our coming and going that occurs in concrete things. Or rather, the journey has already started from the concrete standpoint. We either just co-exist in this time physically and organically or else overtake it, seizing the initiative, rushing into the unreal, as creative beings. For this there is a single movement, universally related in the deepest way if not actually identical, which structurally connects the symphonically framed and the remaining productively historical events. For in either case, the happening presses on into the distance. The end can only come from within, can never come other than from the happening and as a goal. In both, time is entirely a persistence of the Before in the present and thus a saving up, holding out, consolidation, legacy, preparing and gathering until something can be fulfilled. In this way, time which is put tidy, heard from within, fraught with goal, musical-historical and motivated by reason and foresight, rhythm as music within music and as the logical element in the cosmos, achieves its effect. But given some energy in the shaping and the overview, the achieving, too, will pass into a new spatiality so as to usher the accidental succession into the comprehended juxtaposition of a 'developed' schedule. *Musically*, it passes into the sonant-contrapuntal space-substratum of a fugue or collective symphony; *philosophically*, into the lucid, qualitatively discontinuous historical space of a self-contained epoch or even the whole history of the world just as soon as the whole of it, disregarding the decrescendo of the contemporary reality unrolling again with a particular finale, can vibrate in a sufficiently unified, utopian way. Finally, in both the one and the other, active time is heading for an unknown goal. And it is more than likely that within the smaller ambits of music, the same *telos* problem is objectively posed which animates the entire symphonic history – and, more deeply still, the entire philosophical history – of the ethic of inwardness. Consider the movement of the great composers into a spiritual shell, into their native region of the 'I', into the instant of integral selfhood, individually coloured, arrested and prised open, resounding and left to an innermost sanctum, as the thing-in-itself of music, too. This movement is itself nothing other than the passage of music's time into its space, and thus a sudden conversion of its specific temporal form into its specific spatial form. Thereupon, moreover, the ultimate spirit of fugal and sonata rhythm overlying the actual tempo as the spirit of the hierarchies can, being subjective, be inferred in terms of transcending counterpoint.

Bachian and Beethovenian counterpointing as form and incipient ideogram

For if we do not also advance, no note will.

Admittedly a note is able to execute some brief steps on its own. But these will soon end, and the drop of the fifth immediately restores everything to consonant repose. Only the scale leads further, and this is already a purely human structure.

Of course, nothing is easier than to conceive therein a melodic idea. Almost any powerful beat produces one, even the thudding wheels and the rattling of a railway carriage. It is very much rarer to hit upon an idea both *productive of movement* and melismatic. Just as one's first singing lessons make one sing worse, so the spreading of this idea in many parts – a process which by no means has to be 'necessarily' fugal and may content itself with chamber-music delicacy – will initially damp down all melismatic brilliance in order to do away with the false type and to set alight the genuine in its place.

Now does this beginning which starts with ourselves and constitutes a forcible weaving-together possess depth? What arises in this case is not the same thing as a free, song-like play of notes in a single line. The *melos* rises up, the theme holds sway, the development follows, and the creative Beethovenian outburst over the theme, at which the latter becomes a mere facility and not the sole propulsive force. So *counterpoint*, provided it is not a means or formula but a form, carries in its diverse shapes the burden of music's ultimate transcending relation. It is counterpoint, kindled by harmony, from whose shaping energies everything stems. It has just to occur, and the majestic begins – one can part the twigs and branches and thus one sees whence, from what underwood, the blossoms of the marvellous tree have combined to form its crown. But when it is not even the case that sulphur, phosphorus and a striking surface account for a flame, how could we hope to find a Newton of this blade of grass, this organic matter of the highest order? Here again the man using it, the essential Bach or Beethoven availing himself of it, is still the direct yardstick of all things and even the yardstick of transcending counterpoint – indirectly.

To be sure, we have barely understood so far the brilliant flux and heat this produced. We take it for granted that a student will not often need to write a fugue, but we round off our teaching with it nevertheless. That is to say, the metallic, instrumentally rich nineteenth century has not entirely failed to leave a mark on theory. From it, because its great achievement in harmony is immediately evident, we have taken the theory of harmony. Now this does stand higher than the fugue chronologically and also, to a certain extent, in terms of technical developments. But as a mere item with a one-sided stress placed on it in a musical century that was seemingly not so contrapuntal, it must still concede priority to the old counterpoint in terms of sphere. Thus the specific development of sonata technique which the sonata provided still lacks a theory. Here a merely harmonic explanation will not suffice, for Beethoven can by no means be sworn in upon his modulatory tactics and skills. And in view of the old contrapuntal writing, what do we suppose there is about the 'Appassionata' sonata and even the fugued overture, *The Consecration of the House*, that could be comprehended with the new theory of harmony? Precisely in harmonic terms, all this lags a long way behind Bach, who tilled a limited field in an infinitely rich way. If Beethoven's harmonising is more rhythmic, the source of this rhythmicality is not to be sought in Bachian counterpoint. The liberation of the parts as of the dissonances, the new chordal-contrapuntal tensions which transport the music to great climaxes, the succession and thematic duality of the sonata still operate outside the scope of the old *Gradus ad Parnassum*, however much improved. True, the sonata is acknowledged to be in the same class as the fugue. But whereas since the venerable Fux's time the fugue has been constantly allotted its contrapuntal dignity and method, the expounding of sonata theory is confined to the recitation of the mere, extramural, doctrine of forms. And in this theory the construction of sonata form, its own undiscovered counterpoint that starts with rhythmic harmony, is subject to the arbitrariness or, almost worse, the dictatorship of the 'programme' – an almost entirely unmusical line of reasoning. Thus the dynamic theory of the sonata lags far behind the rich but static theory of the fugue and the higher *mathesis* of the musical realm – hitherto always abstracted from the latter theory. It is important for the working to be florid and filled-out, filigrane. Equally, it is highly desirable to hark back at times not only to chamber music but also to the old dialinear style in order to breathe fresh life into a harmony which is easily exhausted in its means of expression and is becoming problematic. But song, enthusiasm, the spirit of love, the new tempest, the colossally pounding ocean of the Beethovenian musical spirit are even more important. If the sonata's part-writing has grown more threadbare, if it still lacks the cultivation of detail in the intoxication of the whole, then logically these defects cannot be cured with the old counterpoint but only ever with its *own specific* counterpoint.

The latter does not bring everything together but divides sound and develops it. Admittedly development already occurs in the fugue as well, as the actual evolution of the parts, but here the theme simply wanders about. One voice begins by briefly presenting its idea, a second voice starts to imitate this theme at the major fifth or minor fourth, but with certain scruples regarding the preservation of key, of which the most important is the reciprocal response of tonic and dominant. During the statement of the reply, the first voice continues with a counterpoint generally exploited fully at a later stage. Then, if the fugue is three-part, the third voice follows with the theme again in its original form, the *dux*, and a fourth will again take up the reply, the *comes*, so that as soon as all the voices have introduced themselves with *dux* and *comes* and thus the full complement of parts is attained, the first development is over. Depending on the theme's productiveness, there can follow another four or five developments. All are determined by exact rules which allow the voices new counterpoints, richly interwoven and dispersed each time (although in Riemann's view this is only good to the extent that at least characteristic motifs recur), until finally the last development appears, the stretto, the master-stroke of *Engführung*, i.e. the compressing within each other of *dux* and *comes* in canon. All this, needless to say, is only a convenient simplification and does not even fully cover the simplest pattern of Bachian working-out, the interpenetration of linear movements as illustrated in Ernst Kurth's excellent analysis of Bach's dialinear technique. But at any rate, here in the fugue there is simply an entry and not an event, only patient working and no impetuous cross-thread. Any surprise element is just as foreign and indeed just as much of a snag to the theme, which is designed to be frequently repeated, as it is to the uninterrupted course of the fugue itself. For as long as the latter is obliged to take all the parts into consideration, it will maintain a certain middle line or neutrality favouring a certain tenacity, an unbrokenness and a ponderous gait and flow in the areas of harmony and rhythm as well. As a whole the fugue, despite its volatile and rich inner character, constitutes repose, solidity, stratification. It is, to stretch a point, the mediaeval idea of society, put into music: and it is not the breathless discovery of a truth but like the careful exposition of a dogma. Only in the sonata, then, does the disorderly, profuse, 'Baroque' element also break through externally, as something external, as overt Gothicism. Here freedom, the person, Lucifer reign, not Jesus and completely rounded theocracy. Thus, with Beethoven, there is a totally different sound, representing what is willed-through, thought-through, grip and attack in general. And Beethoven's development, which rises up over a duothematic tension, snatches us away to the unknown, to an eerily familiar return on another plane. Here, as we have so often described already, the powerful first theme is countered with a softer, song-like second theme and regularly appears in a different but related key, both of them still empty and unconcluded. Most often the first entry is repeated, upon which, after the double bar, the development section arrives, more airy, more immaterial, agitated in tonality, breaking up and creating further contrasts (the ideas live easily with each other). Colourful, rich in modulation, it combines fragments of both themes and by means of their conflict engineers varyingly arresting climaxes from which, with the return to the purposely avoided principal key, the two themes finally re-emerge, but with the second theme's contrast to the first tempered by an acceptance of, or greatest possible approximation to, the first theme's key. Beethoven and nobody else is the greatest master of this art and the first movement of the *Eroica* its eternal model. The question of sonata design can be primarily focused, therefore, on the problem of the new, unsuspected, productive element, the dissipating, mutually overriding and self-surmounting sequence of events in the *development section*, which must therefore represent the entire contrapuntal art of the sonata that we are out to define.

Within it the music grows urgent and heated, spirals upwards; the movement becomes violent. The brass clash and collide, furious detachments meet head-on, glowing with fiery breath. What, above all, is abandoned in the process is mere exposition, the purely expository transformation of initial themes. The only remaining principle is that for the construction of the development, no actually new material is introduced apart from that which has already occurred in the exposition. In the actual selection of it, however, the composer has a completely free hand. He is under no binding obligation towards either an individual theme as a complete, mechanically indivisible structure or even to all the initial themes. He can restrict himself to mere thematic fragments of motifs; indeed he is even allowed to depart from the guiding thread of the tonality provided that after all his divagations, he does re-establish the surrendered key, the secret and, in the end, triumphantly emerging end-cause of the entire harmonisation, which generates not only animation but drama. The theme therefore only pre-exists as that doubly thematic impulse and germ-cell which propagates itself and seeks to become kinetic. Yet it is simply not feasible to suggest that this theme is, if not a fixed structure, at least dormant tension, a storehouse of subsequent energy. In that case it would be easy to break free and progress, even if the only purpose were that the material under such tension would return to the form of simple melody, without any of the new energy found in thematic conflict. This is something that we often see in the sonatas of Mozart, which are not yet authentic sonatas and have not yet come into their own. But neither Beethoven nor Bruckner, nor indeed Wagner, with whom the theme is not even found at the start but overlies it like an *a priori* that is working from a distance, can be adduced as proofs for this theory of thematicism as mere clock-spring or stretched bowstring. Besides, the theme occurs in the finale almost entirely as a product and not as an actual *prius* of the working-out. It all depends on what is done with the theme. Jean Paul's sanguine Wuz the Schoolmaster, being short of money to buy books, had to scribble his own on the basis of titles in a publisher's catalogue in order to acquire a library; but this veritable phenomenologist of thematicism did not thereby acquire a knowledge of contemporary literature. Similarly a rudimentary musical theme, however well chosen, sharply delineated and productive of movement, is no acorn from which – either by itself or in association with other acorns – the forest of the symphony will grow. For the purposes of pressing forward and inward, harmonic development as already exploited is of far greater service. And it is not just because the inner parts give rise to certain unimportant tributaries: these flow into an advancing river that would still exist in any case. Rather there is an intrinsic formally shaping energy here which redefines, reconstructs, the sequence of notes. Indeed, it can render them unrecognisable to the layman, leading one into a completely different climate and thus vigorously stressing, particularly in the development section, the roving, remote and alienated character of the action, together with the yearning for a return to the home key. Above all, rhythm in Beethoven's music has taken possession of harmony, contributed a dynamism with a strong drive and capped it with this dynamism's *rhythmic cultivation of the tonic*. The respiration of the rhythm no longer allows the parts to give themselves out simply in chords, vertically, or even to relax homophonically, any more than it permits all the parts to state a uniform conviction, by which we mean the frictionless fugal self-differentiating of a single idea. Instead the rhythmicising energy constructs in depth. It annexes a polyphonic action by encompassing the vertical segments and, notwithstanding its tendency towards filigrane polyphony, by showing a preference for climaxes which settle in a single layer, passages where the notes fit together to form sonic columns supporting the achieved splendour and are thereby capable of subordinating highly daring, self-intensifying, self-deciding, dynamic-rhythmic harmony to a new form, *sequential counterpoint*. But it is only as a *whole* that this sequentiality represents horizontalism once more. And often this horizontalism is more basically dependent on the harmony's turning-points, transitions or corners, but especially its rhythmically stressed anchor-points, than on the non-decisive part-writing of architectonic counterpointing. Rhythmically, the attention paid to the chord, to the rhythmic dominant which is almost always its unseen collaborator and which it underlines, is not just a matter of chance, an incidental contrapuntal occurrence. This now becomes the sheer *prius* of composition. Melodising that has the richness of chamber music shifts to the centre of things. And thus the glorious white heat of the orchestra, the *prius* of victorious, rhythmically straining harmony, harmonically underscored rhythm becomes, in the end, a *prius* not only of the standpoint adopted but also of the cause at stake, the cause of the dramatically animated sonata from Beethoven to Bruckner. In the *last* place, to be sure, it is not even rhythmically inspired harmonic development which causes the sonata to expand. This may be characteristic of the new energy and may perhaps extensively support it as well. But even the possibilities of tension founded on the dominant and of rhythmically fired harmony, rich as they are, do not have the power to extrapolate solely from within themselves those sudden interventions we are now discussing, the intervention of a new energy of which there is no sign or inkling in the theme. Probably it is only the *contrast in the disposition of the two themes which adds the decisive factor.* We may only penetrate the full interior of Luciferan music, therefore, with the aid of the sonata's *doctrine of two principles* and of that unity wrested from the opposites which, as an 'abstract' of the victory, has only a chance correspondence, as it were, to the signpost of the first theme.

It is at this point that the notes spiral upwards, striking fire, but the impetuous flight does not lack stability. Another element arises continuously and with growing intensity: the struggle or soul of the emergent relationship. Hence in Beethoven's music the detail is nothing and vitality in the broad context is everything – energy, directness, conflict-torn departure and a resolution which is not re-possession but entirely a gain. Thus in his developments, so thoroughly torn apart, Beethoven never acknowledges the theme's opportunity for a delicate, calm, solitary self-enrichment. He recognises only the emotive quality of its exploitation as the boldness, the élan of an adventure stated in the intrinsic harmonic-rhythmic substance. With Beethoven we enter the room and breathe the relationship. We have the most vivid feeling that here, everything is compressing itself by turns, and thus through the changing atmospheric pressure, so to speak, we ascertain the height and depth of the terrain – more than that, we acquire a true sailor's instinct and even genetic instinct for the atmospheric and its laws. We can sense how, from a rapidly vanished cadence or at an apparent full-stop, there grows a tiny structure. At first barely visible and without significance, it then becomes strong, seeks allies, goes to war with the old element, and soon overgrows the whole situation with powerful limbs, with sovereign fulfilment. This music speaks of a rallying, flagging and setbacks, a going astray, argument and victoriousness, presented either in close succession or in sweeping movements – so much so that with Beethoven all the springs and levers apparently applied by the rhythmic harmony alone will become redundant in the face of this wildly torn-apart interior of his and the *productiveness of the two principles* objectively developing through the counter-pressure of the foreign. He hangs the buds over a lamp to force them into bloom. Similarly, perched between two precipices, even the familiar flowers of the adagio never look very natural in the case of this unplant-like composer. That is also why Beethoven does not speak freely in the adagio or the cantabile variation, in his peculiarly burdened, restlessly languishing slow movement, and why his speech is far more typical, and solely definable, in the opening and final movements, where we find the hyper-active 'affects' and the powerful accumulations of a strategy that penetrates the human being. The very slightness of his themes, almost all of which are placed only as the laconic witnesses to a dynamic state, forces him to create something new as he progresses, something other than the mere evolving, unfolding or purely architectonically counterpointed variation of a homogeneous theme. With Bruckner too, although he surpasses Beethoven in terms of the loving cultivation, prolixity and inventive power of the chromatically melismatic element in and above the theme, the intensifying factor lies neither in the themes nor, as we have noted, in the post-thematically established harmony and rhythm, thus rounding things off. Instead, his music displays that other element, quintessential to the symphony, which still lacks a name, although it may be roughly described as the allusive sequence or the efficacy of a counterpoint which is not now architectonic but dramatic. It is a powerful cyclical expansion laid out in several movements. Bruckner thereby stretches the tension based on the dominant, previously confined to a few bars, over a whole movement, thus creating an enormous verticalism when viewed in the perpendicular, and also transforms the successively chased themes into a sequence, and into a juxtaposition and overlaying that only memory can arrest, set in the context of a whole destiny in music. These themes enter into a new, purely ideational horizontal balance of forces, a *horizontalism only visible in the whole of the dynamic-dramatic unity* and comprising flashes of lightning, broad conflagrations, colossal statements under a spell, the magic of the march and an inexhaustibly wide panorama of triumph. The symphony is sound still taking shape. Its form is unrest, disturbance, surmounting, constant sighting without abiding and absolute vision; its counterpoint does not place line against line, but complex against complex. Only upon reaching this retained, 'historical' horizontalism does the symphony afford the simultaneous aspect, the collective impression, the shape that is borne aloft.

Thus the parts had first to become lighter, and frequently make breaks, in order to gather and maintain momentum. But the note has since filled out again, has grown more lyrical and filigrane. Now we have a difficult, fresh simultaneity: an organically interwoven string playing and a violent symphonic blaze with periods of lassitude, climaxes and the spirit of the future. What Schubert had started, however, Bruckner and Wagnerian polyphony carried on, and we can now acknowledge the Beethovenian symphony's occasionally thin writing, lacking in sonority, purely functional, only punctuated by melisma, to be exactly what is most inessential and most easily effaceable about it. Afterwards the right hand could again predominate in piano playing and the individual element, the richly flowering solo passage, in concerted orchestral music-making. To a certain extent it has turned out that there is something we can take as read, a chamber-music delicacy, a contrapuntal minimum located underneath even the fugue, which represents only *one* of its possible forms. At all times this delicacy is only a means, only a non-symbolic reflexive formula with no special significance (just as the entire theory of harmony was); but the specific individual types of its super-structure constitute – in accordance with the rhythm – a form that defines the object. If, however, we make fugal practice absolute, suppressing everything extra that the sonata introduced in terms of sequentiality, meaningful rivalry between the harmonic and contrapuntal realms, and indeed a counterpoint of dramatic harmony, then fugal counterpoint will also become reflexive in response. It will apply to everything and hence to nothing, not even itself, being a mere sleight-of-hand, drawn from a single one of its concretions and hence become neutral, which will have forfeited precisely the transcending quality found in the well-assembled *system* of counterpoints. A mobile yet smooth, transparent activity of the parts can exist once more; Bruckner in particular encourages melismatic diversity again, and all the other signs are that music is approaching a constantly higher level of filigree, new elaborateness of carving and inner massiveness. But this does not also suggest a slavish return to the canon. It is not as though Haydn, for instance, had fashioned a mere smock from Handel's brocade, Mozart had descended from Bachian Baroque to light Rococo and Beethoven to the plain Empire style, and as though, finally, Bruckner's and Wagner's symphonic polyphony had discontinued the old architectonic counterpoint in favour of a minor craft revolving around their illegitimate dramatising. Even the other postulate that the *ultimate music* shall show a practical correlative to the fugue's melismatic-contrapuntal equilibrium, the correlative of reality to the constraint, does not signify any falling away of the dynamic sonata, any 'onwards to the fugue'. On the contrary: the historical Beethoven stands closer to the 'real' Bach than does the historical Bach. The gradual agreement with the old music of space is an *acte accessoire*, a fundamental practical result of Beethovenian music, a purely substantial act of grace crowning the perfected system. And so, as a site for preparations, the *whole of dramatic counterpoint* is still found in front of the ultimate music, of the very ontology of music.

Now here too the ear perceives more than can be explained conceptually. Or, in other words, we sense everything and know exactly where we are, but when it is transferred to the intellect, the light burning in our hearts will go out. In order, therefore, to understand correctly what is contrapuntally purposed, we must institute a new 'I' *above* counterpoints as plain indicative form, the 'I' of the great composers themselves that the listener experiences and that is exploiting the counterpoints, as an authentically expressive-descriptive signet and indeed even as an incipient undistanced ideogram. Here it is not possible to provide a purely intellectual explanation for something and then to relate it immediately to the ulterior world. That the playing occurs in an organised way is certain, but not what is sought from it, behind it, by a man in need. It is claimed, for example, that Beethoven weighs up complementary themes with more discernment than Mozart. But this obviously does not suffice to explain a heard occurrence of the most colourful kind. Not only is it better for Beethoven to err than for a theorist to be in the right. Even where Beethoven is strict and wise, this cannot ultimately be reflected as strictness and wisdom either in terms of counterpoint as form or in terms of kaleidoscopic sequential counterpoint. Equally, what is given formally – always meaning, in this context, what is given in terms of *form* – would fall short if it were a matter of inferring not only the whence, which can still, at a pinch, be 'explained' from the contrary friction and refining of the themes, but also the whither, the tempest in which this music flies off, the wherefore and whereupon of the tempest and anonymous struggle, the deeper how and what of the cheering element in the gain accruing and all the other spiritual energies involved in this activity, which in terms of formal symbols is so meagre and aimless. Everything is certainly well organised; there is just as much 'mathematics' in it as organisation. And to that extent, the varieties of counterpoint can certainly be developed in a theoretical order akin to the systematic relations, structures and orders of a dinner-party, a banquet, formal dance, strategy, functional theory and all systematising. But this kind of thing does not fully account for the essence of music any more than, or even as much as, logic and a theory of categories account for metaphysics. For what we perceive from the scaffolding are the rustic boards upon which Garrick is playing Hamlet. Or, to put it more accurately: Bach and Beethoven, the *great, practising subjects themselves* appear above form, the suggestive pointer, the merely lower object-determinant, as calling, creative, expressive-descriptive 'signets' and indeed – since the compass-needle settles here as if close to the pole – as incipient undistanced ideograms, indicators of the musical metaphysics of inwardness. So little does the compositional layout encompass what a deeply moved hearer registers and grasps at once: music's hall of mirrors and its guests, this theatre of conjuring tricks and illusions. Without the new, autogenous, metaphysical contribution of a subject pursuing further the Bachian or Beethovenian essence, even the profounder forms of counterpoint will remain mere higher powers of mechanics, which can never provide a continuous bridge to the fugue or sonata in the *ideational state*. It is Bach and Beethoven alone who ultimately exist as transcending counterpoint: only Bach, Beethoven and that element in our receptivity which can respond to them as to the productive and undeducible factor, the vital energy by virtue of which all this happens, the one essential tenet of a discontinuous theory of music, the great encountering of a specific subjectiveness impelling us to its sphere, the *individuum* named Bach or Beethoven. So universal and canonical is the latter in respect of its place in the philosophy of history that, like Plotinus's angels, it can stand as the effective category of this one possible transcending contrapuntalism.

Thus there are four great ways of being contrapuntal, and here and now they all possess an objective relation to ethical data. Now it is precisely music, to be sure, that was allotted a distinctly eccentric role in history. But it does not conform historically, after all, simply because its hitherto brief, belated history reiterates the history of our core. In other words, the history of modern music as music which has been 'caught up with' is too large for the modern age. Accordingly, as was already evident in our discussion of rhythm, the distinct historical eccentricity of this art is grounded in the whole of its categorical reiteration of the philosophical history of inwardness and of its ethics.

There are, then, four great hierarchies of contrapuntal technique. The relation which they possess to the ethico-metaphysical spheres of the 'I' is a constitutive one, although it has to be complemented by listening, by creative activity and is thus not direct, not demonstrable without further ado. Mozart, according to this classification, is Grecian and offers the small secular self; he is lightness, Attic counterpoint, pagan joy, the self-aware or sentient soul, the stage of the self that takes the form of play. Bach is mediaeval and offers the small sacred self, built in a sturdy and hallowedly uniform fashion, a musical ruby glass, architectonic counterpoint: filled with charity and hope, the commemorative or authentic 'I'-soul, the expiated soul of Adam, consequently the stage of the self that takes the form of faith. Beethoven, Wagner have revolted against this. They are adjuring and lead into the *great secular*, *Luciferan self*, questing, rebellious, not to be satisfied by anything given, full of militant presentiments of a higher life, bound on an ineffable march of discovery, as yet without obvious booty; they are the masters of dramatic counterpoint and assaults upon the interior, ultimate heaven. But what is still absent, the great sacred self, the upper stages of human essentiality, music that has reached its final destination, will be the art of the later Holy Roman age. And in its arrived state, crowned by eloquence and triumph, this unimaginable music would have to condense sequential counterpoint into the simultaneity of an expressive statement, an understood significance that could be instantly grasped, a *musically* emphatic language of prophecy *a se*, a really telling musical meaning.

The note again, not as a means
but as a phenomenal entity

If, therefore, we do not advance with the note, nothing can continue singing.

The fact that a note has consequences to which one must yield has no basis whatever in the note itself. It is a question of ascertaining

115

with our ears in which direction the phrase would like to turn, how long it needs to cadence, and at what point it will gather its strength for an ascent. And none of this would ever be possible without a sympathetic, energetic bracing of the will, which retains sounds, draws them along with it and anticipates just those consequences which do not yet exist musically.

Granted, even a note in isolation will progress and build itself up in related vibrations. In the sound of bells, which is rich in overtones, it even arouses distant chords; and whenever any other note is struck, it arouses at least the three partials of the major triad. A note spontaneously presses on in this way and possesses an intrinsic movement which reaches for other specific notes with the compulsion of a cadence. It will rejuvenate itself, lay bridges, establish relationships of the fifth. As long as it takes the path of the octave, fifth and third, i.e. that of the primary melody, it will of its own accord settle on certain points in the harmony to which it is drawn on a purely numerical basis, quite independently of our wishes.

But now this, of course, is a meagre singing which will soon die away again. It amounts to a singing of the basses with a sustained key-note, basically a rise and fall of pure fifths, and the riches of dissonance are lacking. Once it has arrived at the tonic, the note will come to a stop. The fall of the fifth is too short, the tonic is like a basin, and its consonant state is the tomb rather than womb of music. So there would be no actual progression at all if purely the natural chord-sequence reigned and no new leading-notes, scales, suspensions, anticipations and fragmentary branchings-off could be intermittently heard and at once pursued purposefully farther. Here what is crucial is to think ultimately only in terms of the scale. This breaks the vicious circle of fifths and thus gives the writing both a voluntarily chordal and a liberatedly contrapuntal character. Certainly we must make use of what we are given; we can even admit that a humming kettle and a gale whistling down a chimney-stack suggest in themselves something akin to a wondrous spirit-language. And equally it is noteworthy that Marschner, Beethoven and Strauss have very frequently used the appeal of the plain basic elements of the triad to great melodic advantage, though simply as raw material which in itself is totally meaningless and extra-musical. In contrast, the explosive melody of the scale, with its thirteen notes in Siam and seven notes in Europe, presents a purely human, unphysiological, not to say non-physical structure.

116

Little may be achieved, therefore, without our doing creative violence to the note and its related vibrations. To become music it is absolutely dependent on the flesh and blood of the person who takes it up and performs it, just like the phantom figures that accounted to Odysseus, not for themselves but for the interrogator himself. The latitude of all the possible partials or of exploded tonality into which modern music is again venturing forth is a benefit which can convey fresh impulses to the spent Romantic and indeed even Bachian system. But any so-called aesthetic physics of the note will be sterile without a new metapsychics of the note, whose servant it is. Hence in the last analysis the life of the note and its own fixedness, its mediumistic, unbroken, material idea is – precisely while it is being played – never basically intended. That is something which, at least up to now, was not evident in painting and sculpture to anything like the same degree. For precisely because seeing and the essence of light do not form the body of the latter, the material side is abandoned to a lesser extent in this domain. Because it is a more distant concomitant, it reappears with greater fidelity when simply broken down to wood, for example, or assimilated as an open-work, forest-like impression of light or in any other still faintly Nature-like terms. Music, on the other hand, just because it reaches closer and deeper, also assimilates the note, the totally broken note, more deeply as the material of the sheer essence of music. For that reason, simply because of the deeper relationship to the note permeated by soul, the note of that which is spiritual, it must show all the more firmness in abandoning the physical note, any trace of a medium acting merely on its own behalf. Thus it is simply because he was actually thinking in terms of wood that Master Erwin abandoned the stones of Strasbourg Cathedral.[20] (Although there is certainly a further motive, for *why* was the Gothic artist thinking in terms of wood after building with stone? He then evaded the issue by harking back all the same to wood, which was still something physical, and staying loyal to it.) With the Beethoven of the B flat major Sonata or the Diabelli Variations, on the other hand, the pre-established harmony between the experience, the material, and the concrete materiality only generated and found in the material is seriously disturbed. People have often remarked on the asceticism of Beethoven's piano writing. It is significant that Bülow, who so often wants to temper Beethoven's 'acoustical atrocities', describes the variations of his last years as the 'most sublime evolutions of musical thinking and imagination in sound'. Bekker is not altogether wrong in his comment that the B flat major Sonata and Diabelli Variations are ultimately unplayable because they are written for an instrument which has never existed and never will exist. These two works, he says, do not employ real sound but incorporeal, purely cerebral abstractions of sound, borrowing the language of the keyboard only as a rough, basically sketchy alphabet. Thus the note's weakness in secular contents, in the power to assimilate the forms of a broad and polymorphous external world, places a corresponding limit on this largely contrived product's deeper ability to appear before the throne of the inner, purely inwardly illumining musical Deity with the works of its *autonomous* fixedness. We enter into it, transfer ourselves hither, twist the sound to the mirror and the floor to the rafters. But it is simply the case that everything lives within us and is *no more* than aroused by the note. We are therefore far too generous if we salute the sound-source, which only surprises us with our own image. It is not, for instance, as though its own significant state of animation were 'experienced' [*empfühlt*], perceived, in the note, namely as something which might have only awakened with our hearing but which henceforth, following this awakening, is condensed by us and woven round with quality, as the prelude to an extra-human physics or metaphysics of the note with an independent existence.

One reason why we cannot expect this is that the external means will start to shut itself off and to perish. To be sure, as can now be stated conclusively, it is no accident that it is precisely the note – as used and radically broken down by human beings – which makes the impact in music, and that precisely this delicate, transparent body is the chosen transmitter of musical states. For when a person is very deeply moved, his eyes will start to swim. He will want darkness, evening to come; all the deeper things we contain are enveloped in twilight. Daylight is something these shun. As drifting, mysterious, humming phenomena, they are better attuned to a misty climate. In exactly the same way, the calls and apparitions of spirits wait for the darkness of night, when the strange interior dream-product can go and strike home undisturbed. But music's different magic resolves this loss of sight in a favourable, personally intimate sense, in the more luminous sense of the concept of a spirit-realm, a concept so uncanny in itself. To quote Shakespeare in a southern clime:

118

How sweet the moonlight sleeps upon this bank!
Here will we sit, and let the sounds of music
Creep in our ears: soft stillness and the night
Become the touches of sweet harmony.

But it is still the enchantment of Death, is music, and allied in a still deeper sense to the Ossianic character, to rain and autumn and the profound delight of darkness falling early, to gloomy skies and heavy clouds, to mist and the heroes who ride over the lonely heath and to whom the spirits appear in the shape of clouds, just as they did to Bach and Wagner – turned to the point of the compass at which this world comes to an end, becomes extinct. It is Wagner's and Schopenhauer's theory of visions which provides the key to this. Behind all dreams, it maintains, there lives a kind of intrinsic prophetic dream which starts with a dimming of our sight and thus enables spirit-shapes to appear in the farthest background of the interior dream-world. We are unable to convey what is now envisioned to the awakening process and our awakened consciousness other than by means of a second dream. This can only transmit the genuine content of the first in an allegorical form, because the phenomenal world's forms of perception in terms of space and time must be already applied when, as anticipated, our brain eventually awakens fully to the outer world – in which event the result would obviously be an image altogether related to our shared experiences of life. Already, however, the great imaginative writers headed by Shakespeare erected their brightly illuminated stage exactly where the more muffled world of sound passes into the more evident, but inferior, world of light. Moreover, the argument runs, the same dream engenders Shakespearean spirit-shapes which a complete awakening of the inner musical faculty could induce to give forth sounds, on the one .hand, and Beethovenian symphonies on the other: symphonies which would be equally sure to inspire in the unveiled, less somnambulistic sight of the hearer a clear apprehension of those shapes, the dense, memorable, surreal spirit-shapes of great poetry. Here we just need to distinguish between two kinds of dream. The one *sinks down* and provides solely a derivative, moonlit impression of daylight contents, a mere recollecting of what existed already. The other *moves beyond* it and constitutes a dawning, a *not yet conscious* knowledge occurring first of all in the sound-subject, the finally ontological word-substratum, of what is coming to pass at

119

some time, out there, in the as yet unbefallen beyond. Even in the latter case, to be sure, there still operates a process of recollection, of finding one's way back to one's native land. This, however, is a place where one has never been before, although it is still native to us. But the substance of this dream in the middle of the night is always golden; it is sound, golden sound. For like the man of significance, who errs more than others because he can never wholly fathom the world's insignificance and lack of affinity with him, the ultimate Deity and this Deity's dominion can no longer be accommodated by any framework of visual and pictorial qualities, the validity of the material. Whereas paint still adheres very strongly to real things and can therefore join them in insignificance, be emptied of spirit, the clash and resonance of sounding brass will spill over. And instead of remaining the latter's hallmark, it will extrapolate itself as a new, man-lent attribute, so that the instruments by which we hear and perceive ourselves are finally closer to spirit than are paint and stone or the questionable nostalgia for God of this material which has become uncategorial. Music can be said to have glorified since olden times the other truth, the white lie, the constitutive imagination, the modern philosophy among the arts. Only the musical note, that enigma of sensuousness, is sufficiently unencumbered by the world yet phenomenal enough to the last to return – like the *metaphysical word* – as a final material factor in the fulfilment of mystical self-perception, spread purely upon the golden sub-soil of the receptive human potentiality. This cannot and is in no way supposed to mean that the physical note in itself is already something metaphysical. It is not even a spiritual enclave within the natural realm. But a relationship is irrefutable because our hearing of the note, our hearing and perception of ourselves in it, and consequently the note's practical possibilities for its spiritual categories, which are alien to it, non-physical, do permit us to establish a similarity between this material and the 'material' of what God signifies. If, however, we seek to discern something with alien laws and an astral character largely from what the note in itself is and provides, this becomes tantamount to the inadmissible relegation of music to mathematical science. And music is no more liable to occur here than a mathematical element could ever be discovered in the phenomenology of musical effects. Hence no road leads from the tidied-up note, in the sense of a subjugation through degree, proportion and quantum befitting a physical and indeed even a psychological object, to the *voluntary and essentially musical* note, the − acoustically speaking, wholly untenable − premises of tempered tuning, enharmonic modulation, the avoidance of potential infinite chaos. Scientific exposition could never account for music's melodic tension, its harmony's dissonant motley, the deliberate incisiveness of its themes. Or for the much-varied, humanly inspired, filigrane, periodistic, horizontal and vertical layering of counterpoint as the most artificial construction on Earth; the *denaturalised* note as an object which is almost purely metaphysical, and as the first phenomenal aspect of all that is mysterious [*aller Heimlichkeit*].

All the same, men did not shrink from making the note land fully in the exterior world only. Not very long ago, we were equating doh, re, mi, fa with the four elements and the seven notes of the octave with the planets. Not only do the Vedas chant their secret rain-songs, not only are the intervals in Chinese music for strings tuned to correspond to the distance between heavenly bodies. For even Dietrich Buxtehude professed 'to have neatly portrayed the nature and character of the planets' in his seven keyboard suites. And lamentably, Shakespeare's Lorenzo goes on to say:

> . . . look, how the floor of heaven
> Is thick inlaid with patines of bright gold:
> There's not the smallest orb which thou behold'st
> But in his motion like an angel sings,
> Still quiring to the young-eyed cherubims.

Here the true, interior night has been abandoned, and the ruling principle is that false, purely *astronomical theory of music* as eventually formulated above all by Kepler. Here even the different registers are supposed to correspond to different planets. The minor mode is supposedly analogous to the perihelion, the major to the aphelion. Indeed, the complete tonal system with all its harmonies is described as a reflection of the solar system and as, in Pythagorean terms, a division by seven of the primordial solar note, the *lyra Apollinis*, and only lawful within the framework of this system.

There is little to be gained by giving such references more spiritual names. The note still fails to land within the being of man. Father Singer, for example, made a serious speculative attempt to deduce the sorrowful sound of the minor mode from the thesis that it is based on a diminishing of the second note in the triad, and thus points to Golgotha as a descent of the second person in the Holy Trinity.[21] True, such claims have a trivial and comical ring to them, while

Christian references to Jesus as the light of the world are deceptive in terms of the incredible astral magic involved. But both here and in the modern theosophy of music, this only echoes that sterilely mystical inventiveness in every quarter which, as Abert has shown, succeeded in subjecting the entire mediaeval philosophy of music to the sway of astronomy, numerical symbolism, instrumental symbolism and astral mysticism. Even with Schopenhauer the ponderous bass is still a reflection of stones, the tenor of plants, the alto of animals, the melody-carrying soprano of the human realm; and the orchestra thus becomes a cross-section of the world. Hence even with this most Christian of philosophers, music's transcending object-relation is still a cosmic aim. Here, after all, man is not the main *point* of Nature but only the strongest, brightest, clearest objectivation of Will and thus has a positive vocation to destroy the semblance of individuation in the face of universal Nature. For Friedrich Schelling, however, music's gold is embedded entirely in the number seven. And Kepler's Pythagorean thinking is so completely victorious in this philosophy of art where it applies to music that Schelling no longer reasons about it from unconscious, yet richly fruitful, Indian convulsive actions, as Schopenhauer did, but straight from the premises of Pythagoras, indeed Egypt itself. It was Schelling who actually conceived the statement that music is nothing but a pointer to architecture, and the latter frozen music. Consequently it is, of course, simple for our philosopher to adulterate music with the overworked large-scale construction of extinct astral relations. He likes only the music of the Greeks, which he appreciates as melody *tout court* and thus relates to the ordered world of the planets. He loathes the music of the modern era, which he brands as confused, unrhythmical harmony and thus relegates to the centrifugal world of the comets. By so doing, he deprives the whole of 'non-architectonic', post-Grecian music of a home in the planetary system, and hence of its chance of a substantial, logically objective arguability. It is all this way abroad that the prosecution of the note starting and carried out from natural premises takes us, into the realms of the absurd and totally unfactual, even when assuming a Christian guise. The impression is that the Christian soul itself, that sheerly musical soul, had not yet woken at all. It is as though the fire, the lamps, of our yearning and our labour had not yet burned through the astral vault of crystal, and as though the deepest thing in the world could still only be conceived as the most objectivistic of a *perfectly cosmic type*. But this should warn us all the more strongly, when it comes to interpreting the factor of the note, to go only by human receptivity, which knows nothing of any astral mysticism in music, and by the unique miracle of genius, which likewise posits a spiritual transcendence that is always of a kindred type.

Therefore it is better to believe that the musical note has only to melt our hearts, that it needs only to soften them and touch us to the quick, in order to bring about its own inner pilgrimage. It is better to believe only in the correspondence between the motion of the note and the motion of the soul. This belief chimes happily with the Church Fathers and especially with St Augustine's doctrine of the note's power to illumine men's hearts, of its enchanted journey and as yet secret landing in the *purely ethico-mystical 'Castel Merveil' of music*. But what this, with the ardent strength of the desire to come home, is exalting is not the fabrication of the ever-gratifying semblance, which has to come below truth simply because of what it is. Nor is it – although here, admittedly, the semblance [*Schein*] is converted into a certain vainly consoling and misleading reflection [*Widerschein*] – the promise of some ulterior world devoid of humans; some sensory reflex of the universal idea deemed since olden times to be free of humans, whether defined as *nous*, as *pneuma* or even as the Will-to-Life, as a contemplatively induced nirvana. For Schopenhauer is still far from understanding music's location in the veritable ground of being as long as he gives it just a passive and cosmic, not an individual, heroic and Christian basis. He grants music the power to supplement the outward show with the thing-in-itself. But he defines this thing-in-itself solely as a metaphysical thing of a kind that is indeterminate, lacking in individuation, unprocessual, indeed already empirically real in the extreme. As a basic concept of moral philosophy the self-encounter, encounter with the 'we' (and in every truly creative being there is a deep passion for making epistemological connections), corresponds ultimately to the apocalypse, the final revelation of the 'we'-problem as the basic concept of the entire system of philosophy. It cannot allow what is true to stand as a straightforwardly inductive logic of facts. Nor can the true be admitted as the totality-logic, definitive for the Greek mind, of a most universal and hence most real substance. On the contrary, there is – and in this sense the responsible artist is closer to the philosopher than is the empiricist devoid of 'subject' – another truth besides the truth of what just exists. This is a truth that concerns only us, that concerns the scope of the world experienced with our colouring of it, swiftly comprehended and consummate in the religious sense, an absolutely 'subjective' and yet extremely substantial world, one exceeding the merely empirio-comparative status of the present condition and its easily reached logic of Being. It is directed not at the elucidation of a thing and not at the elucidation of men but at an initial adaptation of yearning to itself, at the interior life and unknown self-perceiving behind the real world. In music, moreover, man does sustain strong corresponding object-relations. These are mostly still of an artistically specific and – if we extend the concept accordingly – immanent kind, coming before and after the laws of the transcendental synthesis of artistically imaginative apperception and its phenomenal aspect, the material and phenomenal element of its fulfilment. It is the indirect, spasmodic relationship to a man we cannot see; to the approaching shape, perceived in the sound-image, of the Chief, the servants, the eschatological spiritual ground, the restoration of the Great Man, the *secret, absolute figure of mankind out of the maze of the world.*

On the thing-in-itself in music

Only a few people, however, actually reach the stage of pure self-hearing.

People slip from consciousness, plunge into deep sleep and have false and whimsical dreams for the note's duration, inwardly adding touches of colour to things that are buried or have not arrived, in a vague, crepuscular manner.

Granted, the better ones become alert, not bringing themselves just as they are, but at the same time they also grow arid. As cognoscenti they hold on to the scaffolding, and they think that this, the means they have discerned and the forms they have grasped, makes them musically objective. So these rationalists are not on the right track either, and one now almost feels more inclined to put right the flagrant sleepers, who are at least stirring psychically in a realm of the soul, however dully and erratically. For while it is very much form alone which leaves an impression, discloses things and brings what is faintly glimmering to the surface, there is very little to be grasped through form by itself unless there is within it a most expressive personality, the musical wonder, to guide us upwards. The question of the latter lies in the expression of what can be sung.

Unfortunately it was precisely upon the sleeping man with his fanciful notions that a multitude of heard sounds devolved. For it is above all a fact that the falsely associative listener very easily re-discovers himself in the peculiarly hazy essence of Wagner. This is not because with Wagner, even more than with Beethoven, small, long-customary, hitherto respectfully incorporated forms were broken up. For their place was taken by form whose expressive foundation was deeper still. It shows the extraordinary degree to which the musicality of Wagner's disposition exceeded the estimation that this translator of musical into dramatic consistency himself placed on it. Here it will more than suffice to mention the refinements, the floridly spun *melos* and extraordinary craftsmanship in the *Mastersingers*, the harmonic innovations, assimilations and enormous tensions but especially the wealth of syncopation and polyrhythm in *Tristan*, and above all Wagner's extremely distinctive counterpoint, which Bruckner's music exalted. From the purely technical standpoint, even Wagner's genius above all can never be conceived from the evolution of music. Beethoven's symphonies were called operas in disguise, but the justification for that is doubtful. We can say with far more certainty that Wagner's music-dramas, conversely, may be grasped and enjoyed in completely musical terms for long stretches (without knowing the words and the context, which is purportedly their sole foundation), as orthodox intensifications and developments, as evolutions of purely musical logic. This much needs to be said in reply to a mistaken yet fast-growing body of critics. But all the same, we readily admit that Wagner often encouraged those who slept in a haze because he reached the listener falsely, in spite of and even by means of all the technical skill involved. He gave those dreamers with their merely fanciful notions an opportunity to encounter in an all too somnambulistic fashion the fervour, encircling vapour and dream-stratum of a merely animal memory. This illustrates how little a good *working* in itself has a determining or redeeming influence in this domain. For the peculiarly torrid, anti-intellectual essence of Wagner lies beyond *melos*, harmony and rhythm and proves to be the product of his idiosyncratic musical *object-theory*. It was only this which imposed the suppressing of the note, the objective restriction of it to a dull, sinking, drowning, subconsciously unaware, animal state. In striking back, human conscience did not now allow the note to speak to the full its innately spiritual language. It held the note down, choked, inadequate, and it only compensated for the turbidness through the lucidity of the word. Thus the 'motifs' were romantically lodged in the orchestra. But what was actually liberating, expressive about them was invested not in the music, but in the visual element, the word, the drama as the music's ultimate key-note, on outwardly Gluckian classical lines. This again, however, was still only the expressive content of 'confused imagination', the *petites perceptions* of dreaming monads, the *confusa conceptio* of afflicted, unfree emotions guided by inadequate ideas. So with Wagner the pent-up music, denied its full say and cheated 'poetically' out of the proper hour of its self-language, its *humanly absolute poetry a se*, spread further and further into the areas of unfreedom. Not without frequent reversals, certainly, not without vigorously welling up into the spiritual realm and not without a clear inkling of the other, supra-conscious side. But it still had an animal and pagan tendency, which landed it in the unconsciousness of delirium, the screams of fear and ecstasy emitted by oddly frenzied living creatures, the transports of assuaged desire, or ultimately – despite the Grail – in the deceased Pan's shadowy realm, where no men dwell.

So it is in that direction that we are now chasing, and almost the only sound is of greed. Even the proffered renunciation operates with a secular brilliance. Seldom does its heaven appear far above the shore where Tannhäuser is dreaming in the embrace of glowing Love.

Now as we know, Wagner only came late to Schopenhauer's writings, when the alluring shepherd's pipe had already been playing for a very long while. Yet although this composer of the subterranean realm developed completely from within himself, his art nonetheless resembles a vast practical test of the *Schopenhauerian* philosophy of music. In fact almost the entire Wagnerian object-relation is foreshadowed in Schopenhauer; yet the latter does not teach or tell us anything about Beethoven's or Bach's object-relation or, indeed, that of the unsuspectedly expressive future of 'music of arrival'. Even in the world as Idea, it is the world as Will that remains the object of music.

For here we remain beneath the threshold more than ever. The manner of now seeing, instead of being, finds nothing but greed and precious little to assuage it. True, our eyes readily fill with tears, but the interior world that consequently appears in Schopenhauer simply sounds impulsive and frenzied once more, full of fears or short-lived enjoyment; and that is all there is. Here the arts oriented to light and the thesis of sufficient reason reflect the same character from the external angle, but in the shadow of its relations. At best, they have as their model the forms of the objectivations of Will, those curious hybrid forms standing between diversity and unity, between illusion and reality. But just as Schopenhauer's Will announces itself instantly in the scream, and just as time's reflexive eidetic form simply resembles a flowing veil in the way it envelops the core of Nature, dwelling in the hearts of men, so *music* as distinct from the other arts, says Schopenhauer, no longer speaks of appearances and their infinite reference, or of their objectivations or Platonic ideas, which seem almost too rarefied. It speaks of the exclusive essence itself, weal and woe only, the universal Will and that alone as the most serious and the most real thing of all we can find.

Thus here we have no higher cravings. We achieve our purpose in enjoyment, the note being a complete statement of life. Although it is not actually allowed to paint and to copy phenomena, the gradations of the Will certainly project into music so as to provide a mirror of the whole world from its lowest registers up to the human voice, up to the leading melody which expresses the Will's multifariously restless character in the purest and, at the same time, in the most considered way. It is just that, in the last instance, Schopenhauer places no decisive stress on the detailed correspondence between music and the world's divisions of ideas. Rather, it is always one thing that stands out. Everything that takes place is only related to the note like an arbitrary example, music always being only indirectly related to any flesh-and-blood covering, any operatic and worldly scene, expressing the gist of the Will in the abstract, so to speak, without any trimmings and without any motifs; it forms the distilled quintessence of feelings, of passions. In short, music is the melody to which the world *in its entirety* is finally the text. Hence one could call the world the embodiment of music just as much as the embodiment of Will. Indeed, ultimately, Schopenhauer even dissociates music so completely from any kind of parallelism to the objectivations of Will as to maintain that the other arts present the Will only in an indirect, shadowy, external way, by means of ideas. And since our world is nothing but the appearance of ideas in multiplicity, music – because it passes over ideas – is also totally independent of the world of appearance. It simply ignores it and could still survive, up to a point, if the world did not exist at all. In short, music no longer posits perception of its Platonic idea for an appearance, as the other arts do, or a knowledge which is sent endlessly from one thing to another, as science posits. Instead it posits a sameness everywhere and at once, the universally pertinent, the timelessly, spacelessly identical, which is to say the actual Will as the *thing-in-itself*. Upon this rests the ineffably inward nature of music, its power to reveal to the sleepwalker *the world's intrinsic essence*. Although, therefore, the stratification of the world projecting into sound is not ultimately essential to it, sound is still solidly built into the intrinsic essence of the world, and only the world. Thus the calming influence which music now exerts on us goes round in circles. The highest aesthetic elevation above the world tosses man back more than ever into the centre of this world wherein music is deemed to exert its enduring sub-human fascination. Here the shaft of the soul, the crucial turning-point [*Umkehr*], the inkling of higher things, is completely sealed off, and one fails to see what could blast it open. Nothing in this account is more obscure than 'the ineffably inward nature of music', and nothing is more incomprehensible than 'the profound wisdom it contains as a language which reason does not understand', but which Schopenhauer still claims to have fully decoded. It is pointless of Schopenhauer – pointless precisely in view of his philosophy's deepest conclusions – to maintain that all music is achieving its purpose, when its object is still constantly just the Will. Equally pointless is the thesis that music could survive, up to a point, even if the world did not exist. For it could surely survive only inasmuch as music causes the world to emerge once again at this point, with heightened significance – in other words, only inasmuch as it represents just as direct an objectivation of the collective Will as does the world itself. In consequence, music, far from being a panacea for our afflictions, confirms and affirms rather than deflects the universal Will whose cries it utters. Nowhere does Schopenhauer's actual philosophy lead into that shaft of the soul, the complete mental tranquillity and the nothingness which he pronounces to be the location of the universe and which he nonetheless presents as completely transcendent, although it is surely here that the mysticism of a 'universal Christian philosophy' would have its starting-point. In spite of all ultimate negation of the Will, precisely the interior realm finds itself completely repudiated: 'The moment we go into ourselves and, having directed our perception inwards, are aiming at complete recollection, we stray into a bottomless vacuum, turn out to be like the glass hemisphere from whose vacuum a voice speaks but whose cause is not to be found within it; and in thus attempting to comprehend ourselves we will snatch, with a shudder, at nothing but an insubstantial phantom.' In short, while the spirit is certainly the lyre for Schopenhauer, it is always the *objects* that constitute the plectrum. And in the last analysis it is these, the world and its substance, that also provide the only contents which the lyre is entrusted with expressing in sound. Item: *even in the world as Idea, it is simply the world as Will, and never the Idea's secession from the world into itself, that remains the musical object.*

Here human beings, although very much a part of the delirium, are consequently not even capable of acting with the independence this logically entails. Instead they are merely the scenes of the action – battered, ironicised puppets placed on the fist of the one idol and performing in its stage-play. Although they think they are pursuing their most intimate affairs, they are only performing the business of the species. No original 'motivation' at all is operating within them. What is taking place instead is the same fatalism and occasionalism, the same transfer of 'efficient cause' to the first principle alone as applies in the other reactionary Romantic systems; though the terms 'motivation' and 'efficient cause' are inappropriate in the case of somebody who despises the thesis of reason as much as Schopenhauer did. Individuals and their own will, a will not just blindly impulsive, are nothing compared to the one force that wills things, the surge of the universal Will or even universal spirit which alone is real. Therefore it was here that Wagner found his philosophy. As a blind urge, a delirium, a metaphorical glow-worm, a surging, a cloud of vapour and unconscious trance, much *Wagnerian music* sets forth the same frenzied and permanently static automatism, the same Nature-legend remote from a subject. Certainly Schopenhauer breaks through his unbecoming immanence from time to time, and the heavy world rolls to one side. But while many aspects of this life already seem to him like sounds from an orchestra which is about to strike up a great and beautiful symphony, music still does not, to his mind, truly avert any woes. From the angle of both Wagner's music and Schopenhauer's philosophy the world – even as the object of music – is still always that devouring, generative flux of death and birth as which Krishna in his true, divine shape revealed himself to Arjuna. As we have noted, a curiously subject-less

129

animal lyricism emerges, particularly in the *Ring of the Nibelung*. These characters are not dramatis personae advancing into the area of a mutual encounter and their own profound destiny. They are but blossoms on a tree and indeed no more than bobbing ships which passively share in the grief, the struggle, the love and yearning for redemption of their sub-human sea; only experiencing, therefore, the universal wave of the Schopenhauerian Will washing over them at every critical moment. Thus they are swathed in that greed of the thing-in-itself and its tyranny which is not only foreign to the moral will of Beethoven's music but forces the one specifically Wagnerian beginning away from ardent spiritual espressivo.

For all that, the task awaits us of hearing our own selves in a way both pure and deep. It is a matter of training unfocused hearing upon ourselves at last, of grasping the soul. Certainly this will also be furthered by a better technical schooling for the layman, which would give him at least a rudimentary support against the volatile depths.

Ultimately, nonetheless, it will only be himself, grown strong, made intelligible, that the hearer will receive back from the formative equipment. The deeply moved, supremely innocent listener must be preserved and comprehended just as he is in order for him to re-emerge as the man for whose sake the whole thing is happening, behind the tonal framework and its laws, and thus in the place which purposes and awaits him. Even the artist – who, after all, is progressively abandoning the meaningless expedients (like tonality) and only achieving further great things through transcendent forms (like rhythm and counterpoint), even he is simply his own listener in the last instance. As the first man to achieve, on everyone's behalf, the design of meaning upon the interior realm, he is the first to discern – recognising it, just as he is recognised within the shared area – the feeling of wonder as it grows clearer, the utopian ground of the soul drawing closer. This means objectively penetrating to the core of the listener instead of the savant, instead of mere form-analysis. It means *placing at the end of music the interior realm of all that is hearing itself, moulded sound, as simply the aura of the listener re-encountering himself*. It is not before the work that music's spirit-realm stretches, ever, but only behind and above it and also behind its false, pagan area of influence; pressingly far from all mere 'psychology', fundamentally superior to Schopenhauer's paganism as the object of music, pure understanding of oneself-in-existence, with the 'we'-problem and its metaphysics as object and substance. In this way a new self, the perfectly struck self of divination and bringing together, must also be re-introduced behind any concept of musical form, instituted anew as a function of metaphysical aesthetics, if the deeply moving experience is to be saved and consolidated, if the wherefore and spiritual end of music – which is one long tale of heresies in sound – is to attain a concept adequate to it. For music flowered when seeing, clairvoyance, the visible world and also God's traces in the visible world were disintegrating. It is, for a deeper reason than was hitherto evident, the latest of the arts, succeeding visuality and belonging to the formally eccentric philosophy of the history of inwardness, its ethics and metaphysics. At last we can draw our conclusion from this evening lateness and overtaking of every form or species. Now the calling and hearing are themselves emerging, the violence of time and colossal strategy, the shouting, knocking, pounding, visionary hearing anonymously dawning, and the birth of the core, the sonorous, not yet existing, undesignated core of all things, a struggling birth upon the hearth of music. And because, here, the visionary seeing of all ages has now been earnestly transformed, the soulless mind is coming to grief as both artist and thinker. Both the existence and the concept of music are only attained in conjunction with the new object-theory, with the *metaphysics of divination and utopia*.

Granted, we approach this too only in our dreaming, even if it is as near to us as it could be. But it is no longer a dream which recalls bygone things or is tossing about in diverse baser passions. Rather it is that yearning which contains such objects of desire as are not to be fulfilled on Earth at all, the conscious desire for what solely befits us, which is kindled in the well-applied sounding of music. This is deeply familiar to us, bestows goodness and clarity, leads into our hearts, and the exclusive purpose mysteriously confronts itself therein: ' . . . where is Paul, the thief?' asks Matthias Claudius, 'gone into the wood; I followed, looking wildly through bushes and trees, and wanted to punch him the moment I found him, and my blood was boiling – then in the distance the noble lord's huntsmen started blowing their horns. – "Ready cash or no ready cash! I won't hit Paul", and I forgave him in my heart as I stood by the Schmerlenbach and went home again.'[22] Someone who explores on a still higher level the feeling of 'becoming better', becoming oneself, is E.T.A.

131

Hoffmann. He does so through that stranger 'who was telling him of the many far-off, unknown countries, whose speech spontaneously reverberated in a wonderful sounding of music'. A distant realm of the most familiar kind is revealed, the certainty it holds that somewhere and at some time we shall see 'the fulfilment of a lofty desire which surpasses all earthly enjoyment and which the mind, like a chastened, timorous child, does not dare to express'. And pointing us entirely in this, music's most genuine direction is Jean Paul's question: 'Why does the fact that music couples happy and sad feelings, indeed even engenders them itself, and tosses us hither and thither between joy and pain in seconds and without a pause, more potently and forcibly than any art – why, I ask, does this make us forget a higher attribute of music: its power of nostalgia, a nostalgia not for an old country we have left behind but for a virgin one, not for a past but for a future?' Music is so completely the guarantee of the beyond, a song of consolation, Death's enchantment, a yearning and our own arriving simultaneously. It is a nocturnal flower of faith which gives strength in the ultimate dark, and the most powerfully transcendent certainty between heaven and earth. *Thus it is not Leander's ardour, which was all that Schopenhauer meant, but the lamp of Hero which always, and with far greater certainty, burns in the interior of great music*, as the self-illumining dream-heaven of the human soul. Wagner was turning the pages back; Schopenhauer was plunging into a more and more hopeless world. In defiance of Kant's warning, he was seeking the name of the *thing-in-itself in present existence, in Nature*. And although the world deity he had in mind was proving to be nothing short of the devil, Schopenhauer nonetheless assigned to music simply the hearing of this existence, this state of affairs, and not the divination of a mystery, not the discovery of a treasure, our legacy behind the world and the nearest bend in its path. He did not refer to Beethoven, his rhythmically colossal thrusting upwards, his Luciferan-mystical domain. Nor did he refer to Bach, the song of the sacred soul, shining upon its own interior, and to the great organ fugue, a towering edifice with its storeys and staircases, a single self-illumining, colossal crystal splendour,[23] and to the promises of the Messianic home behind all expeditions, all Luciferan heaven-storming. But for us, there is no longer anything other than this to be desired. It is only for the unsayable, for when facial and verbal expression grows torpid, that the musical note is reserved. Spectres and masquerades emerge, caprices of a true vision, the distorting mirror for comic opera and the magic looking-glass for serious opera; 'music, moody food of us that trade in love', and that music which must resound the moment the supernatural appears on the scene, until – in accordance with Busoni's genuine insight – the impossible element in music combines with the impossible, visionary, element in the action, and thus they both become possible. But finally, as soon as everything falls silent on Earth, in the earthly action, completely dispensing with the text and even the Shakespearean dream-world, the world of dance, masks, intoxication and magic, music will articulate features of the other word, deriving from a different larynx and logos. This word is the key to the innermost dream in the chief [*Haupt*] of objects, their own expression that has grown significant, the multifariously one final expression of the generality [*Überhaupt*]. What is still a fervent stammering at the moment will one day share in the eloquent language of music, in increasingly expressive certainty. It is aimed at the word that is our unique solution and that quivers in concealment as *omnia ubique* in every lived instant. The ultimate purpose of music and philosophy is purely the articulating of this basic mystery, this first and last question in all things. For the *thing-in-itself* still 'appearing' in sacred yearning alone, and thus even senior to music in rank, is what operates and dreams in the immediate distance, on the present sky-line of objects. *It is that which does not yet exist, which is lost and dimly sensed, our encounters with the self and the 'we' concealed in the dark and in the latency of every lived instant, our utopia calling to itself through charity, music and metaphysics, but not to be realised on Earth.* The farther and more directly the note goes into itself in this way, the more perceptibly the original dumb man will also emerge from it, telling himself the most ancient of fairy-tales. But he is what he tells himself. If the lived instant, arrested within itself, prised open and left to an innermost sanctum, thus finally begins to resound, then the times will have changed. Music, miraculous and transparent, will have achieved with surpassing art, beyond the grave and the point where this world ends, the first disposition of the human face divine and the quite different naming of a divine name, the name both lost and undiscovered.

THE MYSTERY

We are investigating the whereabouts of clairvoyance, which has disappeared. A river dries up in the soil. Far away, there suddenly appears another river which was never seen at this spot before and which certainly has no source in this arid region. Can we connect clairvoyance with music as positively as we can link those two rivers to each other? We could never catch sight of them simultaneously, but when one of them went, the other slowly grew to a size, and it did so, apparently, from exactly the same energies. We do not know, to be sure, if it came to make the same use of these energies, or grew to the same miraculous form. Thus if we enquire what form music took in an earlier epoch, so as to perceive more accurately what music is, even the acknowledged affinity will not in itself suffice for a closer definition.

For we are gradually becoming blind even to the outside world. We have been blind for a long time to what is above us; even the light of Christian illumination is a thing of the past. It is true that our sense of sight came later than our sense of the supernatural and arrived when the latter was departing. Or rather, as a result of the sense of sight, rebellious and wilfully intrusive, the supernatural world has increasingly receded and gradually perished completely. Earlier, in the times which gave rise to our fairy-tales, exterior things were veiled or completely invisible. But moving behind them in the clearest fashion were their group-souls, the naiads, dryads, guardian angels, Sirius with Orion the hunter, the night-sky's variegated clouds and the whole nearness of the other world. We recall, however, the Roman admiral who dared to do something previously unthinkable and have the sacred hens thrown into the water when, by refusing to eat, they predicted a bad outcome to a naval battle – if they won't eat, let them drink! and this was still in the time of the Sibylline books. So the sensory organs soon developed a greater acuteness. The visible world grew dense, oppressive, definitively real, and the world now invisible to us, the preternatural world, subsided into a belief, a mere concept, a Platonic-Plotinian Jacob's ladder or pyramid of ideas. Even the oracles became ambiguous, indeed unintelligible. And thus a mentality limited to this world, the cultivation of an outlook which reckoned above all simply in terms of military strategy, jurisprudence, calculability and real causality, gained strength in a more and more rational way. By the time of the Emperor Augustus, all sensual or even intellectual contact with transcendence had finally disappeared. Then Jesus was born, the metempsychosis of God Himself, and men could be assured afresh of the preternatural by the grace of this light shining even in the darkness, which is to say this incarnation, earthly journey and spreading abroad of the Word. This was accessible again and perceptible to even the most sensory of organs. But in the four centuries since Luther and the Renaissance – in spite of the renewed prominence of the worldly mentality, and even despite the renewed violence with which a free, virile, active, Luciferan, rationalistic element has been stirring and plunging into the world and over-world, we have been witnessing a twofold process. For on the one hand it is starting to become gradually blacker all around us, and this blackness closed over our heads long ago. Night is advancing further, and not only in a partial sense, as in the Roman era. The natural foregrounds too are beginning to recede, as surely as the higher Christian light they engendered receded long ago. But on the other hand, bright – uniquely bright – is that light of the self which still burns in the interior; and broad is the potential scale of the awakening of the forces within it, which are no illusion. Our soul weeps within us and yearns for the beyond, positing God and the dream. But what the darkness of night is chasing hither, as Orpheus was chasing the shades, is generated purely from the soul and has this intrinsic Eurydice as its only aim. In all the outer and upper darkness, it is only the subjects that cannot be extinguished. The fact that the Saviour lives and *wants* to come a second time is vouched for beyond question as much as ever. Like all that is objective, however, He and God Himself have relinquished their own power to come and to act in the realm of phenomena. The time of the completely pure subject-magic first instilled in us by Jesus, the time for the fullest Luciferan-Paracletian development is at hand. Hence only one thing can save us now, and that is a rebellious alliance in search of itself above everything foreign. We need an alliance between the moral self which alone can still burn a candle in the night of the outer and upper realm on the one hand, and the God who is falling silent, leaving us and hesitating on the brink of His transformation into the Holy Spirit on the other – as constituting the cries, the prayers and the profound designating power of heroic-mystical 'atheism' itself.

Hence whilst we remain in a state of obscurity and expectancy, but are nonetheless reflected in a strangely beautiful way, another kind of clairvoyance has reappeared. It already existed previously and now has a ricocheting effect, so to speak. But everything about it has changed, become more solitary, more unsupported and more productive, no longer mirroring foreign things but radiating into a void before us, in its very function. The seeing eye has been transformed. The Persians, Chaldeans and Egyptians, the Greeks and schoolmen, *all of them without any music worth mentioning*, those masters of the finished and uniform, of firm figures and definitions, reflections instead of productions, have had their deserts, the deserts of figurative clairvoyance and a secure heaven filled exclusively with visible and objective things. To modern man, however, has been given the consoling song of music instead of the ancient realm of images, the ancient homeless exuberance. Hence the great composers' significance grew in proportion to the loosening of the roots and the other firm, sacred, tie of myth. Indeed even the folk-song and chorale are not music's ultimate sources of nourishment, for it is evident from their disappearance that they do not carry its ultimate substance. The latter has increased and grown constitutive to the same extent as philosophy, too, was forced, was endowed with the power, to approach practical action, substance as a process, truth as a universal elevation. Thus a different light obtains in this aural, musical and generative clairvoyance. And in complete contrast to ancient mysticism, which was dealing with realities that were finished and intrinsically clear in the extreme, its planet has not yet revolved enough for us to perceive its other side, which is still averted from both us and itself. We might, in order to recognise whither music is bound and to what end, enquire what it was, in the age of clairvoyance but no music, that is now beginning to appear as music in the modern era. But the affinity perceived between first clairvoyance and then music suffices only to determine the common niveau. It does not stretch either to the new function or to actually stating the contents of the object that has moved on. In this respect we would be going very seriously astray if, on account of the similarity of the two royal roads, we sought to annex the ancient goal; if, therefore, we still sought to populate with the figurations of astral myth, or even of the abidingly semi-astral myth of the Trinity, a daylight altogether generated in sound. This was formerly only for spirit-ears; it was music's vast inner constellation, the primevally divined sonorousness of the celestial world as opposed to the colour-aura of the merely astral world – and thus the extensively, integratedly, sonorously glowing darkness of the lived instant. Instead something different and unnamable, our sacred splendour itself, arises; 'but let's be gone, the dusk is come, the air turned cool, the mist descends, for evening shows a home's true worth'.[24] It is for the profoundest of reasons that only the modern era's perplexities, Luciferan and also satanic ravagings of all higher things, its paradoxically darkened Advent nights have become the birthplace of music. But these have thereby become the birthplace of our very own, historically interior road. It marks a redemption not only from the body but from all mere duty and bare, merely inter-human definability, and a release from any outward essence, any transcendence *in which man does not appear.* It marks a release, finally, towards an ethic and metaphysic of the inner life, the fraternal inwardness, the mystery revealed within itself which will be a complete blasting apart of the world and the dawning of truth over all death and decay.

Here we need not fear any disappointment or even deception. It is no longer legitimate to say that just as dreams fade away as soon as we wake up, so that which lives only in the 'I' and is otherwise uncon-firmed is necessarily unreal. That may be true of our minor states of excitement; it may indeed be the case that the bodily covering which tautly envelops us is what brings all life's torments and pleasures upon us. And just as we imagine in sleep that we are being crushed by an avalanche if a coverlet drops on our face, so this clay, this body of ours besets the immortal soul's sleep of a lifetime with lights and sounds and cold. Out of them it constructs the exaggerated history of its sorrows and joys; and when it wakes up, only a little of it will have been true. Indeed we can add to this statement (from Jean Paul) that not one bit of it was true, that all of it is reflex action and none of it has even an antithetical relevance to the yearningly animated soul, which dissociates itself not only from the body but also from all inter-human definability. But if we are the origin of what the *note of music* says, inasmuch as we insert ourselves within it and speak with this great, makanthropic throat, that is no dream but a firm spiritual circle. It only finds nothing to match it because outside, there is no longer anything with the ability to do so, and because music as an inwardly utopian art is completely beyond the scope of everything empirically verifiable. We do not need to worry, however, that this lofty thing superior to ourselves would rather have another origin, any more than we need be indignant with music – as we still often are, to be sure, with the visual arts – because it has set up a barrier and man is constantly obliged to glimpse it only from outside and stand waiting. Nor must we console ourselves, hypocritically, by saying that we more easily recover from our tears than we could from the ineffable rejoicing of angels. Nor do we need to attack, with a jealousy born of despair, the genuine symbol freely given to us in music, in a way reminiscent of our assaults on the sculpted effigies and symbolic creations of olden times. The back door of mere contemplation has been exploded. The emergent symbol differs from the allegorical symbol which was foreign to man and at least partly extrinsic to him; which would, had it become wholly visible, have throttled and consumed us like the naked Zeus; and whose transcendent elusiveness, still unresolved in the visible realm facing us, was what had constituted its symbolic character. The latter was adulterated, an allegory which only existed for us. Granted, behind it there dwells, as in Egypt, our own obscurity; but also the lethal clarity of error, the foreign light, the astral myth. But a note of music comes with us and does not, in the end, retire allegorically into a province of its own which is foreign or forbidden to us. If musical sound is still only a pointer and lacks authenticity, this is not because it is couched in symbols. Its enigmatic language does not want to hide from us what is already resolved supernaturally. On the contrary, the function of music is the most complete openness. The mystery, the intelligible yet unintelligible, symbolic thing about it is the actual human object, which *in practice* is hidden from its own sight. A note of music comes with us and is 'we'; unlike the visual arts, which seemed previously to point so far above us, out into the realm of the rigorous, objective and cosmic, but which in fact stop at our graves, it emulates good works by accompanying us even beyond the grave. This is precisely because music's sublime element, the new and no longer pedagogical but *real symbol* in music appears so very low-lying in our atmosphere and such a mere fiery eruption, even though it is actually a light in the farthest and of course innermost firmament, and indeed the actual problem of 'I' and 'we'. So moulded sound is not something that confronts us but rather contains something which places our hands on our hearts, adjures and transposes us with our own selves. In this way, it answers our exiguous, eternally questioning receptivity with itself, or at least with its question about our home, a question which is undeflected, grown absolute, an echo of itself. A note of music creates a context of meaning both surreal and unallegorical, and symbolic only with regard to the still imperfect state of its 'I'-ornamentation; a context for what can be humanly intuited of human beings, for a direct gnosis of the 'we'-problem that outruns the species.

So, then: clairvoyance has been extinct for a very long time. But should there not be a visionary hearing at hand, a new seeing from within? Should it not be this which, now that the visible world has become too weak to hold the spirit, will call forth the audible world, the refuge of light, the primacy of the spark to replace the former primacy of seeing, whenever it will be time for music to speak out? This locale is still unoccupied, and so far there is only an obscure echo of it in the metaphysical connections. But a time will come when the note will speak, and speak out, a time when the true vessels of light will be finally installed in the higher self; *when what still strikes Brangäne as the sound of horns will be heard by Isolde as a fountain in the silence of the night*; when the new composers will precede the new prophets. And so let us assign to music the primacy of something otherwise ineffable. Music – this kernel and seed, this reflection of the brightly illumined death-night and of eternal life, this nucleus of the mystical interior sea of the servants, this Jericho and first township of the holy land. If we could name ourselves, our Chief would come, and music is the only subjective theurgy. It takes us into the warm, profound, Gothic sanctum of the interior which alone is shining even in the midst of obscure darkness. Indeed, this alone remains the only possible source of the radiance whose task is to demolish and disperse confusion, the barren power of what merely exists, the crude and ever-persistent groping of the blind demiurge, if not the coffin of godforsaken existence itself, because it was not to the dead but to the living that the Kingdom was preached. And thus on the Day of Judgement, this hardly known, warm, profound, Gothic sanctum of ours will be the same thing as the Kingdom of Heaven revealed.

II

Magic rattle, human harp

The vibrating note travels. It does not remain in its place, as colour does. True, colour is likewise emitted to catch the attention, but then it stays put. For a white to detach itself from a garment, or a wall, is unthinkable. In contrast, the whole of the surrounding air can be full of a sound.

There was a time when the musical note did not appear such a free agent. It was linked quite specifically with the instrument producing it. When first consciously produced, it was wholly attached to its instrument and had no other association. Thus the original rattle rattled as the thing it was; the rattling sound is merely its verb, as it were. The thunder-stick whirred and the drum beat itself: that was the main thing. Thus here the sound is an attribute of the instrument, to which it is linked in a purely material sense. Its sonorousness is used for magical purposes, for healing the sick, driving away evil spirits and summoning good ones. But it is not primarily the sound which performs the spell, but the actual magic drum being used. The crucial element is the sacred instrument, as ancient as possible, specially painted or with special incisions. At the most it is through the power of rhythm, in the dance, that music as such becomes more advanced, itself exerting an immediate influence. Yet, even now, the drum will fascinate by being hollow, subterranean, the cymbal by being metallic.

The more the musical note developed, the more it parted from this foundation. It surmounted its instrument, so to speak, and now used it as merely a means of assistance. Now the ringing and tinkling broke loose from the ringing brass and the tinkling bell; musicians no longer just 'attended on' their instruments but availed themselves of them. This change is marked by the invention of the pan-pipe: the first instrument which did not emit fearsome or muffled sounds in isolation but gave out a well-ordered series of notes. It is at this point that *music* is born, music as a shout of sorrow or pleasure and not as material magically sounding. No longer do we hear the speech of the wood or metal, but neither do we discern the 'soul' of a flute or horn.

Instead the miracle of music is now itself triumphant in every quarter. Previously the 'tricking out' of the rattle with bird feathers 'charged with spirits', and of drums with magical incisions, was at least as important as the frightening or alluring sound that they made; but now, this faith in the material thing disappears completely from the musical viewpoint. On a miniature scale, the rattles, drums and thunder-sticks had even been worn as lucky charms, but not the pan-pipe, which was unconsecrated. The rattling field of the instrument yields to the opening up of the auditory field, in which music had not until now, after its deliverance from the magic of the material thing, made its home. To be sure, the compass, technique and expression of the instruments are and remain of importance, for it is only with amateurs that the instrumentation is a secondary consideration, or even interchangeable. But even where desperate attempts were made to bind the exodus of music to the known realm, a magicking of the instruments or 'natural philosophy' of music in this old style was absent. It is not the tinkling bell but the tinkle itself that now emerges from material deprived of its magic. And in the process, the material can founder completely in the covered orchestra. The musical note evinced much vigour in turning from the attribute of a thing into the very thing that matters, in a developed state; from an adjective into a substantive; from a fortuitous excrescence of objects that were rubbed, struck or blown into a universal, though purely 'artistic', realm with melodic and above all human relations of its own. Music, which to start with only denoted a piece of wood that men shook or sacred implements for their hearing, furthermore became, over and beyond its physical character, a colossal realm whose objective nature was still largely unknown. If one were bent on demonstrating an object for it in the known realm, one no longer referred to sacred instruments, even in the context of magic objects. Rather, notes and their scales were related to whole constellations, to the harmony of the spheres, to the 'Lyra Apollinis' that was supposed to stretch across the seven known planets. But even here, the actual melodies were still floating through space, not located or indeed incarnated in some existing object. Even so-called tone painting 'describing' rain or thunderstorms, where it possesses any musical merit, registers only the psychomorphous action of rain falling, a storm erupting, daybreak or nightfall, without having localised such events in a concrete sense. And as for the 'Lyra Apollinis', the harmony of the spheres as echoed in the scales and

141

harmony of music (a superstition which persisted from the time of the Pythagoreans up to Kepler and indeed Buxtehude), music's real development has confounded all such 'natural', indeed astronomical, object-definitions. Why, even in the much more genuine realm of 'human' object-relations, music still travels under top-secret orders. And assuredly these contain no references, directly or primarily, to an origin linked with material things and the magic of things.

There are nonetheless, amid the fluctuations, some noteworthy remains. Sound's ability to be everywhere and nowhere has asserted its claim, yet it is not necessarily lacking in the instrumental 'where' which bound it to start with. In the first place this is still conveyed by the fact that trumpets are associated with kings and trombones are associated with priests. Trumpets which 'proclaim that kings are approaching' – what we have here is not just convention or external historical association. On the contrary, the trumpet and the trombone are themselves standing for monarchic or sacerdotal might, *almost irrespective of what they are playing.* Granted, the trumpet has ceased to be a sonorous fetish, yet neither is it just the attribute of a king, since it resounds as the actual royal splendour which this king is projecting. And secondly, instruments portrayed as having their own magic still occur on the stage, in magic operas; here they are portrayed with great forcefulness, even. With their diabolical clattering in the orchestra, Dr Miracle's tinkling phials in *The Tales of Hoffmann* belong to this category. They make a light, glassy sound compared to the Doctor's roaring and shrieking, but one that is equally spellbinding. Directly archaic – on the brighter side of the coin – are the horn which plays in *Oberon*, Papageno's bells in *The Magic Flute* and the magic flute itself, carved by Pamina's father 'from the very base of the thousand-year-old oak, by thunder and lightning, gale and tempest'. And once again it is not just their melody which casts a spell, but the fetish to which it is given. In Dr Miracle's case the flute of the Pied Piper is suggested, and in Tamino's the zither playing of Arion and Amphion, not only in respect of their great artistry but in respect of the magic instrument in each case as well. Ultimately, to be sure, this element of the magic object appears to be only a surrogate for the supreme concentration of music at a crucial point in the action, viz. a point effecting some transformation. Take the trumpet signal – scarcely still remembered in terms of a magic object – which, purely as melody, echoes down into Florestan's dungeon in Beethoven's *Fidelio*. At that stage the trumpet is almost completely forsaken, and in it we hear solely the Minister's voice or the realm of salvation which has suckled music since it first became Christian. But even the archaic enclaves which preceded it (in Papageno's bells, in Tamino's flute) no longer qualify as vestigial proofs of ancient magic instruments. They fail to do so at all in terms of the philosophy of musical metal, and they barely qualify in terms of the gnostic-celestial instrumental symbolism that Abert rediscovered in his book, *Musikanschauung des Mittelalters*. It is not the paucity of the remains that contradicts the 'pagan' interpretation of music in the context of magic objects (for the remains are nonetheless lodged in a high, if not the highest, musical authority). But even a consecrated bell, which is another revealing remnant, rings not from the depth of the metal but down from aloft; essentially it is within the church tower that the metal thus dedicated is hanging and operative. In an orchestra, the bell's 'metal mouth' is, rather, a subject for ridicule. Indeed, even music whose aim is black magic (like Stravinsky's *Rite of Spring*) derives its instrumented gruesomeness only incidentally from the clanging brass or resonant bell. –

We are now coming to the actual purpose of our enquiry. For all this harking back brings us to the singer, the problem of the singer himself, especially in opera; he is the 'remnant' which shows the most life. The singer really still is a beating drum, or rather, a harp that plays its own music. Here – in contrast to those previous remnants which were rarely found and faintly bizarre, though important – the musical note has a definite site, namely a body that sings in the process of acting. Here music, in the process of floating, alights on a visible instrumental provenance; it thereby adheres at the same time to other visible objects and denotes them. *By means of the singer*, the melismatic and even the symphonic elusiveness of music finds itself placed in an operatic scene and the action which this localises. In solo song and in oratorio, the human voice is just an instrument like other instruments, and the singer just a mildly stressed vehicle for the music. But as for *opera*, this is not only a place where the human voice will not cause an obstruction. Here – and not just to further the expansion of human song – it is a form of dramatic action which is necessary and supremely justified in a specifically musical context. And in using singers, it puts instruments on the stage that are physically active and significant once more: not sacred instruments, but ones with a natural emphasis. Here *we have on the stage a kind of human harp*. This instrument's voice signifies purely the instrument itself; only on a secondary level do its actions signify the instrumentally detached musical content. Certainly the origins of opera are not archaic in the aforesaid sense. Yet the opera singer is distinctly in touch with the archaic remains, with music as the attribute of an object set in motion and emitting its own sound. Although this parallel may seem an odd one, it is one of the facts of music and has proved to be effective in practice. Apart from the music within whose fabric they are found, soprano and alto, tenor, baritone and bass do in fact 'attend on' the instrument which they represent and with which they are linked through a personal bond. Hence the association of individual *vocal categories*, i.e. individual 'instruments' in the vocal department, with specific *natural* qualities of the *male* or *female characters* corresponding to them is partly extra-musical and, indeed, pre-musical. Here music is not 'formally' self-sufficient at all. Nor does it articulate in an expressive role – as still applies in the solo song – suffering, longing, anger or love 'in general', to cite Schopenhauer's abstract and too emancipated interpretation. Rather, it is now the case that music is attached to the material of its instruments, being the sound and speech of this very material. In the role of soprano or bass, it renders the 'soul of the natural condition' which thus sings of itself. A note on the recorder will never reveal the wood, and a trumpet note will never reveal the 'soul' of the metal, whereas in the case of the lyrical instrument of the body, the voice is also manifested as a revelation of its soprano, alto, tenor or bass character there on the stage. And the associations change in accordance with the way an age views the 'characters of voices'. With Mozart the tenor, for instance, represented a rather gentle cantabile quality: Tamino has it, as does the less powerful Ottavio. The baritone voice, in contrast, represents the very condition of Don Giovanni, the actual hero of an amorous intrigue, as well as the condition of Count Almaviva. Even Figaro's own bass voice is readily reconciled with Susanna the soubrette, whose youth he shares. But when ideas changed in the nineteenth century, the tenor came to the fore. With Verdi, and more 'victoriously' still with Wagner, he became the *aurum potabile* of youth and erotic power – heroic power in fact. Blond hair, a sunny radiance, strange white gods and their fetishes were now the prestige, as it were, of the tenor instruments, the way they looked, and they had a character not previously associated with them. Today, this heroic resolve is fading again. The baritone is regaining ground once more as the instrumental sound of masculine vigour, minus all cello-like smoothness, bland benevolence or acquiescence. This matches our aversion to a high imperious voice expanding in song – even if the actor's name is Radames. But none of these changes would have occurred had it not been for the singer's representation of himself, which affords a lover of operatic voices the presence of a distinct vocal object. Here the instrument's association with a character revealingly arrests, at any rate, the elusiveness which music, even non-Romantic music, still normally possesses. For vocal trumpets, unlike the ones that you blow, really are kings. Indeed Walther Stolzing's high trumpet, which is a sheer paean to himself, almost finishes – even without the *melos* – by transforming the awakened Mastersingers into a love nest's attendant spirits. What has replaced the archaic magic of the object, to some extent at least, is a kind of intrinsic magic of the material, the singing love-poetry or the instrumental live impetus of an especially effusive display of the material itself, which is localised. To be sure it is also this, for its own part, which enables opera music to have its issue in a human world portrayed on the stage and to transform the pan-pipe, or the harp, into actors; these, however, now *voice human material*. They are serving the music above them – with the limiting ideal of the entire theatre itself as a magic flute.

III

Paradoxes and the pastorale in Wagner's music

It isn't a flash and then smoke . . .
But light out of the smoke.
Horace, The Art of Poetry

SOME PRELIMINARY REMARKS

It has always been hard for a new note to introduce and establish itself. Indeed, in Wagner's case, the more he went his own way, the more savagely he was rejected. It took an extraordinary stroke of luck for his actual works to be performed, and when they were, the hostility really began to mount. People were opposed to him not only as the vain show-off that he was in many ways and as whom he identified himself musically in many respects. He was considered above all an awkward musical innovator and also a constantly over-excited one, lacking in both melody and form. This first wave of hostility lasted right into the 1880s. The great ensuing triumph – which in many ways assumed unfortunate proportions – is now history.

This triumph abated again when it was thought that a more cool-headed, more matter-of-fact younger generation was growing up. We are referring to the 1920s, the decade of so-called *neue Sachlichkeit* and the universal trend towards economy that was connected with it. Thus rose the second wave of hostility to Wagner, which was totally unlike that of our grandparents and great-grandparents. To reject Wagner became the fashion amazingly quickly, and the younger generation came to show an uncaring ignorance of his oeuvre equally quickly – this in Germany of all places. His second rejection is more serious than the first because it was instigated by young people, and not by conservatory heads or the kind of audience that hires boxes to see an opera with a ballet in it. For the most part, the conservatory pedants had only meant the likes of Mendelssohn when they had used Brahms as a stick with which to beat Wagner: the same Brahms who found all theatrical make-up and stage effects repugnant, it is true, but who – to Hanslick's displeasure – carried the *Mastersingers* score around with him for weeks on end. Now, however, Mendelssohn's name was the last to be invoked by the anti-Wagnerites, Wagner's often vulgar polemics against him having ceased to count. The entrenched older generation were the last people to take part in the new anti-Wagnerism. Rather it was calm that reigned among the latter group; Wagner was for them no longer the innovator he once had been. His music now stood entirely for late Romanticism and above all for so-called eternal values (a favourite term for all from Pfitzner to Hitler) – values with a stale odour of sanctity to boot. The philistines in particular felt free to inhale this odour, and the Wagner-image was placed at risk all the more when Hitler accentuated afresh the sound and the fury of Wagner, his glorifying of things German, his Aryan hullabaloo – when, in short, Hitler seemed to be cutting Wagner down to 'Blut und Boden'. Fresh pseudo-Gothic, the idea of Hunding's hut as Göring's log-cabin, supplied with mead, the hall of the Gibichungs as Göring's hunting lodge, the festival meadow and Sachs's final address as the *Reichspartei* assembly in Nuremberg: this was all that was needed for the world of Wagner to become entirely suspect – to put it mildly – to the more lucid minds. But prior to this, the anti-Romantic movement or rather the acceptance of the hollow space of existence (expressed in architecture by the house of glass[1] and the aversion to ornament) had already inculcated a hatred of Wagner and his effusion of the soul [*Seelengeschwöge*], as they put it, his bombast. The rejection of all expressive music rendered people *deaf* once more to a master whose whole aim was to raise the orchestra to the greatest expressive power. Transparence and Bauhaus-type economy in the orchestral parts were now at a premium, chiefly in opposition to the over-heated, in fact allegedly poorly written, dangerously torrid Wagnerian score. Yet if we take so objectivistic a view of music that *any expression* is ruled out and *all dynamics* are ascribed to the Devil (it is precisely Mozart who gives the lie to this fresh exaggeration), then we will, of course, cease to show any *differentiated* insight into Wagner's music at all. But in the face of an achievement as colossal and undeniably potent as his, we must find the safest possible starting-point for the aforesaid insight (or else only an uncontrollable, boundless arbitrariness would result). Such safety lies in the *score*. In other words, the *composer* in Wagner is the decisive factor, not the presumed painter or stage designer, not the producer and not even the librettist, who in Wagner's case was always dependent on an advance musical conception. Thus music not only makes the action twice as strong and three times as passionate. It actually dictates the action in the first place (with the visual element following from it). In this connection the latter-day Bayreuth productions really do seem to signify a rebirth of the staging from lighting dictated by the music – with no little success. What we have long been waiting for, the representation of the Wagnerian twilight as dawn and not only as dusk, has at least been taken in hand, and it will continue until all is made clear. The most perilous and at the same time most spectacular of musical achievements (since Handel) demands this, and one can justify any contribution which reveals something to us. So let us proceed to deal less with questions of performance and interpretation than with more basic musical questions, with some hitherto little noted and perhaps even unknown aspects of the music itself; things, that is to say, which are close to the source of the performance material. It is certain that by no means all the profundities of this music have yet been brought out. Only when these have been fully explored, down to the roots of a special 'language within music', might the staging be completely renewed. For the moment, however, let us endeavour to deal with a number of simpler, though similarly unexploited matters. We shall call these 'starting afresh', 'bel canto', 'deep paradoxes', 'the "omniscience" of the leitmotif' and 'the pastorale in Wagner's music'. It is precisely these matters (largely overlooked in practice) which call for a *pre-conceived* lighting plot.

STARTING AFRESH

First of all, in what way should we listen to Wagner? The answer can be stated in one word: humbly. Only then will somebody too raw or too bumptious (these failings often coincide) be capable and worthy of being Wagner's guest. Only then will he encounter to some extent the not uncomplicated drama instead of an impertinent, and certainly clouded, opinion of it. Many people are seeing Wagner's operas for the first time, which is not their fault; they could not afford it before, they need someone to introduce them. But they are different from those young members of the bourgeoisie who, being literally without need and therefore often acting in a priggishly disparaging way, cheat themselves and better minds out of an oeuvre which is at all events not trivial. Those are people who take a dislike to 'mein lieber Schwan' but fail to notice anything else in *Lohengrin*. Accordingly, they have no time for anything which is not sweetly warbled, or actually gasped, but begins by taking a deep breath. An impudent snob neither listens with commitment nor has the ability to hear round corners. Matters are not improved, of course, where it is intended to surprise the vacillating customer with extra stage business. This practice is a bad one; the listener who is new to Wagner will only be enthralled when Wagner does not become artificially woebegone or racked by convulsions on top of it all. What is needed is for new listeners to absorb Wagner in his many striking, brightly coloured passages in an absolutely boyish way. Beards were common at the time that he was composing. But apart from Sachs, who is entitled to sport one, much of it can be removed as having only been affixed earlier. It is also vital to make speechsong absolutely audible, as though it were recitative. The arioso passages will then sound primarily like songs which simply differ less sharply than usual from parlando. Certainly, an artefact is not a doughnut with batter and filling, least of all in the case of the later, through-composing Wagner. But on a first hearing, the doughnut image is undoubtedly better and more helpful than that of a tedious conveyor-belt. With internal cuts, then, the inexperienced visitor may and must enjoy the music at first almost as a sequence of 'numbers'; let us not make these things too difficult for him. Anyway, we must dispose of the uniformly thick sauce of which Wagner is often accused. The ear abhors gluttony and constantly savours distinctions.

THE QUESTION OF BEL CANTO

Bel canto remains unbearable because the singer never desists from shrieking. This is a mistake on his part, a bad habit which leads to shrillness or jaggedness. Apart from some barren stretches of speechsong like Wotan's narrations, in an almost unvaryingly deep register, Wagner's music lends itself to a perfectly melodious delivery. At first it was considered unsingable, and while this notion has long been quashed, it is still considered not really lyrical, i.e. alien to any Italian school of singing. The great sopranos like to yell scoldingly and shrilly, while the great tenors favour a heated and menacing bellowing. Clearly shaped and distinctly gradated tone, a well-prepared rise

149

and fall, subsiding and soaring: such things are seldom instilled in Italian-schooled singers of Wagner. Rather we still have, though maybe in a smoother manner, the bellowing followed by the pompous tone – which is a pointless nuisance. There is a great difference in the same men and women as soon as they perform Mozart, even Verdi; we really cannot skim over this, as any repetiteur worth his salt will confirm. No doubt Wagner himself is partly to blame for these heated and lowering voices and also, in some instances, for their falsely ingenuous cello-like tone, but he did not provide the cue for this school's prevalent manner, or mania. Besides the striving for a more southern bel canto, his works offer enough of the 'song of the nightingale, and tone of red and blue and green,' as David sings in the *Mastersingers*, for the music to be articulated and refined from that angle. If people could sing Wagner more as Lotte Lehmann sang his Wesendonck Lieder, there would be less pedal all round and the shrieking would end. Another pointer comes from the songs of Hugo Wolf, which are very close to Wagner, but not the rhetorical Wagner that singers have cultivated. And what holds true for the singer's delivery applies similarly to the violins, winds or timpani, for then they will no longer be out-shouted or indeed indulge in excessive noise themselves. For some time, moreover, good conductors down in the pit have been achieving a greater lightness and transparence than the suits of armour, the doughty heroes, up on the stage. They are assisted in this by the almost constant dance which protects the *Mastersingers* as an opera against corpulence and also against dragged tempi. They are also assisted by the subtle blending of the sound in all the mature works, and equally by the call for a clear polyphonic texture. There must be a chamber-music 'carpet' underneath; a conductor who smudges the music, blurs it with noise and beats on the drum with might and main is as much an enemy of this mature Wagner as he was of service to the conventional Wagner. Never is the need for delicacy greater than in handling the *Ring*, precisely because of the well-established dangers of the opposite treatment. For instance, an astonishing delicacy is needed, and needs to be heard, when an orchestral interlude like 'Siegfried's Rhine Journey' is swimming against a current as though riding with it, driven only by bliss. Where something with the elasticity of a trout manifests itself, it must be rhythmical and not like an armoured car, for lightness and suppleness cannot be achieved when the music is thickly coated. Equally, those often delectable intervallic changes in the chords require a crystal-clear transition and not the languorous wallowing often added by conductors. Thus a process of clarification is needed in all respects: the course that the real Wagner pursues through his song is ceremonial, but not ceremonious. Rather, an element of lightness and freshness is there for the finding – Moselle wine rather than tepid beer as far as one can make it so. This, among other things, will get rid of the false note so much cultivated by many false throats.

THE QUESTION OF THE PARADOXES

'Someone with much to offer will have something for everyone.'[2] This is a dubious saying, especially where the product shows markedly varying qualities which, as it turns out, go hand in hand. There are undoubtedly many vulgar passages in Wagner, and, from close to, the specialist registers surprise, while the layman clings rather to the old pearls. But even a layman is able to say that Wagner's trouvailles depend on their source. This is true not only of the song to the Evening Star, that banal but at any rate agreeable ballad; it is responsible to a far greater extent for the unedifying rowdyism heard in the cry of 'Hojotoho' or in Sachs's *Jerum* ['lawks!'] with the subsequent hammering. It applies even more to Siegfried's brutal forging songs as well as to all the sensational elements, which have been called music for the unmusical. This is one facet of Wagner and there is nothing we can do about it – least of all, of course, through bel canto. Our only advice (in case it is of any help) is that of Kaspar in *Der Freischütz*: 'A person with any sense doesn't notice that sort of thing at all.' And the specialist, followed by the layman, will attach less importance to this unregenerate character when he knows and recognises a far more predominant facet of Wagner, a Wagner whose ideas and methods are so thoroughly different from the vulgar mind's imaginings. Otherwise the uncultivated, and not only the cultivated, world, would hardly have put up such a strong resistance to Wagner; a predominance of Hojotoho would have made the running at once. Here, however, a subtle but powerful surprise element is greater than the through-composed element. Thus – and this concerns precisely the juxtaposition in Wagner of the commonplace with the astonishing – we find right next to Walther's Prize Song (also a kind of 'Evening Star' at bottom) nothing less than the music of Beckmesser. We refer not to his wretched serenade but many of his other, spiky, melodic lines and above all the music for his pantomime: music which would not be possible without these melodic lines of his, and which is one of the finest and most daring parts of the *Mastersingers*. It is – and this is already entirely contrary to our expectations – significantly more 'modern' and is swimming significantly more against the traditional current than is Walther's Prize Song. This is a mistake from a dramaturgical angle, but musically it is a decided paradox, and one which is irreconcilable not only with the vulgar element. Just what is this paradox meant to signify, set beside the device (so characteristic of Wagner) of the suddenly urgent, arresting musical glance from unexpected depths? It is particularly this esoterically paradoxical element which would have to be heard and illustrated in a far more trenchant way than outward show and grandeur (which need to be repressed): by an inconspicuous illumination and orientation. Take the famous chord in the Prelude to *Tristan* – how strongly charged it is with the shock of the foreign! Such is its nature that not even its key is unequivocally definable, and traditional harmonic concepts like passing chord, chromatic inflexion or suspension convey it only weakly. How often, too, another unresolved 'dissonance', i.e. 'dissonance' which is no longer a part of the harmonic framework, seems doubly surprising: as unforeseen as it is prophetic, almost an unexpected foretaste of composition which abandons the tonic! Take Brangäne's song from the tower, buoyantly extended over the rhythmic or even polyrhythmic unit as though separate, along with 'that ascent of the violins that passeth all understanding' (T. Mann). In its musical *ekstasis*, this goes against the fear and warning it signifies within the framework of the opera. 'Habet acht' is sung from up in the tower, and from this song, of Brangäne's warning, 'Lausch, Geliebter' is registered by Isolde in total contradiction to the song itself, though not to its slow, immeasurably long, arching lines, which do everything to suggest arrival. Likewise, it is time that we acknowledged a much stronger bewilderment, one of precisely this nature, on hearing Wagner than has been usual, our conventional response being prompted simply by the composer's mixture of the vulgar and sublime. When this bewilderment relates to the paradox deep in Wagner, to the fact that he is not timeless but is nonetheless untouched by fashion, it has nothing at all to do with the static established Wagnerism. But neither has it anything to do with the rejected cult insofar as this is always related only to estab-

152

lished responses. The emphatically bright passages strike up the unexpected quite overtly, beginning as early as the first bars of the *Rienzi* overture and extending as far as the 'Let there be light' C major theme of midsummer's day in the *Mastersingers* (a Midsummer Day's Dream, as Wieland Wagner puts it). And it is the emphatically dark passages, as it were, that bespeak really arcane things, as do the pitch-black augmented triads surrounding Alberich, and the Sleep motif, and indeed the 'mysterious ground of unfathomable depth' of which Tristan cannot tell Marke. This arcane quality of the 'one little word "and" ' is handled entirely as a paradox in the Tristan chord itself and specifically left on its wondrous sea-bed. Therefore it is not for us to elucidate the paradox of Wagner's erotic reversal of the will-to-life or indeed the pessimism of the *Twilight of the Gods* by constantly referring to Schopenhauer. For first, this whole connection has been known for many years and indeed has become too normal for it to be called a paradox in the sense of a surprise. Secondly, it is above all the least helpful place in which to look for this particular paradox of the Wagnerian depths, the paradox invoked for the purpose of renewing their work. The point at issue is rather the unexpected nature of the unforeseen-but-anticipatory, as cited. Hence our concern is the individual suddenness of *individual instances*, not the ostensible grandeur of the whole, not the stale bits of Schopenhauer to be found in Wagner and certainly not Wagner's 'religion of art', which is hardly uncommon. We are speaking of totally different things that are coming to light – even, frequently, of a counter-Wagner within the genuine Wagner. Especially these paradoxes in his work, while being episodic and indeed seemingly incidental, do affect some of the colossal surrounding elements or the all too glibly expounded mystery behind it. Certainly they will not remove the lurid colours produced by mere artifice, the stark colours accruing from mere theatrical effect, but these can acquire other nuances through the proximity of what has suddenly deviated from them and is quietly surprising. Wagner does not always achieve this, far from it, and perhaps seldom for longish stretches. Yet the *piano* voice of Siegfried when, in his fear, he perceives the calm surrounding Brünnhilde in the farthest distance, is still stronger than any number of garishly coloured trumpets with the theatrical din they make. At all events, it is now a question of musico-scenic subtleties with an expressive capacity, and pointing beyond any coherent framework of response one might normally expect. True, this kind of paradox is closely linked with the incipient collapse of bourgeois society and would not be possible without it. But precisely that is the source of its frequent change of approach, its sudden difference in expression, the very unforeseenness whereby a Wagner who had been all too clandestine obtained his freedom. The startling interruption plays an important role here, always supplying the paradox with the pattern.

Let us therefore, with some concern, transfer our attention to seemingly incidental episodes. These already appear with startling effect in *The Flying Dutchman*, indeed more so than in the two more mature operas which followed it. Certainly *Tannhäuser* and *Lohengrin* also have many incidental features which excite our sensibilities rather than blunt them. The relevant musical figures are small, altogether modest ones, but they certainly express something in passing. 'Tell me, where have you been so long?' – in reply to this somewhat foolish question from Elisabeth comes Tannhäuser's 'Far from here', and 'oblivion's cloud' appears. But around it we hear, beginning *ff*, incisive violas and cellos, diminuendo: seldom did Wagner succeed in saying so much so quickly. And in *Lohengrin* a very lofty word is set to music equally tersely and unconventionally to match the woman speaking and the far from equable situation. 'God? so you call your cowardice God?' cries the pagan Ortrud to her mediocre Telramund, and 'the word sounds terrible on her lips', that is, infernal. There is also a matching accompaniment of syncopated semiquavers with flutes and violins to hiss the viperish rebuke. But as we have suggested, all this special incidental material is not only broader but much more conscious and also more positive in *The Flying Dutchman*, for this earlier opera is more based on experience, more authentic, as it were, than the next two. Wagner discovered himself in the *Dutchman*: if he had died young and this had been his last music, we would see Wagner as raw and lonely and not at all theatrically-minded. The manner in which he incorporates the traditional song-form is entirely at one with the action, but it has a subtlety we can almost call charming. Take the song of the Steersman (falling asleep when he ought to be wide awake) and the matchmaking song of Senta's father (who surely has less cause for matchmaking than any other father). The contradiction between Daland's and his daughter's respective 'interest' in the Dutchman is already a paradox in itself, and immediately after the wanderer's entrance it makes itself felt in a weirdly comical fashion. 'If you agree with your father, he will be your husband tomorrow' – and Senta, captivated by the Dutchman and carried to him like a sleepwalker, 'moves with a painful jerk'. Daland produces a piece of jewellery and shows it to Senta: 'Is it not something you want, my dear? This will be yours if you exchange rings', and as he is beating a crafty retreat he sings: 'Mark my words, she is as faithful as she is lovely.' Whilst thus praising again the bait that Senta constitutes, he is singing of the same (as it were) 'fidelity unto death' which Senta wanted to maintain, in the demonic earlier ballad; – Daland rubbing his hands, in his calm little song, contrasted with the piercing final cry in Senta's ballad when the Dutchman really enters her soul. The effect of this cry is to convey a message in the best sense; but what is unique is the hush which follows Daland's departure and occurs in the music. Motionless, entirely apart and engaged in a soliloquy, though a twofold one, Senta and the Dutchman face each other, 'engrossed in the sight of the other person'. This long gaze recurs later, in *The Mastersingers*, between Eva and Stolzing in Sachs's workshop. But what is wordless in that scene becomes rapt song in the *Dutchman*, a 'wondrous dreaming' from the depths, reminiscent of *Tristan* in both words and music. 'This maiden's image speaks to me as though from distant, bygone times': the unaccompanied melody climbs boldly up to the ninth, proceeds to a half-close, then reverberates, turned enquiringly to the dominant. What a paradox compared to the operatic duet that would usually occur at this point! And how truly it sets the tone in the way it catches the shattering emotion which travels through the storm and against it, through the contrasting dance of the mariners with the first bar's huzzaing leap to the ninth, through the choruses of the final scene and their sudden change from mirth. At the start of these choruses there appears something else which is totally original, namely a curious echo of a thought, statement or cry that was never voiced. The maidens and sailors call across to the gloomy Dutchman's ship, stifling a rising terror with louder and louder shouts: 'Hey, mariners, give us an answer!' – whereupon there is a 'great stillness' with a solitary C sharp minor chord, *ppp*, long-held. Renewed shouting, increasingly loud and fearful: 'Mariners, mariners, won't you wake up!' – and 'long silence' with the solitary chord again, now in G minor – the answer as a non-answer, again wholly disparate, 'a different world'. At the end the fidelity theme tries to give the answer in the major, but does it in fact do so? The storm goes on raging, and it is within its confines that an uncanny harmony reigns.

It is not our purpose in this essay to record so-called musical pearls. But what does interest us – particularly in *The Mastersingers*, as we shall now see – are the many phrases like 'Now begin' of which these pearls consist. They transmit a sense of surprise even after repeated hearings, often a delight in the fragment, and an abundance of tricks, capers and subtleties that go against the ordinary grain. It is precisely *The Mastersingers*, that melancholy but basically serene work, which provides the most splendid surprise. Even in its sorrowful passages it is only speciously chromatic, being diatonic in a way that none of Wagner's other mature works is – a chalybeate bath in C major, as it was. called in its time, though tastelessly and exaggeratedly. For in spite of the very high degree of organisation, it is still just as rich in examples of the unexpected, in voices and moods which make up a polyphony that is not purely orchestral in nature. Amongst so much else, there is the aforesaid 'Now begin', first in Beckmesser's harsh and querulous tones and then the radiant tone of Walther, with the same fifth but in a brightly ascending F major after the covertly falling fifth in Beckmesser's A minor – a vernal call following a morose one. The same words could hardly be more contrasted in meaning, and the high has never seen off the low more neatly or cheerfully. ('Would that every stout fellow could find such bells', Pamina very rightly sings in *The Magic Flute*.) Then in the second Act we have Sachs's remarkable address to the elder-tree: ' . . . it calls on me to speak. But how am I to find the words? . . . 'twere better, my friend, to let me free.' The lilting, melting melody comes to an end, and the answer to the elder's prompting (all things are in search of their poet) exists only in a yearning melody, in fruitless mental attempts to retain, measure and reach that which Walther has sung. Then there is the splendidly ambiguous dialogue between Sachs and little Eva about the morning at the Song School, with the incessant quavers in the accompaniment and the sweet, apparently innocent, melody. Then a little later in front of the same house, after the onset of so much affliction, there is the difference in Walther himself. Hidden with Eva under the lime-tree, he reaches 'for his sword with an emphatic gesture' on hearing the Night Watchman's horn call, and the bugle's fortissimo is immediately followed by *musica dolce* with muted strings and Eva's line: 'Save your anger, my darling, it was only the Watchman's horn.' (T.W. Adorno rightly drew attention to the fact that there could be a reference to Don Quixote in Walther at this point. Elsewhere, too, we must not overlook this unreal streak in his character, which is unevenly heroic.) To return to Eva beneath the lime, in her surprising comments on Sachs's Paradise ditty: here a curious feminine change of feeling ensues. The ditty tells of the banished mother of mankind, who has to walk on gravel. 'What does he call you?' asks Walther, and Eva says: 'It isn't me, but there's malice behind it.' That is her first reaction, but after the second verse, which has the same theme, she observes: 'The song makes me sad', and after the third, with more intensity: 'The song gives me pain, though I don't know why', and the orchestra adds the Renunciation theme of – Hans Sachs. In passing from her first to her second reaction, however, Eva suddenly becomes hypersensitive to the feelings of Sachs: 'O finest of men, to think I can cause you such distress!' – again underlaid by alien-sounding motifs of renunciation. Later the music signifies a similar transformation – in fact an incognito and a curious ennobling – in the case of Beckmesser, at the end of Act 2 after the brawling and the Night Watchman's call. The theme of Beckmesser's little song ('I see the dawning daylight'), previously so pitiful-seeming, concludes the Act in thoroughly noble fashion, although a very calm tempo and syncopating pauses are the only changes. This is surely a major surprise of some complexity, and it may well be related to something which one would otherwise regard as a remarkable mistake. As noted above, the music for Beckmesser (minus his wretched 'Liedchen', though this proves to be adaptable, and minus his botched Prize Song at the close, though the text of this is extremely striking) is often finer and bolder than some of the music to do with Walther, particularly his ballooning Prize Song. Entirely contrary to expectations, the Beckmesser pantomime in Sachs's workshop exhibits the most interesting music in *The Mastersingers*, although it is meant to poke fun at this 'Jew in the bramble-bush', who thus represents a stain on Wagner's character. A flaw in Wagner – but what a notable purity there nearly always is in Sachs's musical character, compared with Beckmesser's oiliness and even Walther's, which is diminishing. When Walther blasts forth his showy Prize Song, first at rehearsal and then complete on the festival meadow, he almost resembles the 'Trumpeter of Säckingen'[3] instead of the genius at the beginning. In this region, of course, we have plenty of the familiar, all too familiar, Wagnerian *Heldentenor*, and it is not possible to rectify this, unfortunately, by always having the most modern musician compose the Prize Song afresh, so as to insert a different 'Now begin!' into the *Silentium* on the festival meadow. How constantly lacking in convention Sachs's music turns out to be when he is advising Stolzing, and how much the doctrine of the 'interpretation of visions' is purely this music's offspring! So too are the Castalian counsel on vanished dreams, 'Avail yourself now of poetry's art, which many have used to find what was lost', and the auroral words of solace, 'My hope remains as strong as ever, my heart could not be fuller, or else I would have not delayed your flight, but run away with you myself.' All this works towards the Song of the Morning Dream's Interpretation and its quintet, which has little connection with the Prize Song in this mode. Indeed where the Prize Song itself is concerned, we must distinguish between the out-and-out showpiece and the song that – starting with the first glimpse of Eva in church – is taking thematic shape and subsequently permeates the whole score with astonishing subtlety, as different from the showpiece as the first or second phases of Romanticism are from the third to go under that name, the pseudo-Gothic. And before, indeed whilst, the Prize Song is sung a second time in the cobbler's workshop, as a kind of dress rehearsal, its dubious brilliance illumines one of the most vibrant and paradoxical scenes to be enacted by the principal characters. At this precise point we have a repetition of the first scene between Senta and the Dutchman. For the moment that Walther steps into the doorway ('in a knight's shining costume', to be sure), Eva likewise 'lets out a cry and remains gazing fixedly at Walther', hearing nothing, unable to hear what Sachs is now at last telling her. He presents his suit, but in such a way that he can simultaneously say of Walther: 'Listen, my child, that is a Master Song', and indeed, still working all the while on Eva's little shoe: 'Now you can hear the like at my place.' He says this to Walther's truly marvellous octave descent (G–C–E–G) on 'Most hallowed scene', a motif which is so simple and yet conveys in a nutshell the whole radiance of the *Mastersingers* music, Prize Song or no Prize Song. And then comes the paradox in the irradiation of the feeling with which Eva had already entered the workshop. 'Master, there's no risk of that', with the exquisite melancholy of a *dolce* flute figure – in this fresh paradox, the spell of her enchantment is suddenly lifted. She does not fly to Walther, with whom she is in such close accord. On the contrary, 'she now bursts violently into tears, falls on Sachs's breast and clings sobbing to him'; at this point we hear Sachs's Renunciation motif, with which this Act's dark and taciturn prelude began. And the inwardly radiant quintet offers one version of the happy ending, with Wagner providing a unique objectivation of the ideal as both Sachs and Walther, while the festival meadow offers another version, the totally extroverted one. Moreover, the affinity between the quintet's 'dream of the highest glory' and the explicit spectacle of the festival meadow could not be more marked. Wagner secured this affinity through the rhythmically remarkable interlude music, which makes itself felt as the sheer negation of Night, the antithesis of *Tristan*, a communal Midsummer's Day. The back-stage horns and trumpets, placed at a distance and blown very lustily, make a thoroughly carnival-like, not at all 'arty', effect and herald the merriest finale ever composed. Its exposition takes on a fresh intensity time and again until it reaches the chorus 'Awake!' – at which point it starts to focus on the harassed Beckmesser and the successful Prize Song, as well as Sachs's somewhat too forcible apotheoses of German art (this is not the wise old Sachs, who never wears a uniform). But all the imperialistic strains are outweighed by a Handelian lustre, and it is this which holds the final paradox. So effectively has Wagner expanded an inherently private comedy that it is as though not a knight and burghers but a genius and a people are streaming into a shared ocean of C major – and have yet to perform this so well in reality.

There are numerous operas where the orchestra and then the singers sound different from what might be expected. Their music and words do not match, maybe because the former is striking out in completely different directions, maybe because the latter are too silly. Starting from *The Valkyrie*, Wagner pointed to Italian operas as examples of this; largely unfairly, particularly where Bellini and indeed Verdi are concerned. Of course he is quite right, unfortunately, in a few individual instances like 'A gipsy woman dreadful to behold' and its 3/4 accompaniment in *Il Trovatore*. In addition there is a curious sneer at coloratura, and not only at Meyerbeer's but also that of the great Baroque composers. This produces the caricature in Beckmesser's song, where words and music definitely do not match (there is the same broad melisma for 'erscheinen' and the little indefinite article 'einen'). Remarkably, however, this incompatibility is more constructively exploited in *Siegfried*, when – as never before – Wagner needs to express hypocrisy. Here the music does not disturb us in its departure from the text but turns into a new means by which we can really hear that one thing is being said and another meant, i.e. we hear both simultaneously. An example of this is the third scene in

Act 2 of *Siegfried*, where Mime's dulcet melody totally contradicts the words he thinks he is expressing. Siegfried, who now understands the voice of gallows-birds as much as the wood-birds, can hear behind Mime's ingratiating melody the real and completely different text ('I'll chop off the boy's head with a sword'). So here the exceptions to the congruence of words and music in Wagner are fraught with meaning. There are also instances where the music accompanying the words seems to be deliberately inappropriate in a manner that is not simply perverse or devious. This is particularly so in merry scenes or scenes which feign merriment. Take for example – to leave Wagner for a moment – the students' drinking song from the beginning of *The Tales of Hoffmann*, an Offenbach opera where music and words are repeatedly at odds. With its 'Vive la compagnie', the drinking-song has an infernal urgency and is thus a complete exaggeration of the immediate text. No less exaggerated, despite an aura far removed from the inferno, is the light in the music at the entry of the Mastersingers, after the apprentices' dance. For to present such bakers, cobblers, tailors as heavenly hosts is totally incongruous. Indeed we can venture the paradox that our ears and minds will fail to register a straightforward matching of music and words far more often in Wagner than in Italian opera, although this again is precisely because of the expression, which is by no means confined to one level. The leitmotif itself, which is used above all in the *Ring*, fundamentally signifies this plurality of expression between music and words. Its relation to the text is – as we are about to show – partly less than simultaneous, i.e. in the nature of a reminiscence, but occasionally also more than simultaneous, i.e. anticipatory. And this happens particularly in the *Ring*, otherwise so immediate in its effect: the one mature work which, with its bass tubas and *Heldensoprane*, has chiefly determined the standard idea of Wagner's music. Here the verbal language lays itself wide open to an orchestra that is always roaming through the accents of pathos, and this orchestra finds scope for various layers of meaning in just such language. Now and then, admittedly, there is no intelligibly unified text that could lend itself to a musical expansion at all (we need only mention a sentence like 'Glühender Glanz entgleitet dir weihlich im Wag' – 'Glowing splendour escapes from you hallowedly . . . '). Yet, for the most part, ignoring pre-Heideggerian bombast of this kind, between the Rhinemaidens and the Rhinegold, the *Ring* provides such immense opportunities for placing musical emotion far around the word, or in the interstices of the compressed text and its colossal action. Again it is not a matter of 'pearls' but of the paradoxical, which is now carrying on its indirect activity as a kind of para-text. When Sieglinde wonders where she has already seen the guest, the beloved, and has heard his voice, which resembles her own, she sings 'and now I perceive it again' – a song ebbing and flowing in pure chromaticism and quite unexpectedly heightening the style of the expected spring rejoicing which comes before and after. Then in Act 2 of *The Valkyrie* we have Brünnhilde's annunciation of Siegmund's death in notes and rhythms which seem to have forced their way into the text from a different world. The motionless Siegmund and Sieglinde are cowering gloomily and helplessly between the rock-faces, vulnerable almost as a couple of emigrants; the Love motif makes a very lonely sound, and there is profound silence. On the side hidden from them, Brünnhilde appears Athena-like, visible to the audience before she is visible to Siegmund, and it is only with a drowsy, stiff movement that he turns in response to her call. Also, the song in which he questions Brünnhilde is stiffly syncopated in a wholly peculiar way, being as rigid as his movement and relentlessly insistent. The Fate motif resounds, that same motif which is heard when, much later on, Siegfried dies; and, mingled with it in a long-range correspondence which is an astonishing surpassing of what the text can do, are the triplet figures of the funeral march in the *Twilight of the Gods*. Even before his battle, Siegmund is as irredeemably dead as his son Siegfried will one day be. But at the same time, Wagner now unexpectedly takes a leaf out of Beethoven's book. In his behaviour, Siegmund is the most wide awake, freest and least conformist of all the *Ring* heroes, in contrast to Siegfried who is merely 'free' in the sense of a child of Nature. For since Brünnhilde cannot conduct Sieglinde to Valhalla as well, Siegmund does not accept Valhalla's 'freely given bliss' but disdains it – with a statement of the Fate motif in the major which only occurs in this passage – as one who is still living and not confounded even by a death-blow from Wotan. Here we are witnessing in action a part of Beethoven's moral will, that *Quos ego!*, in the midst of figures otherwise driven by impulse, among those *Ring* heroes resembling 'bobbing ships that experience not their character and their musically glowing subject-core but the universal wave of the Schopenhauerian Will washing over them at every critical moment';[4] T.W. Adorno's study [translated as *In Search of Wagner*, 1981] has also acknowledged this particular point. And we cannot fail to hear, of course, the pianissimo with which Brünnhilde – before she herself is turned into a rebel by Siegmund's supremely humane resistance – depicts Valhalla, i.e. in notes very close to humanity, very much lacking in oceanic surges. Here we have noble acceptance, in a virtually Christian-Catholic act of choice, 'with the holiest greeting' – a marvellously simple song, diatonically and quietly subsiding to the tonic that rounds everything off. But the existence of such a palm-branch amid the battling-will is already part of that irradiation of the feelings in which the paradoxical passages in *Siegfried* and *The Twilight of the Gods* are especially rich. Thereupon fresh paradoxes arise, paradoxes which are truly dialectical, deriving from the root idea's antithesis. And Wagner expressed this irradiation of the feelings, or their mutual inner illumination, in beguiling mixtures of orchestral sound, in a curiously pleasant use of the strongest dissonance and in Janus-like leitmotifs. This, understandably, may have prompted Baudelaire's love of this music, and not just because it was 'bizarre' any longer but precisely because it was properly that of a – montage. A salient example of this emotional irradiation occurs in *Siegfried*. When Mime wants to teach Siegfried the meaning of fear, the latter hears, played very quietly, the Fire motif and within it the distant Brünnhilde who is wholly unknown to Siegfried, i.e. a blending of the still completely unknown love with the fear. Her quivering musical image, the chromatically raging semiquavers of Mime's cries and his terror are reserved, for Siegfried, in love ('That must be the strangest of feelings') as though it were the dolcissimo of fear. And, finally, another and quite perfect example of the later identity of the most contrary emotional expression with that which it reveals is found in the Awakening motif (E minor, C major triad) for Brünnhilde and the dying Siegfried. Once upon a time, Siegfried drank the drink of oblivion mixed for him by Hagen, and the demonic power of this drink has the penetrating effect of completely dispelling Siegfried's memory of Brünnhilde just when her name is mentioned; the Oblivion motif is like a ringing sepulchre. But after some ghastly deceit, the handing over of Brünnhilde and the scandalous wedding with Gutrune, Hagen again seasons the same drink for Siegfried, the unwitting perjurer, during the hunt in the Odenwald. And just as the disenchanted Siegfried, his memory restored, his body pierced by Hagen's spear, is about to confront death, we now hear for the second time the same Awakening motif, in the same key of C major and again with the splendid shift to the D minor triad, which had, with the utmost solemnity, conducted Brünnhilde's awakening to the light, to life and the highest form of existence. Yet now, in an identity of the non-identical, the same motif sounds for Brünnhilde's kiss as for the kiss of death. With this ultimate identity of light and death (which is quite different to the Night of the *Liebestod*), we have reached what is perhaps the profoundest paradox in Wagner's musical expression. And it is repeated *suo modo* within the ensuing Funeral March, which recalls the structure of Beethoven's, in its central rejoicing beyond all reason. This funeral march has no validity for Siegfried and Brünnhilde, its middle, where the stage is shrouded in mist, being rather a continuation in a radiant C major of the awakening on Siegfried's arrival. At the same time the previous motif of Awakening, which presents the gateways to morning and evening as so identical, has not even used cryptically ambiguous chords. The Awakening occurs in completely transparent triads – mysteriously in full daylight. And after the grandeur of the concluding song in *The Twilight of the Gods*, which is the most polyphonic of monologues in more senses than one, the end of the work entails another paradox. It is paradoxical in that by virtue of its Redemption theme's constant arching motion, its perspective motion, it never comes to an end at all; notwithstanding the resolved triads and the final fortissimo blow, diminuendo. The primordial stream of sound with which the tetralogy began in *Rhinegold* and which was intended to be the start of all things does not dry up in the towering finale of *The Twilight of the Gods*. Although Brünnhilde has previously sung 'Descend, O twilight of the gods, let the night of ruin fall', the *Ring* music's Awakening, Rapture and Redemption-by-Love themes continue regardless in this concluding night, even as they break off. The Redemption motif at the end of the *Twilight of the Gods*, though weak in melodic propulsion, has much too great a resonance to constitute an end: it is rather the paradox of a repetition that opens up a new vista.

In two Wagner operas which are not operas, everything conspires from the outset to instil a feeling of bewilderment, so to speak. In *Tristan* it is in fact easier to hear the unusual than the conventional. Here the unusual is conveyed by the night and also the daytime Night, which is opposed to the day. Night, the womb of Love, is itself the complete reverse of the daytime law and indeed disparate to it: propriety and honour, tiller and anchor are all lacking as Tristan's ship sails through this storm. The dualistic *Parsifal*, admittedly, does not flout convention in this way, but it has for its location the mount of Monsalvat, vigorously removed from anything conventionally heterogeneous and split into the most violent alternatives. On the Arabic side there is Klingsor's magic garden (a demonicised Tristan-world); on the Gothic there is the temple of the Holy Grail, first darkened, then cleansed of sin. Despite the copious use of familiar associations (a second Hörselberg on the one hand, a second Lohengrin on the other, azure images of asceticism), *Parsifal* again represents the arcane. This is immediately seen in the radical contrast between the northern and southern sides of the mountain and especially in the character of Kundry, who belongs to both sides. The *Tristan* music is, certainly, the more paradoxical on the whole, its expression being caught up in its persistent chromaticism. Right at the start we have the complex '*Tristan* chord' of the Prelude, a chord whose key is hard to determine. Arithmetically speaking, it comes as an altogether awkward fraction. It constitutes a hieroglyph of yearning and of the 'and' linking two people through their mutual perception of the other, and waxing in the advancing night even as it is drowning, foundering. There are constant hiatuses in the course of an 'action' of this kind; after the love potion for Tristan and Isolde, steeped in Night music, everything is heard, and indeed seen, differently. The flaming torch was left for Tristan to find the way to his beloved, but Isolde extinguishes it for the self-same reason, as an 'intimidating light'. Brangäne perceives the horn fanfare from the nearby hunt merely at its face value as C major jostles with F major, but when Isolde is listening, the horns are replaced by violins, *una corda*. First there is the sound of rustling leaves and then of a stream trickling in the nocturnal hush: 'What did I hear?' Isolde asks, 'was that the horns again?' Also part of this continual inversion of meaning (a *compunctio cordis* through the language of love) is the blissful way in which Tristan and Isolde hear Brangäne's warning, contrary to the sense of the words. The world is flooded by miraculous song, and this exhorts reason through its words, which are of the Day, but not through the Night of this *melos* with its series of very remote sounds and arching lines of mystical silver, which do in effect pass all understanding. Moreover the Prelude to Act 3 and the ensuing music up to Isolde's Liebestod turns every consonance of 'Descend upon us, night of love' into a fresh construing of the *Tristan* chord, during the time the hero lies mortally wounded, and up to the hypostatised *and* between Tristan and Isolde in their mutual 'divinely everlasting, primordial oblivion'. A musical nirvana, identifiable with the orgasm – this twofold sense of physical release in the music of Isolde's Liebestod furnishes a paradox which, even in the Romantic death-longing, with its arctic sultriness, is by no means clearly evident, least of all where the present musical characters are concerned. Admittedly there is an excess of the art of consonance in this *Ars moriendi*. For Isolde's Liebestod almost sounds like a kind of transportable concert piece and actually falls short of the sombre, tender Prelude to this Act with the shepherd's lament on the cor anglais and Tristan's tale of universal oblivion and remembrance [*Allvergessen-Eingedenken*]. Yet the linking in this vocal finale of eros and nirvana, and even of nirvana and brahma ('in the world-breath's drifting universe'), by virtue of 'the billowing sea, the ocean of sound' is unique because it never denies the will-to-life, despite Schopenhauer's influence on the music. Consequently all the instruments apart from the elegiac cor anglais are involved in the final chord of the work: Wagner extracts that much richness from the drifting motion. The searching and longing in tranquillity and the wholly successful 'shrouding in noble darkness' that irradiates the action are still stronger than a negation; Wagner's music does not reach a nirvana which lacks ardour. And so the *Tristan* chord's yearning – though with its value completely reversed, of course – once again becomes a dramatis persona in *Parsifal*. This opera, however, because it admits of no continuation into the never-ending, is formally rounded off, does come to an end. In this respect *Parsifal* is, *praeter opinionem*, a far more secular piece of music-theatre than *Tristan* and even the *Ring*. With its final visual representation of a festival meadow of the highest order it is, along with the *Master-singers*, the most worldly of Wagner's major works. All of it is embedded in the kind of eclectic holiness that sought to introduce a Catholic temple of freemasonry and to combine the idea of 'redemption for the Redeemer' with the most rampant Puritanism. The composer takes the place of the priest. The stage becomes the altar for a Christian-Buddhist-Rosicrucian religion of art, or art of religion, Venus-Erda-Brünnhilde receives the rites of baptism, and Siegfried turns into a monk.

To concentrate now on this final opera, it is not the finest of all, but certainly the strangest opera. Here again the Prelude begins with an outright longing and searching, homophonically in tautly syncopated motion. After it has reached the octave there is a grief-laden inversion, and the music climbs anew to the closing note, which is sounded twice. But how significant that the same theme, a thoroughly unhappy-sounding one, later becomes thoroughly reassuring as the theme of the Love Feast! The Prelude itself, in spite of the calmly and very powerfully unfolded Faith motif at its centre, ends questioningly with an unresolved dominant; the resolving tonic only comes later, after the raising of the curtain. But then, the Trans-formation music in Act 1 is meant to lead to something completely different from the mere *temporal* sounding of the tonic. Starting as Gurnemanz is about to indicate the temple to Parsifal, the simple Fool, it glides imperceptibly at first and grows more and more diatonic, indeed homophonic, in construction. Then come Parsifal's words, 'I move apace', and Petrus Gurnemanz replies: 'Thou seest, my son, here time is one with space.' This extremely curious sentence – set over lines of woe (leading to Amfortas, the infirm Lord of the Grail), the sound of incessant steps, summoning bells, Grail harmonies and the summons to awake – has, apart from its own specific significance, a meaning that applies to the whole relationship between the music and the stage-picture in the two outer Acts of *Parsifal*. The specific meaning of the statement is that what is in repose spatially, especially as an achieved state, is set above the step forward in time and indeed seeks to accelerate it, but, upon finding it, slows it down. In the temple of the Grail itself, time acquires its own tempo. It yields to a stratified juxtaposition and hence vertical piling-up until it attains an almost motionless state of presence in simultaneity, which is what the achieved space of the temple is. Thus on the road to the Supper, the Love Feast, Parsifal's forward stride and that of the shield-bearers, knights and attendants are swiftly transformed into the present dimension. Moreover, the forest occupying simply the foreground vanishes. A doorway opens up in the rock-face, stage trombones take up the Quest motif in a shortened and changed form, without the grief-laden inversion, and the columned hall of the Gralsburg appears, a dome-shaped vault emerging purely from archaic, Gregorian song. This also reveals to us the second meaning of the curious statement, viz. that which relates not to a change of *time* into *space* but to a change of *music* into a *stage-picture*. In the outer Acts of *Parsifal*, Wagner no longer mixes the sounds of the instruments and voices but handles them essentially in layers, with clearly delineated themes and frequently a terraced choric structure. Despite the archaising, the ancient style, Wagner's handling of time was inherently a supremely *dynamic* art. The layering was intended to convert it into a hieratic spatial arrangement, the particularly movement-free arrangement of a Byzantine main hall with a cupola. Thus Wagner not only wanted to connect the musical sound with the *theatron*, the art of theatre (which was the largely dilettantish object of a so-called *Gesamtkunstwerk*). He planned, furthermore, to convert it into pure symmetries of space partly by having dynamic rhythm yield to a more chorale-like rhythm and also the rhythm of a slow march, but above all through the layered grouping of the parts. It reminds us of the mythical Amphion, who constructed Thebes in accordance with the harmonies of his singing. This legend aside, there is the physical reality of the Chladnian sound-figures which form themselves out of powder on a glass when stroked, a reality which seemed to render tonal relationships so peculiarly cosmic or at least graphic in the Romantic philosophy of music, or at any rate in Schelling's (and Schlegel's thesis of architecture as frozen music belongs in this domain). At all events – the second meaning of the surprising statement about time and space is realised by music in the spatial dimension occupied by the architecture housing the Grail. This clearly distinguishes the birth of the stage-picture out of transformation music's professed magic from the purpose of the conventional transformation scene such as is found in Weber's *Oberon* and even in *Rhinegold*, where Wotan and Loge are both heard and seen to descend to Alberich. But the harmonic structure is abruptly shattered in Act 2 of *Parsifal*, just where the action shifts from the *temple building* to the Arabic, the *harem side* of Monsalvat, in Klingsor's magic garden. After a wild introduction we hear Klingsor's cry and his chromatic motifs of menace, all of which are to be treacherously softened and suffused with warmth in the magic garden, in the ravishingly tender sounds of the Flower Maidens and in Kundry's Venus song. Then, precisely at this juncture, there comes a blow through a totally surprising event, again representing a unity composed of opposites. Parsifal detects in Kundry's amorous kiss the wound of Amfortas . . . a shrill chromatic descent. With this abrupt initiation, Wagner intended Parsifal to discover not only the spell cast on the Grail but the full calamity of Venus's worldly snare. Admittedly Kundry herself, hunted through all womankind in a transmigration of souls, laughing and despairing, is more inexhaustible than Parsifal as a musical character; but it is Parsifal who, at the most ecstatic moment, is instantly struck by its reverse meaning. Seldom did a totally different element emerge from a smooth sequence of events with the vividness it has here, though – in contrast to *Tristan* – it does so within the well-known proportions of Schopenhauerian-Buddhist nay-saying. Now Parsifal is Tristan's counterpart and indeed an anti-Tristan, as well as a Siegfried in monk's robes. And by the same token, the Kundry-Parsifal relationship in Wagner's last work signifies a retraction of the first of his cardinal musical relationships, that between Senta and the Dutchman. It is not now the restless man who is redeemed by a faithful woman who has fallen under his spell, but the Lilith in every woman who is converted and baptised through a holy-minded man – only in *Lohengrin* do we find this much patriarchal feeling in music so extensively feminised. Just as woman is overcome, so is the power of strongly coveted possessions including, as was shown in the *Ring*, the Nibelung hoard and Valhalla. The curse of the hoard is lifted in the golden glow of the Grail, whose effulgence no longer resembles that of a Rhine-gold submerged in the pagan depths but emanates from heavenly alleluias. And the effect, as it were, that the temple of the Grail is meant to produce, is that of a Valhalla cleansed of sin, Wotan-Amfortas having been saved and restored to order. Only here do heroes meet, as the valkyrie Brünnhilde sang, 'with the holiest of greetings'. This occurs not in a Buddhist but rather in a Catholic sense, and then in a Reformed-Protestant spirit, as in the final 'redemption for the Redeemer', viz. the redemption of Christ from the dross of Church spectacle by means of a – *Bühnenweihfestspiel* [staged sacred festival play]. But in *Parsifal* the genuine paradoxes are salient ones, and particularly those which concern Kundry in her ranging from shrieks to whimperings, from the song of Venus to Good Friday magic. Even the 'Good Friday magic' itself, that rare and curious manifestation of a Christian Nature-music, is entirely the Wagner who specialises in the unforeseen, representing nonconformity.

THE QUESTION OF THE 'OMNISCIENT' LEITMOTIF

When a composer has a capacity for surprising the listener, he will also desire to provide a real sense of familiarity at other points. From time to time Wagner writes passages where the listener feels he is being securely guided. The familiar outline of a leitmotif materialises to play the host, admittedly only for a brief while, but impressively. Some would also say 'importunately'; instead of guidance they sense a hammering away, and instead of a hand, a prodding forefinger. This can even be felt from the behaviour of Wagner's musical heroes, however illustrious and full of virtuous purity. 'You must never question me', intones the motif, and time after time it insists: 'Elsa, did you hear that?' – with the result that even the listener feels that Lohengrin is admonishing as much as guiding him. Where condemnation of the leitmotif is concerned, there are also more up-to-date comparisons in the context of music considered as consumer goods. For the leitmotif now presents itself as a trademark and indeed, because it depends on repetition, as a prelude to modern advertising. And if this is going too far (it borders on insolence to associate Wagner with a formidable slogan like 'Persil washes whiter'), the fact remains that Stravinsky compared the leitmotif to a cloakroom ticket and Debussy the *Ring*, where the examples multiply, to an address book. In his essay *Opera and Drama*, of course, Wagner called his leitmotifs 'plastic elements of feeling', 'pillars of the dramatic edifice' from whose 'harmoniously ordered mutual recurrence even the highest unified musical form' would arise 'wholly of its own accord'. He was not suggesting a pedagogic rule or crutch of any kind; it all lay within the objective area of the form of the work. And contrary to later Bayreuth practice, he never thought of giving every leitmotif a fixed name, a name often so dubious and stereotyped. He would have been alarmed by traces of Mastersinger attitudes ('There seems no end to the code!' – 'Those are merely the names; now learn to sing them the way the Masters prescribed'). But Wagner would have probably accepted comparisons between the acoustical *déjà vu* which is the essence of his leitmotif and what Goethe called 'repeated mirroring' or indeed even, on the grand scale, the concordance passages in the Lutheran Bible. The matter in question goes a long way back historically and yet, as we need to establish from the start, it is something new of Wagner's or at least something he transformed in a very personal way. It already begins in the typical flourishes with which people sang about love, or hate, in the old Singspiel. Furthermore the same figure was often played by the strings or winds at the entrance of a valet, maidservant or old man. The Samiel motif in *Der Freischütz* is a 'characteristic' recurring theme, and the Death motif in *Carmen* also has more to do with this than with Wagner's dynamic model. But the distinctly arresting version, one that has a spell attached to it, is found in Berlioz in his *Symphonie fantastique*, in the theme of the *idée fixe* that crops up again and again in the various movements. All this, however, is still arbitrary allusion in part. What is lacking is a genuinely strict recapitulation (with which Wagner has been credited by common consent), and this certainly derives from the classical sonata. The two or more themes of the symphony in sonata form can always be recognised again in the development section, and the conclusion is obliged to repeat the first theme in full, in the same key. The Prelude to the *Mastersingers* is almost completely sonata-like in structure, with the C major of the Mastersingers theme returning in triumph. Indeed people endeavoured to explain all Wagner's other reprises, particularly those in the *Ring*, from musical symmetries which were supposed to correspond in this way to classical sonata structure. It is reported that Bruckner, having closed the curtain of his box at the opera, believed he could hear the entire *Valkyrie* – including all the vocal parts, of course – purely as a symphony (not as the advertised 'music-drama'). And what was the great, creative exception became the rule – precisely with regard to leitmotifs and their reprise – for musical theorists in their attempts to dissociate Wagner from music-drama as much as Wagner had dissociated himself from opera. In his book *Von Grenzen und Ländern der Musik*, August Halm claimed that at least Act 1 of *The Valkyrie* with its handful of settled motifs had the effect of a colossal sonata movement. According to this view, the return of the leitmotifs always recalled the thematic placing in a classical sonata. Halm put forward this theory in spite of the expressive specificity of many of these motifs, and also despite the fact that Wagner's very leitmotifs reproduce authentic 'motives', as they have been called since olden days, i.e. reasons for actions. And they do so within a conceptual framework which is not that of sonata technique but is nonetheless ruled by musical laws, viz. a musico-dramatic framework. In the four volumes of his study of form in Richard Wagner, Alfred Lorenz attempted something far more radical: the extension of structural links not only to individual Acts but to Wagner's works in their entire breadth. Taking the basic elements, i.e. the leitmotifs, supported by a special type of variation, we then have the arch form, which is meant to correspond to the classical rondo, and above all the form of the *Bar* with its *Stollen* (as they are specifically called in the *Mastersingers*) and recapitulatory *Bar*; when the *Stollen* become polythematic, this form is claimed to be synonymous with classical sonata form. Again, it is of course a great exaggeration blithely to equate Wagner's use of the leitmotif with the thematic development and recapitulation in a symphony in sonata form, and therefore to assume that the latter will ultimately eclipse it – an assumption which is totally form-oriented and ignores the device's significance. It is right and commendable to recognise the leitmotif as an eminently musical 'component' once more, instead of an advertisement or cloakroom ticket. But this must never lead us into underestimating its specifically Wagnerian significance, i.e. into reducing it to the level of traditional symphonic procedures. According to Lorenz, all that matters is what Wagner *does* with his leitmotifs, his 'components'. While being 'equal to the promptings of the will in the action' in some mysterious way, they are, he maintains, basically only there for the purpose of 'constructing a symphony supported by singers and orchestra according to purely musical laws'. In all these reductions, instructive though they are in respect of Wagner's handling of his motifs (which is primarily symphonic, and dramatic only therein), there is still too much equating of the leitmotif with 'absolute music' and indeed treatment of it as a mathematical figure. In *The Decline of the West*, Spengler lent considerable fuel to this argument, not least in his separation of leitmotif and text. And he likewise suppressed the special, signifying, character of these 'components' in favour of something with the inherent character of a variation or transformation. Thus Spengler compared the composer's use of the leitmotif with the numerical diversity in advanced functional theory, 'in which groups of transcendent structures undergo changes that similarly bring out the invariability of certain form elements all the more clearly'. Here Spengler is manifestly using an analogy which is destructive rather than illuminating – destructive because the genuine character of the leitmotif is lost in the process. This extremely forceful device is not entirely definable as a formal element, nor is it 'invariable' in the mathematical sense, despite its relative constancy. Therefore the leitmotif really does have a special purpose in Wagner, i.e. a purpose that is not only expressive and functional in the symphonic sense. The historical analogies themselves make this clear. Similarly, neither the leitmotif's reduction to a trademark nor even its equation with the themes of a sonata on the plane of absolute music (to say nothing of functional theory) exhausts its significance. When it becomes importunate, the leitmotif certainly takes part in capitalist (and not only capitalist) advertising. But is it still an aural advertising of this kind on the many occasions that it conveys a meaning *without insistence?* Certainly, in its development and recapitulation the leitmotif does show its distinguished connections to its precedents, and especially to sonata themes and what they undergo; but does a sonata theme have the leitmotif's range of significant *cross-reference?* We can safely say that this is not so. And we can say with equal safety that Wagner's music with all its special variations and enharmonic changes, above all its motivic concordances, is something other than the development of themes. Although it is very much the music that dictates the action here, the action did influence its conception. The musical element, of course, still has priority and primacy, but the result is an amalgam separating Wagner's music from absolute music, even in the wordless preludes and interludes. Not only is the leitmotif transparent in relation to the text from the angle of its own tonal dwelling-place; it is also, in contrast to the sonata theme, itself metaphorical. And for that very reason there is even a reflection of this metaphorically highly charged quality in what we might call poetic leitmotifs, again in the metaphorical sense. For imaginative literature too is familiar with the musical motion of a submerging and re-emerging, an intermittent recurrence and concord, almost like a Sleep or Fire or Rapture motif and just as full of allegory. Examples of such poetic leitmotifs are the garden in Theodor Storm's *Viola Tricolor* or the little rainbow plate in Gottfried Keller's *Martin Salander*, as indeed are the symbolical cross-references contained in 'biting cold', 'the fair-haired people and their hide-out', 'Hetaera esmeralda' and so on in Thomas Mann's *Doctor Faustus*. It was in a similar fashion that Wagner manipulated his musical leitmotifs, which are stationary and yet pervasive, constituting the paradox of an energetic point of rest, as it were. That is why in the surroundings of these leitmotifs, his work bears the ornate features of the ancient River Meander, twisting back on itself and flowing onwards at the same time. And a point given hardly enough attention so far is that the meandering nature of the Wagnerian leitmotif asserts itself, as we are about to show, not only as a reminiscence, with a *retrieving regression*, but also as a foreshadowing, with an *accelerating anticipation*.

The leitmotif is most widely known, indeed almost solely known, as a reminiscence. Unconscious, *forgotten chords* within the dramatic character are touched and struck, often only in a flash and for a fleeting moment. And this is not just a subjective recollection: a situation from the past emerges, suggested by the music. It need not have arisen long ago – 'The poem? I left it here', says Hans Sachs, glancing at the work-bench from which it has vanished, and we hear Walther's air. Generally, however, the situation from the past lies some distance below the threshold of consciousness, some distance in the past, and announces itself from there. Then it will be announced only in the orchestra, which lies below the actor and the stage. 'Empty it lay before me, my father was not there', sings Siegmund to Sieglinde in Act 1 of *The Valkyrie*, and *ppp* in the very far distance, the trombones strike up the Valhalla motif, with a pause upon the last note which gazes backwards, as it were. In speech and action, the text being sung on the stage is in a totally different place from that of the musical leitmotif. Hence there very often occurs a statement which, though heard all at once, is located in two places – a non-simultaneity in one and the same moment. James Joyce is reported as having developed his technique of the 'interior monologue' under the influence of this two-tiered statement; so extensive, then, is the 'psychoanalysis' of the leitmotif as an agent of recollection and of an objective return to the past. And the regressive leitmotifs undoubtedly predominate in Wagner, particularly in the later sections of the *Ring* cycle, which are built mainly from older motivic material. After all, even the shattering arrival of the Awakening motif in Siegfried's last moment on Earth is a reprise of the motif for Brünnhilde's awakening. Of course a quite different and colossal quality is, as we observed above, added to it in the process: but then, as now, there was the overlapping unity of a metaphysical awakening. And, moreover, by virtue of the fact that the opening of Brünnhilde's eyes to life foreshadows the opening of Siegfried's to death, it is also possible for us to discover the *different character* of some leitmotifs, namely their *anticipatory* character. This relates to a distance in a forward direction, lest it should escape us, and it consists not of exertions of the unconscious but auguries of what is in store. These auguries are particularly fresh where the leitmotif's 'plastic element of feeling' is still emerging, at least for the character in question, and that is why it presents itself in an allusive or fragmentary way. We have already singled out the passage about fearing in Act 1 of *Siegfried* as making this kind of allusion, to something that cannot possibly be already known to the character but is nonetheless anticipated. 'Especially strange this must be', sings

Siegfried with a very timid telepathic awareness of love, and to guide him, the Fire motif is heard around the Brünnhilde rock before him. This music, of course, has already been played, in the last Act of *The Valkyrie*, but there are also leitmotifs in Wagner which first take shape with their associated idea, pristine and unfinished. Among these are Walther's burgeoning Dream Song – soon, unfortunately, to be his Prize Song – at his first glimpse of Eva and the hint of Sachs's resigned *Wahn* motif when Eva exclaims 'The song gives me pain, though I don't know why' in Act 2 of *The Mastersingers*. Another is the Death chord, as yet lacking awareness, at whose fortissimo Isolde throws the torch to the ground, where it goes out. There is also the tentative Love motif when Sieglinde first consciously looks at Siegmund. Above all there is a ravishing utopian power behind the veritable leitmotif-aurora surrounding Brünnhilde's proclamation of the child to whom Sieglinde, who will have to be rescued, is to give birth. Here the Siegfried motif sounds for the still unborn child; and when Sieglinde is subsequently praising her rescue, we already hear the strongly resonant, echoing motif of universal destruction and redemption which will then shroud the last bars of *The Twilight of the Gods* in futurity once more. Also in this category is the prophetic leitmotif in Wotan's 'grand design' in *Rhinegold*, before the entrance into the fortress, when the trumpets suddenly play a C major theme, Siegmund's and Siegfried's later Sword motif. It is the signal – however calamitous – for the intrepid coming hero, the longed-for future breaker of the spear and destroyer of the old world. And when – often very much later – such motifs are fulfilled and recur, it may sometimes appear – and this applies to the destruction and redemption motif at the end of the *Twilight of the Gods* – as though, for their mystical quality's sake, they were still in the process of being born. Only Mahler followed this particular precedent by having themes still in the process of taking shape, scattered signals, melismatic despatches from a distant headquarters. How often Beethoven gives us those remarkable bars where the music is being charged dynamically and harmonically, producing a march like the one in the finale of the Ninth Symphony, where something ineffable is indicated and on the point of arriving, but not yet emerging from its untold spaces! Lastly, another type of anticipatory motif in Wagner is the leitmotif that calls something forth, conjures it up. One example is the magnificent Erda motif (Klingsor's motif being its demonic counterpart): here time did not become one with space, but it does turn into the magic of space. *Vivant sequentes*, we can say as a whole of Wagner's use of the *anticipating* leitmotif. As Mahler too shows, the theme still in the process of taking shape stands, in music's history, not at the close but right at the beginning; and it owes its existence to this unfamiliar aspect of Wagner. Here again there are paradoxes. For the actual themes and their recapitulations, not just the development, are *in statu nascendi*. So indeed is this music's whole specific content, which far exceeds its text.

THE QUESTION OF THE RESONANT PASTORALE

It was not only the internal pulse which sought to beat within these notes, often all too audibly. Wagner vehemently summons the external, the world of things, as well; this is apparent in his style. It trickles, rustles, flickers, glimmers, flashes and thunders: a clangour and even noise of existence, more intrusive than anywhere else. Because of its origin, of course, nothing was easier to imitate. Since Grieg all daybreaks have been similar, and the forest has been murmuring in the salon. Before Wagner, streams and meadows could be stated in simpler terms; in fact the greater economy came closer not only to what was delicate but also to what was robust and certainly to what tasted bitter. It is thus with Mozart, whose music is permanently on the conscience of all out-and-out Wagnerians. There is the duettino for Susanna and the Countess, 'When the gentle zephyrs waft . . . ': here the sweet lyrical exchanges are themselves traversing the paths that meet in the evening garden of love. 'At last the hour is nearing when you, O beloved, will be mine completely': and again, beneath Hesperus's friendly gaze, a melody of the zephyrs is heard, but sung entirely into the night, full of a silver and of roses which exist as much in Susanna's longing as they do in the love-garden. And yet again, as soon as music portrays a Nature which is not amorous but more self-sufficient: how transparently Beethoven achieved this in his *Pastoral* Symphony! Not only the 'Scene by the Brook', needless to say, but also the 'Storm' gets by without any 'pedal' whatever. This storm even follows on from the dance scherzo, which it rudely interrupts. The whole seething tempest is upon us with flashes of lightning in a chain of high sixths, lightning striking twice over in the vicinity, and without a thunder-machine. To a large extent, therefore, pre-Romantic Nature music was relatively simple in character, yet far-reaching in its means – even where it retained the descriptive (not to be confused with naturalistic) features handed down from late mediaeval tone-paintings, French examples in particular. And these features not only occur in Haydn's *Creation*, where the painting has the delicacy of a miniature. They also present graphic figures in Bach's oratorios and cantatas whenever the text leads from subjective experiences to objective events and circumstances (scourgings, the rending of the veil, earthquakes, darkness, transfiguring light). This only altered when – and precisely the Wagnerian element dates from this point – truly Romantic Nature music came into being, music which was Romantic because of the predominance of an initially diffuse 'mood' as well. This marks an overtaking of the descriptive process, and certainly it had starting points in Mozart and Beethoven. But there it was constantly transparent and offered no opportunities for faint glimmerings, dawn awakenings or 'forest murmurs' – in short, Nature's murmurs. Consequently Romantic music's depiction of Nature maintains a very precarious balance between a loss in lucidity and a gain in sound-aura. Yet the loss had already been incurred long before; and the gain, hard though it is to assess, similarly contains an unfamiliar aspect of Wagner, indeed one that may shed a kind of continuing light on the Nature music of previous Romantics. These include Marschner, Weber and also Mendelssohn, insofar as they excelled in the new Nature music. With Marschner, there is the landscape of molten metal introduced by this abrupt, unpolished giant, as in the melodrama of his *Hans Heiling* with its gloomy night and little blue flame on the haunted heath; then in the scorching gloriole when the Queen of the Spirits appears. The path leads on via Weber's polished Wolf's Glen music, that uncanny succession of tone-pictures, music lending itself to the portrayal of horror, racing spectres and sudden silence with almost unprecedented effects of contrast – all of which fascinated Beethoven himself. Nor must we forget the unprecedented moonlight conveyed by the violins in the *Midsummer Night's Dream* overture which Mendelssohn wrote when he was still a young genius: a Romantic translation of Shakespeare which is in a class of its own and, not least, a spectre without horror. All this Romanticism, this surrendering to the mood of evening or night-time even in daylight, now acquired a new grandeur in Wagner. Above all Wagner supplemented it with that peculiarly ringing, reverberant sound which cannot only be described pejoratively as 'pedal' but seeks to manifest itself in a positive sense as a veritable 'sound of

Nature' and does indeed produce this effect in the best passages. Wind, storm, mist, fire and spring appear as dramatic characters, as it were, characters almost homogeneous with the human ones. This was achieved by differing from Mozart and Beethoven, and it was continued more superficially by Wagner's immediate successors. With composers who were further removed from Wagner, it still produced musical images of Nature which would not have existed without the example of Bayreuth. Of course this Wagnerising became wholly trivial in a jingling 'world in harmony' of the kind that embellishes Pfitzner's opera *Die Rose vom Liebesgarten* or mounts up, so to speak, in Richard Strauss' *Alpine Symphony*. Fashionably mythical musical exercises such as the singing laurel in Strauss' *Daphne* are only slightly more profound; delicacy does not drive superficiality away. How much more genuinely related to what had arisen with Romanticism, keeping Wagner at his proper distance, is the mature Verdi's economical art in this respect! The moonlight flitting in octaves before Act 3 of *Aïda* effectively bathes the nocturnal bank of the Nile in eloquent light. And on the other hand, with its increasing remoteness from Wagner and even from Bruckner, Mahler's pastorale proves to be Nature lyricism in the old bucolic, though elevated, sense once more, rather than Nature rendered dynamic or even erotic. We have described Wagner's 'Good Friday magic' (to the text ' . . . dass die entsündigte Natur heut . . . ') as the paradox of a Christian Nature-music. But this rare and curious piece of Wagner again remained linked with eroticised Nature (sickly sweet with enfolding tendrils). By comparison Mahler's several examples of Good Friday magic, as in the first and last movements of his Sixth Symphony, are far superior, beyond all libido – and yet, to be sure, for all this bucolic distance, they owe a profound debt to Wagner's pastorale.' The strangely shifting triads in Mahler's Sixth Symphony, even the introduction to the final part of the Eighth, those mute, seraphically dawning sounds, speak drowsily of the solitude of Nature high aloft. As always with Mahler, they proclaim at the same time that Wagner's *resonant Pan* himself is now acquiring a visionary hearing and transparence in respect of the unknown.

It is always important to consider with what means and to what end this singing is begun. Does it start with humanly conscious notes, or disorderly ones that screen an agitated, if not tormented, sleep? According to Wagner all music begins in the cry with which a tormented dreamer comes round and wakes up. The 'tormented will' is first announced with this cry, that is, it enters as such into the world of sound. Only upon a further awakening does it also enter the world of light. Thus what Wagner expounded in these terms in his essay on Beethoven, where he was adapting Schopenhauer to his own person, posits above all howling, and not singing, at the musical outset. Only after this howling does the note which forms intervals and is formed in intervals arrive, and it then very often re-submits itself retrogressively to frenzy in Wagner, in the actual effect. This accounts for Wagner's retrograde approach even in the domain of Nature, an approach that seeks not only to retrace Nature's own steps to the bass E flat of the Rhine's flowing depths but to trace its primal origins in it, and thus find the way back there. This means that as often as is feasible, large and sharply delineated structures are submerged again in a flux, in a weaving, flickering and glittering, in emotions of the concrete thing, so to speak. Even that which is firm in outline is still bordered by these emotions and lies within the nimbus of Schopenhauer's Will-impulse, which has been reduced to audible 'manifestations'. In spite of the primordial surge, the cry from within sleep or, in this case, from the belly of Nature has become highly rhythmic, harmonised, refined, pursuing within manifestations the relevant musical score of the Will of the universe. This begins with the instrumentation. Wagner chooses heavy brass for the crawling serpent, natural horn notes for the Rhine's undulating depths, extended harp arpeggios for the rainbow, soft woodwind for spring on the Good Friday meadow, and so on. The unprecedented conversion of visual into aural impressions appears possible through the isolation of the active sound of objects, this sound being meant to give the specific rhythm and harmony. The object is now engendered from this, and not only for the ears of spirits, like the new day for Goethe ('to what clangour dawn gives rein!'),[5] but for utterly physical earthly ears, which apprehend not daybreak but the *premier cri* in the objectivations of the universal Will. This is the obverse of what is Amphion-like in the transformation music in *Parsifal*, where time turns into external *space* and music into a *stage-picture*, thus seeking its visible conversion into a sound-*figure*. For it is precisely to these figures reproduced from music that the cry of the thing-will, universal Will, is meant to resound once more through music. It is the aural truth behind a visual illusion, which is inadequate not just from the theatrical standpoint; it is the resonant 'in-themselves' side of things. Fire is now itself entirely chords of the sixth, scurrying up and down chromatically. Storm itself is the pounding sextuplets from which it issues as a manifestation of universal Will; and the tempest itself, harmonic constriction and a sudden discharge into six-four chords in which the music seeks not so much to illustrate it as to furnish its prototype. Hence the intention is for the active sound of things to be 'extended in depth' to their sound-root. But at the same time, this sound-root is meant to be nothing other than the thing-in-itself of the universal Will, discerned almost directly from the manifestations through the medium of music. This going down to the sound-root is Schellingian, i.e. Pythagoras romanticised: music floats in space, as Schelling states in his *Philosophy of Art*, 'in order to weave an audible universe from the diaphanous body of sound and the note'. The other, though not entirely compatible approach, the essentially dominant one with Wagner, is Schopenhauer's: 'Music immediately posits for the phenomenon the thing-in-itself, and this, as the phenomenon's various stages of objectivation, is the craving, despairing, exulting, in short impassioned, Will.' Thus the cry, and with it the sound-root with which everything started, is augmented if not replaced by a thing-in-itself that is no longer causal at all, but meta-causal instead. In other words, the musical basis for the oscillations of the world's Chladnian sound-figures is engulfed by the Will's universal oneness, which knows no time, space or causality. Fire, water, earth, persons, destinies are not so much concrete 'results' of the Will as 'demonstrations' of it. Ultimately, then, Wagner's Nature music does not seek to return just to the *respective* sound-roots but to enter into a *most widespread spell of terror or magic* cast by the universal Will. Schopenhauer's thing-in-itself knows no individuation principle, least of all one removed from its spell and opposing it with a will of its own; and so Wagner's Fate music never, or only seldom, knows genuine persons. As is now perfectly clear, persons belong even as actors to the universal Nature which is the sole driving force. They are prompted by Nature in their actions and thus appear almost homogeneous to storms, mist, fire and spring. Hence an unreliability which also fits in with this unstable, impulsive characteristic, as is evident from the faithlessly faithful Siegfried and even – minus the depth – the mixture of Astarte and Magdalene in Kundry. Even the aforesaid irradiation of the feelings, as represented by 'Sweet distress', 'Exultant death' and the iridescent accompanying chords, has at least some affinity with a universal Will's exclusive fermenting. This kind of musical character-shaping wants to speak in a frenzied, intoxicating way from the fervid thing-in-itself (which is still fervid in the Grail's trans-figured anti-delirium). That is why the Promethean ability to change events is absent from this side of Wagner, in his elective affinity with the arena of natural fervour [*mit Glut-Plan*]. 'To the eternally young', sings Wotan, 'the god yields in bliss', but even Siegfried, who is visualised as representing the 'eternally young', only goes through the motions of doing so. Although fearless and relatively guiltless, he never represents a deliberate counter-attack. Indeed, he is an entangled agent of the entangling *moira*, just as Wotan is its guilty accomplice and victim. And yet, even when faced by this conclusion: it is precisely in Wagner's *Nature music* that the cry and spell do not always have the final word. The latter is not a cry or even a sounding silence but rather a *resonance* – that far reverberation, therefore, which is simply heard at its most powerful in the non-concluding finale of *The Twilight of the Gods*. This resonance is itself equivocal – and now this has the greatest significance. Admittedly, it is still part of the 'infinitely hazy essence of music', as Wagner defined his own music only too accurately, but it has nothing to do with any kind of perfume, or at any rate this does not exhaust its significance. On the contrary, here it is precisely an *open source-sound* and a *newly thrusting sound-root* – having nothing to do with Schopenhauer – that make themselves felt in the end, achieving warmth and daylight. The sound of Nature thus heralds (and it was Mahler who inherited this, testified to it) an element of far-reaching brilliance correspond-ing to the purely individual act of anticipation on the part of some leitmotifs in a more unseeing and also less definite way. Water, fire, air and earth, deep rivers, storm, tempest, rocky crevices, moun-tain heights, night, sunset, dawn, brilliant daylight: all these now exhibit their tonal lineaments as seldom before, lineaments driven out of, expelled from elemental sound. This complements and sig-nificantly extends our pictorial, poetic, landscape images. Hence Wagner's evocation of Nature becomes a special musical touchstone of concrete quality, and one that – *qua* music which bubbles and boils – is very close to the hearth of the qualifying or (in Jakob Böhme's words) its welling up, gushing forth [*Quellen, Quallen*]. Certainly there are other depictions of Nature, thank goodness, besides the kind that are so often satin-quilted or strewn with land-scape painting from Germany's Gründerzeit. Mozart's gardens, the Scene by the Brook in Beethoven's Sixth Symphony, his calm after the storm and even after the trumpet signal in the *Leonore* overture are more quietly and deeply revealing. Yet Wagner does give resonance its full due, like a vibration *ante rem* which continues to give out figured sound *in re*, not to say *post rem datam*; a sound-figure through which it takes up objects of Nature and seeks through art to raise them to a higher power. And in the transparency of the resonance there is always something full of expectancy, which is so peculiar that it is as though even the emphatically subterranean, chthonian, were brewing, spinning, creating something remote. 'Is it daybreak already?' asks the Norn at the start of *The Twilight of the Gods*, in a cry that is eerily muffled – and the musical turmoil is not just subterranean at all. 'Far away, not where we are, vast portals are moved with an echoing sound': this sentence from one of Maeterlinck's neo-Romantic essays would hardly be conceivable without Wagner's Nature music, yet it too is anything but a Romantic regressing or mythicising. 'But it is still the enchantment of Death, is music, and allied to the Ossianic character, to rain and autumn and the profound delight of early falling darkness, the gloomy sky and the heavy clouds, the mist and the heroes who ride on the lonely heath and to whom the spirits appear in the shape of clouds, just as they appeared to Bach and Wagner – turned towards the point of the compass at which this world comes to an end, becomes extinct.' Even this sentence from my *Geist der Utopie* (1918) could not have been formulated in such a way without the Wagnerian landscape, and without the light of another day farther west, aflame in this gloaming. It burns with grandeur, as ultimately happens in the final song of Brünnhilde, flung far into and behind the horizon, using and storing quite different aromatics from those used by fate. Music is a realm where the horizon already begins directly at our feet. This is particularly evident from the Wagnerian pastorale, where music finds so close a resonance in human emotion, so distant a one in the actual sound of Nature. After which, as Stolzing's first song informs us, 'the sound departs from thence in distant waves' – and equally, by the very same token, it does not depart from that place, i.e. it will not have gone near it. As we see, all this is of great complexity and full of a dialectic in the tone pictures, full of a double perception which is both inevitable and startling. The musical pastorale of the future will have Wagner at its rear, but in the way that a ship has the wind behind it, or like the light in the final *Master-singers* chorus, the 'rosy glow of dawn, approaching through the gloomy clouds'. And so as not to shine in nakedness, the light will always take those gloomy clouds upon itself, in order to be charged with colour.

IV

On the mathematical and dialectical character in music
(Essay, 1925)

Even hearing, it seems to many people, best achieves clarity by external means. Happy the person who can simply beat time along with the music. But unfortunately, people also attach to it fondly cherished feelings of which the musical work knows nothing. They attach little images which they have painted in their own minds or hackneyed, allegedly explicatory words, a second kind of tone painting, so to speak. Music is surrounded by groping colloquies that never cease, even though they are no means of comprehension.

Among these are discussions of number and of what relation it might bear to music. This in itself conveys the desire to see sober and even solid fact linked with the dream. Many mathematical brains, we are told, are supposed to have shown a surprising propensity and often a real gift for music. Conversely, though, men who were musicians by vocation did not pursue mathematics as a sideline; so the path is at least not two-way. And a certain embarrassment usually arises if we enquire what type and manner of mathematical thinking does reappear in music, and above all, where. The fugue promptly lends itself as an example; and in Mozart's music the clarity is heavily emphasised, as though a calculation were working out particularly neatly.

Such calculating, viewed as that of a note interweaving itself, has become very much the fashion today. A part is selected for its own energy, for its long drawn-out singing and its readiness to pursue or be led along paths of its own. Dissonance is neither avoided nor actively sought, and a heed for key, the former strait-jacket of the key-note, is disappearing as well. Quarter-tones, the exotic whole-tone scale and the scales of Scriabin and Busoni are breaking into the old harmonic series, changing tonic-relations are appearing and punctuating the process. In short, a kind of arbitrary or unending harmony is arising which does not need to disclose its starting-point and destination; a counterpoint-in-itself, harmonically completely unfettered and also free from all the expression with which it was

183

fraught through Beethoven's restlessness or the music-drama of Wagner. The age of a musical renewal is proving to be also the age of experiments of a technical and rational kind. Thus form-oriented contemplation above all is closer to the musical will-to-the-unknown than is a psychology or even metaphysics, which apparently forces its object under the light of Romantic aesthetics time and again. Just as modern painting began with a hatred of expression, placing the stress on cubes, triangular and cylindrical forms instead of tranquil evenings and other so-called soulfulness, so modern music is returning to the 'direct factors'. It is exploring the as yet subject-alien possibilities of the actual physics of musical notes, without any aim for the time being and also without any prospect of establishing new 'indirect factors', or new metaphysics of music. Thus from this angle, similarly, it is no surprise to find evidence of mathematical proclivities and indeed attempts, by means of a mathematically imbued formalism rendered, as it were, transcendental in itself, to substitute a mathematical hermeneutic for the psychological, historio-philosophical or metaphysical, but at all events spiritual, hermeneutics of music. The result is that ultimately even Bach's counterpoint is, apparently, no longer annexed to the character of Bach as a territorial category of the human realm in music. It only borders on a realm of mathematical or quasi-mathematical laws – without a personal designation and without spiritual, allegedly much too soulful, expression.

Now in every note another also sounds. And each note prefigures specific points to which it is drawn on a purely numerical basis. One to two is a fixed ratio of this kind: two strings of which one is twice as long as the other will cause the tonic to resound in miniature. Further related to this and contained in the tonic is the fifth, which is likewise precisely determined by certain relations of the most simple type between the amounts of vibrations. The clearer these fractions are, the more readily they will blend together of their own accord. But of course no listener will be aware of this and count numbers. Vibrating strings do not explain just how the bare simultaneity of their separate intervals is fused or how the remarkable quality of consonance arises. All that can help us are ideas of the note, which are qualified to conceal calculation, in fact they turn into the opposite in the course of our hearing them. In consequence, even the awkward fractions on which the harmonies of *Tristan* are based

184

appear *suo genere* to be consonant, whereas a strict sequence of pure triads does not sound agreeable but menacing and chilling. There is no way of explaining this from number. The Greek theory of music based on the measurement of clear, simple ratios outlawed the third and the sixth as dissonant because their proportions went beyond the quaternary number. It was only the need of polyphonic song, which did not worry about mathematics, that resorted to the forbidden third, thereby attaining the major chord, that cornerstone of all harmonic development. It was not those who were counting vibrations who discovered this most important of intervals. They were still outlawing and disowning the third long, long after it had already defeated in practice the numerically celebrated fourth.

Now in the second place, notes are of course organised and do not make off as they please. And counting too is an ordering, particularly where it progresses not just in series but in groups. So there is apparently something else in this root which effects a linking together of number and the individual orderings of musical beat, musical construction. A further point is that number appears to prefigure or contain all ordering in general quite readily, reducing it to its most concise expression. Hence we describe number as one of the most ancient symbols of all artistic creation or indeed culture: the latter is like its number and can never escape it. First Lamprecht and then Spengler, often whimsically but often with patent skill, asserted that an age's style of mathematical thinking agreed with the forms of its economy, its ceremonial, its manifold perspective of the world and not least its music. In their view the use, say, of increasingly remote sounds, the Baroque extension of the sound-source into an infinite space, matches the contemporaneous functional extension of number. The eighteenth century's principal instrumental form, the *tema con variazioni*, is claimed to be a formation analogous to the transformation of groups within functional theory. And Wagner's music of the leitmotif finds itself boldly compared with the diversity of numbers in advanced functional theory, where similarly, groups of transcendent structures undergo changes that bring out the invariability of certain form elements. Thus in contrast to the bright daylight of Euclidean geometry, to which no polyphonic, changing, music could correspond, modern analysis appears as a geometry of the night, because infinite space triumphs over individual things, and, by the same token, as a geometry of polyphonic music. More important than all this equating by analogy, the following affinity could, it has been argued, appear within the organising form in general: mathematics is the model for every uniform [*geschlossen*] system and hence also the model for the fugue, as being a uniform system in miniature. In every case, the inferences are seemingly contained in the initial principle. They can be elicited, predicted, calculated from it, in accordance with a totally rational idea of relationships which shows the theme of a fugue to be purely contrapuntal in nature and oriented towards its complete contrapuntal expansion. The epoch of mathematical construction and the great rational systems was also the heyday of the fugue, which made the theme's 'qualities' follow from the set definition of it, as it were.

But pure organisation is empty, applying to all intellectual life and hence to nothing in particular. In substance, number is already a structure *per se* since, unlike a piece of music, it does not signify a time. Counting as a placing of units, as an ordering within a fixed diversity, has nothing to do with musical phrasing or with the time of the present, the appointed time, the time of return as the sonata theme's great moment. It is a rudimentary error to put this time in a relation to arithmetic, just as fluxional calculation is unable to achieve true Becoming, a production which is not only formal but substantial – in short, time as both historical form and sonata form. Furthermore, whereas the *fugue* at least seemed to go on obeying its *initial* law, like 'calculation', Beethoven's *sonata themes* are purely signs of a dynamic condition, seeds of a process which grows primarily out of antithesis. And he himself commands the main theme's triumph in the reprise only as the supreme element within the qualifying process. Therefore mathematics has at any rate no relation to the sonata, that impulsive, dramatic, discontinuous excess of tension, that pure art of time and direction with its productive leaps in the development or travelling. Even admitting the self-developing of mathematical axioms towards the results evolved from them, proceeding via ordered relations: a fugue theme is not an axiom but a character that proves steadfast and evolves in the individual parts – the incidents in its life, as it were, the currents of its world. The most that could be yielded by a mathematical formulation of all the rules and practices of counterpoint would be a new and not especially fruitful branch of mathematics. Within it we would recognise not much counterpoint and even less actual music, just as mathematically conceived logic, so-called algorism, is wholly separate from the real purposes and meaningful contents of logic.

Thus one no longer possesses anything tangible when one's sole consideration is the empty intellectual relationships of pure organisation. Rather, the latter's particular formations are precisely differentiated from one another, that is to say, they are partly dictated by the different contents needed by the different 'orders' in individual cultural fields, and these vary highly. To reduce this richness to a mere formal style of organisation, with a numerical symbol's combinational rules as sole content, is to overlook the fact that history does not flourish for the sake of form-relations. It does so by resolving the tasks and world-themes variously arising within them. But these themes are on various planes. The self-informing [*Selbstverständigung*] of the political man, say, is not quite the same as that of the artistic man, although each is taking place in the general cultural style of an age, and yet is not doing so. That is to say, they belong to different cultural echelons with regard to content. The mathematics of an age in particular and the physics necessarily associated with it are entirely oriented in content to Nature, to the known state [*Gewusstsein*] of what has come into being and has been expanded to the full in her. Never by a long chalk could mathematics be applied as precisely to the military strategy, the art of governance or the recording of history in its age as it can be applied to its 'own' epoch's physics and its understanding of Nature. Only where culture is relegated to an outward aspect of organising, and hence to the common denominator of mere fashion, can the enormous differences of the 'infinitesimal' in number and in Bachian music, the differences of the operative relations and their objects be removed. The musical figure for the character, the essence, of Bach as revealed in the depths of his organ fugues bears the same relation to the forms of known states [*Gewusstseinsformen*] in the mathematical physics of the time as does the higher world of a specific type of vast waking dream, an area of incantation, to the stereotype rotations of the celestial bodies – Kepler notwithstanding.

Now in the third place, a musical note certainly appears greatly to refine those whom it influences. Since olden times people have regarded it as an antidote to gloomy hours, and it is not only the outward serpent that music tames. On the contrary, music renders the soul pure in disposition, both note and soul seeming to be most intimately united in the measure, the roundelay, the beautiful harmony. Just as organising appears to combine musical number in Pythagorean terms by way of logic, so refining appears to do so by way of ethics. In this context Plato praised the Dorian mode as proper to vigorous and well-disposed persons, as the sound of a life that was organised, dignified. But the Phrygian mode too, although it accompanied the dithyramb, was thought by Plato to have a healing influence by causing a discharge of the emotions, thus showing a cathartic power akin to the power of tragedy. Hence, from this angle, the numerically ordered element in music seemed related precisely to the soul's non-fermenting, fully adorned, cosmos-like aspects. Therefore the soul's essence too, according to Plato, is mathematical clarity considered as harmony. Music in general, in this interpretation – a charming of serpents, as it were, combining Orpheus, ethics and Pythagoras – appears a border zone between light and the dark forces of the Earth, whereby the inherently gloomy border area is at least induced to act as a mirror. Only insofar as the soul incarnate takes on a corresponding sheen and prepares to be a mirror does it officiate as a muse and as music, as a sounding of the geometrical-astral light. Thus the Greeks followed Pythagoras and Plato, liberating musical sound from the lower frenzy; and upon 'sophrosyne', by extending the universe's proportional harmony, they established the seven notes, resembling the seven planets. Even the intervals in Chinese string playing are tuned according to the distance between the celestial bodies. Indeed Buxtehude was still claiming 'to have neatly portrayed the nature and character of the planets' in his seven keyboard suites. If, in mediaeval music, the harmony of the spheres was reinterpreted as the song of the heavenly hosts, and if the mediaeval symbolists equated the intervals with the *ordines angelorum*, this was still just a Christian renaming of the harmony of the spheres, not a disruption of it in the sense of the Christian paradox. Kepler even argued that the different registers corresponded to different planets. The minor had its parallel in the perihelion and the major in the aphelion, while the musical scale was both inferred and sanctioned – again, entirely along Pythagorean lines – as a division by seven of the original solar note, as Apollo's lyre. In Schelling's Romantic-reactionary or archaising-Baroque thought, too, the musical gold was still buried in the number seven. Why, Kepler's Pythagorean approach is so completely victorious in Schelling's philosophy of art that the latter presents music as merely a type of incomplete architecture, a still fluid reproduction of the external universe, in contrast to poetry which testifies to unfrozen, vital speaking itself and represents the world's only internal side.

Thus the refining of the audience according to ancient proportion constantly leads from Pythagoras and Plato to music as a kind of auditorium of proportion and of the proportional cosmos above all, taking us away from man and towards a kind of organon for ethical physics. This is the consequence; the price paid for mathematics in such lofty regions. It is also, on the other hand, the laurel which the abstract brightness of figurative thinking bestows.

But the musical note is not only occupied in banishing gloomy hours, whereupon the soul will dance. Bach expresses sorrow and devotion amid tears, more readily than joy, and lingers over this in the St Matthew and St John Passions in particular, plucking sweet fruit from his gall. This is connected with the Christianity in which our rich music first arose. Origen did not seek the proper effect of music in proportion any more, or in a calm and manly fortifying of the soul. On the contrary, he sought it in contrite remorse, that *compunctio cordis* which clearly is alone appropriate to the ex-orbitant [*Über-Mass*]. Only in this way, he argued, were the dark forces of the Earth to be truly resolved along with the barbaric stellar gods, and the human realm was based less on a cosmic façade than it was to the minds of the Greeks. Examined more closely, this reinterpretation and indeed division of ancient harmony has repercussions even for all those Christian celebrations of the cosmos that seem to have merely converted the harmony of the spheres into the music of the angels. For even with Kepler, the achieved Christian paradox brings about a final sabbatising. Above all, the actual musical work that came into being in Christianity, with its eminently historical doings and purely qualitative, unquantifiable structural character, shows even the (ethically speaking) simply crystallising, cosmos-related type of mathematics to be incompetent in this domain. Mathematics remains the key to Nature, but it can never be the key to history and to those self-informings [*Selbstverständigungen*] by the non-equation and the asymmetrical which number was devised to counter, and for whose gradual objectivation the human spirit ultimately produced great music. As regards an undeniable figurative thinking for Nature as well, if not specifically for Nature, the case is rather the reverse! This thinking does not stretch from Nature into history and music but from history and music into Nature, counter-illumining and thus bringing things to light. Without a shadow of doubt, Nature evinces forms which arise out of a process of shaping and reshaping. And they include veritable structures in the fluid domain such as the stream and even the cataract, as well as all relatively constant organic types with their exact construction, even all crystals. They include symbols whose 'significance' does not always (as with most poetic similes and as with the sequence of storm, rosy morn, tempest and light in music) serve merely to express human events and contents but may, in addition, indicate *qualitates adhuc occultae* (in a new sense) in Nature herself. For Plato himself had previously removed the wholly 'pure' form-relations of 'ideas' from the world of phenomena to that *topos ouranios*, that 'heavenly place' of a 'genuine' Being within which precisely the 'pyramid of ideas' is to stand and reach its consummation. Later, in the Renaissance, when it was the natural locale and not a *topos ouranios* that became of importance, these 'ideas' were still, by means of a '*signatura rerum*' in Nature herself, shining through in a supra-mathematical, qualitative sense. But as we have stated, even these 'signatures' – possibly belonging to a type of qualitative categorising – only enter the field of vision methodically speaking by means of cultural and historical counter-illumination. Hence they too represent no cosmic a-historical analogy for the human realm of music. Time and history, innovation and a creative departure from the mere nexus of equations and indeed the final stereotyping, a consciousness of the utopian range, and mounting subject-objectivation as its fulfilment: all these elements of musical awareness are not fundamentally mathematical and are remote from any such contemplation of harmony.

Fourth and lastly, to be sure, calm does appear to provide opportunities for computation. It is in this calm that the light, noble, great song of Mozart has its life, his art being so entirely central to man that it takes part in a game. More than ever, the fugue in its profundity still appears to contain a secret diagram, a mathematics, as it were, of an ultimate, imperturbable pleasure. Indeed this was also intimated by Goethe's curious statement that the Bachian fugue appeared to him like a glimpse of God's heart before the world was created, hence like a play of forms before it has despatched itself to solid things. So perhaps – one might think – this dialinear composing has connections if not with ancient Greek mathematics, then nevertheless with an emanation mathematics conceived on Babylonian and above all Gnostic lines, without our therefore needing to equate the ordered patterns of the fugue with a harmony of the spheres. Moreover, the fugue's melismatic-contrapuntal equilibrium sets the pattern for all music of *arrival*, all music of the object become distinct, the achieved objectivation of its still nameless, unplaced subject. Thus even Bruckner's entirely dynamic counterpoint has a general imperturbability, a mysterious swimming to and fro, an ultimately restful continuity about its movement, as though stemming from arrival. Also, the impulse and God-centred state of mediaeval Catholicism remained alive in this music by virtue of its ability to be construed by even professedly Gnostic hearers as the shaping respiration of Platonic-Catholic spirit-essences, as the vibrant calm at the seat of all production. Accordingly such music of arrival does in fact appear to belong to an ultimate mathematics: a mathematics very much of the past, an eternal leisurely play which reposes in the play of the shaping forces themselves.

But even the transported listener is merely persuaded by others of all this, and it will not occur to him to perceive numbers. It is surely no accident that Beethoven, even when aiming at calm, remains an embarrassment from the mathematical viewpoint, and moreover one that cannot be readily removed from the world of music. For the genuine sonata, for all its resolving in the end, leads away from the essence of mathematics infinitely more than clarity or leisurely polyphony keep suggesting this essence. Again, with regard to the fugue, that indubitably and magnificently leisurely form, we admit that its affinity with mathematical 'deduction' certainly led in the direction of the seventeenth century, when deductive *mathesis* was particularly rife. But as a reproduction of cosmic lines of energy, its purportedly secret diagram – described by the parts entering and leaving the texture – was located in terms of intellectual history in the previous century, in the Renaissance world-picture haunted by magic. There is, however, no source that points to this connection. It is not a connection·between musical harmony and some version of the harmony of the spheres, but a connection existing between counterpoint and that magical *mathesis*, that richly interwoven emanation system by which cabbalistic neo-Gnostic copper and dogma portrayed the governing of the heavenly powers. From a distance, of course, it was possible for Goethe to elucidate music which was not in his line and even Bach's, then quite unknown, by means of cabbalistic images. But with Hegel, the *effected* glimpse 'of God's heart before the world was created' led him not to the philosophy of music but to logic as a 'plan of the world'. And logic alone, for Hegel, has a bearing on the entire world, whereas the philosophy of music in the same system concerns only a part of it, and moreover a 'romantic' part in which the spirit outweighs the cosmic material. It could be maintained that the perfect fugue still corresponded to the mathematics of creative categorical functions, with absolute calm at its centre and in general – a mathematics completely unknown to science and simply mythicised in the cabbala now and then. All the same, it was only the more recent polyphony that suggested an affinity with ancient, magical, emanation mathematics, and polyphony is an exclusive characteristic of Christian music. Thus it was only Christian musical praxis which made such semi-pagan theory possible. Pagan music itself, being always homophonic, did not even permit anyone to propound this theory. This temporally factual contradiction between praxis and interpretation finally indicates that the emanation theory of the fugue is merely a convenient adoption of alien views that not only were distant from music in their time but mask the intrinsic spiritual content of polyphony. Polyphony is a purely Christian product because it was only with Christ that man's spiritual dimension with its implication of a quest was truly entered into. The lofty emanational dimension, the space of creation, is a vault of necessity and not of human freedom – which is the object of music. Music of repose forms a figure which never occurs in the cosmos or is only translated thither anthropomorphically; it is found solely in the human dimension with the realm potentially adequate to this dimension. Even magical mathematics with its kaleidoscopic patterns ultimately expresses merely the mechanism of a kismet. Hence it is still as inferior to music as astral myth is to the Christian mystery of the discovered soul.

As a result we can say that no forming number any longer inhabits the process of sounding. Time as direction demands a different form, above all one that also posits impulse, striding, a barely divined goal. The plus sign is by no means the harbinger of this time, but *contradiction* can be an indication of movement, existing wherever there is life. If the more recent mathematics partly became the organon of quantitatively reified Nature, the situation changed when history, living reality, wholeness finally re-entered our field of vision qualitatively; and *dialectics* dawned as the *organon of the process*. The dissatisfied element in every condition is itself the contradiction which counters the old condition with a new one, with a new theme, although it does not necessarily reinstate the old theme synthetically as a thesis on a higher level, as in Hegel's dialectics. Nonetheless, as any theory of musical forms could have demonstrated to music's mathematicians, the cadence and above all the sonata, the sonata of Beethoven, represent a return from the detour, a uniting of what was separated, almost entirely on the lines of Hegelian dialectics, though as a kinetically modified triad. Not mathematics, therefore, but *dialectics is the organon of music* viewed as the supreme illustration of historical time fraught with destiny.

Notes become divided, a G sharp placed as A flat, and this separation continues. There would also be no moving and advancing in intervals, were it not for the prior unrest of the tonic. The key as it initially appears in the triad is negated, converted into the dominant, for the basic chord has to come out of its shell. As a first subtle dissonance it steps a fifth downwards, the triad thus splitting itself into the pseudo-tonic of the subdominant, as it were. This disruption, separation, urges from within itself the return to the genuine tonic, the basic chord of the beginning, via a resolved contradiction. But it is with some vehemence that this dialectical character persists in the sonata. For the latter, in contrast to the fugue, owes the real climaxes of its counterpoint to the pathos of the recurring principal key. Needless to say, there is still a difference between the richness in contrast this signifies, and what the richness engenders, on the one hand, and the game of question-and-answer that the layman, on the other, readily discerns from the more or less free imitation of a musical idea, especially if this is distributed among various instruments. More essential to the sonata is that unique tension which is manifested in the contrast between the two or three main themes. This goes on working itself out antithetically in the development, far from the main key, and synthetically attains the beginning as its goal only with the unburdened return of the first and main theme. In the development section the energetic character of the first theme suddenly turns, as it were, into the idyllic character of the second, whereby Beethoven heightens this opposition to the point of the most expansive dualism. The contradiction between these 'two principles' fuels the entire dynamics of the development, that area in which the antithesis has fully erupted, whipping itself up more and more fiercely through modulation and counterpoint. Thus the first movement of a sonata is a cadence in the very grandest manner, indeed a syllogism. The confirmation of its theme's victory when the development, the sphere of difference, has done its genetic work corresponds absolutely, *mutatis mutandis*, to the concrete *ergo* of a logical con-

193

clusion. But the syllogism is the primary form of the dialectical method, just as the latter itself is the repeated contemplation of the method of the actual process, which it intensifies more and more strongly in music and philosophy. Ultimately, music which has arrived is only found *behind* the sonata. It constitutes an ontology of music, finally bringing home the subject–object identity in the aesthetic sphere with fully designatory eloquence. This very deep simultaneity, this bringing together at the deepest level of internality, is again, however, no rigid state of relatedness or expandedness. Rather it still bears within it all the scars and marks of the process, enveloped in elevated recollection; the Lamb, not a harmony of the spheres, is its beacon. No more than mathematics is applicable to history can it be applied to this organic element of the highest order, to the cardinal factor of subjectivity guided back within itself and finally itself sounding into its ground, with the flash of eternity as the one and only schema; to be sure, the music and musical form of the latter have not yet come. The essence of the polythematic sonata, however, is still antithetical, dialectical, inasmuch as an elevation must first be achieved. And here again, the truth of this elevation is not a result that can stand on its own but the awaited, utopian, whole of the process. The essence of the monothematic fugue, this self-erecting shrine, and especially of the still unknown ontology of music is an elevation already communicating itself unceasingly. Yet it is one which remains entirely in time and history, and even simply a 'crystal' as long as a *vox humana* joins and entwines with it.[1]

V

The exceeding of limits and the world of man at its most richly intense in music

If I were permitted a wish, I would wish for neither riches nor power but for the passion of Possibility; I would only wish for an eye that was eternally young and eternally glowing with the desire to see Possibility.

Kierkegaard

A note of music comes with us and is 'we'; unlike the visual arts, which seemed previously to point so far above us, out into the realm of the rigorous, objective and cosmic, but which in fact stop at our graves, it emulates good works by accompanying us even beyond the grave. This is precisely because the new symbol in music, which is no longer pedagogical but a real one, appears so very low-lying in our atmosphere and such a mere fiery eruption, even though it is actually a light in the farthest and of course innermost firmament.   Ernst Bloch, *Geist der Utopie*

There is in music something surpassing and incomplete which no poetry has satisfied so far save for the poetry which music, possibly, develops from within itself. At the same time, the openness of this art shows in a particularly impressive way that with regard to the content-relation of the other arts as well, they are not altogether out of the wood.

Ernst Bloch, *Subjekt-Objekt, Erläuterungen zu Hegel*

THE GOOD FORTUNE OF THE BLIND

In order to know itself, the bare self must go to others. Intrinsically it is sunk within itself, and the inwardness lacks its counterpart. But through the Other whereby a normally clouded inner life comprehends itself, it readily enters foreign realms and travels away from itself again. Only sound, and that which is expressed in sound, is referred back to an 'I' or a 'we'. Here one's eyes mist over and it grows significantly darker, so that outward life subsides and only a fountain appears to be speaking. Very often it is that fountain which flows and bubbles in the trying state of being oneself; and this agitated life now *listens* to itself, as a shaped longing and urging in itself, as a song travelling on its own or mingling with others and always portraying invisible human features. This is where the good fortune of the blind begins, both below and above present things. At the same time the note states what is still silent in man himself.

SYRINX THE NYMPH

Here we cannot help hearing a summons in the singing. It began as a cry, a cry expressing an urge and appeasing it at the same time. Originally the human cry was accompanied only by noise, by clanging, drumming and rattling. This kind of thing deafens the ear and remains dulled, for a contrast develops between high and deep but never anything approaching fixed pitch, far less the forming of intervals. This, i.e. music, had modest beginnings in the invention of the shepherd's pipe or pan-pipe. This handy and eminently portable instrument derives from a different social stratum than noise-producing, fearsomely ritualistic instruments. Used primarily by shepherds, the pan-pipe served more immediate, more human emotions and their expression. It was not its function to induce a stupor or to work magic like the wooden clapper, the cymbal or the magically painted and in itself magically venerated drum. Rather it was confined – pure entertainment apart – to amorous longing and to the enchantment of love, the latter being a survival of magic. The sound of the shepherd's flute, pan-pipe or, in the case of the Greeks, syrinx (the meaning is always the same) was intended to reach the distant beloved. Thus music originated in yearning and it began very much as a *call into what has been forgone*. This belief is still widespread among the Rocky Mountain Indians. The young Indian goes off into the plain and laments his love on the pan-pipe; the girl is then supposed to weep, however far away she is. Ultimately the pan-pipe came a long way, being far more than the ancestor of the organ: it is the birthplace of music as a human expression, a sonic dream-wish. Not only a Red Indian belief attests to this but also – filling exactly the same role – one of the loveliest of ancient legends. This legend represents the origin and content of music in a charming allegorical form. In his *Metamorphoses*, Ovid gives the following account of the Arcadian flute and its content. Pan was chasing about with some nymphs and ambushed one of them, Syrinx the dryad. Fleeing from him, she found herself cut off by a river and implored the waves, her *liquidas sorores*, to change her appearance. Pan tried to seize her but was left with only a reed in his hands. As he was lamenting the lost beloved, the wind produced notes in the reed-bank, and the god was gripped by their beauty. Pan broke the rushes, saw reeds of varying lengths, bound a suitable selection together with wax and played the first notes just like the wind, but with human breath and as a lament. This engendered the pan-pipe, and Pan's playing gave him the consolation of a union with the nymph (*hoc mihi conloquium tecum manebit*) who had vanished and yet not vanished, since she was still present in the sound of his flute. Thus the version by Ovid. His legend was a recollection of primitive times and the primeval history of music viewed as the pathos of loss, a recollection which makes the story unsentimental and, like all genuine allegory, objective. Leaving Pan aside, the pan-pipe did not of course originate in Greece but in the Far East around the third millennium, and it quickly spread right across the Earth, especially among nomadic races. But while the legend indicates, in a manner both elegant and profound, the *need* for music, it also truly denotes the invention of music as *human expression* – a minor invention, but one of great consequence. There is an important contrast between the syrinx and ritualistic or percussive instruments with their dull, bellowing, howling and rattling noises. Into this ritualistic sound-world was now thrust an instrument giving out a well-organised series of notes. And by uniting syrinx and nymph, Ovid designated the goal towards which the note-sequence – always a tracing of lines in the invisible – is moving. It is something contradictory and utopian, for this flute-playing constitutes the presence of a vanished entity; that which has exceeded the *limit* is regained by this lament and contained in this consolation. The vanished nymph has remained as sound, adorning and preparing herself within it, and sings in the face of want. The sound comes from a hollow space, is produced by the fructifying breath of air and remains in the hollow space, which is made to resound. The nymph became the reed, and the instrument is called her syrinx. It is simply that, up to now, we have not really known what music itself is called and who music is.

BIZARRE HERO AND NYMPH: 'SYMPHONIE FANTASTIQUE'

Something is lacking, and sound at least states this lack clearly. Sound has itself something dark and thirsty about it and blows about instead of stopping in one place, like paint. The shifting and drifting can also have the bad effect that longing, in its musical guise, becomes blurred and flaccid. But while the note is not precisely fixed

197

spatially, it can be placed very precisely in time, in the beat, in the song we are aiming at. It is precisely the acute shapes of disquiet, well-known to us and exceeding limits, which are unmistakable in their musical disposition. Hoffmann's Kapellmeister Kreisler put into music that which wanted leaves of gold in every tree, that unconditional element which surrounds every starving wretch. In its most recognisable form, namely the erotic form, this unbridled longing reappeared with Berlioz, in his youthful *Symphonie fantastique*. Hence this may be put at the threshold, with its own special nymph, a bizarre one. All 'excessive' figures have a particularly strong utopian leavening, and with Berlioz this is isolated in a musico-erotic form. So Syrinx the nymph makes another appearance as the theme of the girl which permeates the five movements of the *Symphonie fantastique*. This early work is by no means first-rate music as a whole but highly significant from the angle of longing, because it is occupied in a sensational manner with a *utopian idée fixe*, which it realises in a bizarre hero and through a strange Helena. The 'programme' conveys the composer's intention and the outermost and, as it were, still extra-musical doors to the work. A young artist glimpses the girl who is the embodiment of all his dreams. The image of the beloved always appears to him together with a musical idea, a theme that has a passionate, yet refined and reserved character. It is this melody which constitutes the *idée fixe*, both pursuer and pursued. The contrast to the principal theme is found in the middle subject, and this second theme is not manifested in gentleness, as it normally would be, but as haziness, sleep and immobility. After the lurid, often abrupt workings-out the first theme's idea returns, darkened at first and sinking to deeper and deeper registers, and then with great splendour – a splendour, however, which is always that of a mere image of longing grown sharp and significant, and evanescent. The theme's return in C major at the end of the first movement represents happiness, but an unattained happiness; it is a star, but distant as a star is. And Stella leaves the first movement, which is headed 'Dreams, sorrows', to pass through the Scherzo ('A Ball'), through an Adagio which is certainly unique in its way ('Scene in the Meadow') and through the march finale ('March to the Scaffold') to the fugal finale ('Dream on a Witches' Sabbath'). In the Scherzo, the theme is heard in dance rhythms. The Adagio converts it into isolated recitatives, a dialogue in musically audible meadows – then one solitary voice, with the other no longer responding, complete silence – distant thunder on the horizon. A vast plain separates the melody of the theme and the remote, mysterious, disparate thunder; in this Adagio Berlioz wrote a pastorale equalled only in the mysticism of Chinese landscape art. The fourth-movement march and the bacchanale of the fifth, with its double fugue comprising the *Dies irae* and a witches' sabbath, batter and hack at the theme. Finally the melody of the beloved appears once more, debased on the clarinet, faded, sullied and vulgar. Always, and even in the last movement, the music conveys Stella's absence as much as her presence. She is still heard among the grinning faces, the bacchanalian tolling of bells and the parody of the *Dies irae* with which the *Symphonie fantastique* closes. This great musical 'penny-dreadful' is filled with an unattained joy; and the aerial roots of sound provide the 'Not-yet', indeed even the 'Never', with its intrinsic existence. The pneumatic fabric of sound forms the location of the *idée fixe* or the jungle which its chase is traversing. Merlin heard fleeting voices that others could not hear; Berlioz, one of music's magicians, brought them to sonorous life. That tracing of lines in the invisible we mentioned becomes glaringly apparent with Berlioz, and the lament for Syrinx grows demonic. Here the element of loss, the absolute element, does not reside in the finale, which is in any case the most questionable part of a symphony. It lies in the soft thunder of the scene in the meadows, in the response which is tacit but encompasses the unattained, in the context created in this coda by the significant pause before the thunder. And Berlioz achieved this with a delicate Adagio and its drawn-out, extensively alienated heathland of sound at eventide, a heath where the rest is not silence.

HUMAN EXPRESSION AS INSEPARABLE FROM MUSIC

It is not the purpose of a note of music to be either vaguely emotional or merely the result of sawing a fiddle. In the first place, it is not meant to wash over the audience in a melting, effeminate way. If a violin sobs like a human breast, this is not only a bad image: the violin is playing badly or playing bad music. A note-sequence whose expressiveness is lost when it is performed lucidly and objectively will never have had any expression other than a fraudulent one. But in the second place, we must not allow our repugnance against torrid music and an emotionally charged morass of sound to lead us into denying the psychically charged nature of the whole business of music. A note-sequence posits spiritual contents as matters of the will

199

to such an extent that in its archetypal forms it already announces a *striving* or a *movement*. We can sense a distinct fall between the keynote and the fifth; the seventh begs to be led downwards and the third upwards, and chords tend to associate with other chords. Not everything hinges on our empathy in this respect. On the contrary, the tonal relation itself already contains an objective factor which ineluctably determines our empathy. Even the relation of vibrating strings is heard emotionally, and this relation itself determines the first attraction of notes, as also their first friendly consonance. What started as such a physical event, independent handling and a social art which is even more independent take a stage farther. Otherwise music would never go beyond descending fifths. Having started as a physical phenomenon, musical tension turns into a psychical one. And melody's most remarkable attribute – the fact that in each of its notes, the immediately following one is latently audible – lies in human anticipation and hence in expression, which is now above all a humanised expression. There might still be music if there were no listeners, but certainly there would be none without the musicians to supply the musical movement and its psychical energy, its pounding energy, in the first place. Composers turn music not only into an expression of themselves but also into an expression of the age and society in which it originates. So naturally this expression is not just romantic or quasi-freely subjective. Any number of *human tensions* are added to the tension of the fifth to create a more complicated cadence and thus the history of music. *Social trends themselves* have been reflected and expressed in the sound-material, far beyond the unchanging physical facts and also far beyond a merely romantic espressivo. No other art is conditioned by social factors as much as the purportedly self-acting, even mechanically self-sufficient art of music; historical materialism, with the accent on 'historical', abounds here. The dominance of the melody-carrying upper part and mobility of the other parts correspond to the rise of the entrepreneur, just as the central *cantus firmus* and terraced polyphony corresponded to the hierarchical society. Haydn and Mozart, Handel and Bach, Beethoven and Brahms all had a social mission which was very specific; it extends from the form of performance to the *ductus* of the tonal material and its composition, and to the expression, the statement, of the content. Handel's oratorios reflect, in their proud solemnity, the rise of imperialist England and her claim to be the chosen people. There would have been no Brahms without the middle-class

concert society and even no musical *neue Sachlichkeit,* no purportedly expressionless music, without the enormous increase in
alienation, objectification and reification in late capitalism. It is
always the consumer sector and its requirements, the feelings and
aims of the ruling class which are expressed in music. Yet at the same
time, thanks to its capacity for such directly human expression,
music surpasses other arts in its ability to absorb the manifold griefs,
wishes and rays of hope common to the socially oppressed. And
again, no art so outstrips a given age and ideology – although this, of
course, is an outstripping which never abandons the human sector. It
is inherent in the material of hope, even when the music is expressing
sorrow at its times, society or world, and even in death. The sound of
the Bach cantata *Schlage doch, gewünschte Stunde* traverses the
darkness and, by virtue of its very existence, offers a mysterious
solace. *Evidently, therefore, expression of a human content is not
restricted to romantic expression,* as though this were all that
mattered and music would otherwise be only a sewing-machine. We
must not suppose that it was only Beethoven who supplied this
element, in some of his slow movements, and then, in the most exor-
bitant way, Wagner; with the result that in stretches of Wagner,
expression turns into a veritable parading of the soul, where he bares
his all. As it is time to demonstrate, we find the following instead.
Pre-Romantic music, in connection with its social contents, actually
aimed at an expression which turns out to be far more spontaneous
than modern expression. For the ancient Greeks regarded even the
flute as exciting, but the lyre as idyllic. The Dorian mode was considered powerful and propitious, and the Lydian mode feminine, the
mode of passive emotions. Then we have the vocalises and jubilations of mediaeval music, which were not just decorations and
melismatic excursions but went beyond words, in the interests of a
wholly exalted expression. Hence St Augustine says of the *jubilus* of
the Alleluia: 'When joy moves a person in the jubilation, he lets forth
some sounds which do not belong to speech and have no actual
meaning, and then bursts out into an exultation without words, so
that it seems he is moved by joy in such song but cannot sum up in
words what moves him.' In the first operas around 1600, Peri's and
Monteverdi's recitatives were still adòpting mediaeval vocalises and
tropes precisely because of their expressiveness. And the earlier and
far more complex music, the Flemish fabric of contrapuntal movement, was by no means averse to an expression *sui generis,* namely

late-Gothic and Christian. What has been stigmatised as 'artifice' or even 'study music' in the Flemish contrapuntists, their 'decadent late-Gothic formalism', may be partly accounted for simply by the fact that they have not yet been successfully revived from the purely technical viewpoint. Josquin wrote a 24-part motet which contains a strict six-part canon in each of the four voices. And yet his contemporary, Luther – who was generally hostile to scholasticism – said: 'Josquin is master of the notes and they have to do as he wanted; the other masters of song have to do what the notes want.' This sentence can only refer to the fund of will-power and expression pervading Josquin's mammoth filigree and mammoth, multi-tiered structure. With the beginnings of the harmonic style in Palestrina and Orlando di Lasso, we see quite clearly the unity of the *anima christiana* and its musical framework, Raphael-like in the one instance, incipiently Baroque in the other. Even Bach, who composed the most learned and at the same time most deeply inspirited music, makes nonsense of the antithesis of expression and canon. While it is absolutely wrong to romanticise Bach in the way Mendelssohn did, we do not come any closer to understanding him by merely dismissing Romanticism out of hand, as though we would then be left with nothing but reified form. Bach's composing can by no means be interpreted by partisan opponents of all expressive statements as a line-weaving in itself, indeed a prototype for the mechanisation at which late capitalism has arrived. With an ostensibly positive slant, this so-styled *neue Sachlichkeit* is reproducing an estimation of Bach which was common fifty years after his death and virtually buried the greatest of composers. In this estimation, Bach's music was unnatural and merely for the head, a 'sexton's music without spirituality' and mere periwigged arithmetic. (This view, incidentally, bears some similarity to the view of the great Flemish contrapuntists still current at the time of writing.) Such attributes are now praised in Bach as 'absolute music' in a supposedly positive sense, and always with that polemical contrast to purely Romantic espressivo which is totally irrelevant to the essence of Bach and *his specific espressivo*. As long ago as the 1870s, Spitta's Bach monograph was permeated and led astray by the same contrast, the same unfruitful repudiation of all emotional and expressive lines, although these make up almost the whole of Bach's music. Miserably defeated, Romanticism took its revenge by reintroducing expressive interpretation nonetheless, but now not even along Mendelssohnian lines but along those of the

202

Gartenlaube,[1] allegedly pure form plus *Gartenlaube*. Take the sinfonia at the beginning of the second part of the *Christmas Oratorio*. According to Spitta, normally a great supporter of absolute music, it is 'the charm of oriental idyll and the sobriety of a clear, starry Northern winter's night' which form 'the atmospheric background to this sinfonia'. This, in view of the rude vitality of the flutes and violins, is untenable not only technically but even as a pictorial association. And it is instructive that Albert Schweitzer's later Bach analysis, stemming entirely from his own performing experience, demonstrated the music's specific espressivo in the greatest detail. Down to the graphic character of the score and the perceived *gestus* of the action and emotion, Schweitzer shows what Bach's espressivo involves, in the cantatas and chorales and in the instrumental music. He presents us with a catalogue of documented expression, in which the melodic-rhythmic figures actually spring up and take shape, arising from 'affect' and also from its outward agitation. Thus we have figures of languor, agonised or proud grief, spontaneous or transfigured joy, horror and triumph. We find in Bach an incomparable expressive spectrum ranging from the fear of death and longing for death to solace, assurance, peace and victory. No form, however unified, is obstructing this, and no ground-bass is thwarting the leap from one extreme to the other – extremes occurring and contrasting only in love and in the domain of religious emotion. The contrast between *O Golgatha, unsel'ges Golgatha* and *Der Held aus Juda siegt mit Macht* is the range covered by this Baroque espressivo: Baroque in its sudden peripeteia and Baroque above all in its turbulent, Christian, emotional content. To this category belong not least the cantatas containing dialogues between Jesus and the soul or between solace and despair, allegorised in music. Indeed the prevalence of expression in Bach is so strong that the following verdict by Schweitzer on the chorale movements in Bach's cantatas and Passions may not appear extravagant: 'From the standpoint of pure music Bach's harmonisations are wholly enigmatic, for he does not work upon a tonal succession that in itself forms an aesthetic whole, but follows the lead of the poetry and the verbal expression. How far he lets these take him from the natural principles of pure composition may be seen from his harmonisation of "Solls je so sein, dass Straf und Pein", in the cantata *Ich elender Mensch, wer wird mich erlösen* (No. 48), which as pure music is indeed intolerable, Bach's purpose being to express all the wild grief for sin that is suggested in the words . . . Before he decides simply to write beautiful music to a text, he searches the words through and through to find an emotion which, after it has been intensified, is suitable for musical representation.'[2] While such statements may still be influenced by neo-Romantic expression rather too strongly, Schweitzer is nevertheless wholly correct on the central issue, that of the *verbal dictate which governs the music*. Indeed, in addition to the expressive power of the individual tone-drawings, of which Schweitzer cites a particularly large number, there is – hardly less importantly – the expressive power of veritable tone-paintings, and precisely where dissemination of the emotion in mythical terms is concerned. Key-changes often occur purely in order to reflect mythical processes of rejoicing. This is seen at its plainest with the theme of the Resurrection. In the music for *Et exspecto resurrectionem mortuorum* in the B minor Mass, the 'exspecto' makes a hesitant, uncertain appearance, the bass sings a descending six-note scale, and a pause ensues. Then comes the transformation which confirms the expectancy: the keys undergo modulation via G minor, A major and D minor to the D major of a Vivace allegro, at which we hear trumpets, whose timbre, with Bach, always signifies victory. And the primacy of expression is merely more latent in any music by Bach which is purely instrumental and not emotionally coloured by words. Granted, the fugue does not have any lyrico-emotional expressive tension. But it does contain a dynamic expressive tension which is condensed in the theme, and the development whips up the theme to eight parts contrapuntally and resolves it triumphantly. So, even here, we never find an adherence to rules for their own sake or indeed a formalistic exclusion of man, who was heavily burdened at that time but was crying to heaven all the more ardently. Equally expressive in nature, although still unconquered in its ultimate expression, is the crystal music in the organ fugues, in all their translucence; this is the least self-sufficient of all. And the more convivial works from Bach's Cöthen period – especially the Brandenburg Concertos in their magnificent and elegantly wrought construction, the variations they work and their heightened thematic richness – evince a supremely socio-dynamic expression, which does not flower from arithmetical problems. Thus expression is part of pre-Romantic music as well, being inherent in well-constructed music and an accretion only where the music is badly constructed. In well-constructed music it is never introduced through an emotional delivery. The performance – however much it must allow the 'mind' of the lines and forms to be heard – discovers expression in the lines and forms themselves, and within these alone. Expression is realised in forms regarded not as reifications and an end in themselves but as means to a word-surpassing or wordless statement and always, ultimately, to the *utterance of a – call* [*Ruf*].

On Biedermeier soil the emotionally charged voice often interposes, of course. This produces a great stir or much superfluous heat, yields soulfulness without expense and is an effect without a cause. It is found in Romantic music and Romantic music only, but never, significantly, in its well-wrought passages. And the demand not for lack of expression but for genuine, musically founded expression revolts against an accretion that makes Syrinx the nymph slimy and cheapens music's inherent sense of loss. Of course false emotion did have better origins, probably connected with the heartfelt popular style at the start of the folk-song's demise. The damage begins with the Count's accents in the last Act of *The Marriage of Figaro* ('Contessa, perdono!'); it continues with Florestan's 'In des Lebens Frühlingstagen'. It culminates in such pieces as the Prize Song of *The Mastersingers*, otherwise an opera of such solid power, and it makes itself felt in the 'Recordare Jesu pie' of the otherwise thoroughly genuine Verdi Requiem. Finally, Strauss presents this emotion, if not cynically, then with all the fervour that cellos can muster in the caressing tone of the Dyer's 'Mir anvertraut, dass ich dich hege' in *Die Frau ohne Schatten*. These are all merely episodic examples, but there would have been no room for their pastoso at all before Romanticism, and within the latter it constitutes a peril. For all Wagner's genius, this applies to many passages in his music, especially in *The Ring* where we have shrillness or the unctuous Wotan. The unique expressive gains, the Sleep motif, Erda's motif in *The Ring*, the motif of midsummer madness in *The Mastersingers* and so many musical gems and insights, the powerful unrest and nostalgia in this music and its pronouncements were not infrequently paid for with lengthy wallowing in self-sufficient lyrical rhetoric. Of the great poets, only Schiller was haunted by the spell of a distortedly expressive monstrousness, a spell which is by no means synonymous with pathos or even false pathos. The virus takes different forms: it inhabits the senseless fervour of Romantic violin tone and the bloated imprecations of Wagnerian heroines, and it is always effect composed of affects or affect composed of effects. Arch-Romantic music, then, was without doubt peculiarly threatened by this, and no doubt there were causes behind it which were at least recognised and no longer approved in more advanced regions. Its social cause was the broad urban bourgeoisie with its need for vague titillation and above all the lower middle class with its retailing of emotions at bargain prices. Technically speaking the psychical, all too psychical virus was carried by middle parts inserted for the sake of colour instead of plasticity, by thick instrumentation and by basically torrid or over-excited rhythms. Tchaikovsky's music often constitutes a whole monument to this kind of espressivo (not forgetting the first Act of *The Valkyrie*). But such extreme cases, needless to say, are not the *real* expression of Romantic music. Nor is its *real* expression divorced from, or added on to, the *great technical construction*. Expression is always music's *terminus a quo* and *terminus ad quem* to such a degree that good music will shape it as inevitably as bad music will counterfeit it and turn espressivo into its opposite: meaninglessness. So we are not concerned with any of this unformed, illicit, expression from the Romantic period, which discredited the term 'expression'. It was mere bodily warmth, or a herd-warmth ['Kuhwärme'], as Thomas Mann put it, and it lacked strict control and a pleasure in orderliness. This was the garbage of the Romantic movement, not that classical face which *is* portrayed in its music. The quartet in *Fidelio* and the quintet in the *Mastersingers* provide expressive music that is both canonic and Romantic; for this reason the two pieces are also the most finely constructed. We cannot miss the part-writing on account of the soul-searching, any more than we can miss the pathos inherent in a very great contrapuntal marvel like the *Crucifixus* of Bach's B minor Mass. True, Romantic music did sometimes also endow its expression with *literary* signposts which are redundant (Beethoven's headings to the *Pastoral* Symphony) or not in fact conducive to the best results (the out-and-out programme symphony from Berlioz to Strauss). But even this was a means of pursuing intrinsically musical interests: the object was to instil in music an ever-greater expressive precision by means of the series of ideas provided. Admittedly, another danger was that music would be comprehended as a mere illustration of literary imaginative devices, contrary to its latent power of expression far beyond all the words in the dictionary. Even here, however, as in all more exalted use of a text, the charm of the verbal expression is wholly subservient to music's deepest concern: to be, discover or become a language *sui generis*. Since, indeed, its power of expression lies beyond anything we can put a name to, the final issue at stake is no longer expression in music at all but *music itself as expression*. That is to say, the *sum total of its meaning, signification and representation and of that which it represents so mistily and yet, in both senses of the word, so grippingly*. And it is with this sole purpose that music – such a recent art in its polyphonic form – is approaching the hour of its own special language and its poesis *a se*, prefigured in powerful expression but still unknown all the same. This language, of course, comes solely from absolute music, not from some fixed text that is superimposed. To borrow a comparison from Wagner, any literature which is set to great music bears the same relation to music's ineffable expressive power as a commentary by Gervinus[3] bears to a Shakespeare play. In the last analysis, then, musical expression as a whole *is the viceroy for an articulate utterance which goes much farther than is currently understood*. This has occurred, in different contexts, in all great music. But it will only be fully perceived when the hour of eloquence has come, in the form of a revelatory music. What Isolde hears as a fountain, in the nocturnal silence, still sounds like a fanfare of horns to Brangäne. That is to say, should visionary hearing of that kind be attained through successful musical poesis *a se*, then all music we already know will *later sound and give forth other expressive contents besides those it has had so far*. Then the musical expression perceived up to now could seem like a child's stammering by comparison, a language of an ultimate kind that is seeking to take shape but has come close to doing so only in a few, very exalted places. Nobody can understand it yet, although it is occasionally possible to surmise its meaning. *But nobody has as yet heard Mozart, Beethoven or Bach as they are really calling, designating and teaching*; this will only happen much later, with the fullest maturation of these and all great works. It will happen, therefore, with the ear-muff removed that intensively besets music, an ear-muff which stems from the fact that the note does not yet have, or give forth, the full eloquent light of its understanding. Among the arts, music contains a very special ingredient lending itself to the quotation of that still wordless element which achieves expression instrumentally and can penetrate within the sung word to both its undertone and overtones. Thus the utopian art of music, which as polyphony is so recent, is itself still making for a special, utopian course, that of fully-fledged *exprimatio* (within and instead of

207

emotional or descriptive espressivo). The *utopikum* of this expression is the *hour of eloquence through music, understood as visionary hearing*. It is a poesis *a se* with passwords affording entry into the material tonal nature of everything that flows, before, while, and indeed after, it becomes more or less adequately manifest. This something that is adequate to our own and to all core has not yet emerged; its conscience, throbbing affectively and yet not just affectively, its rhythmic-melodic summons, produced by great masters: this is finally music. 'If we could name ourselves our Chief would come, and music is the one subjective theurgy',[4] i.e. one whose purpose is to sing and invoke the essentiality most in the likeness of men. This song and its expression are subjective, far more so than in any other art save for lyric poetry. To this extent, the experience of musicians provides the best access to the hermeneutics of affects and in particular the affects of expectancy. But music is also subjective in a significantly different sense, in that its *expression* not only mirrors the *affective looking-glass* reflecting *a given society and the world as it occurs* in *affective correlates*. Music also comes close to the subject-based *hearth and driving force* of events, as a subject-based exterior. This *agens* is still in a state of ferment beneath everything already determined and has not itself emerged yet in an objectively stated form. Hence musical expression, too, is still fermenting and has not emerged yet in a finished, definable form. This objective-indeterminate element in the expressed, represented, musical content is the (temporary) defect of its qualities. Accordingly it is the art of pre-semblance [*des Vor-Scheins*][5] which is related to the flowing existential core (instant) of that-which-is-in-being most intensively, and to the horizon of the latter most expansively. *Cantus essentiam fontis vocat* – music names the essence of the fountainhead.

MUSIC AS CANON AND ORDERED WORLD;
HARMONY OF THE SPHERES, MORE HUMANE POLE-STARS

Because of the aforestated dangers it was all the more necessary to handle the note's drifting character in a thoroughly sober, impassive manner. Craftsmanship remained highly esteemed in music when it was dying out or totally forgotten in painting. Playing the recorder is something that needs to be learnt, and one has to know the rules of the waltz or of jazz, for every mistake is audible. All the same, musical craftsmanship – while far removed from the spectre of emotionality – never led an independent or abstract existence. Human needs, socially changing tasks, have been behind it ever since the days of the syrinx. It is clear that the means and techniques of so companionable an art are largely determined by the given social conditions, and that society will extend far into the sound-material, which is in no sense self-active or Nature-given. Equal temperament restricted to octaves is so much a product of history that it is only a few centuries old. Sonata form with its conflict of two themes, its key-note, development and reprise, presupposes a capitalist dynamics; the multi-layered and totally undramatic fugue, a static hierarchical society. So-called atonal music would not have been possible in any other era than that of the late bourgeois decline, to which it responded in the form of a bold perplexity. The twelve-note technique, which forsakes the dynamic relationship between dissonance and consonance, modulation and cadence in order to form strict, immobile rows, would have been inconceivable in the age of free enterprise. Indeed, only the history of music from 1600 onwards, or even from 1750 to 1900, is a history of the dissonance and cadence. Hence each musical form itself and not just its expression depends on the given relationship of men to other men and is a reflex of this. To be sure, such a reflex is often reified and curiously removed from the actual expression and even the *humanum* of music. This is why it could seem as though there were two kinds of music: that of soulful emotion vented in song and that of pure, almost mechanically self-sufficient, form. Hence the dispute between the two is manifested not only with regard to musical works but also in the different and perhaps even incompatible meanings of the word 'music'. On one occasion the word will be used to designate the *wholly unformed*, the pure mood, and the note's spectral character is appropriate to this. On another, conversely, it will signify *a mastery in the learned skills* of combination, a concern with the part rather than the heart. Sometimes music is regarded as a diffuse vagueness, as in the context of Schiller's observation: 'A certain musical frame of mind comes to me first, and only then does the poetic idea follow.' Christian Weisse, the Hegelian, expressed this in his aesthetics by placing music in the lowest category of the arts; by saying that in the tonal realm the spirit of the ideal still lacks shape and is weaving within itself, only expanding in the plastic arts and only expressing itself in a concentrated way in poetry (see Lotze, *Geschichte der Ästhetik*, 1868, pp. 455f). At other times, on the contrary, music is regarded as a supremely finished construction, in fact a piece of mathematical logic which has strayed into the flimsy carryings-on of art almost by mistake, like Saul among the prophets. This is a repercussion of music's academic status in the quadrivium of mediaeval studies, where it constituted a science together with arithmetic, geometry and astronomy. It was the Pythagorean, mathematical-astronomical, theory of music which gave the art its place in the quadrivium and indeed elevated it to a very superior, cosmically governed science. In this view, music was anything but a shapeless rushing or a warm bank of mist. Kepler connected it rather with the firmament, the realm of the purest cyclical motions, which were also the most objective in the world. Here, music did not well up out of feeling but gushed forth from the planets, pouring itself on the Earth first and only then on human beings. 'It is the task and predisposition of the Earth-soul to provoke the Earth into sweating so that rain will arise and the Earth will be usefully moistened. It is impelled to this through the attraction of the aspects, which is rather like a heavenly music; it will not stir until encouraged by a celestial tune . . . But the reason for the comparison of the astronomical aspects to music is that both the circle divided according to the aspects and the monochord divided according to the harmonies have divisions' (Johann Kepler in his *Letters*). So whereas music lacks all precision when taken to mean a mood, it has been treated as mathematics when it has meant proportion and also composition. Men have thought that music as a mood ceases to be music as soon as it assumes an intelligible shape, hence turning into architecture and poetry. Music as form and proportion, on the other hand, is deemed to become all the more itself, the more orderly its utterance and cosmographic nature are. Whereas music as a mood remains buried within the soul and seems the most chthonian of all the arts, so-called *musica mathematica* becomes wholly Uranian and steps off in heaven. These, then, are controversies which are quite different from the dispute between expression and form, although they are related to it on an elevated theoretical plane. And the upshot is that in ages where expressive contents are rare, the great formal achievements of musical craftsmanship will be reified with particular ease. It has been said that a composer is a combination of a shaman and an engineer; at all events, after the discrediting of Romantic exuberance, it is the engineer who makes the more modern impression. Thus musical craftsmanship itself is denied its expressive task and becomes allied totally to a physical theory of notes, though a very highly developed one. The problem raised is not only *melos* without expression but – deriving *from the self-sufficient canon's ideal and image of perfection* – *melos* without an 'I', music dictated by rules. The Pythagorean and Keplerian background dimly but insistently makes itself felt: music is presented as a framework of parts following or rotating in an extra-human order. This order can be of the most prosaic kind, in fact a regulating of mere chance. A popular example is Scarlatti's *Cat's Fugue*, said to have taken its theme from the keys depressed by a cat which was crossing the keyboard. The ordering, however, can be extra-human in a more elevated way. Then even the keen disciplinarian will not frown upon its appearance in expressive music, as in the Adagio of Bruckner's Sixth Symphony, where three octaves of a scale slowly pass each other the gold buckets[6] – a favourite example (even Beethoven offers a similar one in the *Pastoral* Symphony's finale) of music that exists on well-tempered tone-physics and, on the face of it, nothing else. Generally speaking, music as expression is not so much rejected as outstripped or at least replaced through a purportedly extra-human order. Instead of expressing the soul, it now manifests itself as *a copy of the cosmos, a reproduction of cosmic conditions*, much as it was thought that architecture would reach its grandest consummation when it copied a cosmic system. If formalistic music does not take the structure of the world as its model, it does believe in subject-less order, i.e. in music as a set of rules instead of music as existence. From this standpoint, harmony and counterpoint appear to be both self-sufficient and transparent – and always transparent in mathematical-physical terms. True, we do not hear numbers and formulae, but we are at least supposed to discern forces in music which also occur in mechanical processes, in dynamism and stasis, e.g. falling, discharging, equilibrium and the like. But dialectics of Nature are less often mentioned in this context, in spite of the dichotomy in the sonata's thematicism and structural layout. Nor does Nature as a human symbol, heard through music, come into the reckoning for what is now a one-sided external series. For *in a theory of rules which is as reified as this theory is*, mechanics alone will still be visible on the horizon, a mere reflex of mechanisation in a secularised, formerly Keplerian Nature. Thus in the late-bourgeois anti-expression theory of music and its reification of form, the extra-human very easily turns into the anti-human, and there is a clear fun-

211

damental relation. Matter-of-factness [*Sachlichkeit*] is interpreted entirely as a system of rules governing something alien. 'Music, moody food of us that trade in love,' says Shakespeare; and yet there is no connection between the hypostatised *Cat's Fugue* and Syrinx the nymph or the stage of self-transcending, the utopian sound of one's source and existence. Nonetheless, this distinction too is an artificial one and just as artificial and abstract as the distinction between expression and well-wrought form, which are in truth one and gladly support each other. And similarly, music as a world of harmonic-contrapuntal rules is only at odds with music as the utopian sound of existence if the world of rules (i.e. a specific perfection of its means) has been reified and absolutised; if the target of creating the best music is lost within a music without a designation, a mere intrinsic guarantee of melodic-contrapuntal consistency. When counterpoint has become an aural form-fetish, the two musics are at war. But let us avoid this absolutising. Let us assume that we have neither music in which we cannot sense anything expressive, nor a corresponding science from which our minds cannot derive anything enlightening. Then it is precisely in music's *theory of forms* that its deep-seated and far-aiming intention will instantly emerge and be set in motion. To counter the purely drifting and vaguely warm element in the note, musical craftsmanship will then transmit what is *indeed a world of rules – not however an automatic one, but the world of the human personages of Mozart, Bach and Beethoven*, which will have now become not a canon, but canonic. Then even the ultimate transparence of an absolutised handicraft, music in its cosmic relation – which is to say the harmony of the spheres, which has been secularised time and again – will do no more damage in the end. Indeed it must serve the best of purposes, serving as a prefiguration that will allow Nature, too, to be heard as a . . . pastorale, i.e. in humanly significant terms.

Thus the note is now going far afield, and it has equipped itself for its journey. A note that is formed possesses – and painters have always envied it for this – exact rules and firm understanding. Of all the crafts, music was the *earliest to be rationalised*; it did not only consist of empirically tested devices and the trade secrets of the masters. *Mutatis mutandis*, the geometry and rules of correct proportions explored by Leonardo and Dürer had dwelt for a long time within the musical canon. The ancient tradition that promulgated music as a science was a principal reason for this salutary rationalisation of it. So music became one of the seven 'liberal arts' in the mediaeval university, and it entered the quadrivium. Certainly this tradition was acquired at a high cost, the exaggerating of numerical relations, and it had hardly any connection with the practice of music, to which Pythagorean speculations were a downright hindrance. All the same, the traditional rationalisation of music was a boon for the polyphonic style that appeared in the eleventh century. Not Pythagoras but in all likelihood a closeness to the scholastic way of teaching and thinking made possible the miracles of ingenuity that were constructed by the contrapuntists of Burgundy and Flanders. Painters went their empirical way through the studios; the stonemasons had their lodge, where practical geometry and an oral tradition of gnosis were combined in an often mysterious fashion. But in music, the enrichment of the polyphonic style went hand in hand with the penning of its rational theory – a *Speculum musicae* by Jean de Muris, and from Jacob of Liège in 1330, and an *Ars nova* and *Ars contrapuncti* by Philip of Vitry. And there arose a connection which so far has never been followed up and yet has sustained the proud rationality of counterpoint right up to the present: a connection with *scholastic logic or, to be more precise, with its forms of combination.* It is significant that Boëthius, who passed on the tradition of Greek music theory in his *Ars musica*, translated and wrote commentaries on Aristotelian logic for the same world and, in many cases, the same people. Abelard praised Boëthius as showing absolute insight in musical matters; if this verdict changed in the subsequent centuries of counterpoint, it was supplanted by the authority of the manifold *conversiones* and *contrapositiones* of a doctrine which Boëthius was again the first to pass on. The difference between artistic rules in counterpoint and the laws of truth in logic was no obstacle to this cross-connection. For, leaving aside the status of music in the quadrivium as one of the seven liberal arts, scholastic logic had for some time ceased to maintain epistemological aims like those of Aristotelian logic. Rather it had extensively developed into a theory of formal consequences, especially in changes of judgement, as we see in the textbooks from Petrus Hispanus onwards. Counterpoint was a variation on a theme in several parts, *ex una voce plures faciens*, through inversion, imitation, cancrizans and so forth. Scholastic logic laid down variations and combinations of elements of formal judgement, *ex uno judicio plures faciens*, through conversion, contraposition, subalternation, modal consequence and so forth. To these consequences were added the conclusions, or modes of the concluding figures, which rest upon the different combinational possibilities of the premises; the actual art of combination had been borrowed from mathematics back in Alexandria. Admittedly we cannot compare more closely the 'arithmetical model' of the fugue (also called *conseguenza* in fourteenth-century Italy) and the 'jigsaw puzzle' of scholastic logic, because the material is too disparate. But in both fields we find a remarkably similar spirit; it was, after Petrus Hispanus, essentially one of a formally correct working out in logic as much as in music. It was a rationalism of sorting-out [*Auswicklung*] and subsumption as opposed to the more recent rationalism of development [*Entwicklung*] and generation. It is this legacy which brings to musical form – besides the aforesaid danger – a special dignity, particularly if this dignity is linked with the essential articulate expression which it is its sole purpose to embody.

And now we return to the most famous argument behind all this revelling in musical laws: *the harmony of the spheres and its offspring, the cosmic theory of music.* For in its mythical-utopian archetype, we find another character besides the half Pythagorean, i.e. besides the apparent correlation of musical laws *per se.* It is a matter of opening up this other character by human means and thus disrupting the connection with the cosmic theory of music. This theory held sway for all too long, but it taught the musical work to think a very great deal of itself. Through the Pythagorean ban on thirds and sixths it hindered music's development, but it gave the music that came into being the ambition to achieve an enormous correlate. Although it was an ungodly astral myth, it provided the dream of musical perfection with a counterpart to what was for so long the purported canon of the cosmic system in architecture. Indeed whereas this canon (up to the temple of Solomon) often applied only in a poetic sense or in esoteric schools, heavenly music was actually associated with earthly, learned music and served as its ideal model in scholastic reasoning, from the beginning of the latter until long after its heyday. 'Early mediaeval musical theory was as staunch an adherent to the music of the spheres as the Pythagorean school itself . . . Thus the proposition of the Church Fathers that Church music comes from God and has its model in the singing of the heavenly hosts found a certain degree of philosophical support' (Abert: *Die Musikanschauung des Mittelalters*, 1905). Music's temple of Solomon was the song of the planets and, after St Augustine, the song of the angels; intervals, which the Pythagoreans equated with the distances between planets, now corresponded to the *ordines angelorum*. But even in Christian thought, the link with the planets was never broken. St Ambrose, the founder of Christian church music, actually taught that the mysterious music of the universe was the archetype and prototype of earthly music, and King David was supposed to have introduced the art of psalmody in imitation of the song of the planets (the heavens praise the glory of God everlasting). The Carolingian music scholar Aurelian of Réomé, one of the most influential revivers of the Greek modes, always connected the eight modes with the heavenly motions, but his doctrine also stated that 'In hoc (sc. cantandi officio) angelorum choros imitamus'. Thus music acquired a framework which was both cosmic and sacred, with gradations, and which united Ptolemy and mystical emanation. Already, Boëthius had taught the following classification: first, *musica mundana*, the universal motion determined by proportion and number; next, *musica humana*, the ensemble of body and soul; and lastly *musica instrumentalis*, the lowest, audible emanation. The celestial heptachord was associated with the intervals and modes, and the angelic choir with the ancient Christian antiphonal and responsorial chant. Even the innovation of the polyphonic canon did not lack the sound of the spheres as a model. From the Arabic theory of music (al-Farabi) had come the parable of the flowering tree whose branches were finely proportioned by means of numbers, whose blossoms were the different kinds of consonance and whose fruits were the dulcet harmonies (see Abert, opus cit.). The universal tree is an age-old oriental simile, probably far older than that of the planetary spheres, but it could be linked with the Gothic trellis pattern that was now appearing in music. When the mensuralist Marchettus of Padua uses it around 1300, there is a connection with the art of singing several differently measured notes in the upper part against one note, i.e. the beginnings of the art of counterpoint. Music itself thus became a richly sub-divided structure and a tree with many branches. But this polyphony and its ramifications still did not abandon the astral order: the polyrhythmic, polyphonic ground-bass included choirs of angels. This was in spite of the completely new musical form and also in spite of that scepticism about the harmony of the spheres which arose at the end of the Middle Ages. An intended copying of *musica mundana* as being the best music is found in the motets of Philip of Vitry, the contrapuntist we have mentioned.

Although published as an *Ars nova*, i.e. an art giving free rein to the native imagination, the melodies showed a strict uniformity and periodicity and no changes of rhythm, in conscious 'imitation' of the rotation of the stars. Such music had its theoretical basis in the contemporaneous aforementioned *Speculum musicae* by Jacob of Liège, a complete demonstration in notes of the universal hierarchy. The universality of music was defended and scholastically classified. It now extended from the *res transcendentales et divinae* to cover the whole cathedral of the universe via stars, people, animals, plants and stones. And when the hierarchical world-picture reflected in the heavens had shattered, the harmonies of the spheres were still heard in art. There were still 'touches of sweet harmony', as Lorenzo described the stars to Jessica, still these sublime lines of recollection: 'Die Sonne tönt nach alter Weise / In Brudersphären Wettgesang'.[7] And natural science, which deprived the world of these divine attributes, was itself still deeply embedded in Pythagorean doctrine to begin with. Even Kepler, one of the men who shattered the old image of the world, adhered to the music of the spheres, and went so far as to describe it in terms of the counterpoint of his age. With Kepler, the *Lyra Apollinis vel Solis* became the Baroque orchestra with all its polyphony. 'The celestial movements are therefore nothing but a constant sounding together, . . . all in a six-part texture, as it were' (with the six planets as individual parts), 'and organising and interrupting infinite time with these notes. And so it is not surprising, furthermore, that man, who copies his Creator, has gained an insight into polyphonic song which was denied to the ancients, reproducing the constant flux of world-history with a polyphonic musical structure of much artistry in the brief fraction of one hour, and thus vicariously savouring the Creator's delight in his work through the delicious feeling of bliss that music, as it copies God, imparts to him' (*Harmonices mundi V*, chapter 7). Finally, and as was to be expected, Romantic natural philosophy gave a fresh boost to the ancient celestial magic. This is most audible in Schelling. His *Philosophy of Art* again sought 'to establish the supreme meaning of rhythm, harmony and melody' in an astronomical fashion. In so doing Schelling associated rhythm and homophonic melody, as possessed by the ancients, with the world of the planets, but harmony and counterpoint, as an allegedly confused movement, with the – comets! This apart, however, his endeavour constitutes a fresh revival of the astronomical theory of music in its entirety – although, to be sure, it is already as foreign to the music of the age as it is cosmic in construction. 'Heavenly bodies float on the wings of harmony and rhythm; what has been called centripetal and centrifugal force is nothing else than – this rhythm, that harmony. Lifted up by the same wings, music floats in space in order to weave an audible universe from the diaphanous body of sound and the note.' Item, *the history of the harmony of the spheres is still the history of the canonic system of the cosmos in music and hence the history of the temple of Solomon in music*, i.e. the most highly conceived form-utopia. This form-utopia, of course, is only utopian because distant in space. Its wish-dream applies to a location which is not already present. Ideal time [*Wunschzeit*], and consequently real utopia, infiltrates this changing harmony of the spheres, the avowed harmonic-integrity of Creation, only inasmuch as one conceives its ideal space [*Wunschraum*] as being filled not simply with the music of angels but with that of a *future Jerusalem*. This occurs in the earlier accounts of a – blissful end in which the departing person, when well on his way, seemingly succeeds in hearing from the beyond a song of the joy to come. The idea survives until far into the Baroque era in the diverse references to musical miracles, as in the book *Of the Three Ages* (1660) by Sperber, a Joachite and Rosicrucian: 'When, in 1596, a doorless chapel was accidentally discovered in Jerusalem, people heard an agreeable harmony like an angelic or celestial music coming from within. So they were in no doubt that in a few years would commence the new age and joyful era when they would constantly delight in hearing all that celestial music of which earthly music is only the beginning.' Moreover we may recall, in a context which is anything but heretical, the exclamation of Pius IV on hearing Palestrina's *Marcellus* Mass: 'Here a John in the earthly Jerusalem is giving us an idea of that song which the holy Apostle John once perceived in prophetic ecstasy in the heavenly Jerusalem.' There is an epigone's echo of this at the end of Act 1 in Pfitzner's opera *Palestrina*, where he portrays the creation of the *Marcellus* Mass. Here, first one angel's voice, then several, and then angelic choirs stretching to dizzying heights sing the music to the 'inspired' composer. And Bruckner's majestic triads imply a background of heavenly sovereignty still based in real faith; a burst of cherubic voices seems to be reflected in the octave leap divided by a fifth which pervades his *Te Deum*.

To sum up, then: the hypostatizedly mythical element in the *orien-*

tation of both astral and astral-Christian longing is undeniably obvious, although it has not to this day died out theoretically. All the same, we should not overlook the positive element in this ungodly astral myth of music – that which denotes its disintegration, its human and utopian breaking up, and that element alone. The positive element in a very large-scale form-correlate of true music must be fully appreciated, but with a concrete-utopian *change of function oriented towards the makanthropos* or Great Man. There are certainly stars in musical sound, but stars which have only taken shape as the names of human beings. There are certainly illustrious orders in harmony and counterpoint, but they are called Mozart, Bach or Beethoven. Their intrinsic value is the *existere* expressed through these categories, in the medium of sound close at hand. Certainly there is a transparent relation of rhythm and counterpoint, if not of harmony and counterpoint. This, however, obtains not from some isolated structure of these forms themselves, far less from the universal music in which we believed for so long, but from the great composers and their universe, which objectified itself in these forms. After such objectifying, a counterpoint can be related not to a realm of higher laws but to the musically utopian subject–object content as articulated in Mozart, Bach or Beethoven; – by virtue of this inner factor a universe will still resound. And what of the temple of the universe that was supposed to reverberate as music? It was a useful notion in that it prevented this art, which appeared to be so tied to a subject, from being a private music. This was the best service that the harmony of the spheres could and did perform: it snatched music out of the pure inner light and indeed pure psychology. But architecture based on 'cosmic proportions' constantly reminded one that it was oriented first and last to social needs and human dimensions. And this is even truer of music, which is related to the latent subject and the object perfectly matching it as no other art is. Hence the language sought and implied in music lies much farther than any other art beyond the existing terms as well as the achieved contents that they designate. It surpasses the agreed and known facts of the emotional contents and any scenic realisation that is already cut-and-dried. This still applies where music seems only the accompaniment to a text in a song, oratorio or opera. Music reflects reality in the aura-manifestations of its 'naturalising': manifestations which are not yet controlled or comprehended on the pictorial or, often, poetic level. What informed sound thus reproduces, in a statement as illuminating as it is affective, is an intensive root, a signalised social tendency or – in the manifold pastorale – a natural world discerned as a musical figure and newly de-reified. Hence even when, precisely when, music constitutes a revelling in the rules of composition, it is transmitting the prophetic language of that which fills the human and man-related bosom of all existence and which, in consequence, belongs extensively to the *insistent disquiet and dawning possibility which are lodged in reality.* Hereby, music is undoubtedly jeopardised by mere animal warmth in respect of its intensive features as much as it is by an all too amorphous and generally indistinct character in respect of its vast horizons. yet both are (temporary) defects of its expressive qualities, which are venturing forth on so profound and so broad a basis. And above all: since Gregorian chant, music has been borne along by a tendency towards moral order and – even without the myth of the spheres and astral myth – a perfect harmony. Both historically and objectively, then, music proves to be essentially a Christian art. Its harmony of the spheres simultaneously disintegrates and reveals itself, becoming the *source-sound of self-shapings still unachieved in the world.*

TONE-PAINTING; WORK OF NATURE AGAIN; THE INTENSITY AND MORALITY OF MUSIC

It does not go without saying that the note can indicate external things and be related to them. After all, it inhabits precisely that region where our eyes can tell us nothing more and a new dance begins. Nonetheless, sound is not just inward. It is rather the case that its inward nature has a subterranean relation to that exterior which is not just outward. This is true of all tone-painting, providing that it does not confine itself to a mere trifling copy of a few available noises or voices like the trickling of water, the sound of thunder or the nightingale's voice. In tone-painting, good music always reproduces something other than a superficial impression. Rather it extracts a sounding and demonstrating which is surplus to the real object that has come into being. This kind of tone-painting is as old as good music, and it does not embarrass it in any way whatever. Tone-painting also takes the lowest forms, certainly. And the thinner the instrument, the cheaper the music and the more vulgar the listener, the more this practice was assured of popularity. Timotheus, the Greek cithara virtuoso, is reported as imitating the sounds of

219

battles; he was even banished from Sparta for this reason, and rightly so. Sixteenth-century English virtuosi of the spinet used to copy birds' voices, thunder and lightning – although they also portrayed fine weather, to which there was more than cheap imitation. From a very early stage, however, other musicians besides virtuoso performers have gone into the tonal side of the external world, with aims other than the amusements of fireworks or waxworks. Jannequin, a pupil of Josquin, went so far as to turn tone-painting (and even the mighty Josquin had not despised it) into a genre of its own, composing hunting, bird and battle pieces with mimicry and counterpoint. In 1529 he wrote the once-famous *Cris de Paris*, which include the noise of the streets and the hawkers' shouts. In 1910, Erik Satie was to write an equally acceptable piece titled 'Dining on the Pump-Room Terrace', while Honegger takes a locomotive as his *musicae personam* in his *Pacific 231*. Such compositions may seem the exception, and a mere reinvigorating of music with noises instead of new notes. Yet the exception immediately becomes the rule when it is constantly found in the greatest of composers. Now Bach did not just practise tone-painting but offered what is literally tone-drawing [*Tongraphik*]. That is to say, he added a musical figure to the figure described in the text and realised in the visible world, thereby enabling this real figure to speak in notes, in the unfrozen speech-flux of its content. Hence the musical images of striding, collapsing, descending, ascending and so forth in the cantatas and Passions, a constant aural demonstration of the scene – *in fluxu nascendi*, that is. One example typical of hundreds is Cantata No. 39 with its setting of the text, 'Das Unglück schlägt auf allen Seiten um mich ein zentnerschweres Band' ('Misfortune casts all around me the weightiest of bonds'); from nearby and out of the distance there come, respectively, a helping hand and the light of solace. Now Bach's music employs three descriptive figures. We have not only the rising figure of the rescuing, helping, hand and the typical flickering figure of a light but also a symbolic figure of encircling, to represent the state of one around whom a heavy bond has been cast. In lesser music such tone-drawing could easily appear ridiculous, but with Bach it is part of the de-reifying musical movement. That was how he audibly realised the sound-image that matched visible or frozen images and was still in a state of flux, still only just taking shape.

This continued without interruption in music's new and more agile form, although it seemed to withdraw from description to some extent. After Bach's seriousness, the downright incessant tone-painting in Haydn's *Creation* looks like mere sport. And the depiction of 'mood' had a sequel in the new, naturalistic musical style, ranging from the specific genre-picture to the specific fresco. This style allowed entire, connected emotional processes to be related musically to the causes and consequently to the objects as well. Barbarina's cavatina in *Figaro* comes into this category. So do Beethoven's strongly motivated burlesque, *Rage over a Lost Penny*, and Rocco's aria in *Fidelio* where, even without words, gold is clinking in the orchestra and preying on his mind. Most notably, this category includes – with its thoroughly virile style – the 'Awakening of Joyful Feelings on Arriving in the Country' as the countryside itself. It includes Beethoven's 'Scene by the Brook' and certainly the *Pastoral* Symphony's portrayal of the storm, perceived through the elective affinity with the composer's own nature. The sulphureous warning note in the sultry atmosphere which interrupts the dance of the countryfolk, the double eruption of lightning (not thunder): these convey an electricity that only music, the art which is its own *agens*, is able to discern underneath the phenomenon and match artistically. The sound-world awakened in this way has not been achieved since. Along with and instead of trivial detail, Nature – both charming and violent – is reproduced in that world out of its sound's fluidity. But at a somewhat lower level (in the chthonian sense, too), this was also the cue for the start of Romantic tone-painting. Here we have a partly hesitant and in part strongly vaporose, crepuscular invocation through dark tonal registers, through Nature's nocturnal facets. Via the Wolf's Glen music, this dealing in spectres and magic was to culminate in Wagner. There it no longer occurs in fluent motions but rather in ferment, thunder, phosphorus, fire and brimstone. Hence the music, no longer graphic but distorting or floating, of autumn and mist, the ponderously raging storm at the beginning of *The Valkyrie*; hence the crudely decorative Ride of the Valkyries and the magic fire. But hence too so original a start as the E flat major triad of the gushing Rhine from whose depths the Nibelung music rises. Or the glinting, whispering and confusedly jagged music of the Erda scene, one of the most powerful manifestations in sound of the subterranean. All these locales have indistinct lighting and are reproductions of Nature deriving from the surging element and bound for a dreamed-of, mythical realm – notwithstanding the 'naturalism' with which Hans Sachs hammers away at Beckmesser's shoes and

Alberich's dwarfs hammer on their anvils. With Wagner the tone-painting remains essentially chthonian; the light in which it occurs is a fiery glare from the depths. And this glare remains dominant even where it overflows into the autumn's popular rejoicing or the springtime light on the meadow. Here Wagner differs in turn from late-Romantic Nature music or musical natures, which were far closer to the surface or wedded to the daylight. It is thus with Richard Strauss, the master of the superficial, as in the curious sounds that represent the bleating of sheep in his *Don Quixote*. It is thus with Mahler, the master of a universal Holy Night – especially in spring where he allows voices of Nature to infiltrate, always with a ray of hope or salvation. Peculiarly non-Wagnerian in this respect, for all the Romantic affinities, are the Alpine heights in the first movement of Mahler's Sixth Symphony, otherwise so deeply tragic. Over a static bass we hear chords without a key, chords of the second that alternate with triadic harmonies, interspersed with cow-bells, flutes and kettledrums; high above, a musical portrait of the solitude of Nature. Nowhere is Wagner's relation with Nature attuned to these Aeolian harps. And neither is it attuned to a signal of liberation that would break Nature's spell. Nearly all Wagner's human beings are at home in the volcanic world of impulse, in the Schopenhauerian Will, acting and talking from within this natural dream-state. Not only the magnetic Senta and Elsa but also most of the *Ring* characters, in their fervid lyricism, and even Eva and Walther resemble the glow-worm that (to quote Sachs's words) is finding or missing its mate. Such was the cost of achieving – the reverse of a music of the spheres, namely a music that comes from the belly of Nature. These people come of the same stock as the unillumined Nature which acts and resounds through them, sounding in a unique surge or flickering flame. In accord with his musical depiction of the elements, Wagner's musical characters all too often become 'bobbing ships which passively share in the grief, the struggle, the love and yearning for redemption of their sub-human sea and experience only the universal wave of Schopenhauerian Will washing over them at every critical moment, instead of a mutual encounter and their own profound destiny'.[8] This, then, was the price that Romantic composers paid for the constantly remarkable phenomenon of a *copying of Nature as the unearthing of Nature*, i.e. as the depiction in notes of her dark side only. Bach had rendered audible the musical figure for what was visible or frozen, *in fluxu nascendi*, as we have observed. For their part, the Romantics painted *natura naturans* not as a diagram but as phosphorus. All the same, we find the sub-real, as something pre-real, even in Bach. Goethe captured this in his famous statement: 'I told myself it was as though everlasting harmony were conversing with itself, as may have been going on in God's heart shortly before the creation of the world. I too felt this inner animation, and it seemed as if I neither possessed nor needed ears, far less eyes or any of the other senses.' This latter regression or unearthing, however, is far from being something chthonian. It was heard not by Schopenhauer (who, significantly, never mentioned Bach) but rather by Hegel (who, equally significantly, praised Bach for his 'sturdy genius'). Romantic music's unearthing of Nature – which in Wagner's case was also oriented in theory towards Schopenhauer and his ground of the Will – had a completely different result. Here a downright savage core of things was depicted and reproduced. Certainly, what sprouted from it was only the inhumane world once more, the world of the Norns, a fate from which this music knows no means of escape. When Siegfried, himself a child of Nature, breaks the spell, he is only accomplishing a predetermined fate. When Parsifal extricates himself from it, then it is the universal world-will that is changing, time and again – changing to a voluptuous sound of harps and bells, and with a theatrical display of felicity which, even when it goes beyond kitsch, is still entirely part of the world-libido. *Natura naturans* in Romantic music thus turns once more into *natura naturata*, endowed with the improved brilliance which its actualised state affords, and with the archaising utopia that is peculiar to the regression into imagined myth. This rebirth of present world, too, was effected in accordance with Schopenhauer's philosophy of music, or rather, his world-correlate for music. Here music does comprehend the root that is growing in dark secrecy; but it ends in a portrayal of the unillumined world-tree, is finally oriented to the pure 'objectivations of the will'. Even the orchestra is, in a strikingly cosmomorphic way, related to natural realms with a ground-bass (corresponding to stone) underneath, harmonising voices in the (organic) middle, and the melodic upper voice above. In essence, Schopenhauer simply based his analogy on the style of Italianate opera. But it has something more far-reaching to tell us, namely that the all too murky rooting of music in the Will, as presented by Schopenhauer, remained in *natura naturata*. What this leaves us with is always the existing world of the Will and never anything new-born, except through the immateriality of the sound. In Schopenhauer's view, not even the Beethovenian symphony broke away from the ancient Will and the well-trodden paths, in spite of all the dissension. 'It is a *rerum concordia discors*, a faithful and complete reproduction of the world as it bowls along, supporting itself in the unfathomable confusion of innumerable shapes and through constant destruction.' But although it seldom departed from the myth of Nature or the nature of myth, Romantic music's eagerness to gush forth, or its stressed ferment, could not be prevented from arriving at a world with a different effervescence – right within the sounding archaism of its Nature. When it is musically implicit, *natura naturans* or the natural subject always renders the afforded tone-painting transparent. Not in the sense of escape or liberation, which is never found in Wagner – not even, or perhaps least of all, in his Christo-theatrical works. But in that of a constant boiling over into the archaic-utopian sphere, into unrealised meanings of a hermetic, mythical Nature. Authentic, i.e. human, will is of course totally absent from this Nature, discounting Sachs and the defiantly dying Siegmund. 'Drowning, sinking unawares, supreme pleasure' – for all the utopia enclosed in it, this underworld-relation is the opposite of Beethoven or the world of virile will. Where, on the other hand, music is related to man as the core of Nature, it will of necessity become related to a Nature which is fissured and cracked open, a Nature which can be illumined as the *regnum hominis*. And it happens that Wagner, precisely because of his closeness to the source-sound, presents music not only as drowning but also, in crucial passages, as a kind of supernaturalising process in the midst of Nature herself. That is to say, we have the transparence of a peculiar resounding which occurs nowhere else and is projected far towards and behind the horizon, a resonant pastorale which is less a matter of Schopenhauer's Will than of an orbiting to a homeland. Brünnhilde's last aria is an example of this in the expansiveness of its final vast, homeward-bound, arching motions at the end. Yet with Wagner, even this Nature will still be vaguely seductive unless we hear in her sound a corresponding echo, Beethovenian and true to man, for which there arises a resonant source-area, huge in its dimensions. The narcotic effect will then give way to an ethical influence and illustration through music. And instead of the powerful *tone-painting* of a great, primevally dark Nature-dream, we discern a *morality of music*.

224

After all, man also wanted to be depicted in his dealings with others, and how could this depiction be closer, better, more improved than in notes? Sound will then return from its outings once more, arrive at its own doorstep and light a fire in the house. Tone-painting and its profounder associations have their counterpart in the self-portrait through notes, in an exemplary solidarity. Music was always expected to have this moral effect, as though there were wild beasts to be tamed in man or a dullness that needed enlivening. This hope stretches from Orpheus to *The Magic Flute*, where the Three Ladies sing: 'Hiermit kannst du allmächtig handeln, der Menschen Leidenschaften wandeln' ('With this can all deeds be performed, the passions of men be reformed'). In a less magical form, such expectations ran from Plato right across the Middle Ages. They preserved the old, controversial association of the good with the beautiful in a considerably grander style than was possible in imaginative literature, not to mention the musty form of moralising literature. In itself the art of a period always obtained a better insight into the association than pure moralising did; when it lent itself to the latter, the result was Gottsched[9] or the cast-iron broom. But art was no more perspicacious than the unconfined energy of humanity in any given age. And when it was married to the latter there emerged a Schiller and a Beethoven, that musical embodiment of morality. Indeed, even pure moralising was forced on to a higher plane through music's ability to be a morality. The philistine call for fig-leaves cannot be compared to the Platonic campaign of the Church Fathers against torrid music, or to the campaign waged by Pope Marcellus against over-ornamented music. It was Plato, then, who began to take a really earnest view of music, in accordance with his not very liberal State utopia. A sound with a languorous effect was an annoyance to him, not a folly (*The Republic*, Book III). He rejected the elegiac and tender modes and commended 'the modes of vigorous and well-disposed minds which can imitate extremely well the voices of unhappy and happy men, wise men and brave men.' All this stemmed from a respect for music that certainly corresponded to its object more closely than the harmony of the spheres. Or rather, it got right the human part, the harmony between body and soul. For Plato, this ideal rendered 'musical education of the greatest importance because rhythm and harmony sink right into the depths of the soul and take hold of it with all their might, bringing beauty of form with them and imparting this beauty to the soul when it has had the benefit of proper instruction.' The Church Fathers took over this rigorous musical ethos, now oriented not to the objective of a disciplined *polis* but to that of a religious *civitas Dei*. They always considered music to be dangerous, and hence in need of supervision. There were 'songs of the Devil' (described in terms which suggest a *Tannhäuser* orgy), and there was 'true music', i.e. music which was curative and purifying, the *praeludium vitae aeternae* praised by St Augustine. The image of David, who cured Saul of madness by playing a harp, pervades the whole musical ethics of the Church Fathers and the Middle Ages. 'True music' was intended to arrange a rapport with the salvation of the world in imitation of Christ, in succession to Christ. Pseudo-Justinus offered the following guidelines for moral and psalmodising music: 'Song awakens ardent longing connected with pleasant sensations, soothes the bad emotions aroused through the flesh, and banishes the bad thoughts induced by invisible foes. It irrigates the soul so that the divine estates bear rich fruit, and it renders the champions of piety steadfast in times of danger. Song is a medicine to pious men amidst the hardship of earthly life.' The supreme purpose of the singing of psalms was the *compunctio cordis* – the sinner's contrite remorse, but also conformity with angelic music; thus 'true music' appeared to implant in disorder something highly desirable. Likewise, the tonal relation with its moral use and effect steered entirely towards human grounds. The self-portrait was appointed to snatch us up into the substantial realm, raise our essence. No great composer has proved closer to this than Beethoven, whose music is full of moral passion and therefore the will to achieve clarity, not mindless life. Hence Beethoven's declaration: 'Few men understand what a crown of passion every single musical phrase is, and few know that passion itself is the crown of music'. Or again: 'Few men attain to this, for just as thousands of them marry for the sake of love, without even so much as the revelation of love within them, so thousands conduct an affair with music and still do not have their revelation. Like every art, it is founded on the exalted auspices of moralism, all genuine invention being a moral advance'. And so this, the art closest to man, always evinces – besides the chaos and gloomy turbulence in which its kind of inwardness is certainly not lacking, and which lodges itself in mythic nature – the vision of man which rises above the spell. Music even evinces it in the great impulses of the spellbound Romantic Nature-relation, that spell notwithstanding. Ultimately, after all, the world-root growing in music is the human root of a world-Being adequate to it – a root that is absolutely utopian in tendency, and not archaic and fixed. And the creative darkness in which it still resides is not the gloom of the Schopenhauerian Will. It is that incognito of the present which pulsates through everything and is concealed in the world itself. *In its incomparable proximity to existence, music is the most closely related and the most public organ of this incognito*, as the streaming *existere* now seeking to refine itself in concentric preludes. And the world, or outwardness, to which the *moralitas musicae* has its underground relation, the relation of the permanent sub-current or tonal flux *ante rem* – this is not the world which has already come into being but the world circulating within it and, as the *regnum hominis*, just lying ahead in futurity, anxiety, expectancy. Music's connection with this world means that it is nothing less than a seismograph of society. For it reflects any cracks beneath the social surface, expresses desires for change, and is synonymous with hoping. No angelic music will arise in the process and not even a *compunctio cordis*, as the great epoch of the Church Fathers had hoped. The self will constantly encounter disorder below the surface or diagrams of another order, in which the awareness is no longer amenable to any object but an alien one. That is music's place in the world and the place of the world in music, even during the musical Nature-relation. There is no music of fire and water or of the Romantic wilderness that does not of necessity, through the very note-material, contain within it the fifth of the elements: man. Music posits a Nature which includes the fleeting, hunted, native Syrinx and the lamp of Hero, shining over the waters of the Hellespont. Indeed, even the brightest morning music supposes Nature to be approaching evening, when the world is terminating and music itself is crossing over as though to a pre-semblance [*Vor-Schein*] of its future mystery. Here the streaming essence of the subject-ground and of the questing world-ground work together, in a pre-semblance which, unlike that of the other arts, contains a permanently apocalyptic momentum. Painting and even imaginative literature can miss this momentum because of their language, which is sated with phenomena and already or still extensively localised. Music with its overt flux, full of the beginnings of something as yet unrepresentable, necessarily posits the ex-territorial at the same time. No Nature-relation mounts any opposition to this, unless it is endowed with the realism of the humane ciphers and real symbols in Nature, at the limits of visible, known things. Thus only the counterpoint named after, and containing, Mozart, Bach or Beethoven goes to such limits. And the categories of Mozart, Bach and Beethoven are only at home on a level where material which is present nowhere else, and quite certainly fully formed nowhere else, crosses over to another cosmos. *These are the figures of the exceeding of limits in tonal spheres.* They are articulations of man's existing, in a developing language of intensity that seeks, by visionary listening to itself and by an act of expansion, to achieve *its whole essence* in a world which has come to its senses. In consequence, music contains the morality and universality of a centre which is pervasively and thoroughly intensive. Melody effects this lyrically, the fugue epically and the sonata in a dialectical-dramatic manner. But the experiment of the perceiving-in-existence of observer and world remains common to all musical forms, particularly the strict ones. What it represents is a figuring-out *in fonte hominum et rerum* that is utopian and fermenting, in an area of intensity which is so open only to music.

THE HOLLOW SPACE; THE SUBJECT OF
THE SONATA AND FUGUE

The note began as something which was pulling and stretching, but does it want to go on like this? Indeed it wants to and will do so, but maybe not along the old lines, which have become both convenient and awkward. That is to say, is there any life in that chordal tension and resolution which seems to have been inherent in the note for so long? Using the familiar route, dissonant–consonant, from the dominant via the subdominant back to the tonic? No, this approach has run its course; as we know, it ran out of steam from a social and hence technical standpoint. The society of clashing rivalries expressed in classical-romantic tonality has expired. It was replaced first of all by so-called atonal music with its abandonment of the tonic. Then music which no longer cadenced appeared in the form of Schönberg's twelve-note technique with new sound-material fully worked out to the last detail. The twelve-note technique, too, no longer acknowledges a connection with the tonic and resulting resolution of harmonic tension, which was essential to the sonata. Dissonance and consonance have grown meaningless, while the dynamic relationship between modulation and cadence has yielded to a more gliding, quietly austere pattern of note-rows. The tempered

228

scale is preserved, and in principle all twelve notes in the traditional space of an octave are used (hence no quarter-tones or eighth-tones), but with the awareness of key eliminated. Thus there arises a limited, well-organised multiplicity of ground-rows. One of these always takes priority in the music, through a continuous, uninterrupted and constantly repeated process. This repetition does not result ultimately in monotony for the reason that all twelve notes of the scale can easily be transposed. Nor is it simply monotony of which the unprepared listener complains: on the contrary, his reaction is a shocked one. Monotony would be more liable to induce drowsiness, and even the celebrated lack of expression which the aforesaid *neue Sachlichkeit* has foisted on modern music would never produce a shock. The latter is rather a response to what has been abandoned outright, in the face of an imminent, uncomprehended future which cannot be gauged by conventional means. Schönberg's *Theory of Harmony*, written in the period prior to dodecaphony, already reflected this in the words, 'The melody concludes with something new, endless or unfulfilled', while the harmony ceases to communicate the place of departure, and also the destination. And once achieved, even the twelve-note method, because it gave equal status to every note and made any chord feasible, no longer had any tonal point of reference, a home key implicitly containing the cadence and theme, as in the sonata. We cannot start with a theme as the basis of something that would be recognised again, as in the sonata or indeed the fugue. Music becomes a kind of existence which takes shape only as it happens. 'This is why,' Křenek rightly remarks (*Über neue Musik*, 1937), 'this is why the shaping of modern music has something fragmentary about it, with all the resultant impression of sadness and dissatisfaction which fragments leave.' But hence, too, the hard life of something unending in this unfulfilled something; twelve-note music represents both, in their most authentic technical state. In this way Schönberg's music remains outright expression and in particular an expression of the position of the subject in this transitional age. Though unclear, the position is not denied or suppressed. If the atonal era failed to do away with this *espressivo* (an example of which is Schönberg's monodrama, *Erwartung*), then so did music composed with twelve notes, however rational its constructional principles. It too is 'atmospheric music', not 'machine music' like that for which Stravinsky was aiming, alongside rigid neo-classicism. Schönberg's music is decidedly not the familiar

229

machine-like art of this period, disguised in an equally familiar neo-classicism. Rather it reflects the hollow space of this period and the atmosphere brewing within it, with its noiseless dynamite, long anticipations, suspended arrival. Thus Schönberg's music is never uplifting. Indeed, it was found wanting in the capacity for expressing the sublime as well as patently unable to express the hackneyed round of aesthetic enjoyment. It was even said that the sole surviving key-note in this music was that of despair, a purely temporary and ephemeral despair reflecting bourgeois hopelessness and, ultimately, its concern to deprive its victims of any will to change things. But all such views are themselves hopelessly exaggerated. The only true point they make is that this music, which is distinguished at once from total nihilism through its boldness and logic, bears all the scars of a hard, far from paradisical transitional age – while being marked just as strongly by the indefinite or as yet undefined, scintil-lating figure of its vision. Had this vision been expressed socially, then Schönberg's art would at once have been more immersed in beauty and more simple. For this purpose, however, music needs to be allied with moralities that have a totally different fibre. What we find in Schönberg's oeuvre, *rebus sic fluentibus*, is a light that is wholly honest and productive. It is a valid light for its age and the only one in which the burgeoning substance of modern music can thrive at all; scintillating in the hollow space. Before being aware of it, modern music showed a mastery in the breadth of its motivic relations and the unconfined power of the vagrant chords; its expressive character was one of complete openness. Already in Schönberg's first String Quartet and in the first Chamber Symphony, music evolves in such a way as to detach itself from its beginnings. Motivic relationships now convey the overall context, and the thematic material spontaneously originates from the nucleus of a single idea. In the three Piano Pieces, especially the third, even the motivic linking ceases. No theme is repeated, and new ones are enter-ing continually. In the monodrama *Erwartung*, thematicism has been abandoned altogether, and we are witnessing the start of the fundamentally athematic style which Alois Hába and his followers then went on developing on a basis of retained atonality. But even with such serial structures as are found in the second Chamber Sym-phony and its hapless mysticism, the twelve-note technique does not sacrifice total openness with regard to what ensues; the retrogression of the note-rows is very different from a thematic reprise. Twelve-note technique rules out sonata form, which has such a reprise. And the attempt to renew sonata form that began with the Wind Quintet (which also appeared as an authentic sonata for violin and piano) remains superficial by comparison with Schönberg's Variations for Orchestra. Of the old forms, only the variation and the suite match the line which, without tracing any loops, moves straight in the direction of something new, unending and unfulfilled. And only hence, out of the *fragmentary-unending*, does the antithesis to the shock proceed. By that we mean a reunion with an old form that has been reborn, newly heard and employed with an open ending. What we have here is not variation technique and not only the deliberate, radical liberation of a purely contrapuntal polyphony. But through its expressive content, music which is still taking shape does have a formal relationship to the ultimate striving of classical-romantic art, and to the law which governs not its start but its ending. For while the sonata principle of a conventional thematic exposition and its reinforcement in a reprise is utterly alien to serial form, its striving does lead more and more to an open ending when manifested as a finale. Unlike a theme of Mozart's or the theme of a fugue, the Beethovenian theme is itself an undeveloped one from the *Eroica* onwards. It only discovers itself in the development section, and it only assumes a dialectical form at this stage. Mahler, as the last, and often transparent, user of the old tonality, never pursued thematic development from an established beginning. And for this very reason, his *espressivo* does not derive *from* something but is moving *towards* something. The conventional expression of tension and emotion disappears, and the reprise and mostly very broad coda (Seventh Symphony) have their life in a new region, or in distant regions. Suggestively long introductions often precede the thematic complex – 'from airy tones wells up a mystery'.[10] The development section abounds in modulations and new motivic patterns (first movement of the Third, last movement of the Seventh Symphony), and the coda represents Holy Night but also Advent. Mahler's very music is an act of self-approximation, mixed with the cries of sentinels, alarm-calls, funeral processions, military signals, with a kind of melismatic intelligence beamed from a distant headquarters. His last message, in the *Song of the Earth*, enters with an unresolved suspension upon an immeasurable 'Ewig, ewig'; and this is despite the retention and final release of the key-note. The new music no longer contains Romantic music's dynamism but appears in the paradoxical

231

guise of an extremely extroverted Adagio, as it were. Yet it implies just as much that is unattained as dynamic music does, if not more.

And so now what historical tradition presents as the old note resounds anew. Precisely because it is impossible to work within it, except for unconcerned epigones, it is constantly growing more beautiful. Here we have an enormous legacy and one which does not fizzle out on reaching maturation. Its roving and atmospheric attributes never desert it, nor do conflict and inconsistency by a long chalk, even if they are no longer pursued in an entrepreneurial spirit. They no longer go by the name of free enterprise; they are, on the contrary, a revolutionary campaign against inconsistencies. Thus the musical form embodying the essence of conflict, the *sonata*, is also heard in a new way. It is not an indulgence in fervour, but something explosive. In a crucial sense the style of the sonata – that bourgeois-revolutionary style – was heralded and even initiated by a change in the performing style, the orchestral style. When, towards 1750, Stamitz trained his Mannheim orchestra in nuances of light and shade and in the art of the crescendo and diminuendo, he was opening up the way for sonata style. Terraced dynamics based on a sequence of contrasting, but inherently inflexible, loud and soft accents were replaced by gradual dynamics and an atmospheric character. Then with Beethoven, a very long time afterwards, the duothematicism and its conflict which are the technical basis of sonata construction came to maturity – or reached the conscious stage. So through its peculiar atmospheric character and gradual dynamic changes, the sonata divorced itself *ab ovo* from its predecessors, the orchestral suite and the Bachian concerto, and indeed from its antithesis, the fugue. By itself, of course, the atmospheric quality would have led to chaos. Or else – since the music of the *Sturm und Drang* period lacked this period's literary eloquence, apart from a surprisingly early foreshadowing of it in Stamitz – it would have become simply a medium of composed hysteria. To counter this, the incipient social antagonism was sublimated into a conflict of two souls in one breast (as in Goethe's *Faust*): a conflict which was going on simultaneously in music. And in the sonata, the conflict became dialectical. As we know, the principal theme in the main key is followed by a softer, lyrical, contrasting second theme (often a mere patch of oil with insipid symphonists like Schumann). The development section gives rise to thematic dissension, divagations and highly charged digressions. When the main key has been restored, the reprise leads back to the first theme, which is now triumphant. In the *Eroica*, 'the two principles' in the thematic material are put fully to work; the antagonism derived from society is at the same time that of the explosion which led to it in the first place: the French Revolution. It was for the same reason that the *Eroica* became the first conscious and the most consummate sonata-symphony. Its first movement in particular represents the Luciferan world of the Beethovenian sonata. Thus it is not the will of the entrepreneur that lets loose its socially warring subject here, but something which supremely exceeds that and comes from a far more ancient level: the will of Prometheus. The maturation of Beethoven, which affords the sight of a greater explosiveness, a more revolutionary music than with any other composer, has its basis in this legitimate Titanism. Only later could the subject of the sonata turn into an élan that was smartly ambiguous, like that of Siegfried in the *Ring of the Nibelung*. Eventually, in Strauss' *Don Juan* and his *Hero's Life*, an entrepreneurial energy alone was manifested, discarding all Promethean excess. But a genuine sonata subject means, *in terms of musical technique*, the power to develop and shape all the possibilities implied by the thematic material. And *in terms of musical content*, sonata subject means the Beethovenian category as the exceeding of limits, which is expressed in this power in an especially precise and canonic way. It is a musical cousin of Faust, an immensely charged and forward-urging character clad not in the civilian dress of Faust, so to speak, but completely preoccupied by rhythm and strategy. It also provides sonata form with the urgency whereby it not only surpasses, naturally enough, the unpolarised note-row formations and parallel displacements of post-Romantic music but also outstrips the great achievement of the monothematic style, the fugue. Apart from containing the fervent élan of diverse rivalries, the sonata was, let us remember, full of revolutionary tension, a tension imposed by its two contrasted themes and the antithesis of their respective harmonic zones. As we have noted, that kind of tension no longer exists in modern music. Hence it was imperative for music in this age of strife to achieve a new kind of tension. And since the superficial adoption of sonata form is not enough, other means must be found precisely in order to withstand the revolutionary élan of the authentic sonata, though at the cost of such aristocratic values as elegance or smooth compactness. Atonal music attempted to maintain tension through a string of catastrophes. But a more legitimate way of finding the necessary motive power is through the element least affected by the demise of the old tonality: through rhythm. It is not disturbed by ametrical composing (without bar-lines), and in polyrhythms adopted from primitive music, it works independently of the abandoned harmonic music, and beyond it. There is even a special, very deep-seated, still barely discovered *rhythmic tonic-relationship*. Were one to find this, one would again achieve not only the sonata's far-ranging expeditionary character but also its other, decidedly non-fragmentary quality, signified by the triumph of the theme. In modern music there is no longer a reprise and restoration of the main key whereby a triumph can be appreciated. Its whole grandeur and its future lie in the fact that its theme has not been decided once and for all, and stated at the outset. This music is still taking shape and is quite determined to conclude with something new and endless. But the sonata's reprise had signified not only a return but also an arrival – just that element, therefore, without which the revolutionary tension would be meaningless. The reprise contained the climax of the sonata: to achieve this without having the reprise to jog our memory is only truly possible with the aid of a rhythmic tonic-relationship. Now for both *tension and resolution* – at a new level – the *sonata* remains the model. Thus its legacy survives not merely in the maturation of hearing but also in the continuing production of music. And the *other model*, but with regard to the *existence* [*Da-Sein*] , *the safe-keeping of music*, is still the *linear polyphony* of the old counterpoint prior to the sonata style, and hence the *fugue* above all. This is, as we know, monodic – a single theme, *dux* with *comes*, roving through the parts, inside which it evolves without dissension, without conflict. Even double and triple fugues with two or three themes never present them as antithetical, and the dynamic development is smooth and leisurely. Granted, the reduced tension and more solid deliberateness reflect a hierarchical order which has died out as such and is hardly canonic. It is therefore true that fugal form, in overcoming dynamism without having known it, lags behind the sonata as a reality; and with its overt dialectics the sonata, as we have noted, surpasses it. But it is equally striking that the fugue was able to part from its old foundation precisely *within sonata form* and then contained no tranquil ground-bass whatever. The fugato, which is only an approximation to fugal form, will or can produce something uneasily rigid, most eerily so in the fugued chorale of the Men in Armour in *The Magic*

Flute. Mozart was forging a new expression. It had its sequel in the fugato of the *Eroica* funeral march, which would scarcely have been conceived without Mozart's precedent and is an altogether dynamic cortège, no longer a *quietas in fuga.* Even more striking is the fact that authentic fugal form, too, conveys a marked degree of impatience, viz. a private feuding, when used within a symphonic context. Take the brawling fugue in the *Mastersingers* and the veritably nagging fugue in Strauss' *Sinfonia domestica;* both fugues moreover are especially learned and complicated. Or let us take an example from the new music itself. Berg's *Wozzeck,* that extremely dramatic and atmospheric work, incorporates inventions and passacaglias; and the singing voice in particular, intensified to the highest degree of dramatic expression, has a dynamic part in the working out of a double fugue without any stylistic incongruity. Its very feasibility shows us how decidedly the maturation of fugal form throws up an element not confined to a leisurely organisation whereby the parts comprise the *dux* and *comes* alone. And what of the old fugue itself, the art of the masters, not the schoolmasters, of fugue? The *Bachian organ fugue,* filled with the *sursum corda?* Its ultimate expression (see the fourth section of this essay) is still unconquered. And if it implies patience, then it is a paradoxically heaven-storming patience, without dramatics but showing a lofty ambition. Thus while the fugue shows no impatience in its monodically articulated 'continuo', it does have an aim and indeed *is* an aim or, to be more precise, its constraint *ante rem.* Instead of disappearing, the legacy of sonata style will be tackled in a new form, without any of the Romantic debts it incurred; but the *safe-keeping of music or its existence [Da-Sein]* as represented by *architectonic counterpoint* will remain pre-eminent. It will be a corrective primacy of space over time and of realm over situation, now as before. It will remain a primacy of that distant simultaneity *[Zugleich-Sein]* which within music, in a style which is still harmonic-linear, is signified by Palestrina, being a constraint of seraphic equilibrium. For even in art, the ordering of freedom is superior to freedom when it has not yet attained this absolute space, behind change. Change and the atmospherical as a whole belong to time, not to the sphere of fulfilment. Only dissension is real in time – both music's time and historical time – but only the supremacy of developed monody is real as a product. In the music of the future, everything will depend on causing the theme of that monody to take shape in encirclements. But this, in incessant new experiments and fragments, is the basic theme that will finally speak: the core of human intensity. It is the fugue subject in its desire to become situation-less, as signified by the Bachian category and its maturation, an edifice towering up into the supreme order. Thus it is to a *struggle* against fate and to an ultimately envisaged situation-less state, to an *absence of fate*, that both of the two traditional forms, sonata and fugue, are pointing. Indeed, even in the battle of the sonata, at least the quiet movement – the *Andante* or *Adagio* – rests from the conflict. These movements already evince the slowly travelling arrow of beauty and – as in Schubert – musical substance which is prepared to stay and bestow blessings for ever. In their strongest manifestations they even comprise something that is denied to the sonata's first movement, as it is to the fugue: a sojourn in the unheard. Consider the Adagio of the 'Hammerklavier' Sonata, the corresponding movement of convalescence in Beethoven's A minor Quartet and the Adagio with variations in his Ninth Symphony. These mirror the subject's act of hearkening at a point reached neither by the theme's triumphant reprise nor by a single finale written so far. Thus the great Adagio is the symphony's true finale, a last dance which is leading towards the music and not away from it. Instead of humming towards an agreed conclusion, the Adagio epitomises in advance the finale's aerial perspective, as a kind of supreme good in music. It is quite legitimate for great Adagio movements to traverse the region of a figured chorale or to contain this chorale behind their slight, unemphatic caesuras. For in spirit, the Adagio of a symphony is the chorale of the latter's intensity. With regard to their object, music's slow miracles are also the deepest. They are travelling and aiming beyond time, and hence also beyond decay. And in a true . . . finale, more light is shed on the following process. On the golden sub-soil of a most distant, yet direct, remembrancing [*Eingedenken*] that penetrates to the primary and most intensive, a place where painting and literature are merely served up, music is digging out its treasure: the *intensive essence*.

FUNERAL MARCH, REQUIEM, PROCESSION BEHIND DEATH

For this digging, the note itself strikes the light that it needs. It does not need any external light and can bear darkness, whose silence it actually seeks. Silently, at night, treasure is dug up, and music does not disturb the silence because, being the light in the tomb, it knows this tomb well. Hence its proximity not only to the fortune of the blind but also to death, or rather the deep desires that endeavour to illumine it. If death conceived as an annihilating scythe is the hardest non-utopia, then music is pitted against it as the most utopian of all the arts. It contests it with a concern that is all the greater because precisely death's mysterious territory is filled with night, a generative force which seems so profoundly familiar to music within this world. However firmly the night of death may be distinguished from any other, music rightly or wrongly feels itself to be a Grecian fire that will still burn in the River Styx. And when Orpheus strikes up his harp against death, and victoriously so, his playing is only victorious in death, that is to say, in Hades. It may be a mere fable that dying people perceive music when they are slipping away from life. Or rather a graphic expression, like the corresponding and considerably more sober one according to which a man in distress will hear angels playing their flutes. It is an expression which, like much in our world, directly rebuffs the harmony of the spheres. Equally, the idea of the legendary Aeolian harp at death's door, on the other hand, often takes that ancient myth in too conventional a way. Now it may be an open question whether dying people hear music. But the fact is that, in music, the living hear a dying which bears the strongest of elective affinities to it; death's region borders indirectly on music. It borders on its frequent introvertedness, and it borders above all on its non-visual material, on its constant tendency to designate a universe without external features in the invisible realm in which it begins and which remains its further objective. This kind of thing can be merely a vague feeling. Then it will, by itself, be little more than a negation or a general travelling outwards or upwards which is uncontrolled in its course, if not itself in the grip of death. But music really does approach death, with a definite position and no vague emotionalism, with the ambition of having – to take an appropriate phrase from the Bible – *swallowed it in victory*. The love-song, which above all expressed the yearning for a union transcending obstacles or provided solace in hope, hope in solace, goes as productive death-music into the night to come and lights the lamps of one who is stubbornly undismayed. Rain, storm, clouds, lightning, even disintegration become, for this homeland, a mysterious path or an enigmatic, concordant environment. How much profound music derives its darkness and, indeed, its light from this element of the night of death, and emits from its blackness a brilliancy manifestly different from that which is normally in light! What is denied to almost any pictorial imagination denies so little of itself to music. Hence even in front of the Sostenuto assai of its greatest happiness, there is waiting a covert funeral procession – the slow movement's most serious tune. Then we come to the requiem's many overt airs of lament, of mortal sickness with an inherent overcoming of death. The requiem gives us the funeral march, the change effected by the magic of dread and the transforming dialectics of terror. *Schlage doch, gewünschte Stunde*: in Bach's cantata,[11] Man goes through the ultimate fear with a feeling of homesickness. A sheer ferrying-across is ventured in the funeral march of Beethoven's *Eroica*; it returns in some measure in the funeral march in the *Twilight of the Gods*. Beethoven was venturing the paradox of Heraclitus's dream-wish that the way downwards may be the same as the way upwards. We have the gloomy uniform C minor of the beginning, the C major of the middle section with its bright oboe theme, the dancing triplets, the return to the funeral theme, and the shy, oscillating, unrepeated melisma of happiness in the violins shortly before the end. This state of surrender and this azure colouring amount to two manifestations of the same content. Nor is their relationship such that the darkness manifested is cancelled out by the brightness, i.e. provided with an other-worldly transfiguration as its facile apotheosis. For after the great forte, the brightness again fades to a single, pianissimo violin part and into the dark of the funeral march, as if this were on the point of collapse. So the succession of events is actually meandrine or the continuation of the same thing in death conceived as both ogre and friend. In the funeral march which the *Eroica* takes for its Adagio, the Baroque sequence of *lamento e trionfo* is superseded. Both are present, but both the convention of the lament and the downright superficiality of the triumph – which remain stubbornly separate – have become invalid in the light of death and for the amazing mystery that it irradiates (Allegretto of the Seventh Symphony). The intricacy of the concept of depth is also seen at work in the actual Grave tempo: as a *De profundis* and as that depth by which we mean the ether, as a profundity of height.

Dying has itself evolved darkly brilliant images for music to fathom. These are not locked in themselves and mundane like the death of a hero and the funeral march, or even the accompanying dirge. Instead the Church offered *perfected* images of death which, now that they have grown transcendent, apocalyptic, are rivalled by the *requiem*. The liturgy furnishes contrasts in the face of which the meandrine duality of death as foe and friend is dispelled. Through it, to be sure, the music of the requiem seems to maintain a pious conviction that no longer exists as such and in any case has nothing in common with the complicated profundity of the said meander. In fact most people have not believed the Church's account of death and damnation for a hundred, almost two hundred years. Yet it lives on in music. Mozart, Cherubini, Berlioz and Verdi still wrote their masses for the dead in the grand style – and thoroughly genuine masses at that. There is no trace in these masterpieces of decorative pretence, not even in Verdi's, where theatricality would most be expected. Certainly this poses a problem, and one which cannot be solved by resorting to the so-called illusoriness of art, which permits one to enjoy at a discount what men previously paid the full price for believing, with fear and trembling. It therefore seems to be the case, oddly enough, that the same musical dressing-out which had run riot earlier and was banned by the Church for this reason, as a distraction, was now rescuing the liturgy and making it enjoyable. But this is not really the reason behind the requiem's late flowering. The austere Cherubini and the bold, meticulously explicit Berlioz offered no illusions. The music of the great requiem masses does not purvey aesthetic enjoyment but affects people and moves them deeply. And the liturgy, an offshoot of the early periods of chiliastic fear and longing, issues to music its great *archetypes*, independently of the transient patristic forms it has taken. Thus music itself reproduces the symbols of expectancy at work in the requiem; they are written into it. The reason why a musical Last Judgement is not a merely mythological topic or a mere motif of an upward movement as with Rubens, the reason for these moral contents lies in the *problem of death and the utopia·to counter it which is perennially present for music*. In consequence, apocalyptic contents emerge even where, and precisely where, the text is very different from the liturgy. Beethoven is the prime example and proof of this. Beethoven, whose oeuvre does not include a requiem, did compose one in his *Fidelio*, and one that is wholly unambiguous *with its Dies irae for Pizarro and Tuba mirum spargens sonum for Florestan*. As the spirit-world in revolution, this particular world is not closed to music; nor is the archetype of the apocalypse closed to music. Even the thunderclap in Cherubini's Requiem that proclaims the exploding of the universe is nothing extrinsic to music – it knows all about the world's end.

239

A mystical brutality is lacking in neither Berlioz nor Verdi. With Berlioz, it appears in the Horsemen's trumps of doom which blaze down on the audience from all four main points of the compass. With Verdi, it comes in the shattering blows, the plummeting cries of the *Dies irae*. But then there is the contrasting *Sed . . .* in Verdi's Offertorium, the *Sed* before the *Signifer sanctus Michael*, sustained for seven bars, plus the celestial melody which weaves around it not in triumph but in buoyant hope. So music works out stories of despair and rescue with an ultimate Baroque tendency; these stories are wedded to neither the baroque spirit nor the Judgement theology of the liturgy. They are, however, bound up with an awareness of death and of the ideal answer to death which is more genuinely present in music than anywhere else. It last appeared as such, freed from the traditional liturgy, in Brahms, in his German Requiem. *If one is seeking a musical initiation into the truth of utopia*, then the first, fully comprehensive light is *Fidelio*. The second – covered by a shade and suitably distanced – is the *German Requiem*. The choir sings 'Here on Earth have we no continuing place, howbeit, we seek one to come' – and beneath it we hear a progressive groping and searching, the tracing of a path into the unknown, the awakening. 'Behold, I shew you a mystery; we shall not all sleep, but we shall all be changed, in a moment, in the twinkling of an eye, at the last trump.' The mysterious music for these words from St Paul in the Brahms Requiem spontaneously includes the clangour of the last trumpet in a visionary hearing, a metaphysical counterpoint of Hell and victory, of Hell swallowed up in victory. This is not lacking in restraint and in what amounts to the same thing with Brahms: a precious depth that avoids apotheoses. It does not allow even Jubal's harp and Miriam's notes and sound to accept the light easily or just to present it as a consonance. The second movement of the German Requiem takes as its text: 'The redeemed of the Lord shall return again, and come rejoicing unto Zion; gladness, joy everlasting, joy upon their heads shall be'. But the music for this 'joy everlasting' proceeds fortissimo to G minor and certainly not to unmitigated radiant consonance. This is because Brahms's treatment of joy is even more complex than Kant's treatment of pathos (for the same un-Catholic reasons), and because his heaven has a piquancy which prevents it from being conventional and simple-minded. These are by no means the wan joys that Nietzsche mistakenly perceived in Brahms. Nor are they a 'late autumnal light above all joys', since they display far too

240

much ardour amid the uncertain darkness. To be sure, the happiness that turns into a mystery is manifestly enveloped in dissonance, and inherently, dissonance may in fact be a stronger expression of the mysterious than a familiar triadic harmony. This music is telling us that there is a shoot – no more but also no less – which could blossom into joy everlasting and will survive in the darkness, which it actually constrains within itself. This signifies no certain answer whatever to the most callous non-utopia, but it does signify a capacity for confuting it on its own basis. No part of this response is free from doubt, and the sound-formations are still drifting ones. But they contain live particles of an end, live particles that would not be possible if decay and death were the only final answers. In the medium of the note, which still has no fixed abode, there is manifested a freedom from oppression, death and fate which has not expressed itself in a specific visible form and is not yet able to do so. That is precisely why all music of annihilation points to a core which, since its seeds have not yet blossomed, cannot decay either; it points to a *Non omnis confundar*. Within this music's darkness are glinting those treasures which are safe from rust and moths. We mean the lasting treasures in which the will and the goal, hope and its content, virtue and happiness could be united, in a world without disappointment and in the supreme good: – *the requiem encircles the secret province of the supreme good.*

MARSEILLAISE AND TWINKLING OF AN EYE IN 'FIDELIO'

There is one work in which the note simultaneously loads and aims in a quite exceptional fashion. This is *Fidelio*, where it is a matter of making one call audible and every bar is tensed towards this. In the light and superficial prelude between Marzelline and Jaquino there is already a disquiet and a pounding that is more than superficial. Everything is future-oriented, 'then shall we rest from troubles', and every note is symbolic. 'Think you I cannot read your heart?' Rocco asks Leonore; and then the scene contracts as four voices build up pure inwardness. 'I feel so wondrous strange, my heart is stifling me', begins the quartet, the Andante sostenuto of a song giving vent to absolutely nothing but its 'wondrous', borne upon darkness alone. Marzelline sings it for Leonore, and hope illumines the goal, though the danger is great. 'Now I see a shining rainbow resting on the gloomy clouds' – Leonore herself is speaking within this light in the truest aria of hope, rising and falling above sombre agitations of sound, her face turned to that star which comforts the weary. The star's influence was already felt in the timid 'wondrous' with which the quartet began. It influences Leonore's aria and the Prisoners' Chorus, when not only Leonore and Florestan but all condemned men on this Earth look up to the light of the morrow. But the star is dazzling and high in Florestan's feverish ecstasy, being Leonore herself. To this star belongs the visionary cry, 'to freedom, to freedom, into the kingdom above', soaring with superhuman cadences, then collapsing unconscious and dying away. Then comes the start of the subterranean monodrama, the scene of the wildest suspense; Florestan confronts Pizarro, 'a murderer, murderer stands before me', Leonore shields Florestan with her body, revealing her identity; renewed onslaught of the murder theme, the pistol is pointed at Pizarro, 'one more sound, and you are dead'. Were the spirit and dramatic scope of this music to give rise to nothing further, then the pistol shot would be both the symbol and the act of rescue, and its tonic the answer to what was called and the call itself from the outset. But on the basis of the music's imperatively apocalyptic spirit and scope, this tonic obtains a symbol from the requiem: more specifically, from the Easter mystery in the *Dies irae*. We refer to the *trumpet signal*. If one understands this signal in a superficial sense, from Pizarro's earlier order to sound it from the battlements as a means of warning him, then it is merely a literal herald of the Minister's arrival from Seville. But in Beethoven's mind, it is the *tuba mirum spargens sonum* announcing the Saviour's arrival. That is how it penetrates to the dungeon below, to the torches and lights which accompany the governor upwards. Thus does it penetrate the 'namen-, namenlose Freude', the ineffable joy where Beethoven's music no longer holds back, and the chorus of 'Hail to the day, hailed be the hour!' in the transformed courtyard of the fortress. It was an inspired idea of Mahler's to play between the dungeon scene and the final liberation the third *Leonore* overture, that overture which is really a utopian memory, a legend of fulfilled hope, with the trumpet signal at its centre. The signal is sounded, without and after the staging, and the music answers with a melody of calm which cannot be played sufficiently slowly. Then the signal is sounded a second time, and the same melody answers, mysteriously modulated, in a remote key out of a world already changed. And now back into the scene of liberation, the Marseillaise over the fallen Bastille. *The 'twinkling of an eye' is come*, the star of fulfilled hope in the here and now. Leonore removes Florestan's chains: 'O God, what a moment this is' – and at these words, which Beethoven has raised to metaphysical heights, there arises a song, a veritable tarrying moreover, which would deserve to go on arriving for ever. First the sudden switch to a distant key, then an oboe melody expressing fulfilment; the Sostenuto assai of time standing still and absorbed in the moment. Every future storming of the Bastille is implicitly expressed in *Fidelio*, and an incipient substance of human identity fills up the space in the Sostenuto assai. The Presto of the final chords just adds the reflected glory, the rejoicing around Leonore-*Maria militans*. Beethoven's music is chiliastic, and the form of the 'rescue opera', which was not uncommon at the time, only furnished the superficial material for this music's moral contents. Does not the character of Pizarro bear all the features of a Pharaoh, of Herod, Gessler, the demon of winter and indeed that same gnostic Satan who put Man into the dungeon of the world and keeps him prisoner there? Here and nowhere else, on the other hand, music becomes a rosy dawn, militant-religious, the dawning of a new day so audible that it seems more than simply a hope. It shines forth as the pure work of Man, as one which had not yet appeared in the world surrounding Beethoven, a world that existed irrespective of men. Thus music as a whole stands at the farther limits of humanity, but at those limits where humanity, with new language and *haloed by the call to achieved intensity, to the attained world of 'we'*, is first taking shape. And this ordering in our musical expression means a house, indeed a crystal, but one derived from our future freedom; a star, but one that will be a new Earth.

Translator's notes

The philosophy of music

1 Singing at this primordial stage is suggested in Colette's portrait of Debussy (*En Pays connu*): '. . . a sort of bee-swarm buzzing, something like the sound you hear from telegraph poles, a groping and hesitant murmur'.

2 Balzac: *La Peau de Chagrin* ('The Wild Ass's Skin').

3 Kleist: *Die heilige Cäcilie oder die Gewalt der Musik* ('The Legend of St Cecilia').

4 No quotation marks in the German text; but this is the opening line of Klopstock's poem (and Schubert's song) *Dem Unendlichen*.

5 *makanthropos*: 'Great Man'. Discussed in Bloch's *Atheism in Christianity* (translated by J.R. Swann), pp. 151–60.

6 Karl von Piloty (1826–86). German painter specialising in realistic historical scenes.

7 Translated by H.E. Krehbiel.

8 Hebbel: *Zwei Wandrer*, written in 1837.

9 Wilhelm Jordan (1819–1904) completed a modern version of the Nibelung legend in 1874. Felix Dahn (1834–1912) was a historian whose novels include *Odhins Trost* ('Odin's Consolation'), 1880.

10 Obviously a pun on 'August'; perhaps also on *Halm*, meaning 'blade of grass' (*Tannhäuser*, Act 1: . . . *den Halm seh' ich nicht mehr, der frisch ergrünend den neuen Sommer bringt*). See the comment on August Halm in David Drew's introduction. Of the other writers on music mentioned in this section, Leopold Schmidt (1860–1927) became the leading critic in Berlin. Paul Bekker (1882–1937) was chief music critic of the *Frankfurter Zeitung* until 1925; an English translation of his *Beethoven* dates from that year. Karl Grunsky (1871–1943) and Friedrich von Hausegger (1837–99) were active in Stuttgart and Graz respectively. The latter's *Die Musik als Ausdruck* took issue with Hanslick (see n. 15 below). Hugo Riemann (1849–1919) published a music lexicon and some important theoretical works, beginning with his *Vom musikalischen Hören*. Moritz Hauptmann (1792–1868) is chiefly remembered for *Die Natur der Harmonik und Metrik*, 1853; English edition, 1888. Hauptmann rejected mathematics as a tenable

244

basis of music and applied Hegelian dialectic to harmonic theory, taking the major triad as smallest intelligible musical unit.

11 Friedrich Theodor Vischer (1807–87). Swabian author of the voluminous, Hegel-influenced *Aesthetik oder Wissenschaft des Schönen*, 1846–57.

12 An allusion to a line in the opening scene of Goethe's *Faust*, Part One: 'Allein der Vortrag macht des Redners Glück' (Solely the delivery 'tis that wins all ears).

13 Spoken by the Astrologer in Goethe's *Faust*, Part Two, Act 1.

14 A nineteenth-century periodical much favoured by the German middle classes.

15 In his thirtieth year Eduard Hanslick (1825–1904) published an internationally acclaimed work entitled *Vom Musikalisch-Schönen* ('On the Beautiful in Music'). As a music critic in Vienna, he turned against Wagner. Johann Friedrich Herbart (1776–1841) occupied Kant's former chair of philosophy in Königsberg for a quarter of a century. Author of *Psychologische Bemerkungen zur Tonlehre*, he is now considered less dogmatic in musical matters than earlier opinion held him to be.

16 Epimetheus, the brother of Prometheus, unwittingly released the contents of 'Pandora's box'. Bloch is referring to Goethe's verse fragment, *Pandora*. Here Pandora's daughter Elpore visits Epimetheus in a dream and eludes his embrace.

17 An allusion to the close of the first scene in Goethe's *Faust*, Part Two: 'Am farbigen Abglanz haben wir das Leben' (Our life consists in the coloured reflection).

18 A quotation from the second monologue in the opening scene of *Faust*, Part One.

19 Wilhelm von Kaulbach (1805–74). A cartoon of his inspired Liszt's tone-poem, *Hunnenschlacht*. August Bungert (1845?–1915) entertained the notion of a festival theatre at Bad Godesberg. His magnum opus was an operatic tetralogy, *Die Odyssee*, 1898–1903.

20 Although extolled in Goethe's influential *Von deutscher Baukunst*, Erwin von Steinbach is not now thought to have built more than parts of the west façade of Strasbourg Cathedral.

21 Pater Peter Singer (1810–82). Composer and organist at the Franciscan convent in Salzburg. His *Metaphysische Blicke in die Tonwelt* appeared in 1847.

22 From a reflection on music entitled 'Ein sonderlicher Kasus von harten Talern und Waldhorn', published in Claudius's periodical *Der Wandsbecker Bote*.

23 In Expressionist thinking, the crystal building assumed a mystical and utopian significance. See Wolfgang Pehnt's *Expressionist Architecture* (London, 1973), pp. 35–41.

24 Spoken by Wagner, the famulus, in Goethe's *Faust*, Part One.

Paradoxes and the pastorale in Wagner's music

1   A celebrated example was the glass pavilion designed by Bruno Taut for the Cologne Werkbund exhibition of 1914.
2   Spoken, in a very slightly different form, by the Director in the Theatrical Prelude to Goethe's *Faust*. 'Wer vieles bringt, wird manchem etwas bringen.'
3   A reference to a vapid verse-epic by Victor von Scheffel (1826–86) that enjoyed popularity in the latter half of the nineteenth century. It even yielded a *Spieloper*.
4   A self-quotation from the 'Philosophy of music' in *Geist der Utopie*, 1918 edition. Cf. pp. 63, 130 in the present volume.
5   Spoken by Ariel at the beginning of Part Two of Goethe's *Faust*.

On the mathematical and dialectical character in music

1   See n. 23 to 'The philosophy of music'.

The exceeding of limits and the world of man at its most richly intense in music

1   See n. 14 to 'The philosophy of music'.
2   Ernest Newman's translation.
3   Georg Gottfried Gervinus (1805–71). Liberal thinker expelled from Göttingen. An English edition of his Shakespeare commentaries appeared in 1863. In 1868 he published *Händel und Shakespeare: Zur Aesthetik der Tonkunst*.
4   A self-quotation from 'The philosophy of music', 1918. Cf. p. 139.
5   A key term in Bloch – see his *Aesthetik des Vor-Scheins*, edited by Gerd Ueding (2 vols., 1974).
6   An allusion to the opening monologue in Part One of Goethe's *Faust*:

> Passing gold buckets to each other,
> How heavenly powers ascend, descend!

7   'The sun gives out its ancient sounds / In rivalry with brother spheres.' From the Prologue in Heaven, *Faust*, Part One.
8   A self-quotation from 'The philosophy of music', 1923. See p. 63.
9   Johann Christoph Gottsched (1700–66) produced a major treatise on the German language. His criticism reflects an extremely rationalistic and moralistic bent. Bach set his *Trauerode* to music.
10 See n. 13, 'The philosophy of music'.
11 Now attributed to Melchior Hoffmann (c. 1685–1715). Cf. p. 201.

Index